Critical Incidents in Counselor Education

Teaching, Supervision, Scholarship, Leadership, and Advocacy

edited by
Jacqueline M. Swank and Casey A. Barrio Minton

American Counseling Association
2461 Eisenhower Avenue
Alexandria, VA 22331
www.counseling.org

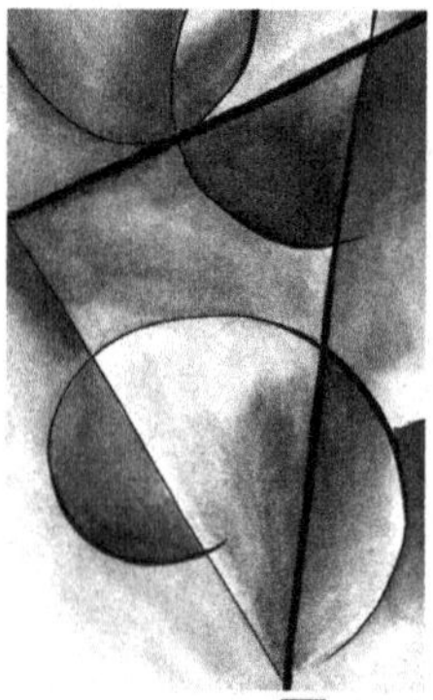

Critical Incidents in Counselor Education

American Counseling Association
2461 Eisenhower Avenue • Alexandria, VA 22331

Associate Publisher • Carolyn C. Baker

Digital and Print Development Editor • Nancy Driver

Senior Production Manager • Bonny E. Gaston

Copy Editor • Beth Ciha

Cover and text design by Bonny E. Gaston

Library of Congress Cataloging-in-Publication Data
Names: Swank, Jacqueline M., editor. | Barrio Minton, Casey A., editor.
Title: Critical incidents in counselor education : teaching, supervision, scholarship, leadership, and advocacy / Jacqueline M. Swank, Casey A. Barrio Minton, editors.
Description: Alexandria, VA : American Counseling Association, [2022] | Includes bibliographical references and index.
Identifiers: LCCN 2021019222 | ISBN 9781556204029 (paperback)
Subjects: LCSH: Counseling—Study and teaching (Graduate)—United States. | Counseling psychology—Study and teaching (Graduate) —United States. | Counselors—Training of—United States. | College teaching—United States. | Universities and colleges—United States—Graduate work.
Classification: LCC BF636.65 .C75 2022 | DDC 158.3071—dc23
LC record available at https://lccn.loc.gov/2021019222

Dedication

To current and future counselor educators and to counseling supervisors, scholars, leaders, and advocates who continuously navigate ethical and professional dilemmas to enhance the counseling profession and those we serve.

To God for his continued blessings; my family and friends for their unending encouragement and support; and my mentors, students, and colleagues, who help me continually grow both professionally and personally.

—Jacqueline M. Swank

To the mentors and students who have made me a stronger teacher and leader.

—Casey A. Barrio Minton

Table of Contents

Preface xiii
Acknowledgments xv
About the Editors xvii
About the Contributors xix

Part I • Teaching

Section 1 • Student Engagement and Dispositions

Chapter 1
I Don't Have a Clue:
Responding to Unprepared or Unengaged Students 5
Critical Incident 5
Jonathan H. Ohrt and Kathryn P. Linich
Response 10
Samir H. Patel

Chapter 2
I Did My Part:
Responding to Inequitable Group Project Contributions 13
Critical Incident 13
Linwood G. Vereen, Clewiston D. Challenger, and Nicole R. Hill
Response 19
Vaibhavee R. Agaskar and Jean Georgiou

Chapter 3
It's Not Their Work: A Case of Plagiarism 21
Critical Incident 21
Tiphanie Gonzalez
Response 26
Casey A. Barrio Minton

Chapter 4
Too Much Information:
Maintaining Boundaries During Skills Practice 29
Critical Incident 29
Kathryn L. Henderson
Response 34
Linwood G. Vereen, Clewiston D. Challenger, and Nicole R. Hill

Chapter 5
I'm a Counselor . . . Well Almost:
Boundary Extensions in Service Learning 37
Critical Incident 37
Mark B. Scholl
Response 42
Kathryn L. Henderson

Chapter 6
I'm Here, I'm Not Participating:
Student Resistance to a Group Experience 45
Critical Incident 45
Samir H. Patel
Response 50
Olga R. Dietlin and Jenny L. Chien

Section 2 • Dynamics Related to Diversity and Inclusion

Chapter 7
Whose Cultural Competence?
Students' Needs in Multicultural Courses 53
Critical Incident 53
Carlos P. Hipolito-Delgado
Response 58
Mark B. Scholl

Chapter 8
A Cohort Divided:
Navigating Tensions Related to Race and Ethnicity 61
Critical Incident 61
Catherine Y. Chang, Erin C. M. Mason, and Vanessa Placeres
Response 67
Jonathan H. Ohrt and Kathryn P. Linich

Chapter 9
I Need a New Partner:
Addressing Cultural Encapsulation and Racism 69
Critical Incident 69
LoriAnn Sykes Stretch and Denita N. Hudson
Response 75
Carlos P. Hipolito-Delgado

Chapter 10
Interacting With Me:
Title IX and Faculty-Student Consensual Relationships 77
Critical Incident 77
Imelda N. Bratton
Response 82
Shawn L. Spurgeon

Section 3 • Instructor Preparedness

Chapter 11
Embracing the Digital World:
Instructor Preparedness for Online Delivery 85
Critical Incident 85
Olga R. Dietlin and Jenny L. Chien
Response 90
Catherine Y. Chang and Erin C. M. Mason

Chapter 12
Does It Apply to Me?
Instructor Competency to Teach Specialty Courses 93
Critical Incident 93
Vaibhavee R. Agaskar and Jean Georgiou
Response 97
LoriAnn Sykes Stretch and Denita N. Hudson

Chapter 13
Something to Share: Promoting Unethical or Illegal Practice 99
Critical Incident 99
Shawn L. Spurgeon
Response 104
Jacqueline M. Swank
Resources 105

Part II • Supervision

Section 1 • Supervisee Dispositions and Behaviors

Chapter 14
This Is Cool, Does It Work?
Using a Technique With Limited Training 111
Critical Incident 111
W. Bradley McKibben
Response 117
Jane M. Webber

Chapter 15
I Don't Believe in That: Addressing Counselors' Values Conflicts 119
Critical Incident 119
Anita A. Neuer Colburn
Response 124
W. Bradley McKibben

Chapter 16
I'm an Emotional Person: Determining Counselor Impairment 127
Critical Incident 127
Jane M. Webber
Response 133
Anita A. Neuer Colburn

Chapter 17
Don't Watch Me:
Not Bringing Session Recordings to Supervision 135
Critical Incident 135
Devika Dibya Choudhuri
Response 141
Gülşah Kemer

Section 2 • Issues With Site Supervisors

Chapter 18
I'm Getting Different Messages:
Incongruence Between Supervisors 143
Critical Incident 143
Joel F. Diambra
Response 149
Heather J. Ambrose

Chapter 19
The Other Side: A Supervisor Presenting Differently to Students 151
Critical Incident 151
Derrick A. Paladino and Leigh D. DeLorenzi
Response 156
David Julius Ford Jr.

Chapter 20
To Tell or Not to Tell: Site Supervisor Impairment 159
Critical Incident 159
Heather J. Ambrose
Response 164
Derrick A. Paladino

Section 3 • Doctoral Student Supervisors

Chapter 21
Biased: A Doctoral Student Supervisor's Struggle
With a Supervisee's Lack of Awareness 167
Critical Incident 167
Gülşah Kemer
Response 173
Joel F. Diambra

Chapter 22
I'm Attracted to My Supervisee: A Doctoral Student Supervisor's Struggle 175
Critical Incident 175
David Julius Ford Jr. and Matthew Tirrell
Response 180
Devika Dibya Choudhuri

Part III • Research and Scholarship

Section 1 • Collaboration and Authorship

Chapter 23
That's My Idea: Taking Someone Else's Work as Their Own 187
Critical Incident 187
Melissa Luke and Sherrie L. Bruner
Response 193
Richard E. Watts and Jacqueline M. Swank

Chapter 24
Who to Include: A Case of Contested Authorship 195
Critical Incident 195
A. Stephen Lenz, Diana Camilo, and Megan Speciale
Response 201
Sherrie L. Bruner and Melissa Luke

Chapter 25
Is This How It's Supposed to Be? Collaboration Gone Wrong 203
Critical Incident 203
Erik M. Hines and Paul C. Harris
Response 207
Jesse Fox

Section 2 • Client Interest and Well-Being

Chapter 26
I Need Your Approval, but I Don't Want to Do That: Getting IRB Approval 209
Critical Incident 209
Sam Steen and Shekila Melchior
Response 213
Diandra J. Prescod

Chapter 27
Should He Be Included? I Know His Sister 215
Critical Incident 215
Elizabeth A. Prosek
Response 221
Sam Steen and Shekila Melchior

Chapter 28
Do We Stop the Study?
Best for the Client vs. Best for Research 223
Critical Incident 223
Diandra J. Prescod
Response 227
Kelly L. Wester

Section 3 • The Publication Process

Chapter 29
A Little Bit Here, a Little Bit There: The Least Publishable Unit 229
Critical Incident 229
Kelly L. Wester
Response 234
Erik M. Hines and Paul C. Harris

Chapter 30
It's Already Published: Can I Still Submit My Manuscript? 237
Critical Incident 237
Richard E. Watts, Jo Lauren Weaver, and Jacqueline M. Swank
Response 241
Elizabeth A. Prosek

Chapter 31
Do I Compromise to Get Published?
Responding to Reviewers' Feedback 243
Critical Incident 243
Jesse Fox
Response 248
A. Stephen Lenz, Diana Camilo, and Megan Speciale
Resources 249

Part IV • Leadership and Advocacy

Section 1 • Professional Organization Leadership

Chapter 32
Is There a Conflict? Balancing Fiduciary Responsibility 255
Critical Incident 255
Leigh Falls Holman
Response 260
Philip B. Clarke and Michelle R. Ghoston

Chapter 33
Who Are You Representing?
Serving Two Professional Organizations 263
Critical Incident 263
Kristopher M. Goodrich and Renée C. Howells
Response 268
Marty Jencius

Chapter 34
True to Our Mission:
Establishing an Identity as a Professional Organization 271
Critical Incident 271
Marty Jencius
Response 277
Natoya Hill Haskins

Chapter 35
It's All About Mentorship: Managing Professional Journals 279
Critical Incident 279
Cirecie A. West-Olatunji and S. Anandavalli
Response 284
Kathy Ybañez-Llorente

Section 2 • Leadership and Advocacy in the Local Community

Chapter 36
What Should We Fund?
Addressing Budget Issues on a Community Board 287
Critical Incident 287
Nicole R. Hill
Response 294
Renée C. Howells and Kristopher M. Goodrich

Chapter 37
My Hands Are Tied:
Navigating University Prohibitions on Advocacy 297
Critical Incident 297
Kathy Ybañez-Llorente
Response 302
Nicole R. Hill

Section 3 • Diversity and Inclusion Within Counselor Education Programs

Chapter 38
Do We Practice What We Preach?
Diversity and Inclusion Plans 305
Critical Incident 305
Christian D. Chan
Response 311
S. Anandavalli and Cirecie A. West-Olatunji

Chapter 39
Maybe I Can Change This:
Addressing Marginalization in a Program 313
Critical Incident 313
Natoya Hill Haskins, Unity Walker, Aiesha Lee, and Huijuan Li
Response 318
Christian D. Chan

Chapter 40
You Can't Treat Me That Way!
Microaggressions and Bullying 321
Critical Incident 321
Philip B. Clarke and Michelle R. Ghoston
Response 326
Leigh Falls Holman

References 329
Index 363

Preface

Counselor educators have multiple roles and responsibilities as teachers, supervisors, scholars, leaders, and advocates for the counseling profession. Doctoral programs in counselor education and supervision have the challenging task of preparing students to embrace each of these roles with all their complexities. Despite rigorous instruction and experiential learning opportunities, counselor educators and supervisors, especially those new to their roles, often struggle with complex situations that they feel unprepared to address.

The challenging, complex critical incidents counselor educators navigate within their multiple roles become learning opportunities for growth and development. As we have trained and mentored counselor education doctoral students and new counselor educators, as well as reflected on our own experiences as counselor educators, we have been reminded of the similarities in the challenging situations we have experienced. Learning from others' experiences may help aspiring and new counselor educators and supervisors avoid pitfalls in addressing similar situations. Thus, we designed this book to help you navigate critical incidents commonly experienced in counselor education and supervision. The cases are largely fictitious or composites, but the situations are real and are experienced by counselor educators frequently in their work settings.

This book focuses on critical incidents experienced by counselor educators across four unique areas in which they must develop specialty skills: (a) teaching, (b) supervision, (c) research and scholarship, and (d) leadership and advocacy. Within each chapter, experts in counselor education identify key issues relevant to the case; analyze the critical incident with overt attention to the *ACA Code of Ethics* (American Counseling Association, 2014), existing literature, and diversity and inclusion; and discuss actions and outcomes. Experts also provide a response for each chapter that focuses on reinforcing decisions made, introducing additional literature, and providing contrasting opinions.

The first part is focused on teaching and includes 13 chapters within three sections: (a) student engagement and dispositions, (b) dynamics related to diversity and inclusion, and (c) instructor preparedness. The second part is related to supervision and encompasses nine chapters within three sections: (a) supervisee dispositions and behaviors, (b) issues with site supervisors, and (c) doctoral student supervisors. The third part pertains to research and scholarship and includes nine chapters within three sections: (a) collaboration and authorship, (b) client interest and well-being, and (c) the publication process. The final part focuses on leadership and advocacy and includes nine chapters within three sections: (a) professional organization leadership, (b) leadership and advocacy in the local community, and (c) diversity and inclusion within counselor education programs.

We expect you will find the stories and analyses helpful in multiple ways. Counselor educators may use this book throughout the doctoral curriculum in courses focused on each of the four domains as well as in more general professional orientation and ethics courses or internships. This will provide an opportunity to facilitate exploration of critical issues commonly experienced in counselor education and supervision. These conversations may help students develop an understanding of the complexities of the roles of counselor educators and supervisors. We expect counselor educators and supervisors will see themselves in many of the stories, perhaps using the book to explore multiple perspectives on common critical incidents they find themselves navigating.

The authors address challenges and opportunities counselor educators must navigate on an ongoing basis. The book also focuses on integrating multicultural and social justice issues through the inclusion of diverse counselor educators as authors, the inclusion of diverse individuals within the scenarios, and overt discussion of cultural dynamics and considerations across topics and issues. This book supplements existing textbooks within each of the four domains by focusing on real-world application of theories, concepts, and techniques. In sum, we believe you will find the book beneficial for preparing counselor education doctoral students and fostering the further growth and development of practicing counselor educators and supervisors.

Acknowledgments

A special thanks to the 61 authors who contributed to this text and to the mentors, counselor educators, teachers, supervisors, scholars, leaders, advocates, students, and clients who inspired this book and the case studies within it.

About the Editors

Jacqueline M. Swank, PhD, LMHC, LCSW, RPT-S, is an associate professor of counselor education at the University of Florida. She has extensive experience working with children and adolescents and their families in various counseling settings, including outpatient, day treatment, inpatient, and residential treatment facilities, and has worked clinically in both the United States and England. Her research interests focus on the holistic growth and development of children and adolescents, counselor competency, assessment, nature and play-based interventions, and international counseling.

Dr. Swank is the author of more than 70 articles and 16 book chapters and is currently working on a second book. She has been recognized for her scholarly work, having received nine awards for specific research projects from professional organizations, including the American Counseling Association, the Association for Assessment and Research in Counseling, the Association for Counselor Education and Supervision, the Association for Adult Development and Aging, the American Horticultural Therapy Association, and Chi Sigma Iota. She has also received a University of Florida University Term Professorship. She is currently the principal investigator on two federally funded grants totaling nearly 1.2 million dollars.

She has a strong commitment to service and has served as president of two national counseling organizations: the Association for Assessment and Research in Counseling and the Association for Creativity in Counseling. She has also served in several other leadership capacities at the local, state, and national levels. She was recognized for her service and contributions to the field of creativity in counseling with the Association for Creativity in Counseling Professional Service Award and the Samuel T. Gladding Inspiration and Motivation Award, her contribution to the field of play therapy with the Viola Brody Award, and her contribution to assessment and research with the Association for Assessment and Research in Counseling Professional Level Exemplary Practice Award. She has a passion for international work and has trained teachers and church leaders in using helping skills in Haiti. She enjoys teaching and mentoring students and has been recognized for her teaching with the Diane E. Haines Teaching Excellence Award at the University of Florida. Dr. Swank lives in Florida with her two cats, Holstein and Piper. She enjoys going on mission trips and volunteering, photography, playing games with friends and family, and going on adventures in nature.

• • •

Casey A. Barrio Minton, PhD, NCC, is a professor of counselor education and the counselor education unit coordinator at The University of Tennessee, Knoxville. Her scholarly work focuses on crisis intervention, clinical mental health issues, and professionalization through teaching and leadership. She most enjoys teaching doctoral courses in professional orientation and teaching and master's-level courses in multicultural counseling, diagnostic issues, and crisis intervention.

Dr. Barrio Minton is the author or editor of five books, including *Practical Approaches to Applied Research and Program Evaluation for Helping Professionals*, *DSM-5 Learning Companion for Counselors*, and *Professional Counseling Excellence Through Leadership and Advocacy*. She has been recognized for her scholarly work twice each by the American Counseling Association, the Association for Counselor Education and Supervision, and Chi Sigma Iota.

The founding editor of the *Journal of Counselor Leadership and Advocacy*, Dr. Barrio Minton is a past-president of Chi Sigma Iota International, the Association for Assessment and Research in Counseling, and the Southern Association for Counselor Education and Supervision. She continues to actively serve these organizations through their mentorship programs and committees. At the time of this printing, she was serving as president of the Association for Counselor Education and Supervision. Dr. Barrio Minton began her service to the profession as a Chi Sigma Iota Leadership Fellow and chapter president in 2003, and she received the American Counseling Association's Arthur A. Hitchcock Distinguished Professional Service Award in 2017. She is a Fellow of the American Counseling Association. Dr. Barrio Minton lives in Knoxville with her partner Joel, child Leah, and dog Rosie. She enjoys exploring new food and drink, going on adventures with Leah, and setting running goals that feel just out of reach.

• • •

About the Contributors

Vaibhavee R. Agaskar, PhD, LPC, NCC, is an associate professor at New Jersey City University. Currently she is serving as the principal investigator for a Behavioral Health Workforce Education and Training grant funded by the U.S. Health Resources and Services Administration to expand the behavioral workforce in integrated health care at primary care settings.

Heather J. Ambrose, PhD, LCMHC, LMFT, AAMFT Approved Supervisor, is a core faculty member in the School of Counseling at Walden University. Her expertise is in training clinical mental health counseling supervisors.

S. Anandavalli, PhD, NCC, is an assistant professor at Southern Oregon University. She holds leadership positions in the American Counseling Association and serves as cochair for the Writers' Consortium for the Association for Multicultural Counseling and Development.

Imelda N. Bratton, PhD, is a faculty member at Walden University. Her expertise is in play therapy.

Sherrie L. Bruner, PhD, LPC-MHSP, is a clinical assistant professor and director of the Counselor Training Clinic in the Educational Psychology and Counseling Department at The University of Tennessee, Knoxville. Her research interests focus on the intersection of counselor education practice and persistence for traditionally marginalized populations in higher education.

Diana Camilo, EdD, LPC, NCC, is an assistant professor at CSU San Bernardino. Her expertise is in school counseling, student services, and administration. Her research interests focus on culturally responsive practices for school counseling and college and career readiness.

Clewiston D. Challenger, PhD, is an assistant professor in the Department of Counselor Education and Counseling Psychology at the University of Connecticut. His research interests focus on high school to college transition, college adjustment, sense of belonging and inclusion, self-efficacy, mental health, institutional attachment, academic buoyancy and motivation, and student athletes at predominantly white institutions.

Christian D. Chan, PhD, NCC, is an assistant professor at the University of North Carolina at Greensboro. His research interests focus on intersectionality; multiculturalism in counseling practice, supervision, and counselor education; social justice and activism; career development; critical research methodologies; and socialization/communication of cultural factors in couple, family, and group modalities.

Catherine Y. Chang, PhD, LPC, NCC, CPCS, is a professor at Georgia State University and director of international programs for the College of Education and Human Development. Her research interests focus on multicultural counseling competence and social justice issues in counselor training and practice.

Jenny L. Chien, PhD, LPC (MI), LMHC (FL), QS (FL), is an assistant professor in the Clinical Mental Health Counseling Program at Cornerstone University. Her expertise and research interests focus on university mental health and counselor wellness.

Devika Dibya Choudhuri, PhD, LPC, NCC, CCMHC, ACS, is a professor of counseling at Eastern Michigan University. Her expertise is in sexuality, trauma, and identity. Her research interests focus on multicultural issues in psychotherapy, supervision, and pedagogy.

Philip B. Clarke, PhD, LCMHC, is an associate professor in the Department of Counseling at Wake Forest University. His expertise is in counseling individuals with substance use disorders, individuals with co-occurring disorders, and persons with dementia and their families. His research interests focus on wellness, addiction, older adults, and creative teaching approaches.

Leigh D. DeLorenzi, PhD, LMHC, LMFT, NCC, is an assistant professor at Rollins College. Her expertise is in the treatment of trauma, and she has spent her career counseling children, adults, families, couples, and groups. Her research interests focus on the effect of well-being initiatives within medical and mental health training environments.

Joel F. Diambra, EdD, LPC-MHSP-S, NCC, is an associate professor at The University of Tennessee, Knoxville. His expertise is in group counseling and clinical supervision. His research interests focus on student development, group counseling, and clinical supervision.

Olga R. Dietlin, PhD, is an assistant professor in the Higher Education and Student Development Program at Wheaton College. Her expertise is in graduate counseling and student affairs training. Her research interests focus on the pedagogy of care in online settings, student development worldwide, and conflict in politically divided relationships.

David Julius Ford Jr., PhD, LCMHC (NC), LPC (VA, NJ), NCC, ACS, is an assistant professor at Monmouth University. His expertise is in culturally responsive counseling and supervision. His research interests focus on Black men attending predominantly white institutions, Black Greek life, Black men in counseling/counselor education, queer men of color, and HIV/AIDS.

Jesse Fox, PhD, is an assistant professor at Stetson University and executive director of the Episcopal Counseling Center. His expertise is in spirituality, religion, and mental health. His research interests focus on theory of religious and spiritual integration, spiritual bypass, and religious and spiritual struggle.

Jean Georgiou, EdD, LPC, NCC, ACS, is an associate professor in and chair of the Department of Counselor Education at New Jersey City University. She is currently involved in a project in Western Kenya, where she conducts mission work and psychoeducational groups.

Michelle R. Ghoston, PhD, LCMHC, LPC, ACS, is an assistant professor at Wake Forest University. Her interests focus on equity and neuroscience education.

Tiphanie Gonzalez, PhD, is a tenured assistant professor in the Department of Counseling and Psychological Services and diversity coordinator for the School of Education at State University of New York at Oswego. Her expertise is in multicultural competency and working with P–16 students/clients. Her research interests focus on multicultural counseling, advocacy in counseling ethics, and creative counseling.

Kristopher M. Goodrich, PhD, LPCC (NM), ACS, is a professor and department chair at The University of New Mexico. His expertise is in lesbian, gay, bisexual, transgender, queer, and intersex (LGBTQI+) issues in counseling, clinical supervision, and professional identity.

Paul C. Harris, PhD, is an associate professor at the University of Virginia. His expertise is in issues related to promoting equity in schools and in the college and career readiness of Black males and student athletes.

Natoya Hill Haskins, PhD, LPC, NCC, is an associate professor at the College of William & Mary. Her expertise is in counselor education, culturally responsive teaching, and support structures for Black and Brown students. Her research interests focus on culturally responsive counselor education experiences for graduate students of color, critical race theory in counselor education, and school counselor advocacy efficacy assessment tools.

Kathryn L. Henderson, PhD, LPC, NCC, is an associate professor of counselor education at the University of Saint Joseph. Her expertise is in ethical and legal issues in counseling, in particular in gatekeeping.

Nicole R. Hill, PhD, LPC, is a professor in and dean of the College of Education and Human Services at Shippensburg University. She focuses on cultivating faculty and student development, championing humanistic engagement in professional communities, and advocating for excellence. Her research interests focus on leadership, mentoring, counseling identity, and social justice and access in higher education.

Erik M. Hines, PhD, is an associate professor at Florida State University. His expertise is in college and career readiness for African American males and in improving and increasing postsecondary opportunities for first-generation students, low-income students, and students of color.

Carlos P. Hipolito-Delgado, PhD, is a professor at the University of Colorado Denver. His research interests focus on the sociopolitical development of students of color, the cultural competence of counselors-in-training, the ethnic identity development of Latinx youth, and the internalization of racism in communities of color.

Leigh Falls Holman, PhD, LPC-MHSP-Supervisor, RPT-S, is the Clinical Mental Health Counseling Department chair for the Dallas campus of The Chicago School of Professional Psychology. Her research interests focus on counselor burnout, trauma interventions with addiction and offending behaviors, and teaching and supervising students and emerging counselors who are working with forensic populations.

Renée C. Howells, PhD, NCC, is an assistant professor at The University of New Mexico. Her expertise is in crisis and trauma counseling. Her research interests focus on traumatology and disability identity and inclusion.

Denita N. Hudson, PhD, LPC, is an associate professor at The Chicago School of Professional Psychology. Her expertise is in multicultural counseling and social justice and in counseling student development. Her research interests focus on global counseling, the effect of racial trauma on Black families, career choice, and development.

Marty Jencius, PhD, is an associate professor at Kent State University. His expertise is in the application of technology to the practice and teaching of counseling. His research interests focus on teaching and technology innovation in counseling and on the study of counselor subjectivity using Q methodology.

Gülşah Kemer, PhD, NCC, ACS, is an associate professor in and director of the Counseling Doctoral Program at Old Dominion University. Her expertise is in clinical supervision. Her research interests focus on counselor and supervisor training and development with a specific focus on beginning and expert supervisors' thought processes.

Aiesha Lee, MA, NCC, is a doctoral student at the College of William & Mary. Her expertise is in trauma and systems theory. Her research interests focus on trauma, spirituality, and multicultural counseling.

A. Stephen Lenz, PhD, LPC, NCC, is an associate professor at The University of Mississippi. His expertise is in youth development, holistic approaches to counselor training, and community-university partnerships for public mental health promotion. Additional interests focus on using multiple modalities in research and evaluation for cultivating practice-based evidence.

Huijuan Li, MEd, is a doctoral student in counselor education and supervision and a research assistant at The University of Iowa. Her expertise is in school counseling. Her research interests focus on trauma-related and multicultural issues in school counseling.

Kathryn P. Linich, LPC, is a doctoral student at the University of South Carolina. Her expertise is in grief and loss. Her research interests focus on grief education and wellness interventions for clients experiencing grief and loss.

Melissa Luke, PhD, LMHC, NCC, ACS, is Dean's Professor in the Department of Counseling and Human Services and the associate dean for research in the School of Education at Syracuse University. Her research interests focus on effective preparation and supervision of counselors to more effectively respond to the needs of underserved clients.

Erin C. M. Mason, PhD, LPC, is an assistant professor at Georgia State University. Her research interests focus on school counselor professional identity, pedagogy in counselor education, technology, and social media.

W. Bradley McKibben, PhD, RMHCI (FL), NCC, is an assistant professor at Nova Southeastern University. His expertise is in clinical mental health counseling and clinical supervision. His research interests focus on professional counselor development and relational/cultural issues and attachment strategies in clinical supervision.

Shekila Melchior, PhD, NCC, is an assistant professor and academic program coordinator at George Mason University. Her expertise is in school counseling, social justice, and immigration. Her research interests focus on social justice identity development, undocumented students/immigrants, the professional identity development of school counselors, human trafficking, and activist wellness.

Anita A. Neuer Colburn, PhD, LPC (VA), LCMHCS (NC), BC-TMH, ACS, NCC, is a clinical associate professor at The Family Institute at Northwestern University. Her expertise is in clinical supervision competency. Her research interests focus on lesbian, gay, bisexual, and transgender advocacy; spiritual integration in counseling and supervision; and group approaches to career management.

Jonathan H. Ohrt, PhD, is an associate professor at the University of South Carolina. His expertise is in school counseling. His research interests focus on mental health in schools, wellness promotion, and group work.

Derrick A. Paladino, PhD, LMHC, NCC, is a professor at Rollins College. His expertise is in college counseling, identity development, and crisis assessment and intervention. His research interests focus on college student development and multiracial identity.

Samir H. Patel, PhD, LPCC-S, LMHC, is an associate professor at Murray State University. His expertise is in clinical mental health counseling. His research interests focus on wellness within a multicultural/social justice framework and counselor training to enhance clinical efficacy.

Vanessa Placeres, PhD, LPC, Certified School Counselor, RPT, is an assistant professor at San Diego State University. Her research interests focus on multiculturalism and school counselor training.

Diandra J. Prescod, PhD, LPC, CCSP, is an associate professor at the University of Connecticut. Her expertise is in mental health and career counseling. Her research focuses on effective career development interventions for science, technology, engineering, and mathematics students and minoritized students in higher education.

Elizabeth A. Prosek, PhD, LPC, NCC, is an associate professor of counseling at The Pennsylvania State University. Her expertise is in clinical mental health counseling. Her research interests focus on counseling military populations; the diagnosis and assessment of co-occurring disorders; and ethics, competence, and professional identity development in counseling and counselor education.

Mark B. Scholl, PhD, LMHC (NY), is an associate professor in the Department of Counseling at Wake Forest University. His expertise is in providing career counseling to members of the ex-offender population. His research interests focus on culturally responsive counseling, promoting career development among ex-offenders, and constructivist career counseling.

Megan Speciale, PhD, is an assistant professor at Palo Alto University. Her expertise is in sexual wellness and lesbian, gay, bisexual, transgender, queer, and intersex (LGBTQI+) children, adolescents, adults, and families. Her research interests focus on feminist and queer perspectives on counseling and counselor education, sexuality counseling/education, and LGBTQI+ issues.

Shawn L. Spurgeon, PhD, NCC, LPC-MHSP, ACS, is an associate professor at The University of Tennessee, Knoxville. His research interests focus on African American male development and counselor identity development.

Sam Steen, PhD, PK-12 License in School Counseling, is an associate professor and academic program coordinator at George Mason University. His expertise is in school counseling, group work, and multiculturalism. His research interests focus on group counseling in school settings, school counselor identity development, and the achievement of students of color.

LoriAnn Sykes Stretch, PhD, LCMHC-S, NCC, ACS, BC-TMH, is a clinical associate professor at the College of William & Mary. Her expertise is in issues of social justice, international counseling, telehealth, and online pedagogy. Her research interests focus on educational equity, global counseling, telehealth, and clinical supervision.

Matthew Tirrell, MS, LPC, NCC, ACS, is the director of field placement and an adjunct professor in the Department of Professional Counseling at Monmouth University. His expertise is in counseling people with comorbid disorders and supervising counselors-in-training. His research interests focus on lesbian, gay, bisexual, transgender, queer, and intersex (LGBTQI+) people in recovery and contextual factors in multicultural supervision.

Linwood G. Vereen, PhD, NCC, is an associate professor in the Department of Counseling and College Student Personnel at Shippensburg University of Pennsylvania. His research interests focus on leadership, Black existentialism, group work, and humanistic counseling.

Unity Walker, MEd, NCC, is a doctoral student at the College of William & Mary. Their expertise is in marginalized advocacy, transpersonal issues in counseling, and counselor development. Their research interests focus on marginalized advocacy and transpersonal development.

Richard E. Watts, PhD, LPC-S, is SHSU Distinguished Professor and Texas State University System Regents' Professor in the Department of Counselor Education at Sam Houston State University. His research interests focus on the integration of Adlerian, cognitive, constructivist, humanistic-existential, and psychodynamic theories and applications in work with individuals, couples, and groups; supervision; education; and leadership. He is also interested in ethical, religious, and spiritual issues related to counseling.

Jo Lauren Weaver, MS, ALC, NCC, is a doctoral student and research assistant at the University of Florida. Her research interests focus on effective treatment modalities for children and adolescents, restorative justice, generational impacts of social media, and creativity in counseling and counselor education.

Jane M. Webber, PhD, LPC, is an assistant professor and doctoral program coordinator at Kean University. Her expertise is in trauma counseling; disaster response; and child, adolescent, and school counseling. Her research interests focus on trauma training and counseling approaches and on trauma-informed supervision.

Kelly L. Wester, PhD, LCMHC, NCC, is a professor at the University of North Carolina at Greensboro. Her expertise and research interests focus on researcher identity and research self-efficacy development and on nonsuicidal self-injury.

Cirecie A. West-Olatunji, PhD, is a professor at Xavier University of Louisiana and a past-president of the American Counseling Association. Her research focuses on the relationship between traumatic stress and systemic oppression.

Kathy Ybañez-Llorente, PhD, LPC-S, is an associate professor at Texas State University. Her expertise is in ethics, multicultural supervision, advocacy, professional leadership and service, and licensure regulation. Her research interests focus on professional identity, clinical supervision, ethics, and licensure regulation.

Part I
Teaching

Section 1
Student Engagement and Dispositions 5

Section 2
Dynamics Related to Diversity and Inclusion 53

Section 3
Instructor Preparedness 85

Counselor educators spend more time teaching than in any other role. The 2016 Council for Accreditation of Counseling and Related Educational Programs (CACREP) Standards (CACREP, 2016) specify teaching as a core area, including coverage of a more traditional knowledge base (e.g., models of adult learning) alongside specialty skills for delivering coursework, assessing skills, and addressing problems of professional competence. Likewise, the *ACA Code of Ethics* (American Counseling Association [ACA], 2014) addresses ethical issues counselor educators may encounter within the classroom, including the importance of self-growth, clear expectations for students, and gatekeeping responsibilities. Furthermore, the Association for Counselor Education and Supervision Teaching Initiative Taskforce (2016) provides *Best Practices in Teaching in Counselor Education* to guide these processes.

Like many tasks in our complex profession, teaching is about so much more than delivering content and ensuring aspiring counselors have the knowledge to pass licensure examinations. Rather, counselor educators must create environments in which students learn content, establish foundations for complex skills, and cultivate the dispositions they need to succeed. Even in courses with a high level of content, counselor educators require self-growth and awareness exercises, model elements of counseling relationships, and navigate intricate intrapersonal dynamics and interpersonal peer relationships. Furthermore, counselor educators engage these tasks in the context of holistic, professional programs, thus adding a layer of complexity to our teaching tasks. This part of the book encompasses 13 chapters grouped within three primary, although sometimes overlapping, areas: (a) student engagement and dispositions, (b) dynamics related to diversity and inclusion, and (c) instructor preparedness.

Student Engagement and Dispositions

Most counselor educators in graduate, professional programs focused on human relationship and communication expect a level of preparedness and engagement from adult learners in the classroom. A number of issues or situations may lead students to not meet expectations for engagement. Whether in part-time programs in which many students navigate work and family demands or in full-time programs in which they may be deluged with coursework (and also navigate work and family demands), students may manage their workload in ways that impact peers and course processes as a whole. In "I Don't Have a Clue: Responding to Unprepared or Unengaged Students," an instructor flounders when students have not read or prepared for class and thus cannot engage the lesson he prepared for them. Next "I Did My Part: Responding to Inequitable Group Project Contributions" features a group member who stops engaging with group members, who initially do her work out of fear for their grade; the instructor must decide how to address this, including considering strategies for balancing both the collaborative group process (an important work skill for any workplace) and the content of the assignment.

Counselor educators also encounter situations in which students intentionally or unintentionally violate the *ACA Code of Ethics* (ACA, 2014) as part of course experiences. These situations raise critical questions regarding student retention and remediation processes. Instructors must discern how to address concerns related to dispositions or ethical comportment in ways that are developmentally and culturally sensitive yet protect the public. "It's Not Their Work: A Case of Plagiarism" features an instructor who balances ethics and care when responding to a case of blatant plagiarism, adjusting course materials and processes to prevent future instances. Not all disposition concerns are so clear. In "Too Much Information: Maintaining Boundaries During Skills Practice" a student repeatedly shares her own trauma with peers, even after the instructor sets limits for sharing to help students practice appropriate self-disclosure. Likewise, "I'm a Counselor . . . Well Almost: Boundary Extensions in Service Learning" involves a student who oversteps her bounds of competence and parameters outlined as part of a service-learning engagement, raising questions regarding her self-awareness and willingness to follow supervisory directives.

As is also illustrated in the previous cases, counselor educators have unique responsibilities to help students develop self-awareness, intrapersonal understanding, and interpersonal skills. The *ACA Code of Ethics* (ACA, 2014) also directly states that "self-growth is an expected component of counselor education" (Standard F.8.c.), noting the importance of ethical principles and allowing students to decide what to share or withhold in class. These responsibilities are further highlighted in the 2016 CACREP Standards (CACREP, 2016) for experiential learning within multicultural counseling coursework and the requirement for at least 10 clock hours as members within a small-group experience. In "I'm Here, I'm Not Participating: Student Resistance to a Group Experience," an instructor must decide how to address a student, older than many of her peers, who chooses not to engage in small group.

Dynamics Related to Diversity and Inclusion

The counselor education curriculum must include clear and specific attention to the Multicultural and Social Justice Counseling Competencies (MSJCC; Ratts et al., 2015). The CACREP Standards (CACREP, 2016) require attention to the MSJCC in programs' admission processes, in the social and cultural diversity core area, and throughout other core areas, an expectation for infusion that is echoed in the *ACA Code of Ethics* (ACA, 2014). All counselor educators must have skills for facilitating growth in the MSJCC and broaching cultural issues and dynamics within programs at large. "Whose Cultural Competence? Students' Needs in Multicultural Courses" features a multicultural counseling course instructor whose attempt to meet a white student in their developmental space raises questions among peers of color regarding how their needs are met in the course. Likewise, "A Cohort Divided: Navigating Tensions Related to Race and Ethnicity" illustrates how dynamics regarding students' race and ethnicity can play out even in coursework not expressly focused on cultivation of the MSJCC. In both cases, instructors need to navigate tensions related to student dispositions and development.

At times, students will demonstrate dispositions that raise significant questions regarding their ability to work with diverse clients. Even when not nested within "the" multicultural course, instructors have a responsibility to respond in a timely, ethical manner. "I Need a New Partner: Addressing Cultural Encapsulation and Racism" features a student who requests a new partner for skills practice because she has difficulty understanding her peer's accent and cultural experiences. The doctoral student facilitator and instructor work to respond to the white student; however, they struggle to address the needs and experiences of the student of color.

Finally, the very nature of adult learning and of self-growth exercises inherent in counselor education can create situations in which students and faculty members feel connected with each other. This dynamic is compounded given the apprenticeship nature of relationships between doctoral students and faculty members. "Interacting With Me: Title IX and Faculty-Student Consensual Relationships" features a case in which a faculty member and doctoral student develop an increasingly flirtatious, personal relationship that ends in a Title IX complaint. Although university policy does not disallow such connections, the case raises important questions regarding boundaries, modeling, and aspirational ethics.

Instructor Preparedness

A final set of critical incidents encountered by counselor educators feature instructor preparedness and competence to engage teaching assignments. Many established counselor educators never engaged in sustained study of teaching and learning. Rather, they use their understanding of human development and relationships to navigate the teaching and learning process, often becoming highly skilled instructors. Although written before the coronavirus pandemic, "Embracing the Digital World: Instructor Preparedness for Online Delivery" highlights a critical issue experienced by the majority of counselor educators in 2020: expectations to move courses online with no or minimal preparation in online teaching and learning.

An additional issue related to instructor preparedness relates to balancing counselor-first and specialty identities. Many counselor educators develop specialty skills in one work setting (e.g., clinical mental health counseling, school counseling) yet teach core curricular coursework for students as a whole. In addition, last-minute budget or personnel issues may force counselor educators to teach courses for which they have little specialty expertise, creating tensions regarding scope of practice. This raises important questions regarding how instructors can ethically and competently help students apply material to their specialty areas. "Does It Apply to Me? Instructor Competency to Teach Specialty Courses" features a counselor educator who helps his department by teaching fieldwork courses outside his specialty area.

Even when they are well prepared in teaching methods and content, counselor educators experience tensions related to intersections of best practice and real-world practice. Often counselor educators lean on guest speakers to help make these connections. At times, however, guest speakers may inadvertently promote problematic practices. In "Something to Share: Promoting Unethical or Illegal Practice," an instructor must decide how to respond when a protégé discloses a well-intentioned yet fraudulent payment practice.

Section 1
Student Engagement and Dispositions

Chapter 1

I Don't Have a Clue: Responding to Unprepared or Unengaged Students

Jonathan H. Ohrt and Kathryn P. Linich

2014 *ACA Code of Ethics* Standards Addressed

- F.7.a. Counselor Educators
- F.9.a. Evaluation of Students

• • •

During his first semester teaching in a counselor education program, Professor O had been very excited for every class. He had spent hours preparing and updating handouts, developing experiential activities, and reviewing videos to show in class. On the day of class, he would review assigned readings to make sure he was up to date on the material. Although he did not spend nearly as much time preparing for courses currently, he continued to be enthusiastic about teaching and was very well prepared to engage with students. He hoped that students shared his enthusiasm and were equally prepared to engage in a shared learning experience.

Professor O primarily adhered to a humanistic (C. R. Rogers, 1969) and experiential (Kolb, 1984) teaching philosophy. He tried to facilitate warm, empathic, genuine, and trusting relationships with students. He attempted to facilitate an open environment in which students felt comfortable sharing their perspectives and enjoyed inquiring about course topics within a learning community. Professor O viewed student learning as an active process that included both cognitive and affective components. He believed students learned best by doing, reflecting, and trying new approaches.

On the first day of class, Professor O reviewed the syllabus and discussed requirements, including reading and assignments. He explained that he would not lecture directly from the book and expected that students would read and be prepared to discuss the content. Professor O emphasized his belief that active learning was most helpful and class was most enriching when everyone was engaged. Professor O liked to start each class with a check-in and a brief discussion of students' perceptions of the topic. For example, he might ask about personal or professional experiences related to the topic or how the topic related to other aspects of counseling. In the first few weeks of class, he often facilitated brainstorming activities to engage the class in discussion.

One particular semester, Professor O taught the course Critical Issues in School Counseling. The course was an overview of current issues and concerns school counselors encounter. The content for the class session included environmental risk factors K–12 students face related to academics and overall well-being. Professor O started class by asking students to share some thoughts about the reading. He inquired about which risk factors surprised them most and how they believed school counselors could help prevent student distress related to them. Although he typically started class this way, the discussion during this class related more closely to concepts covered in the required reading.

After about a minute of observing the glazed looks on students' faces, Professor O realized most were unsure about how to answer the question because they could not recall specific risk factors in the reading. In an attempt to encourage participation, he half-jokingly reminded them "Participation is 15% of your grade—let's make sure we all get our points today." A few of the students laughed nervously while others continued to stare with blank faces. After a few more moments of silence, he asked, "Is any of this ringing a bell?" He still did not get a response. It became clear that students either had not completed the assigned readings ahead of time or did not comprehend the material well enough to share their perspectives.

Professor O was confused because the discussion had been rather lively in previous class meetings. When it became clear nobody was going to volunteer, he asked students what was keeping them from sharing. After another moment of silence with no real response, Professor O blurted out, "Did anybody read?" He noticed guilty looks on students' faces as some reluctantly shook their heads. He then asked, "So what's going on? Why aren't we reading?" Finally, a more vocal student jumped in and explained, "We just finished a big paper that was due yesterday for another class, and we have an exam in our class tomorrow. We have just been really busy this week." Although the student was not speaking on behalf of everyone, there appeared to be somewhat of a consensus among the students.

Professor O's genuine internal reaction was to be a bit offended. He had spent time planning his class, and he felt disappointed that students were not invested in his class. Professor O was careful not to shame the students. Instead, he tried to empathize with them: "You are overwhelmed this week. Sometimes in graduate school things are piled on all at once and it is hard to get to everything. Reading can be hard when it's not directly tied to a grade or assignment." He spent some time talking about how reading ahead is imperative to having fruitful class discussions. Professor O eventually moved on to the content of the class. Students were engaged in the discussion throughout the rest of the class when prompted or when asked to work in small groups.

Case Analysis and Discussion

Many instructors assign readings to help students prepare for class so they can use class time to focus on discussion and activities without spending time reviewing concepts students can easily read. Although it is not uncommon to encounter students who are unprepared, it can be frustrating. Instructors know how and why the material is important, and they can see how it plays into the bigger picture of learning outcomes. Instructors get excited to hear students' perspectives, and it can take the wind out of their sails to be met with blank stares and silence. Silence can cause instructors to have to think on their feet, rearranging plans to account for students' lack of preparation. This is a skill all instructors develop throughout their careers.

There are some important considerations in this case. It could be helpful to consider students' learning preferences. Some students may feel intimidated to speak up in front of the whole class, even if the class is small. Students may do better in pairs or small groups, where the focus is not solely on them. Although it might be nice to have a full class discussion, not all students are initially comfortable participating in this way. Another consideration is that some students learn better through experiences and discussions rather than reading. They may not get as much out of reading because there is nothing to apply it to in the moment. The relevance of topics at hand may become clearer once a discussion begins, an activity is done, or experiences are shared that can better contextualize the meaning of the concepts learned (Kolb, 2015). Finally, some students may not have actually completed the reading. Many professionals cannot honestly say that they have completed all assigned readings. Sometimes students simply do not want to do it, and so they do not. Other times they may feel overwhelmed; readings get cut from the to-do list in favor of something of higher priority. Sometimes students forget about the readings. Regardless, students are coming to class with no introduction to the topic, and they may be secretly hoping other students will contribute and save the class.

Critical Analysis

Regardless of which of the aforementioned issues applies, the reality is that the instructor is faced with a room full of students who are not prepared. Educators should question realistic expectations when it comes to classroom preparation. The *ACA Code of Ethics* (American Counseling Association [ACA], 2014) states that counselor educators should be "skilled in applying . . . knowledge; and make students and supervisees aware of their responsibilities" as well as serve as role models for the profession (Standard F.7.a.). Instructors provide a syllabus that clearly outlines expectations for the course, but it can be tricky to address students when expectations are not being met. As counselors, students will be faced with clients or students who are not following recommendations or putting in work outside of session. It would not be appropriate for them to scold or punish their clients for not meeting expectations. However, counselor educators are ethically responsible for modeling counselor characteristics while still evaluating student progress and assessing for competency (ACA, 2014). Instructors who gently remind students about the importance of participating and explore their reasons for not doing the reading can model professionalism while holding students accountable and working toward a solution, just as they might with a reluctant or resistant client.

What appears to be a lack of student preparation can also be misleading. An important part of experiential learning is reviewing readings assigned in class (West et al., 2013). West et al. (2013) suggested spending 15 to 20 minutes at the beginning of each class going over important topics and referring to specifics in the readings. This can help students understand the most important parts of a lesson prior to engaging in discussion and activities. West et al.'s approach is interesting because they posited that students who react to prompts in the ways described in the case above may not be unprepared. Rather, they may have read without knowing what they were looking for; thus, they were not able to retain key topics or concepts. This is students' first exposure to the material, and they may also be taking other classes in which they are flooded with new information. Providing an overview of why assigned readings matter or what to look for may be key to helping students retain information in the long run.

It is also important to remember cultural considerations that may impact students' preparation. Ng (2006) found that the three most common concerns for non-Western international counseling students were English proficiency, adjustment, and conflict with Western understanding and approaches. Students may not understand readings or questions because English is not their first language. They may be dealing with concerns around cultural adjustment. They may also be struggling to relate to Western conceptualizations of cases and solutions. Sharing conflicts or personal experiences with a group of strangers may also be inappropriate from a cultural standpoint. It is important to check and provide assistance as well as consider the unique perspectives of non-Western students in the context of class discussion (Ng, 2006).

When instructors consider cultural differences, it is important that they think about aspects of U.S. culture and history that may make international students and English language learners uncomfortable (Interiano & Lim, 2018). Historical inequalities and experiences of marginalization may cause students to feel uneasy asking or answering a question in class. In this same vein, dominant white American culture tends to strongly favor assimilation, encouraging people of color to abandon their culture of origin in favor of adopting dominant norms and values. Students may worry about their English not being good enough or their perspectives going against white American values. These concerns can lead to students being rejected by peers and faculty members. Instructors can combat this by viewing the material they are teaching through a multicultural lens. Incorporating multiple cultural perspectives into lessons and opening the door for conversations about culture may encourage students to share their views.

There are also considerations for working with minoritized students from the United States. In one study, Black doctoral students suggested that having white teachers who were invested in them and their success helped them feel supported and have more trust in their mentors (E. M. Brown & Grothaus, 2019). White faculty members may leverage networks and resources to help minoritized students access opportunities that are more difficult to access as a result of systemic oppression; this is a way to show investment in their success. Instructors can also demonstrate investment in students' success and experience by reaching out to students outside of class to check in, which may help them feel more comfortable speaking up in class.

Actions and Outcomes

Professor O spent some time processing students' lack of preparation. He empathized with their heavy school workload and reiterated the importance of coming to class prepared. These actions were consistent with his teaching philosophy. In this case, the incident could have been mitigated with better planning on the part of the instructor. Although Professor O discussed expectations, more explicit directions may have been helpful for students. For example, he could have provided discussion prompts prior to class to help students prepare ahead of time rather than relying on students' ability to recall specific concepts from the reading.

As a result of this incident, Professor O provided more guidance by developing questions for review prior to class. He adjusted the class format to give students an opportunity to engage in small-group discussion prior to large-group discussion. Students discussed prompts with a partner before coming together for class discussion. This helped accommodate students who were not comfortable speaking in front of the large group. In future courses, Professor O tied class discussions based on readings to course credit to help students feel more invested in the activity.

Professor O confronted students about being prepared, but he ultimately did not hold them accountable by reducing participation points. He also could have required students to complete readings or an additional activity or assignment to demonstrate understanding of the topic as opposed to moving on with the class. Although he processed students' reactions, he could have spent more time processing expectations for active participation. For example, he could have started by getting a sense of students' preferences and their comfort sharing in large groups. Professor O could also have sought more explicit feedback on course readings. It could have been that the readings were not interesting or were too difficult for students to understand.

As a result of the incident, Professor O gained insight into more effective ways of interacting with students. The students were honest with him about feeling overwhelmed. This interaction is encouraging within a humanistic teaching philosophy. Students seemed to appreciate an empathic response and became motivated to participate in the class. However, Professor O also learned that his student-centered approach required adjustments to fully work. He recognized the need to be especially clear about expectations. Students may know they will be expected to contribute to class discussions, but they are more engaged when they know which topics from the reading might be discussed.

Conclusion

Active student engagement is a fundamental requirement in essentially all counselor education courses. There are a variety of reasons why students may hesitate to participate, and instructors are responsible for fostering active engagement in the classroom. Doing so will help instructors avoid disappointment when students do not prioritize their specific class. In Professor O's case, guided questions helped provide structure and organization for discussions, which subsequently flowed more smoothly in future class meetings. Overall, the empathy of Professor O and the intentional design of experiential activities helped everyone feel more comfortable with expectations and with participating in learning with their classmates.

Reflection Questions

1. What are some challenges you anticipate when promoting student engagement in discussion?
2. What are some additional helpful strategies for engaging students in discussion?

Critical Incident Response

Samir H. Patel

A common expectation across academic disciplines is that students will read assigned materials prior to the start of class. Despite being a necessity for most, if not all, counselor education courses, students do not always follow through with this requirement. Professor O experienced a conundrum when his approach to teaching did not account for student noncompliance with reading expectations. The case provides dialogue around potential reasons for readings not being completed, ethical issues this might pose, and cultural considerations of which to be mindful. These components are critical, and there are other opportunities to explore: (a) limitations of pedagogies, (b) specific techniques to increase reading compliance, and (c) cultural competencies to enhance student-teacher relationships.

Professor O took a humanistic and experiential approach to teaching. Major tenets of humanistic education include (a) creating learning environments that promote achievement by actualizing the full potential of students; (b) fostering a culture in which self-directed learning results in deep learning of new material; and (c) cultivating relationships in which cooperation, not competition, is center of the classroom experience (Khatib et al., 2013). In addition, the experiential teaching philosophy provides a path for assisting students in challenging personal beliefs while exposing them to diverse worldviews (Greene et al., 2014).

Professor O can use humanistic constructs to design courses and deliver content to promote student learning. Although he could penalize students for noncompliance by deducting participation points, this strategy would be out of character for an orthodox, humanistic counselor educator. Thus, an argument for considering limitations of the humanistic teaching philosophy is warranted.

There are a number of strategies for increasing student compliance with reading. For instance, Hoeft (2012) discussed the efficacy of attaching quizzes to readings, providing supplementary assignments tied to readings, and discussing readings in class prior to assigning them (e.g., hyping up chapters before students leave class). Kerr and Frese (2017) encouraged instructors to create collaborative apps (e.g., word clouds, wikis, Google Docs) to promote dialogue around readings outside of class. These types of self-directed learning activities are foundational to both humanistic and experiential teaching and might help Professor O view strategies to remedy student noncompliance through a student-centered lens.

The authors also noted the importance of viewing participation through a cultural lens. It is critical that instructors continue their professional development as it relates to the Multicultural and Social Justice Counseling Competencies (Ratts et al., 2016). Instructors should consider strategies to promote access for students of color. For instance, they can bring awareness to student research focused on social justice issues. Finally, instructors can demonstrate investment in students by checking in with them outside of class, which may create stronger relationships and increase student engagement in and outside of class.

Professor O considered the use of small-group experiences to promote in-class dialogue. This approach may also be culturally responsive for promoting dialogue among international students, who may not always feel comfortable engaging in classroom discussion because of cultural norms, language barriers, or concerns about not being able to accurately articulate their thoughts (Kwon, 2009). To circumvent some of these issues, instructors can create small groups, provide prompts to the students in advance, and provide feedback during group discussions to reinforce continued dialogue (Corse, 2011).

This case illustrates a common experience for instructors. When students do not follow through with expectations, the onus is on instructors to make changes to promote learning. Counselor educators are tasked with meeting students at their developmental levels while providing experiences that promote a professional counseling identity. All in all, Professor O's adjustments modeled roles of counselor educators and expectations for counseling professionals without placing negative judgment on students.

• • •

Chapter 2

I Did My Part: Responding to Inequitable Group Project Contributions

Linwood G. Vereen, Clewiston D. Challenger, and Nicole R. Hill

2014 *ACA Code of Ethics* Standards Addressed

- F.8.d. Addressing Personal Concerns
- F.9.a. Evaluation of Students

• • •

Mary was a first-semester master's student enrolled in a group counseling course taught by Professor Jack Madden. A single parent of a teenager, Mary had completed her undergraduate degree in the early 1990s and had been working full time as a case manager for an assisted living center for the past 10 years. The group course was designed to meet 2016 Council for Accreditation of Counseling and Related Educational Programs (CACREP) Standards (CACREP, 2016) regarding foundational group counseling skills and fundamentals in designing and developing curricula for psychoeducational groups. As part of the course, students were part of a learning triad in which they worked collaboratively to design a group. Professor Madden used this assignment to prepare the counseling students with skills needed to conceptualize group format and practice curriculum development. The assignment was clear: Each group was to create a curriculum focused on a theme of interest. Professor Madden emphasized that each group should have eight distinct sessions to educate members and allow space to process their thoughts, feelings, and experiences.

During the first week of the semester, Professor Madden emphasized that "each group member is expected to work in full cooperation with the others and share the workload equitably on this assignment by doing their part." Mary was grouped with Kyle and Jennifer, who were also first-semester master's students; all group members immediately liked one another and were excited to work together. Understanding Mary's situation, Professor Madden encouraged her to have an open discussion with her group members about workload distribution and the coordination of schedules. Mary, Kyle, and Jennifer met off campus to discuss their approach to the assignment. The group decided that Kyle and Jennifer would each develop three plans while Mary was responsible for completing two. Kyle and Jennifer said they wanted to respect Mary's limited availability and her roles as a parent and full-time professional.

As the semester progressed, Mary, Kyle, and Jennifer developed rapport and seemed to work well together. Meeting weekly, each member communicated well and contributed their thoughts, ideas, and comments equally to the project. Initially it appeared as if the group's chemistry was paying off as the project progressed smoothly. However, Mary began accepting overtime hours and was less available to attend group meetings in person because of her obligations. Mary requested that the group transition to virtual meetings; Kyle and Jennifer accommodated the virtual meetings so Mary could continue to be included.

After several weeks of virtual meetings, Mary expressed appreciation for how efficiently the group was working together but subsequently withdrew from the virtual meetings altogether, citing her overwhelming work and parental duties. Kyle and Jennifer continued meeting regularly to work on the assignment while trying to practice patience and understanding toward Mary. Both assumed Mary was responsible and would get her sections of the project done.

One week before the due date, Kyle and Jennifer had growing concerns about making the deadline even though both had completed their sections. Mary's communication with the group had been minimal for a few weeks, and Kyle and Jennifer were left in the dark regarding the status of her assigned sections. Although the group members saw one another in Professor Madden's class each week, Mary often appeared preoccupied and unable to talk with her groupmates, leaving class immediately after dismissal. Kyle and Jennifer tried unsuccessfully to contact Mary for updates.

Three days before the due date, Mary emailed her group to update them on her progress. Mary said that her work hours and daughter's extracurricular school activities had hindered her ability to give her full attention to the project. She admitted that she had only completed one of the two sessions assigned to her. Mary expressed disappointment in her efforts and acknowledged Kyle and Jennifer's disappointment. She requested that Kyle and Jennifer complete the plan.

Kyle and Jennifer privately expressed their frustration with Mary's nonchalant approach. Concerned about their grades, they reluctantly agreed to complete the final group session, channeled their energy, and submitted the completed assignment on time. Nevertheless, Kyle and Jennifer felt uneasy; neither thought the workload was equitable or balanced. Kyle suggested they make Professor Madden aware of the group dynamics and workload distribution. He felt this information would inform how Professor Madden graded their assignment. After all, Professor Madden had been clear about his expectations that group members contribute equitably and collaboratively. Jennifer did not wish to rock the boat and pleaded with Kyle to reconsider mentioning this to Professor Madden and to be more understanding of Mary's situation.

A few days after the project was submitted, Mary reached out to Kyle and Jennifer to express her gratitude for their flexibility and understanding. Rather than taking responsibility for her shortcomings, Mary continually praised her peers for their ability to spring into action when it had come down to the wire. Mary sighed and said, "Whew, that was a close one. Talk about cutting it close. But I think we will get a good grade on the assignment." Her comment did not resonate well with Kyle and Jennifer. They disclosed that they had privately requested that Professor Madden grade their assignment independently and not as a group. Mary felt disappointed, ambushed, and misunderstood. She exclaimed that her time was limited and she had done her part. Mary told Kyle and Jennifer that they did not understand that she did not have the same freedom as them and that she felt singled out because of her age, parental status, and employment status.

Case Analysis and Discussion

Promoting effective group work has been a long-standing challenge for many counselor educators because of the difficulty of assessing individual contributions while focusing on the overall collective assignment. Professor Madden expected students to gain knowledge of effective development of group curricula while also promoting their development as coleaders who navigate group dynamics. Given the explicit and implicit student learning outcomes of this experience, the response to this case should be viewed from multiple perspectives, namely, the ethical framework of the case, the assessment protocol implemented by Professor Madden with an emphasis on group process, and the impact on student growth and development.

Although there were no egregious ethical violations, there was a series of minor concerns that could morph into a more complex concern regarding Mary's growth and progress through the program. None of the participants in this case study were put in harm's way, and no one experienced significant trauma as a result of the class assignment. Yet the Preamble to the *ACA Code of Ethics* (American Counseling Association [ACA], 2014) specifically identifies one of the guiding principles of professional ethical behavior as fidelity, or "honoring commitments and keeping promises, including fulfilling one's responsibilities of trust in professional relationships" (p. 3). Mary's behavior during the group assignment did not fulfill her commitments to her peers. Although many graduate students are willing to help their peers, it seems as if Mary took advantage of the situation. She made unilateral decisions that impacted her peers without consulting them.

As an emerging counselor who will be expected to follow the *ACA Code of Ethics* (ACA, 2014), it is imperative that Mary also understand that "counselors aspire to open, honest, and accurate communication in dealing with the public and other professionals" (p. 8, Section C). During the assignment, Mary stopped actively and accurately communicating with her peers. As she continues to develop as a counselor, she will need to cultivate and demonstrate that critical area of ethical comportment.

The role of the instructor is another important consideration. Specifically, Professor Madden could have put measures in place to better support and protect the interest of all students. This includes recognizing dynamics of group projects in which the distribution of work is ultimately inequitable. As in other areas of professional life, an equitable distribution of work may not be realistic, yet it is important to consider. Professor Madden might have provided information to enhance the learning environment and better support students by clearly stating expectations and providing "ongoing feedback regarding their performance throughout the training program" (ACA, 2014, Standard F.9.a.) Similarly, CACREP Standards emphasize the critical role of assessing student learning and dispositions throughout the program (CACREP, 2016, Section 4, Standards F and G). Professor Madden could have integrated specific assessment protocols and feedback processes to mitigate some of the challenges of inequitable work distribution.

Professor Madden comes across as having developed an assignment, assigned students to work groups, and provided direction and expectations with attention to a final due date. What is missing are the steps he could have taken to ensure that all students had a fair opportunity for success as group members and as individuals. There could have been one or two benchmark opportunities for group members to receive instructor support for their work. In addition, groups could have clearly delineated individual tasks or responsibilities in writing with Professor Madden.

The group counseling course and the corresponding project are ideal for the development and implementation of a rubric or set of rubrics that clearly articulate goals and expectations of the project. Assessment rubrics should also clearly articulate how each student will be evaluated. Learning outcomes are important to graduate education and counselor training, as the role of a professional counselor is action oriented. With this being said, it is important to have a defined set of outcome measures within each course. Students need to know whether they are being assessed on the group process or the group product. The rubric in Table 2.1 provides an example of how to assess group performance.

The students could have been better supported in their experience if Professor Madden had developed a few benchmarks for the assignment. For example, the students could have turned in work plans that outlined the type of project they intended to complete, the timeline for completion, and the distribution of tasks among group members. This could have supported the students' efforts and also allowed Professor Madden an opportunity to lend support and have a working knowledge of what each group intended to accomplish. Professor Madden could have developed a rubric to outline what aspects of the final assignment needed to be present in the benchmark. The rubric also could have delineated whether any assessments were individual rather than group based. This would have assisted each student in a self-assessment of their work and helped them begin to answer the overall question of whether they had done their part.

Impact on Student Growth and Development

Another perspective to be addressed is how this case impacts student growth and development. Both the CACREP Standards (CACREP, 2016) and the *ACA Code of Ethics* (ACA, 2014) clearly discuss the evaluation of students and the importance of experiences for self-growth. This includes an assessment of academic, clinical, and dispositional growth throughout the program. Course assignments that require a high level of self-awareness and collaboration provide an opportunity for students to be assessed on their professional dispositions. The first step in this is the identification of such dispositions. Spurgeon, Gibbons, and Cochran (2012) operationalized five dispositions: commitment, openness, respect, integrity, and self-awareness.

TABLE 2.1

Sample Rubric for Group Process Contribution

	Skill Level Rating Scale			
	4 (*Always*)	3 (*Almost Always*)	2 (*Sometimes*)	1 (*Rarely*)
Task completion	Always brought needed materials Always ready to work Consistently stayed focused on the task and what needed to be done Could be counted on by other group members all the time	Almost always brought needed materials Almost always ready to work Focused on the task and what needed to be done most of the time Could be counted on by others most of the time	Sometimes brought needed materials Sometimes ready to work Focused on the task and what needed to be done some of the time Could be counted on by others some of the time	Rarely brought needed materials Rarely ready to work Rarely focused on the task and what needed to be done Let others do the work most of the time
Contribution	Completed an equal share of the work Strived to maintain equity of work throughout the project	Contributed significantly but other group members clearly contributed more	Contributed some toward the project	Contributions were insignificant or nonexistent
Communication	Consistently responsive to requests for input and feedback Initiated communication among the group Shared work for feedback	Usually responsive to requests for feedback and input Sometimes initiated communication Usually showed work for feedback	Sometimes responsive to requests for feedback and input Occasionally initiated communication Sometimes showed work for feedback	Rarely responsive to requests for feedback and input Rarely initiated communication Rarely shared work for feedback
Preparation	Often cited from readings Used readings and experiences to support point of view	Occasionally cited from readings Sometimes used readings and experiences to support point of view	Rarely able to cite from readings Rarely used readings and experiences to support point of view	Unable to cite from readings Could not use readings and experiences to support point of view
Demonstration of professional attitude and demeanor	Always demonstrated commitment through participation Always arrived on time Often solicited others' perspectives Always had a positive attitude toward the project and the group	Rarely unprepared Rarely arrived late Occasionally solicited others' perspectives Often had a positive attitude toward the group and the project	Often unprepared Occasionally arrived late Rarely solicited others' perspectives Usually had a positive attitude toward the group and the project	Rarely prepared Often arrived late Never solicited others' perspectives Rarely had a positive attitude toward the group or project
Cooperation and interaction	Was consistently courteous and valued others' opinions Routinely volunteered point of view Always a willing participant Worked to minimize conflict and was effective at resolving personal issues within the group Responded frequently to questions	Was mostly courteous and valued most opinions Occasionally volunteered point of view Minimally involved in either starting or resolving conflicts Responded occasionally to questions	Was sometimes courteous and valued some opinions Rarely volunteered point of view The source of conflict within the group Rarely able to respond to questions	Was not courteous and did not value others' opinions Never volunteered point of view Participated in regular conflict that interfered with group progress Never able to respond to questions
Quality of work and leadership	Exhibited excellent listening and leadership skills Provided work of the highest quality Comments were relevant and reflective of knowledge, previous comments from students, and learning Comments frequently moved the research project forward	Provided high-quality work Comments were mostly relevant and reflective of knowledge, previous comments from students, and learning Comments sometimes moved the research project forward	Provided work that occasionally needed to be checked or revised by group members to ensure quality Comments were rarely relevant and were only slightly reflective of knowledge, previous comments from students, and learning Comments rarely moved the research project forward	Provided work that usually needed to be checked or revised by group members to ensure quality Comments reflected little understanding and betrayed a lack of preparation Comments did not move the research project forward

The dispositions most applicable to Mary are commitment and integrity, defined as "investment in learning; development of counselor identity; advocacy; professional excellence; civic engagement; collaboration; scholar/practitioner; interpersonal competence" and "personal responsibility; personal and professional maturity; honesty; courage; congruence," respectively (Spurgeon, Gibbons, & Cochran, 2012, p. 103). It is important for Professor Madden to be knowledgeable about the scholarly discussion of dispositions (Miller et al., 2020; Spurgeon, Gibbons, & Cochran, 2012) and how accreditation and ethical standards inform the manner in which counselor educators provide feedback to emerging counselors about their dispositions. From this perspective, each assignment has the potential to address significant parts of student development and opportunities for self-growth.

The impact of failure to address student growth can be significant. Mary's choices provide an example of the importance of being aware of one's impact on others. Mary engaged in a set of behaviors seemingly without much care or concern for the impact her choices would have on those in her group. She unilaterally decided that Kyle and Jennifer could complete the assigned project in her absence. In addition, she shared comments of support and congratulations after not fulfilling her commitment to the group or the project. This could easily be seen as being patronizing or not taking Kyle and Jennifer's individual needs into account. Professor Madden's lack of clarity regarding learning and growth expectations could also have a negative impact on the program's ability to assess key performance indicators or engage in remediation should concerns about Mary's dispositions continue.

Conclusion

Group assignments are an integral component of counselor training programs. Requiring students to complete group projects assesses two discrete domains: learning of the assignment (content) and individual contributions of students toward the completion of the group assignment (process). Proactively discussing how group assignments will be evaluated and how individual contributions will be assessed is a critical skill counselor educators need to cultivate. Group assignments can provide dispositional data for counselor trainees, and it is vital that counselor educators understand and see how failure to act could impact student growth experiences. Lack of intentionality, clarity, and communication in framing the evaluative framework for group assignments can create challenges for how counselor educators assess key performance indicators and student dispositions and for how students perceive the equity of work expectations across the program.

Reflection Questions

1. What steps could Jennifer and Kyle take to raise and express their concerns about their group project experience?
2. What would help Professor Madden assess students' level of participation, knowledge acquisition, and content understanding?

Critical Incident Response

Vaibhavee R. Agaskar and Jean Georgiou

The authors considered three important factors: Mary's ethical behavior, the role of the instructor in assessment, and students' growth and development in the graduate program. Although Mary did not commit any serious violations of the *ACA Code of Ethics* (ACA, 2014), students who aspire to become professional counselors must follow ACA's guiding principles of fidelity and professional responsibility.

Professor Madden needs to support students in completing their work and assignments. Rather than turning in an entire project at the end of the semester, it might be beneficial for students to turn in sections so instructors can give plentiful opportunities for students to revise their work before it receives a final grade (Bain, 2004). Professor Madden may also work on a rubric that specifies group members' tasks and responsibilities along with learning outcomes for the assignment. The rubric in Table 2.1 will help group participants evaluate their contributions to the group process. Considering the intricacy of group projects, it might be beneficial for students to receive grades both individually and as a group.

The crux of this analysis is the impact of group process on student development. Per CACREP Standards (CACREP, 2016), an adviser is required at all times during the program. Professor Madden may consider working with Mary's adviser to assist Mary in understanding her responsibilities as a graduate student. In addition to her academic and clinical skills, the program faculty need to evaluate Mary's professional dispositions. If needed, an adviser could create a remediation plan with Mary, with periodic accountability check-ins regarding other coursework until she progresses satisfactorily. An academic adviser could also suggest students seek supplementary services (e.g., in the writing center or counseling center) to support their academic and personal growth.

As a single parent who was working full time and returning to college after some life experience, Mary was a nontraditional student. Nontraditional students may face a variety of concerns and special needs requiring different approaches and methods (Rash et al., 2008). Mentorship plays a valuable role in the optimal development of students and may be helpful when working with nontraditional students across disciplines (Mullen, 2005). ACA (2012) and CACREP (2016) have also highlighted the importance of mentorship in the counseling profession. Faculty mentorship and contact are especially valuable for helping females and minoritized students feel connected to their programs in ways that may improve the retention and graduation rates of these students (Butler et al., 2013; Lechuga, 2011). Mary may benefit from working with faculty members who can advise or mentor her in the graduate program. Similarly, peer mentorship may be advantageous to Mary (Boswell et al., 2015). For example, membership in Chi Sigma Iota might help Mary build a strong support network with peers during the program and beyond.

Part of ensuring student success is not only providing students with necessary tools but also showing them how to use them. Some students will require different tools or more time learning how to use them than others. Through various stages of guidance, advisement, mentorship, and professional development, students like Mary can triumph in academia as well as in the counseling profession.

• • •

Chapter 3

It's Not Their Work: A Case of Plagiarism

Tiphanie Gonzalez

2014 *ACA Code of Ethics* Standards Addressed

- F.9.a. Evaluation of Students
- G.5.b. Plagiarism
- G.5.c. Acknowledging Previous Work

• • •

Professor P was a first-year faculty member at a local college in a city environment. While grading for the Multicultural Counseling course, one paper struck Professor P as very familiar. The assignment was so impressive and of such high quality that their initial thought was that it could be published. Professor P did not have the software that allowed them to check for plagiarism. Rather, students submitted paper assignments during class. Although the content, language, and flow of the paper felt familiar, the fact that Professor P had received the assignment in this way made it feel new as well.

Professor P considered the student's past in-class contributions and assignments while evaluating the suspicious assignment. It was clear that this assignment was not in the student's voice. Unsure of how to move forward, Professor P started with a simple Google search using the most familiar sentences. Rather quickly, Professor P found an article that had been published in a well-known journal by a well-known author whom they had personally met at conferences in the past.

After finding the identical article via a Google search, Professor P emailed a request to the student to meet after the next class to talk about their submission. This was new territory for Professor P. Before meeting with the student, Professor

P took several steps to build a plan of action for addressing the plagiarism. After notifying the department chair, Professor P printed out the original published article and the student's paper for comparison. Professor P showed both the article and the paper submission to the student, addressing the plagiarism directly. During their meeting, the student shared that they did not understand the rules around plagiarism, noting that they were returning to graduate school after having an entirely different career and that writing these kinds of papers and citing in this way was foreign to them. The student asked Professor P not to report the plagiarism to the administration or fail the student in the course. The student offered to redo the assignment instead.

Because Professor P was teaching a graduate course, they had never considered teaching their students about plagiarism. Professor P thought plagiarism was something students already knew about. Plagiarism was something that could end the student's college career. Professor P wondered whether there might be a technology gap based on age, socioeconomics, or limited access to technology (Burt et al., 2011). For Professor P, this kind of plagiarism meant the student needed to at least fail this assignment, which in turn meant they were going to fail the course. Professor P was clear with the student that although this was the first time the student had been found plagiarizing, failing the assignment was fair. Professor P moved forward with some discomfort, wondering what they could have done differently to prevent the situation.

Case Analysis and Discussion

"Plagiarism occurs when a student intentionally or unintentionally uses another person's words or ideas without properly crediting their source, an offense that most university officials consider to be a serious breach of appropriate academic conduct" (Youmans, 2011, p. 749). Plagiarism is common among students. In a review of the literature, Youmans (2011) found that 7% to 55% of college students had knowingly plagiarized. Universities recognize the slippery slope of academic dishonesty during students' careers, noting that academic dishonesty can hinder the completion of degrees and contributions to potential fields of work (Youmans, 2011).

The *ACA Code of Ethics* (American Counseling Association [ACA], 2014) makes it clear that counselor educators need to be well informed in the areas they teach (Standards F.7.a., F.7.b.). Many students and faculty members are drawn to certain authors, sometimes networking with them while attending conferences and programming. This is why Professor P easily realized that the student had submitted a work that was not their own. Counselor educators and supervisors also have an ethical responsibility to ensure aspiring counselors have the academic skills and professional dispositions to be in the field (Standards F.6.b., F.9.a.). This includes remediating incidents of academic dishonesty, which is a reflection of students' work and their moral character. Even when reproducing language from their own published works, authors need to properly cite and quote (Standards G.5.b., G.5.c.).

Vehviläinen et al. (2018) discussed how faculty members who work with students who have plagiarized can use one of two approaches: a rules ethical approach or a care ethical approach. The rules ethical approach is "based on the notion of the universal application of a rule viewed as detached from the subject" (p. 2), whereas the care ethical approach "places the act in relation to the actor's intentions and understandings" (p. 2). In deciding how to work with this student, Professor P was torn between being student forward or rule forward. As a counselor educator who was largely person centered, Professor P leaned toward a care ethical approach. Instead of sending the case to a disciplinary committee, Professor P created a lesson on the ins and outs of plagiarism and strategies for avoiding plagiarism. In accordance with a rules ethical approach, Professor P gave the student a failing grade for the assignment. However, they did not report the incident to the administration.

This decision to use a care ethical approach in assessing the student's explanation for why they had plagiarized the assignment but a rules ethical approach in handling grading was in line with a student-centered approach to teaching. It is important for instructors to be mindful of student diversity and needs (ACA, 2014, Standards F.11.b., F.11.c.). In this case, Professor P was mindful of this student's socioeconomic and age diversity. The student was older than their peers and admitted they were struggling with this type of writing and unfamiliarity with plagiarism. The student also appeared to have a technology gap compared to students who had moved directly through their undergraduate program and into their graduate program in a time of very easy access to journal articles, books, and websites (Burt et al., 2011). This increased the chance that the peers had been formally educated about plagiarism in a way this student had not. Although their peers may have been accustomed to plagiarism-checker reports, the entirety of this student's prior work may have been graded by hand, thus limiting the student's learning opportunities in comparison to peers who had access to this technology, which was normalized in their work.

Preventing Plagiarism in Future Classes

Graduate students have a wide variety of backgrounds, and counselor educators should consider strategies for preventing plagiarism. Faculty members may teach minilessons on plagiarism early in their classes and include tips on how not to plagiarize in their syllabi. They can also use worksheets and widely circulated plagiarism materials available through programs like Turnitin. Most colleges and universities also have preventive information. For example, the City University of New York at Hunter offers information on their website (see www.hunter.cuny.edu/studentaffairs/repository/files/What%20is%20Plagiarism.pdf).

Counselor educators can assess students' understanding of plagiarism early in their classes. Often they may be surprised by how little students understand plagiarism in its many forms. Unlike the blatant plagiarism in this scenario, more subtle forms of plagiarism often become a problem.

By sharing information in their syllabi, counselor educators can ensure that students have resources they can lean on when they are unsure about whether they are plagiarizing. When going over the syllabus during the first week of class, educators may have a short introductory discussion of their expectations for the quality of student work. At a minimum, students should receive a quick overview of cut-and-paste plagiarism, paraphrasing plagiarism, citing of quotations, and self-plagiarism at the beginning of the course.

Later counselor educators can discuss proper paraphrasing and how, even with in-text citations and references, paraphrases too close to the original source may be considered plagiarism. Taking a sentence and changing one or two words is common practice among students in early submissions of their work. Counselor educators may also notice overquoting within an assignment. These more subtle forms of plagiarism may be honest mistakes students have not had a chance to learn about within their undergraduate education.

Counselor educators may find that students misunderstand the appropriateness of resubmitting assignments (i.e., self-plagiarism) to multiple professors when they teach similar topics, in particular graduate students who often have limited time in their busy schedules. The idea of resubmitting the same work or cutting and pasting large parts of the same idea for a new assignment can seem both attractive and time effective. Students are often surprised to learn that they cannot cut and paste from their own work without citing the original work. Counselor educators should be creative and build assignments in ways that minimize the possibility of student plagiarism through duplication. Brainstorming with colleagues who teach similar courses at their own and other institutions can allow professors to gauge how common an assignment is. Instructors can also build assignments that require a thorough understanding of course materials while also allowing for self-reflection, as doing so can give assignments depth. To add these reflections, students must understand the material well enough to create connections. It is difficult for students to unknowingly plagiarize reflections when connecting them to course content, even if they are retelling an experience they shared in another class.

It is important for professors to share the rules students need to follow regarding academic honesty as an important part of their dialogue and rapport building. For example, Professor P could share how part of their professional requirements include the publication of articles and research. Like students in their classes, professors cannot submit the same work to more than one journal at a time. Even reworking an already published piece is discouraged and toes the line of self-plagiarism. Faculty members may also help their students understand that it is common practice to reformat course papers into articles for specific journals; this is acceptable and is not considered a form of plagiarism.

Steps After Plagiarism

Even the very best writers may misstep with regard to academic integrity and plagiarism. In addition to educating students, counselor educators must challenge themselves to follow five recommendations for discussing and assessing student work around plagiarism.

First, educators should keep reading and studying. Professor P was able to catch that the assignment was plagiarized because they were familiar with the author and the article. There is nothing wrong with having go-to articles, books, and authors, but counselor educators need to continue feeding their minds in the same way they encourage students to learn and grow.

Second, faculty members may use free-write assignments in class and have students hand them in before the first big assignment. The free-write assignments allow counselor educators to learn about students and their writing styles. They also allow students to hone their creativity around an assignment. Through free-write assignments, students can build depth by forming their own ideas prior to the due date. A student who is crunched for time may inadvertently copy an idea from another source because their memory is pulling information from documents, audios, or programs they have reviewed. This type of plagiarism is connected to something called *cryptomnesia* (Dow, 2015). Although it is controversial, there have been discussions on inadvertent plagiarism through memory in extremely public cases, in particular around music (Yin, 2016).

Third, instructors should be thorough while grading and openly discuss the grading process. This includes making an active decision not to skim student assignments. In addition to being able to fully hear what students are saying in their submissions, reading the entirety of students' work is an act of respect for the work they do. As counselor educators become more familiar with students' styles, it becomes easier to distinguish whether they are using their voice. Openly discussing the grading process may encourage students to be mindful of their work while reassuring them that the instructor is being thoughtful about the care they are putting into the grading process.

Fourth, instructors should have students submit large assignments online. Grading online allows counselor educators the opportunity to hear the assignment through text-to-speech software. By listening this way first and then cycling back to read through on their own, counselor educators can hear an assignment in its entirety without the stop-and-go of marking. Counselor educators may use text-to-speech software so they do not become fatigued from reading each document twice. Often as we pause our reading while grading tone, mood, and flow can be disrupted, which can change the voice intended by the student.

Fifth, counselor educators should use a plagiarism detection program. Many university learning management systems provide screening programs such as SafeAssign or Turnitin. These programs provide a percent count of original student content to content likely written by someone else. These works can include published professional works or previously submitted student works.

Conclusion

These recommendations serve the dual purposes of ensuring the academic integrity of student work and enabling counselor educators to genuinely get to know students beyond their interactions in the classroom. Assignments can showcase student thought, which is deeper than what is shared in the classroom. In particular, students who often do not speak may use assignments to ask questions, brainstorm, and share ideas they may not be brave enough to say in front of their peers. These practices may prevent plagiarism and allow counselor educators the privilege of learning to better hear student voices through verbal discussion and written voice.

Reflection Questions

1. To what degree do you agree with Professor P's approach to handling the plagiarism violation? Why?
2. What are some additional remediation strategies counselor educators can use in instances of blatant or incidental plagiarism?

Critical Incident Response

Casey A. Barrio Minton

As a first-year faculty member, Professor P is navigating a dynamic nearly all counselor educators will navigate at some point in their careers. The academic integrity violation of focus in this case was egregious, but the author recognized that violations occur on a continuum ranging from what seem to be unintentional mistakes to clear stealing or cheating. I see two key considerations related to Professor P's actions: deciding whether to report and coordinating responses.

Counselor educators often develop caring relationships with students they conceptualize within their developmental and cultural context. Professor P easily cued into plagiarism and approached the student with care and consideration. After exploring with the student, they issued a failing grade on the assignment and decided not to report the violation. From a dispositions perspective, students who are willing to steal or purchase assignments may also be willing to lie about their actions. Although the student may have been genuine in interactions with Professor P, they may also have intentionally misled Professor P regarding this experience.

In deciding against taking a rules ethical approach, Professor P may have inadvertently violated university policy. Many systems require faculty members to go through formal student conduct processes when assigning academic penalties, including simple grade reductions on an assignment. These policies often leave the consequences of first violations to the discretion of faculty members; however, following due process policies can protect faculty members from claims of arbitrary or unfair decisions. University reporting systems are also intended to allow the administration to detect repeat violations that warrant higher, system-level action.

Even if Professor P's actions did not violate policy, faculty members should think carefully about the possible role of implicit bias in deciding whether to use a formal process. Professor P considered socioeconomic and age diversity as reasons not to report the incident; these and other cultural understandings of academic integrity may have been at play. It is also possible that privilege based on race, ethnicity, or other identities led the student to feel comfortable (or even entitled) to plead for an exception. These same dynamics may have led Professor P to accept the plea. Although the student's identities are not disclosed, one could ask whether Professor P and the student would have had a similar process and come to the same conclusion if elements of identity had been changed in some way (e.g., if the student was a traditional-aged man of color). Just as there are well-documented disparities at all steps throughout the criminal justice system, systematic disparities are at play in identifying students who have cheated, reporting them, and assigning penalties.

Counselor education programs are somewhat unique within higher education systems given their programmatic approach to preparing students for practice. Professor P notified their department head of the plan to address the concern; however, there is no evidence of consultation with other faculty members regarding prior concerns related to the student, program precedent for handling academic dishonesty, or the need to activate the program's remediation plan. Instead, Professor P took the issue on themselves, first working with the student to not report the case, then building multiple systems and structures into their courses to protect against future violations.

Although Professor P's responsiveness is commendable, faculty members should consider working with their programs to address academic integrity on a systems level. Professor P might discuss the incident during a faculty meeting, ascertaining whether there have been previous disposition concerns about this student while also exploring the degree to which academic dishonesty is an issue within the program at large. This process could ensure mentorship for Professor P as they adapt to life as a counselor educator, pointing them to university resources, advising on helpful and not helpful responses, or even helping Professor P understand that there is already explicit coverage of plagiarism within required orientations. Professor P might have chosen a very different course of action had they discovered that the student had had similar violations in the past or had already completed mandatory academic integrity training much like what Professor P built into their courses.

If consultation with faculty reveals that academic dishonesty is a concern across students, this may point to the need for a unified plan for addressing it as a program. A collaborative discussion may help the program to set clear, fair expectations for students. If there is not a university procedure for addressing academic dishonesty, the program could develop a policy, place it in handbooks with clear ties to the *ACA Code of Ethics* (ACA, 2014), and address it in orientation. This may even result in an orientation assignment for a first-semester professionalism course that frees faculty members to attend to course orientation and relationships rather than plagiarism prevention in their first meetings.

All in all, Professor P expressed care and diligence in their individual response to the student and preventive steps in their courses. By converging their efforts with university policies, peer consultation, and a program-level response, Professor P can ensure fairness, clarity, and appropriate support as they continue in their new role as a counselor educator.

• • •

Chapter 4

Too Much Information: Maintaining Boundaries During Skills Practice

Kathryn L. Henderson

2014 *ACA Code of Ethics* Standards Addressed

- F.1.a. Client Welfare
- F.7.g. Student-to-Student Supervision and Instruction
- F.8.c. Self-Growth Experiences
- F.8.d. Addressing Personal Concerns
- F.9.a. Evaluation of Students
- F.9.b. Limitations

• • •

In a first-semester counseling skills class, master's students routinely practiced basic microskills in triads, rotating the roles of counselor, client, and observer. On the first day of class, Professor X discussed the important role of the mock client, noting that students should come to class prepared to discuss real-life topics they were comfortable sharing. Topics such as substance use and trauma were off limits for role plays. This restriction was essential to assist students in developing professional boundaries as well as identifying areas in which personal concerns may intrude into the counseling relationship. Also, personal unfinished business might indicate issues that could use attention in personal counseling, which this course did not provide. Professor X indicated that if role-play practice sessions transitioned to such topics at any time, the client should hit the pause button on the dialogue and say they wanted to talk about something else. Professor X had the same responsibility while observing in-class practice sessions and providing live feedback. The course syllabus included details about these rules, including the expectation that students would notify Professor X if such incidents happened.

A few weeks into the semester, Professor X became concerned about Jessie while watching recordings of in-class practice sessions. Although the role play began on a simple topic—Jessie's current lack of a romantic relationship—it transitioned to a history of sexual abuse she described in a detailed manner in a calm and matter-of-fact voice. The student in the counselor role looked uncomfortable and asked whether they should switch to another topic, which they did. Neither student discussed this incident with Professor X.

After seeing the video clip, Professor X emailed the students in this triad and asked to meet with them individually to discuss the recording. Jessie initiated the conversation with Professor X, saying she had realized after the fact that her history of sexual abuse might qualify as an off-limits topic. She added that she had received a lot of counseling and felt OK about sharing. Jessie said she thought it was helpful for her peer to hear "this sort of stuff" before practicum.

Professor X thanked Jessie for sharing her perspective. She appreciated that Jessie had received counseling and shared that many counselors have experienced hardships; the work they did on those issues in their own personal counseling was vital for their professional competence. Professor X also noted the importance of maintaining boundaries with clients. Discussing her personal history of abuse in such a detailed way could cause harm to a client who also might be traumatized. There were varying opinions on self-disclosure with clients; best practice at this stage of development suggested consulting first and disclosing deliberately and for the benefit of the client. Professor X shared that because self-disclosure can be a social habit and a more advanced skill, it was off limits in this course. Students were expected to maintain the same boundaries with their peers as they would with future clients. In fact, the class would review the topic of self-disclosure in the upcoming weeks. Professor X shared that she would like to see students asking in advance whether a topic was permissible; this expectation paralleled the expectation to consult when encountering ethical dilemmas.

Jessie said she had not thought of the possibility she might harm someone by sharing her history, and she was concerned she might have caused harm to her peers. She wanted to speak with them and apologize. Professor X let her know she would be meeting with them about it and encouraged her to be in direct discussion with her peers. In separate meetings with the other students, Professor X processed what it had been like for them when Jessie had begun discussing her trauma history and asked what it would have been like for them to notify her about it. Both students shared feeling uncomfortable, overwhelmed, and out of their depth. They also worried about getting Jessie in trouble. Professor X thanked them for sharing their experience and expressed how important consulting was. Professor X stated that the priority was learning and growing; if she had not known this had happened, there would have been no opportunity for growth.

The following week during practice sessions, a student came to get Professor X, saying it was urgent. When Professor X arrived, one student was crying and another was consoling her while Jessie was sitting in the practice room alone. During the role-play session, Jessie had brought up the topic of her trauma history again and seemed to be on autopilot discussing details of the abuse. She said it was not on purpose, and it seemed to happen before she realized it. Professor X asked if someone would go see if other professors were in their office and could join them. Professor Y came and consulted with the crying student while Professor X spoke with Jessie.

Professor X expressed concern that this had happened again. Jessie seemed numb and detached when responding, not answering directly. Jessie said she would contact her counselor the next day and asked whether she would be kicked out of the program. Professor X shared that dismissing a student was a last resort and there were other options to consider. As class ended, Professor X said that it was important that she consult with other faculty and that she would be in touch to set up a time to meet. Before leaving, she confirmed that Jessie had a support she could contact.

Case Analysis and Discussion

The case illustrates the dilemma of assessing the potential for competency concerns that could impact future client welfare while helping new students develop effective personal boundaries. Students are not expected to arrive in their first-semester courses fully formed as professional counselors; counselor educators often look for students to be actively working to meet expectations while demonstrating growth and responding to feedback. Jessie's history of abuse illustrates how the very nature of life we experience as humans comes with us into our new roles. The critical incident demonstrates the need for ongoing self-care, as this new role may have unexpected consequences for previously settled personal history.

Analysis of the Critical Incident

The *ACA Code of Ethics* (American Counseling Association [ACA], 2014) offers guidance on many aspects of Jessie's case. Section B, Confidentiality and Privacy, calls for counselors to establish and uphold appropriate boundaries with clients to contribute to trust in the counseling relationship. Counselors' disclosure of details about their personal worlds is often referred to as *self-disclosure.* A basic expectation of new counseling students is to learn and demonstrate basic counseling skills while also respecting boundaries for interpersonal disclosures. This expectation parallels the future obligation to maintain boundaries with clients, as excessive self-disclosure is ineffective and potentially damaging to counseling relationships (Remley & Herlihy, 2020; Young, 2017). Given the natural role of self-disclosure in social relationships, I restrict self-disclosure in beginning skills classes so students rely on their new counseling skills to build rapport instead. A foundational ethical obligation of counselors is to avoid harming clients (ACA, 2014, Standard A.4.a.); this is mirrored in Standard F.1.a., which holds supervisors responsible for monitoring supervisees' performance. In this case, Jessie's pattern of sharing detailed information about her history of abuse raises concerns regarding her ability to maintain professional boundaries, which could impact client welfare.

On a related note, counselor educators are also responsible for addressing potential competency concerns and providing remediation as needed (ACA, 2014, Standard F.9.b.). Professor X's decision to reach out to Jessie after the first incident is aligned with providing formative evaluation and clarifying performance expectations for students (Standard F.9.a.). Another responsibility of counselor educators is to protect all students during experiential activities. Placing limits on topics allowed during role plays assists with upholding the spirit of practicing skills, not providing professional counseling, which is beyond the development of first-semester students. An additional benefit is avoiding exposure to content that may be triggering for students. Standard F.7.g. addresses the need for counselor educators to protect the rights of students when peers lead experiential activities. Professor X's follow-up with Jessie's peers reflects a desire to assess their experiences and provide guidance for the future.

Another important element is that Jessie may have a disability due to undisclosed mental health diagnoses. The Americans With Disabilities Act protects students who enter counseling programs with any disability, including a mental health diagnosis. It is not known whether Jessie has a current diagnosis; however, the circumstances of her incident imply that she could. Professor X initiated a dialogue with Jessie that sought to normalize Jessie's history of trauma, sending the message that professional counselors can experience personal hardships and also become counselors.

Discussion of Actions Taken and Not Taken

Professor X acted diligently in offering clear and timely feedback to Jessie on the problematic nature of her disclosure. At their meeting, she could have discussed other topics related to gatekeeping as a reminder of counselor educators' obligations when competency concerns arise. Students often do not recall details of gatekeeping policies, which many programs only review during orientation sessions (J. M. Foster et al., 2014); having them indicate their acknowledgment and understanding of them at multiple points, both orally and in writing, is recommended (Pease-Carter & Barrio Minton, 2012). At the first incident, there was no indication that the concerns would develop into a gatekeeping issue; however, a reminder of Professor X's role in evaluating students could have been helpful. In addition, if the program designated the course a gatekeeping course, a reminder of this fact could be included as well. Given Jessie's possible undisclosed disability, offering broad information about accommodations available to all students could help Jessie learn about potential options she could pursue.

Professor X may have also consulted with other faculty after the first incident. Consulting is best practice for the continued growth of educators and supervisors and also has the benefit of offering support in challenging scenarios. Given that a colleague was asked to help during the second incident in the classroom, making sure colleagues were aware and up-to-date on the circumstances would have been useful to ensure effective intervention in the moment. After the second incident, it would be advisable for Professor X to consult with colleagues and document the competency concerns noted (Homrich & Henderson, 2018). Regardless of a student's initiative in terms of seeking personal counseling, Professor X could have recommended or required counseling as part of remediation. Counselor educators are responsible for requiring students to address personal issues that might impact their professional competence, and faculty may help students identify appropriate clinicians (ACA, 2014, Standards F.8.d., F.9.c.).

An additional concern is Jessie's rationale that her peers could benefit from her disclosure. This perspective seems to indicate a lack of abiding by course policy and could be viewed as similar to refusing to incorporate feedback, a common competency expected of students (Homrich & Henderson, 2018). Professor X indirectly broached this topic but did not directly connect it to Jessie's decision-making and lack of abiding by course policy.

Professor X and a colleague met with Jessie the next day. Jessie shared that she realized she needed a new counselor who could better help her as she was transitioning into her new role as a graduate student. She realized the two incidents probably indicated she needed at least a few tune-up sessions regarding her trauma history as well. The faculty members validated her self-awareness and encouraged her pursuit of self-growth and her decision to re-enter counseling. They shared information about the campus counseling center, where all students could obtain counseling from licensed clinicians. Professor X suggested Jessie consider consulting with her instructor regarding possible accommodations for triggering course content when she enrolled in the Crisis and Trauma course. Jessie devised a formal written plan with the note that any additional concerns would result in a review for formal remediation. Jessie entered personal counseling and fulfilled the agreement. The faculty did not note any future disclosures of too much information or any additional concerns.

Conclusion

Encountering the key issue of students sharing too much personal information can be common and challenging. Important considerations accompany this critical issue, including professional boundaries, professional competence, harm to future clients, and gatekeeping. These considerations contribute to the need for counselor educators to address the key issue of disclosing too much personal information early on with students and with care.

Reflection Questions

1. How do you differentiate between the nature of self-disclosure with clients and students?
2. How would you have handled approaching Jessie and her small-group partners regarding what happened? What would you have done similarly or differently? Why?

Critical Incident Response

Linwood G. Vereen, Clewiston D. Challenger, and Nicole R. Hill

Counselor educators are tasked with preparing professional counselors who must approach their work with a high level of competence. Professional competence emerges from the cultivation of professional dispositions, clinical and ethical skills, depth of knowledge of professional constructs, and professional identity (Miller et al., 2020; Spurgeon, Gibbons, & Cochran, 2012). This case highlights dialectics between dispositions and clinical skill development and between assessment and growth commitment many counselor educators encounter. As Professor X works with students in the counseling skills course, she must promote skill development, boundary setting, and ethical competence while also evaluating dispositions and skill proficiencies.

The author identified critical standards from the *ACA Code of Ethics* (ACA, 2014), specifically relating to confidentiality and privacy, nonmaleficence, supervisory responsibilities, and assessment and remediation by counselor educators. It is important that Professor X ground herself in department and professional policy, ethical standards, and accreditation mandates regarding students who exhibit signs of impairment. It is imperative that Professor X follow policies and procedures as stipulated in student handbooks and program communications.

Professor X needs to balance the potential disability rights of the student with a consideration of counselor impairment as outlined in the *ACA Code of Ethics* (ACA, 2014). Impairment would impede Jessie's ability to provide competent care for clients, necessitating that her instructor and program work with her to address concerns that would hinder her ability to focus on the needs of the client. Furthermore, the 2016 Council for Accreditation of Counseling and Related Educational Programs (CACREP) Standards (CACREP, 2016) discuss the importance of departmental policies regarding student review, remediation, or dismissal from a program for nonacademic reasons. If the department does not yet have a robust and formal policy for nonacademic gatekeeping, Professor X could actively advocate for the adoption of a process that is comprehensive, transparent, and grounded in the literature on professional dispositions (Miller et al., 2020; Spurgeon, Gibbons, & Cochran, 2012).

As Professor X raises concerns with Jessie, she needs to be clear and direct on programmatic expectations and policies. This provides a foundational extension of the case. This process is vital and important for fostering student development. Informing Jessie about the focus of the meeting and the reason for the concerns is critical. Transparency is a vital part of the learning process, and each student has the right to know the reason for any scheduled meeting in advance. It is important that Professor X inform Jessie that she has engaged in a pattern of sharing too much detailed personal information about past trauma that is beyond the scope of the practice activity. Jessie should be reminded about the initial class experience in which she was provided with information and pointed toward resources to assist her in seeking help outside the classroom. Professor X needs to document all concerns and identify next steps and share this information with Jessie verbally and in writing.

Because of the critical role program faculty play in gatekeeping, Professor X could also be very transparent in informing Jessie that her progress will be discussed at the next faculty meeting. Jessie needs to know that she could be placed on a Professional Progression Plan if she does not respond to feedback. If Professor X's department does not already have a gatekeeping policy, it is recommended that it establish a systematic structure for articulating professional competencies that need to be met and evidence of how this will be accomplished in an identified time frame. The Professional Progression Plan needs to include a set of guiding developmental principles and dispositions each student in the program can be expected to adhere to (principles) and possess (dispositions). As part of this process, the faculty could provide Jessie with a copy of the *ACA Code of Ethics* (ACA, 2014) with sections on student impairment (Standard F.5.b.) and addressing personal concerns (Standard F.8.d.) highlighted for her review. Jessie could also be provided with an opportunity to clearly articulate her understanding of the current dilemma and how she will be expected to exhibit a different pattern of behaviors in the classroom.

• • •

Chapter 5

I'm a Counselor . . . Well Almost: Boundary Extensions in Service Learning

Mark B. Scholl

2014 *ACA Code of Ethics* Standards Addressed

- A.1.a. Primary Responsibility
- C.2.a. Boundaries of Competence
- F.1.a. Client Welfare
- F.4.b. Emergencies and Absences
- F.6.a. Evaluation
- F.6.b. Gatekeeping and Remediation
- F.7.i. Field Placements

• • •

Beth was a white, middle-class, first-semester student in a master's program accredited by the Council for Accreditation of Counseling and Related Educational Programs. She was taking five courses: Human Development, Counseling Theories and Models, Professional Orientation, Counseling Skills, and Research and Statistics. Her Human Development instructor, Professor Edwards, informed students that one course requirement would be a 25-hour service-learning (SL) project. This was the first time he had included SL in his course. Professor Edwards had spent the summer meeting with partners to establish SL placements in local schools and community agencies. He informed the students that the SL project was directly related to the course objective of understanding how the psychosocial development of individuals potentially enhances their cognitive development. Students were required to complete a poster describing their experience and what they learned, and they would present their posters at a special event at the end of the semester.

Beth enthusiastically approached Professor Edwards and told him she would like the SL placement at Champion Middle School (CMS) that involved helping facilitate an after-school program. Professor Edwards explained that this would be an excellent opportunity for her to gain experience working with children in a program designed to foster psychosocial development. Professor Edwards connected Beth with the school counselor at CMS, Suzie Mitchell.

Ms. Mitchell informed Beth that the primary purpose of the Success Program was to assist students in developing social competence (e.g., waiting one's turn to join a game, decreasing inappropriate verbalizations) and related behaviors in classroom and nonclassroom settings. During program sessions, cofacilitators promoted healthy peer interactions. In addition, the Success Program was part of a larger initiative to improve the overall social climate at CMS, a school in which 70% of students came from families of low socioeconomic status. The after-school program consisted of three groups of 20 students from sixth, seventh, and eighth grades. A full-time CMS school counselor and one graduate student volunteer cofacilitated each group. Beth was assigned to work with Ms. Mitchell and the sixth-grade group.

Beth completed two 90-minute facilitator training sessions co-led by Ms. Mitchell and another school counselor. Beth learned that one of her primary responsibilities would be to interact with students in ways that promoted and modeled competent behaviors. She was informed she should verbally reinforce good behavior, inform students when they broke rules, avoid long conversations with individual students, and model socially competent interpersonal behaviors (Rathvon, 2008). In the training sessions, student volunteers learned and practiced fundamental skills that were essential for working with the middle school students. Some of these skills included engaging in active listening, reflecting meaning and feeling, providing praise and encouragement, and giving constructive feedback. The volunteers also learned about a variety of evidence-based games and activities to use during the program.

During the first group session, Beth cofacilitated a game in which students received coupons for exhibiting prosocial behaviors. Afterward, Ms. Mitchell praised Beth and provided some constructive feedback to promote her growth as a cofacilitator. Ms. Mitchell shared some information on the background of students in the group, including information about a 12-year-old boy, Quetzal Rodriguez, who came from a Latinx family, was of low socioeconomic status, and had recently sprayed graffiti on an outer wall of the school. The graffiti incident had resulted in his referral to the Success Program. Beth was curious about Quetzal and asked several questions about his behavior, academic performance, and personality.

The following week, Beth returned to CMS to cofacilitate another session. However, Ms. Mitchell was out sick, and Ms. Davenport, a sixth-grade teacher, co-led the session with Beth. Ms. Davenport looked to Beth to fill her in on the procedure for the session. Beth asked Ms. Davenport whether it would be OK to pull Quetzal aside for a one-on-one conversation during the group activity. She explained that she would like to work on developing rapport and providing him with individual support. Ms. Davenport did not see any harm in Beth talking privately with Quetzal, and Beth and the student had a conversation in an available office. They played a popular game called Dots and Boxes, during which Beth inquired about the graffiti incident. During their conversation, Beth asked him to tell her what had happened and his motivation for drawing graffiti on the wall. Quetzal shared that he had artistic interests in painting, creative writing, and music. Their one-on-one meeting lasted about 20 minutes before Quetzal returned to the group.

A few days later Beth again cofacilitated the group with Ms. Davenport and invited Quetzal to meet with her for a one-on-one conversation. This time the conversation lasted 30 minutes and included talk about holistic wellness and healthy eating habits. She made several recommendations based on an article she had recently read. These included choosing food brands with less sodium and sugar, engaging in mindful eating, and ensuring that fruits and vegetables made up half of one's plate. Beth was certain that the conversation had gone well.

When Ms. Mitchell returned, Beth learned that the school had received a telephone call from Quetzal's parents. Mr. and Mrs. Rodriguez were concerned about the individual counseling their son had been getting from the school counselor and the fact that he had been taken out of the beneficial group activity. Ms. Mitchell reprimanded Beth for counseling Quetzal without proper training and authorization from the school. Though Beth met the hour requirements for her SL project, Ms. Mitchell gave her a very poor evaluation of her performance.

Case Analysis and Discussion

Professor Edwards met with Beth to process the completed SL project, during which he encouraged Beth to reflect on her actions in light of specific standards in the *ACA Code of Ethics* (American Counseling Association [ACA], 2014). In only the first semester of her master's program, Beth was practicing outside the boundaries of her competence in violation of Standard C.2.a. This standard is related to the general ethical principle of fidelity, and because competence is essential to good practice it is also related to the principles of beneficence (the obligation to benefit clients) and nonmaleficence (the obligation not to harm clients). Beth's actions created a greater likelihood that she might harm, or fail to benefit, Quetzal. Professor Edwards added that counselors should also understand their own cultural identities and how these "affect their values and beliefs about the counseling process" (ACA, 2014, p. 4). For example, Beth ostensibly believed that taking Quetzal out of the group setting would be more beneficial than having him remain in the group. She did not appear to understand how her own cultural values might have contributed to this belief. Furthermore, Standard A.1.a. states that counselors should "respect the dignity and promote the welfare of clients." By meeting with Quetzal individually, Beth was reducing his opportunity to develop interpersonal competence. There was thus a greater likelihood that, rather than promoting his welfare, she might harm, or fail to benefit, Quetzal. In addition, she gave Quetzal advice regarding eating habits. Beth's recommendations were outside the scope of acceptable practice and also disregarded the important role the family's cultural heritage played in influencing his diet.

Additional areas of concern pertain to Beth's responsibility to communicate in open and honest ways (ACA, 2014). Beth did not appear to communicate honestly with Ms. Davenport when she asked to talk privately with Quetzal. One of the salient, fundamental rules for session facilitators explicitly stated that facilitators should avoid long conversations with participants. Beth appeared to take advantage of Ms. Davenport's lack of understanding of the rules when she requested to speak with Quetzal. Beth repeated this action in a subsequent session when Ms. Mitchell was absent; she might have sought permission either from Ms. Mitchell by distance communication or from another school counselor at CMS. This example pertains to the ethical principle of veracity, or "dealing truthfully with individuals" (ACA, 2014, p. 3).

Although an important distinction should be made regarding Ms. Mitchell's role as an SL supervisor as opposed to an internship supervisor, it appears that she neglected her responsibility to provide Beth with adequate SL supervision. Ms.

Mitchell cofacilitated sessions with Beth and gave her immediate feedback on her performance following the first session. However, when she missed two group sessions and did not provide Beth with distance supervision or an alternative qualified supervisor, there was a lapse in the monitoring of Beth's performance. Ms. Mitchell was neglectful in that she did not provide Beth with a method for maintaining contact or a contingency plan in the event that Ms. Mitchell was unable to cofacilitate the group session. This contingency plan could have included having an alternative method for distance supervision or arranging for another school counselor to monitor Beth's performance and provide her with feedback.

Professor Edwards recognized that in some instances Beth acted inappropriately, and in other instances her developmental needs had been neglected or underserved. In processing these events, he distinguished between these two sets of issues. He acknowledged that there were ways he could improve as an instructor with regard to supporting Beth during the SL project. He also encouraged Beth to use these events as an opportunity for learning and to incorporate them into her final reflection paper. He reminded her that her course evaluation and grade would be based primarily on the quality of her reflections on her SL project and her poster.

Instructor's Role and Responsibilities

A key component of well-designed SL experiences is the quality of the preparation that instructors provide their students (Cavazos Vela, 2020). Providing Beth with more preparation might have reduced the potential for some of the problems she experienced. It is important for participants in SL to understand that they are expected to work collaboratively with their community partners (Kaye, 2004) rather than function independently. Professor Edwards might have provided his students with reading assignments to familiarize them with the nature and purposes of SL projects in general and the specific programs in which they would be participating. Professor Edwards might also have required his students to meet with or interview community partners prior to beginning their SL experiences (Cavazos Vela, 2020). Although CMS provided Beth with training that prepared her for her role as a cofacilitator, the preparation she received from Professor Edwards for the SL project was inadequate.

Instructors are responsible for ensuring that SL experiences are integral to the course they are teaching (Caruso et al., 2006; Cavazos Vela, 2020). Professor Edwards appropriately connected the SL project to a course objective. He ensured that students understood the SL project as an integral component of the Human Development course. As a final requirement for the SL project, students presented a poster session; this ensured that the project was integral to the content and structure of the course (George et al., 2015).

An essential characteristic of SL projects is students' reflections on their SL experiences (Caruso et al., 2006; Kaye, 2004). Professor Edwards included reflection assignments before and after the SL project, which is key to ensuring that students incorporate SL experiences into their own identity development (Caruso et al., 2006; Kaye, 2004). Examples of reflection prompts before a SL project might include "What do you anticipate your relationship with your SL supervisor will be like?" or "What do you hope to learn or accomplish?" (Cavazos Vela, 2020). Examples of reflection prompts after a SL project might include "What did you learn from your SL project?" or "In what ways did the project influence the development of your professional counselor identity?" (Cavazos Vela, 2020). In addition, Kaye (2004) recommended that students complete daily written reflections during the project. It is essential for students to continually reflect on what they are learning and how it is affecting their values, learning, identity, and feelings. Written daily reflections help students make connections between their experiences and course content and promote the incorporation of learning into their identity development. Instructors should require students to submit these reflections as they are completed so they can continually support and monitor performance in a timely manner throughout the experience.

Instructors should ensure that they maintain good relationships with school and community partners (Lloyd-Hazlett, 2018). Cavazos Vela (2020) recommended giving partners the opportunity to provide feedback on the quality of their relationship with the student, feedback on the quality of the student's performance, and recommendations for improving SL projects. Requesting feedback communicates that community partners are valued and strengthens relationships. This case illustrates the importance of maintaining open communication throughout the SL experience. Professor Edwards could have achieved this by providing the SL supervisor with an evaluation form to complete at the project midpoint, including questions related to the student's strengths and challenges and recommendations for improvement. It is also good practice to schedule intermediate conversations in which SL partners can share their impressions of the student's performance. These measures strengthen communication and the quality of the relationship between the instructor and SL supervisor and improve the quality of support provided to the SL student. In the present case, the quality of this relationship was not good, and Beth's developmental needs were underserved.

Finally, instructors should recognize that student evaluations are based on the quality of their reflections and related assignments (e.g., papers, poster sessions) rather than the quality of their on-site performance (Cavazos Vela, 2020). In the current case, Professor Edwards recognized that it would be unfair to evaluate Beth on the basis of the quality of her performance at CMS. In addition, it is worth noting that the SL supervisor's illness and the lack of communication between Professor Edwards and Ms. Mitchell were beyond Beth's control. Professor Edwards's emphasis on the quality of her reflections was appropriate, and it also potentially ameliorated Beth's feelings of embarrassment and shame. As a result, Beth was more likely to be able to fully reflect on and process her decisions and actions and to learn from her SL project.

Conclusion

SL projects have the potential to contribute to meaningful learning. Instructors are responsible for providing students with adequate preparation prior to SL projects, structuring during projects, and reflective opportunities throughout projects (Cavazos Vela, 2020; Kaye, 2004). The quality of reflections should be used as the primary criterion for evaluating student performance (Cavazos Vela, 2020). In addition to maintaining open communication with SL site supervisors, instructors are advised to comment on students' written reflections and meet with students during projects to provide ongoing support and supervision.

Reflection Questions

1. What additional content might be added to training sessions to better prepare SL students for working effectively with students from diverse populations?
2. How could Ms. Mitchell have used Beth's interest in working with Quetzal to intentionally promote Beth's professional development?

Critical Incident Response

Kathryn L. Henderson

Unanticipated issues are bound to pop up when creating assignments as detailed and involved as SL projects. The author identified several critical issues related to ethical principles and standards and critically examined how the roles and actions of the SL supervisor and instructor either supported or hindered Beth.

Examining the scenario through the lens of the *ACA Code of Ethics* (ACA, 2014) is critical for ethical practice. The author identified Beth's boundaries of competence as a student who is not yet an intern, potential harm to her SL clients, and her lack of cultural competence and awareness. He also highlighted the ethical principle of veracity, which has important implications for Beth's decision-making process. Beth's lack of disclosure to Ms. Mitchell regarding her decision to hold individual sessions with Quetzal is dishonesty by omission. Failure to truthfully initiate contact with supervisors can impact trust and lead to a rupture in the relationship. Not only did Beth ignore the rules of the SL site, but she did not appear to realize that her independent decision-making and subsequent action were inappropriate or outside the boundaries of her competence. These factors speak to the ethical principle of fidelity; Beth's actions could lead to Ms. Mitchell not trusting her. This scenario could result in dismissal from the SL site.

The site supervisor's absence created a space for this ethical dilemma to occur. The author provided a thorough analysis of Ms. Mitchell's lack of adequate supervision during her absences. This circumstance has implications for the instructor's role in planning for supervisors' absences. As he might for an internship, Professor Edwards could have developed clear, preventive parameters for site supervisor absences that applied to all students.

Given the ethical violations that occurred, Professor Edwards might also consider formal remediation for Beth. Professor Edwards did ask Beth to reflect on her actions through the lens of the *ACA Code of Ethics* (ACA, 2014), which can be regarded as summative evaluation and informal remediation. However, additional options are available. The student's performance at the site was not included in the evaluation of the assignment. One way to address how students' behaviors impact their performance is through gatekeeping and remediation. The *ACA Code of Ethics* instructs counselor educators to remediate students when necessary (ACA, 2014, p. 15). One way to determine whether students' behavior warrants remediation is by consulting with faculty; consultation with peers is best practice as well as ethical practice (ACA, 2014). Questions for Professor Edwards to consider during consultation include the following: Is Beth demonstrating similar or new problems in other courses? If Beth repeats these behaviors, would there be different outcomes or consequences? If Beth behaved in a similar way during her clinical internship, what would be the consequences?

The author identified many ways in which Professor Edwards could better prepare students for the SL assignment. In addition, he could have clarified at the beginning that students would not be engaging in counseling, which is outside the boundaries of their competence. This clarification is often made in skills-based courses prior to practicum to reinforce that students are practicing skills and not offering counseling. Professor Edwards could also have provided an overview of ethical principles and standards pertinent to the SL experience. Beth was concurrently learning ethics in a different course, but she may not have been exposed to ethical standards relevant to SL sites. Professor Edwards should consult with his colleagues prior to the start of the SL assignment about what content on ethics has already been covered. Any content on ethics not yet taught should be included in Professor Edwards's course prior to the beginning the SL project.

The very enriching nature of SL demands complex considerations of instructors and students unique to these assignments. Beth's dilemma highlights the unique opportunities and challenges inherent in SL. The aftermath of such dilemmas provides space for fundamental growth and learning for faculty and students.

• • •

Chapter 6

I'm Here, I'm Not Participating: Student Resistance to a Group Experience

Samir H. Patel

2014 *ACA Code of Ethics* Standards Addressed

- F.7.c. Infusing Multicultural Issues/Diversity
- F.8.c. Self-Growth Experiences

• • •

Professor Dev Dixit, a 41-year-old Asian American counselor educator, was teaching Group Counseling for the second time. The class was made up of 23 students who ranged in age from 21 to 43, with the mean age around 24. Per program requirements, students were required to participate in an experiential counseling group in which wellness was the focus. Each group consisted of seven or eight students, and groups were facilitated by doctoral students. After each session, the students (i.e., group members) submitted a reflection to Professor Dixit.

After the first group experience, one student's reflection gave Professor Dixit more pause than the others. Carla, the oldest student in the class at 43, reflected on some logistics regarding group: completing ice breakers; establishing group rules; setting goals; and discussing consent, confidentiality, and limits to confidentiality. On several occasions, Carla noted age differences between her and the rest of the group, including the group facilitator. Carla noted that all her fellow group members were in their early 20s, and the group facilitator, Thomas, seemed to be in his early 30s.

Carla reported that she felt some frustration toward the other group members concerning their "current station in life." She pointed out that when the group members introduced themselves they all spoke about aspects of their social lives and coming into their graduate studies directly from their undergraduate programs. In contrast, Carla noted that she was married with children and had been awarded her undergraduate degree "nearly two decades ago." She ended her reflection by stating that she would keep an open mind but that she had reservations regarding "this group thing."

Professor Dixit observed the great detail Carla put into her reflection. As he thought back on her presence in the first few face-to-face classes, nothing remarkable struck him. She was polite, participated in discussions and activities, and had passed her first quiz (which indicated that she was reading the assigned chapters). Thus, he decided not to give her any direct feedback, as people were sometimes slow to warm up.

In Carla's second reflection, Professor Dixit observed that Carla's distance from the group continued to widen. She opened by describing Thomas's check-in and his intervention of exploring progress made on their established goals. Previously Carla had stated her goal was to be more consistent with physical wellness. However, in this reflection she noted that she had "little to no room to change" her routine. She discussed how her job as coordinator of the university testing center was "extremely demanding" and the fact that because her husband was the chair of the chemistry department she bore most of the child-rearing responsibilities.

Carla also wrote about Thomas's effort to connect wellness and counselor efficacy via *The Indivisible Self* (Myers & Sweeney, 2004). She stated that despite feeling supported by Thomas during the session, she still did not experience a sense of connection with the group. Carla explained that she was feeling out of place because she and other group members were "in totally different places . . . developmentally speaking." She closed the reflection by stating, "I wonder if I could just come to group to meet requirement expectations but not participate like the others."

Professor Dixit pondered Carla's experiences in group and her closing statement in the second reflection. He was mindful of the 2016 Council for Accreditation of Counseling and Related Educational Programs (CACREP) Standards (CACREP, 2016), which note that students need to participate as group members for a minimum of 10 hours (Section 2, Standard F.6.h.). In addition, the *ACA Code of Ethics* (American Counseling Association [ACA], 2014) indicate that counselor educators should assist students in a timely fashion when professional competency is in jeopardy (Standards F.8.d., F.9.b.). However, his decade of clinical experience informed his awareness of how forcing self-growth may lead to resistance, the antithesis of what he wanted for Carla. He was aware of the truth in Carla's reflections: She felt disconnected from the group because of differences in age. Although she was aware of this disconnect and the requirements of the course, Professor Dixit believed she was not fully in touch with the consequences of nonparticipation, both personally or professionally.

Case Analysis and Discussion

The *ACA Code of Ethics* (ACA, 2014) suggest that counselor educators integrate multiculturalism into all classes (Standard F.7.c.). The Multicultural and Social Justice Counseling Competencies (MSJCC; Ratts et al., 2016) include an examination of the role intersectionality has in the development of one's identity (C. D. Chan et al., 2018). Central to the MSJCC is the idea that one must be willing to explore one's subjective understanding of self (Melamed et al., 2020).

Manis (2012) argued that didactic multicultural education alone may not be enough to promote the competencies necessary to understand mental health and wellness from a framework of cultural diversity and social justice. Rather, innovative teaching strategies across the curriculum should task students with critically exploring subjective understanding of their intersectionality and in turn understanding and accepting the subjective experiences of their clients (Melamed et al., 2020). It is critical that counselor educators adopt a pedagogical approach that provides instruction while infusing aspects of the MSJCC.

In the early 1990s, Ladson-Billings began to research the integration of cultural competence and pedagogy. Ladson-Billings (1995a) viewed culturally relevant teaching (CRT) as an action-oriented process that empowers students at the collective level as opposed to traditional pedagogy, which focuses on the individual level. This approach includes three main propositions (Ladson-Billings, 1995b): (a) Students are viewed as a community of learners, and thus they are responsible for one another; (b) the classroom is viewed as a communal learning environment in which success becomes the focal norm; and (c) transformative change comes by way of critical interaction and dialogue. Thus, a persistent emphasis is placed on collaboration within the classroom.

hooks (2003) stated that to promote a collaborative experience the classroom should become "a place of liberating mutuality where the teacher and student work in partnership" (p. xv). A central tenet of CRT is that the educator authentically believes that if students are treated competently they will demonstrate high levels of competency (Ladson-Billings, 1994). Thus, counselor educators who practice CRT should (a) examine teaching practices that reinforce one student's value while denigrating another (e.g., "All students must participate at the same level"), (b) experience students' culture as an asset as opposed to a deficit (e.g., "How can I use this student's culture to engage them?"), and (c) integrate fluid teaching practices that promote competency and reflection (e.g., "What strategies can work in concert with the student's values and stimulate self-awareness?"; Howard, 2003). Counselor educators who promote ongoing and continual self-reflection in their classrooms will enrich the development of emerging counselors (Odegard & Vereen, 2010).

In terms of critical dialogue, students gain positive cognitive outcomes in a classroom community, especially when they have the opportunity to meaningfully share how the subject matter connects with them (McKeachie & Svinicki, 2006; Tenenbaum et al., 2001). If a counselor educator experiences resistance from a student, it may behoove the counselor educator to pay particular attention to the disconnect between the student and the communal learning environment. A counselor educator can then use CRT to create a dynamic space in which students, as a collective, can explore their values and understanding of self while learning course content.

Given that Carla did not yet experience a sense of communal safety, Professor Dixit was aware that he needed to help her resolve this disconnect, and it was important to him that he do it from an inclusive stance. With CRT in mind, Professor Dixit reflected on his teaching approach to this point. He then explored potential strategies that could accentuate group counseling and group work while also drawing from the MSJCC. Ultimately, Professor Dixit wanted Carla to explore the issue of being disconnected from her group not only to help her become more self-aware but also to facilitate the development of her professional identity. If this approach did not work, Professor Dixit knew he would need to pursue a more direct strategy, such as having a formal discussion with Carla and encouraging her to seek out her own counseling outside the group experience. At this time, Professor Dixit believed he should place his trust in his pedagogical approach, as this might engage and elicit Carla's strengths and resources within a communal experience.

Actions and Outcomes

Prior to the next class meeting, Professor Dixit decided to use a teaching strategy known as the *3-2-1 assignment* (Rutherford, 2002) designed to help students form independent, critical thoughts about material and share their learnings with others (Alsamadani, 2011). Professor Dixit sent out an announcement to all students and emphasized the importance of mindfulness and intentionality when reading the assigned chapters. He explained that after they had read the chapters, he wanted them to (a) identify three words that captured the essence of the chapter, (b) develop two questions around challenging aspects of the reading, and (c) summarize one concept from the readings that had been experienced in a meaningful way during the counseling group.

When the class met the following week, Professor Dixit intentionally formed eight breakout groups of two or three students each so no breakout group consisted of members from a single counseling group. These breakout groups would serve to build a communal experience within the classroom. He asked the students in the breakout groups to share their reflections from the 3-2-1 assignment and any other thoughts associated with readings focused on the stages of the group process. Carla shared that her one meaningful takeaway was how she was afraid of the storming stage. There were things she wanted to express to her group, but she did not feel comfortable doing so. The other two students in Carla's breakout group expressed similar thoughts and feelings.

Before making an announcement to end the breakout groups, Professor Dixit instructed students to "jot down one or two important or meaningful points from this breakout session." He invited the students to rejoin as a whole class for that day's lecture. As a supplement to the stages of group, Professor Dixit discussed Johari's window (Luft, 1961) and connected the stages of group with how likely a group member was to expose content that was contained in each quadrant of Johari's window. "For example," Professor Dixit explained, "during the forming stage, it is more likely that group members will expose aspects of themselves that are held in the arena quadrant, the area that is open to yourself and others. But folks are not as likely to share aspects of themselves that are contained in the façade quadrant, as the group members have yet to develop the norm of pushing one another to be authentic. Authenticity typically arises when the group creates an environment of true trust, and this happens as a result of the storming stage."

Professor Dixit went on to discuss Johari's window in more detail and then returned students to their breakout groups. He encouraged them to discuss how the points they had identified in their initial breakout session fit within Johari's window and group stages. He also challenged them to consider implications of their new learning for their development as professional counselors (i.e., an intersectionality of their identity development).

When she rejoined her breakout group, Carla shared that she was hesitant to disclose aspects of herself that were contained in the façade section of Johari's window (aspects known to self but not known to others); however, she recognized that she was able to share in the breakout group because students in the group were connected around the idea of not feeling "totally safe." Carla also made the connection that to be OK with the storming stage as a facilitator, she needed to be OK with going into the storming stage as a group member.

In her next counseling group reflection, Carla described her experience of sharing the effect Johari's window had on her understanding of self. Although she was nervous, Thomas, the group facilitator, helped her "to make links with various group members." She also described how her courage in talking about age differences created "external and internal conflict within the group, but the conflict led to deeper and honest conversations." She concluded her reflection by noting that group dynamics "are now shifting toward the transition stage of group development" and that she was "more open to trusting the group process . . . even if the journey is challenging."

Conclusion

When interacting with students who demonstrate resistance or difficulty engaging with class content, structure, or experiences, counselor educators must examine the process of teaching and learning. Just like counseling, teaching warrants reflection and intentionality. As demonstrated in Professor Dixit's work with Carla, having a sound pedagogical approach helps counselor educators be reflective and also invites opportunities to use dynamic teaching strategies. As a result, the classroom becomes a community in which comprehensive learning is the shared goal.

Reflection Questions

1. What concerns might you have about a student who does not participate fully? What are instructors' responsibilities when encountering students who participate minimally?
2. How did Professor Dixit encourage his students to explore their subjective understanding of self?

Critical Incident Response

Olga R. Dietlin and Jenny L. Chien

This case highlights the importance of considering the unique experiences and challenges of graduate students who enter master's studies with significant life and career knowledge. Counseling programs attract a high percentage of older adult students (Schaefers, 2012), and experiences like Carla's are likely to occur.

Older adult students sometimes display characteristics such as "respect, experience, enthusiasm, perfectionism, rigidity, greater need for faculty support, and a high number of demands external to the program" (P. J. Jordan, 2018, p. 5). Carla's discouragement, disconnection, and resistance, coupled with her conscientiousness, mirror these characteristics. Older adult students may struggle to consider feedback from students who are younger than themselves, and they may have a tendency to "talk down," be "motherly," or show impatience with younger students (P. J. Jordan, 2018, p. 113). Older adult students may also have a tendency to develop stronger bonds and be more comfortable with same-age peers than with their younger colleagues (P. J. Jordan, 2018). Improving collegial relationships, rapport, and a sense of safety for older students is important. Professor Dixit needs to monitor and discuss these group dynamics to ensure all students are engaged in the experiences they need to be effective counselors. This would include exploring and challenging assumptions about commonalities and differences between groups.

In keeping with the MSJCC (Ratts et al., 2016), Professor Dixit could support Carla and encourage group development by exploring students' beliefs, attitudes, knowledge, and skills. An exploration of beliefs and attitudes includes self-growth experiences as recommended in the *ACA Code of Ethics* (ACA, 2014, Standard F.8.c.). Students should be encouraged to understand their experiences of self and their personal perspectives before beginning learning experiences (C. D. Chan et al., 2018; Melamed et al., 2020). This can be accomplished using case vignettes and reflection activities (Mitcham et al., 2013).

Professor Dixit may also introduce the concepts of bracketing and broaching. "Bracketing revolves around the counselor's ability to take [their] own personal values and set them aside—suspend them—but not give them up or change them" (Kaplan et al., 2017, p. 116). This is a necessary skill for students to develop as they work with peers with different values and life experiences and transition to working with clients. It will be important for Professor Dixit to model and teach students to honor their own values while also keeping their professional obligations (Kocet & Herlihy, 2014). By directly addressing Carla's age-related apprehensions, Professor Dixit could strengthen rapport and a sense of safety in the classroom, helping his students realize that age-related issues and other culturally specific issues need to be openly discussed. He could also model broaching behavior, demonstrating specific skills to initiate and respond to cultural concerns and "facilitating a kind of cultural catharsis" (Day-Vines et al., 2020, p. 108).

In closing, adhering to a pedagogy that simultaneously honors students' life work and experiences (P. J. Jordan, 2018) and provides opportunities for growth and development is imperative when educating master's counseling students. We recommend that Professor Dixit use a balanced dialectical approach that affirms and validates Carla's experience while also stretching her skills and comfort zone. This instruction methodology will benefit Carla and encourage all students to achieve greater counseling competency.

• • •

Section 2
Dynamics Related to Diversity and Inclusion

Chapter 7

Whose Cultural Competence? Students' Needs in Multicultural Courses

Carlos P. Hipolito-Delgado

2014 *ACA Code of Ethics* Standards Addressed

- F.7.c. Infusing Multicultural Issues/Diversity
- F.8.c. Self-Growth Experiences
- F.11.b. Student Diversity
- F.11.c. Multicultural/Diversity Competence

• • •

Professor Malcom was a first-year assistant professor in counselor education at Teachers State University. He identified as a Latinx, cisgender, heterosexual male of middle socioeconomic status. His teaching philosophy was grounded in Socratic questioning. In an attempt to deconstruct power dynamics in the classroom and help students think more deeply about issues, he avoided lecture in favor of guided discussion and asking questions.

Professor Malcom had taught multiple graduate counseling courses during his doctoral studies in a well-respected counselor education program. Despite being warned by his mentors against teaching multicultural courses, Professor Malcom was passionate about the topic and jumped at the opportunity to teach the multicultural counseling course his first year. This was his first time teaching multicultural counseling. Students in the course were relatively ethnically diverse, much to the appreciation of Professor Malcom, who thought that diversity led to richer discussion.

During Week 3 of the course, the class engaged in a discussion regarding how acculturation impacts clients' worldviews and the counseling process. Anne, who identified as a white woman and later life career changer, expressed a lack of understanding of why minority communities were not able to better assimilate into the United States. She said, "Eastern Europeans and Jews all successfully integrated in the past. Why is assimilation such a problem for communities of color today? I mean, look how successful Jews are." This statement produced audible moans of disbelief from classmates. Professor Malcom asked Anne to consider whether skin color might play a role in easing the acculturative process for certain ethnic groups. To this, Anne commented that Asians also appeared to be successful in assimilating and succeeding economically. In a calm and inquisitive tone, Professor Malcom asked Anne to consider whether she was buying into stereotypes about Jewish American and Asian American folks. He also asked her to consider whether differences in migrants' socioeconomic status and U.S. immigration policies might make it easier for certain groups to experience success. Anne did not respond. The remainder of the class was tense, with few students volunteering to participate.

After class, Bell, a student who identified as a queer first-generation college student of African American descent, told Professor Malcom how disappointed she was with class. Bell said she had hoped the course would push her white peers to confront their biases, especially because the course was being taught by a person of color. Furthermore, she told Professor Malcom, "You went too easy on Anne and let her get away with being blatantly racist." Professor Malcom told Bell that he thought students were on a spectrum of awareness, with some possessing limited knowledge and awareness and others being very knowledgeable and experienced. He told Bell that his approach with Anne was guided by an attempt to meet Anne where she was. He said he hoped his questioning might plant a seed that would lead Anne to think more deeply about her comments and beliefs. Obviously dissatisfied, Bell said good night and left the classroom.

Next week at office hours, Chris, a student who identified as a white male with disabilities, came to speak to Professor Malcom about what had happened in the last class. He told Professor Malcom that he no longer felt safe in class. He said, "I feel like you were rude to Anne, like you did not respect her opinions, which totally goes against the ideals of multiculturalism." Chris said he was not the only one who no longer felt safe: "I am on a group chat with a few of the white students in class, and none of them feel safe speaking in class after last week." Professor Malcom asked Chris whether he could differentiate between safety and comfort. He asked Chris specifically whether he feared for his physical and emotional well-being or whether he was uncomfortable with having his ideas questioned. Professor Malcom also asked whether his own identity as a male of color might have been impacting Chris's perceptions. Chris immediately said he did not think Professor Malcom's race was an issue, but he had a hard time explaining why he no longer felt safe. He said, "I just feel like you won't respect my opinions and will attack me if don't say the right thing."

Later Bell came to office hours. She told Professor Malcom that she had given thought to their conversation after class last week. She expressed frustration, saying, "I feel like multicultural counseling was designed to educate folks who don't get diversity. Like this class was not designed for people from oppressed communities and those who have an understanding and appreciation of diversity." She told Professor Malcom that she got that beginners needed an introduction to diversity and social justice, but she hoped he would do more to facilitate the growth of students who were more advanced. Professor Malcom thanked Bell for sharing her thoughts and said he would do better at meeting the needs of students across the spectrum of multicultural competence.

Case Analysis and Discussion

Professor Malcom was challenged with balancing the educational needs of more advanced and novice counseling students. This critical issue can present itself in any counseling course, but it is prevalent in multicultural counseling courses, which are rife with opportunities for students from more privileged backgrounds to aggress against students from marginalized backgrounds. Instructors must balance the learning needs of students, facilitate growth, and redesign multicultural counseling courses. Considerations for faculty members in counselor education from marginalized backgrounds are also discussed in this case analysis.

Balancing Student Needs

Counselor educators must promote the cultural competence of counseling students (American Counseling Association, 2014, Standard F.11.c.). Too often discussions of diversity are focused on the learning of naive and privileged students, like Anne and Chris, and do not attend to the educational growth of students from marginalized backgrounds, as Bell asserted during office hours.

Naive students lack experience with diverse communities. It is not that they are actively biased or hateful; they merely endorse dominant ideology out of lack of active consideration (Hipolito-Delgado, 2009). Privileged students have unearned advantages based on a dominant identity; this bestows a sense of entitlement, a lack of identity, and freedom to ignore the other. Because privilege is bestowed and viewed as a lack of identity, it can be hard for students to see how they benefit from social inequity, leading to rugged individualism and the belief that meritocracy is valid. It is helpful to remember that bias among naive and privileged students can be the product of generalization based on limited information. Thus, these students might not actively endorse biased beliefs; they merely have not taken the time to question them. Faculty members can use instructional strategies to promote questioning to inspire students to reexamine their beliefs. Professor Malcom did this to some extent; however, he missed helping Anne question whether assimilation is the desired goal for ethnic communities. What is it in Anne's experience that leads her to believe that a loss of one's home culture in favor of U.S. culture is best?

Students from marginalized communities are often frustrated by their experiences in multicultural counseling courses and typically do not experience gains in multicultural competence from such courses (Chao et al., 2011). Perhaps this is because students of color feel tokenized, as if they are expected to educate their more privileged peers (C. A. Baker et al., 2015). Like Bell, students of color describe frustrations with surface-level discussions of diversity, desiring more depth and breadth (Seward, 2014). To engage students from marginalized communities, Hipolito-Delgado et al. (2017) called for counselor education faculty to broach differences in ways that foster a sense of inclusion.

To promote the learning of students from marginalized communities, it is helpful to include considerations of sociopolitical power and oppression. This moves discourse beyond cultural values and difference and toward the social construction of power and privilege and the perpetuation of oppression through education, politics, and culture. This approach can promote the sociopolitical development of all students, increasing their critical consciousness and the need for social action to facilitate the liberation of oppressed communities. For students like Chris, this will clarify the fact that multicultural counseling is not simply about respecting opinions but about being an advocate for social justice.

Growth Can Be Challenging

Every human has a right to physical and emotional safety. However, there is a difference between safety and comfort—a point Professor Malcom attempted to convey to Chris. Growth occurs through disruptions of existing schemata, often as a result of questioning previously held beliefs. This notion is exemplified in cultural identity models that describe encounters or experiences in which dominant ideology is challenged and the reality of cultural complexity comes into focus (Hipolito-Delgado, 2009). These growth encounters are cognitively and emotionally uncomfortable, as one is forced to reconcile new information and the realization that previously held beliefs were incomplete. It is unrealistic for students like Chris to expect to experience growth in cultural competence while maintaining a sense of comfort.

In the case, addressing Anne's comments can be uncomfortable for Anne, Professor Malcom, and the class; this is probably why the remainder of the class period was tense. Still, faculty members need to be intentional about addressing bias and microaggressions through classroom activities, readings, and discussion (Hipolito-Delgado et al., 2017). When bias goes unaddressed, students from marginalized communities can feel alienated and unwelcome (Haskins et al., 2013). Thus, the comfort of privileged students is maintained at the expense of students from marginalized communities.

Engaging in critical conversations around bias presents a learning opportunity. Students can more deeply question their beliefs, learn how their words and actions impact others, and experience how to engage in conversations about difference. Professor Malcom did a good job of asking Anne to think more deeply about her biases. However, he might have used this as an opportunity for the class to engage in a deeper conversation about racial bias and sociopolitical opportunity. This may have allowed the class to investigate the origin of biased thoughts and the role of dominant discourse and propaganda in furthering bias. In addition, Professor Malcom might have invited students from marginalized communities to share their thoughts and feelings, allowing them to process their emotions. Although such a conversation might have been uncomfortable, Professor Malcom could have better attended to the needs of all students in his class.

Rethinking Multicultural Counseling

Multicultural counseling courses are typically taught from a group-of-the-week perspective, in which each week a new cultural community is the focus of learning. This approach can lead to generalization and reinforce bias by treating cultural groups as monoliths. Instead, Vontress (2009) encouraged a conceptual approach that honors the distinctness of individuals while attending to key concepts such as degree of acculturation, collectivism and individualism, emic versus etic diagnosis, and the need for autoplastic versus alloplastic interventions.

I encourage faculty members teaching multicultural counseling to promote dialogue and authentic intergroup contact in their courses. The great Brazilian educator Paulo Freire (1970) argued for a problem-posing education that relies on discussion to disrupt educational hierarchies and promote critical thinking skills. Such an approach may not seem natural, as students have become accustomed to being lectured to throughout their education. Professors must create conditions to foster dialogue by eliminating lecture and allowing classes to be guided by questions. I set this tone at the outset of my multicultural classes through an activity that entails lyrical analysis of a punk rock song (see Hipolito-Delgado, 2016); this activity also serves as a metaphor for unpacking assumptions and aids in practicing critical questioning. Although this will not eliminate bias in the classroom, it will create expectations and help students develop the skills needed to process incidents when they occur.

Authentic intergroup contact is also vital for diminishing bias (DeRicco & Sciarra, 2005) and increasing cultural competence (Hipolito-Delgado et al., 2011). To this end, Hipolito-Delgado et al. (2011, 2013) argued for a cultural immersion project, the Multicultural Action Project (MAP), as a method to promote intergroup contact and increase the cultural competence of counseling students. For the project to be meaningful, extended contact between groups is required, marginalized groups should not be expected to educate more privileged parties, and counseling students should provide services with and on behalf of the marginalized group. The MAP would be useful for aiding Anne in better understanding the experiences of communities of color. It would also provide Bell with the depth and breadth of experience she desires; it might also challenge her to engage with a cultural community with which she has less experience.

Considerations for Faculty From Marginalized Communities

Faculty members from marginalized communities are often expected to be the voices of diversity in counseling programs. Counselor educators from marginalized communities are often expected to teach courses and serve on committees related to diversity and social justice—yet this can be a risky proposition. Faculty of color typically receive worse course evaluations than their white male peers, and courses that explore issues of diversity and inclusion also tend to yield worse teaching evaluations (Perry et al., 2015). Given that Professor Malcom is a person of color and is teaching a course on diversity it is likely that he will receive worse course evaluations. This is one reason why his mentors advised him against teaching multicultural counseling. Because course evaluations are typically considered as part of promotion and tenure, Professor Malcom should be concerned about how low marks might impact his professional advancement. I am not suggesting that faculty from marginalized communities not teach multicultural counseling if it is an area of passion and expertise for them. However, I am cautioning counselor educators to consider how being a member of a marginalized group and teaching a course on diversity might negatively impact their course evaluations and hurt them in terms of attaining tenure and promotion.

Conclusion

The challenge of balancing the learning needs of students is not easily resolved. My hope here was to provide insights into the needs of students from more privileged and marginalized backgrounds, suggestions on engaging in critical conversations and rethinking multicultural counseling courses, and considerations for faculty from marginalized communities. In addition, I hope to have provoked thoughts about the experience of students and faculty from marginalized communities in counselor education programs.

Reflection Questions

1. What other strategies could you implement in a multicultural course to better balance the needs of all students?
2. Should untenured faculty from marginalized communities teach multicultural counseling courses? Why or why not?

Critical Incident Response

Mark B. Scholl

The author made a cogent case for providing students with a climate characterized by egalitarian dialogue to promote a transformative expansion of consciousness for learners (Freire, 1970). This recommendation is echoed by counselor educators (e.g., Dollarhide et al., 2018) who assert that egalitarian teacher-student dialogue facilitates the incorporation of social justice principles into counselor training. Similarly, Lai et al. (2014) noted the importance of egalitarian conversations in multicultural counseling courses and related training, emphasizing the importance of providing factual information and experiential learning consistent with the MAP.

It is important for Professor Malcom to inform students of ground rules for the classroom and his rationale for emphasizing dialogue. I agree that growth in cultural competence cannot occur if one maintains a sense of comfort. The concept of creating brave spaces complements the author's recommendations (Arao & Clemens, 2013). Creating a classroom environment in which students openly share their authentic experiences, beliefs, and feelings requires courage, and this should be identified as an aspirational value. At the same time, it is helpful to provide students with ground rules to promote mutual respect and civility. A typical ground rule for brave spaces prohibits making personal attacks (i.e., criticizing individuals rather than behaviors; Arao & Clemens, 2013).

The author effectively contrasted students who are naive and students who have experienced oppression in their everyday lives. When Professor Malcom corrected Anne, the naive students were inclined to believe that he did not respect their opinions. By contrast, Bell, a student who had experienced oppression, believed Professor Malcom had gone too easy on Anne. These widely differing perspectives illustrate the considerable skill and experience needed to effectively lead egalitarian consciousness-promoting discussions (Williams, 2019).

The author aptly emphasized and addressed the difficulty of balancing the needs of both groups of students. I also appreciated how he distinguished between feeling unsafe and feeling uncomfortable. Instructors of multicultural courses can normalize and validate feeling uncomfortable by noting three common reasons for these feelings (Williams, 2019): (a) Counseling students are caring people who want to avoid offending others, (b) students with firsthand experiences of oppression may find these experiences particularly difficult to talk about, and (c) counseling students are highly invested in their own growth and development. Sharing these reasons can normalize feelings of discomfort, self-consciousness, and reticence.

Students from diverse populations can feel an unfair expectation to educate their more naive peers. I believe an important point can be added about Paolo Freire's (1970) philosophy of education. Freire advocated for empowering students from oppressed populations to openly share their authentic inner voices and opinions, including opposing viewpoints, with classmates. Professor Malcom might have spent more time talking in depth with Bell about the classroom climate he envisions and how much her authentic responses can contribute. I believe it is important for Professor Malcom to balance encouraging Bell to share her authentic perspective with showing empathy regarding her feelings of safety. It is difficult to know precisely how Bell is feeling. Inviting Bell to share her feelings outside of class would provide an opportunity to practice sharing her authentic inner voice and might also increase her comfort in the classroom. Because many people of color feel an unfair expectation to educate white peers, it is important that Professor Malcom clearly communicate that he is extending an invitation that Bell has permission to decline.

Overall, the author provided clear, coherent recommendations for meeting the needs of students. The MAP is an excellent way to promote learning that can be tailored to the unique needs of individual learners. The author's recommendations for using authentic, egalitarian practices to empower students also reflect attitudes and practices that will empower future clients.

• • •

Chapter 8

A Cohort Divided: Navigating Tensions Related to Race and Ethnicity

Catherine Y. Chang, Erin C. M. Mason, and Vanessa Placeres

2014 *ACA Code of Ethics* Standards Addressed

- F.9.a. Evaluation of Students
- F.11.b. Student Diversity
- F.11.c. Multicultural/Diversity Competence

• • •

Jessica, a white woman, was an assistant professor with several years of school counseling and teaching experience. Veronica, a Latinx woman, was a third-year counselor education doctoral student and a practicing school counselor. Jessica and Veronica were coteaching the spring Classroom Management, Collaboration, and Consultation course for school counseling students. Jessica was the instructor of record, and Veronica was the teaching assistant.

Jessica and Veronica used a constructivist teaching style for the course. Their goal was to be student centered. They designed class activities to align with learning objectives, the 2016 Council for Accreditation of Counseling and Related Educational Programs (CACREP) Standards, experiences at internship sites, and students' own personal life experiences. The course included both didactic and experiential components. Jessica and Veronica shared responsibility for presenting content and facilitating activities throughout the semester. There were also several sociopolitical factors to consider at the time, including Donald Trump's presidency; mass shootings in schools in Florida, Texas, and Southern California; targeted arson attacks on African American churches in the Southeast; and the continued advancement of movements like Black Lives Matter and Me Too.

Students were in the second year of the school counseling master's program. They were in the final phase of their training and entering their first semester of internship. The cohort consisted of 16 women, most of whom were in their middle to late 20s; four students identified as second-career students. The cohort was split demographically, with a little less than half self-identifying as students of color and a little more than half self-identifying as white. All students in the cohort took core courses together and had navigated the school counseling program with minimal overt conflict up to this point. However, the instructors observed several incidents that implied underlying tensions within the cohort. White students and students of color self-segregated during in-class activities, during group work, and outside class.

For the second to last class meeting, Jessica and Veronica planned a video and group discussion. Jessica played a video that presented a white school counselor who incorporated inclusion into her classroom management to engage students who felt excluded or disinterested. The school counselor's use of classroom management skills ultimately led to a positive relationship with a Black student who had previously been disengaged, uninterested in the classroom, and frequently in trouble. The video continued to highlight the school counselor's role in supporting the student's success.

After the video ended, Jessica attempted to lead a discussion on strategies used by the school counselor. Beatrice, a 27-year-old self-identified African American woman, described her disappointment and frustration toward white peers who glorified the school counselor for helping the Black student. Some white students explained their hesitation in speaking up about topics related to marginalized communities. What followed was a broader conversation around cohort dynamics related to race/ethnicity, expectations of school counselors for advocating for and supporting students with marginalized identities, and the disappointment felt by all students.

A few students of color explained that they felt they had to serve as spokespeople for their racial groups. They shared that they felt dismissed by white students who did not make an effort to understand the lived experiences of people of color or build genuine connections with cohort members who did not look like them. Amy, a 23-year-old white woman, explained that she was tired of having discussions of multicultural awareness because she did this all day at her internship site and did not see why the conversation was necessary in the classroom. Amy proceeded to put on her jacket and beanie, and she physically disengaged from the conversation.

Jessica and Veronica worked to address comments about the need for multicultural awareness and tried to maintain a space in which this conversation could continue. They were also having reactions to cohort dynamics, each other, and the topics discussed. Their intention behind explaining the importance of multicultural awareness was twofold: to relate the conversation to their work with diverse students and staff in schools and to remind students that the work was ongoing at both personal and professional levels. Veronica was frustrated, and she was afraid that if she expressed her opinion about what Amy had just said, it would have been fueled by emotion in a way that would not have been beneficial to the learning environment.

Following Amy's comment, a few students of color expressed frustration and disappointment with cohort members of the dominant culture. Students of color diverted the conversation to matters about their lived experiences, isolation within the cohort, and sadness about the disconnect between cohort members in and outside class. The group spent the remainder of the class processing feelings and thoughts around the cohort rupture, race relations, and their work as school counselors. By the end of the class, no clear conclusion had been reached. It felt like Jessica and Veronica were outsiders in this conversation as they watched the group take the lead and go where they needed to go while also trying to ensure no harm was done. Following class, Jessica and Veronica processed what had happened and were perplexed as to how to move forward with only one class session remaining before this cohort moved on in the program.

Case Analysis and Discussion

There are several salient issues in this case study. The direction the instructors ultimately take will be based on their teaching philosophy, classroom management style, relationship with the students, and understanding of multiculturalism and ethics. This incident occurred at the end of a course during students' first semester of internship, so the timing and extent of the rift in the cohort will be important to consider. The instructors also want to be cognizant of relevant codes of ethics (e.g., American Counseling Association [ACA], 2014), the CACREP Standards (CACREP, 2016), the ASCA School Counselor Professional Standards and Competencies (American School Counselor Association [ASCA], 2019), and the Multicultural and Social Justice Counseling Competencies (MSJCC; Ratts et al., 2016).

Counselor education programs must monitor the development of their students and serve as gatekeepers for the counseling profession. All counseling programs must systematically assess and address students' knowledge, skills, and professional dispositions throughout their program of study (CACREP, 2016). According to the *ACA Code of Ethics*, counselors "explore their own cultural identities and how these affect their values and beliefs about the counseling process" (ACA, 2014, p. 4); more specifically, Standard F.11.c. requires that students be trained to "gain awareness, knowledge, and skills in the competencies of multicultural practice." ASCA's standards echo the need for awareness and knowledge of the impact of cultural, social, and environmental influences on student success (ASCA, 2019, Standard B-PF 6). These standards provide a road map for what counselor educators must assess in their students.

The importance of multicultural and social justice counseling competencies is implied in the *ACA Code of Ethics* (ACA, 2014). The MSJCC have been endorsed by ACA and several divisions, which signifies that these competencies are integral and relevant to all aspects of the counseling profession. The MSJCC outline four developmental domains, with self-awareness being an essential tenet of and the starting point for the other domains of client worldview, counseling relationship, and counseling and advocacy interventions. New to the MSJCC are quadrants that reflect the diverse identities professional counselors and clients bring to the counseling relationship with specific recognition of privileged and marginalized statuses. In this case, Jessica and Veronica will want to consider how their various identities relate to each other and the students. The cultural climate of the class is essential to promoting ethical practices and multicultural and social justice counseling competencies.

The safe and supportive schools model of school climate (National Center on Safe Supportive Learning Environments, n.d.) provides a helpful framework for promoting educational environments that optimize school climate and learning. According to this model, a positive school environment includes engagement (relationship, respect for diversity, and school participation), safety (emotional safety, physical safety, and substance use), and environment (physical environment, academic environment, wellness, and disciplinary environment).

In addition, researchers have called for the evaluation of dispositions in counselor education programs. *Professional dispositions* are "the commitments, characteristics, values, beliefs, interpersonal functioning, and behaviors that influence the counselor's professional growth and interactions with clients and colleagues" (CACREP, 2016, p. 43). Using an intensive case study approach, Spurgeon, Gibbons, and Cochran (2012) identified five core dispositions for counseling students: commitment, openness, respect, integrity, and self-awareness. Jessica and Veronica's school counseling program has a list of dispositions on which faculty evaluate each student. These dispositions are similar to the ones identified by Spurgeon and colleagues: (a) integrity; (b) self-awareness; (c) the ability to successfully complete the academic coursework and achieve required expectations; (d) sensitivity to individual differences and respect for diversity among fellow students, staff, faculty, and clients; (e) respect for and adherence to the *ACA Code of Ethics* (ACA, 2014); (f) the ability to accept and make use of feedback from faculty regarding one's progress in the program as it relates to academics, interactions with fellow students and faculty, and clinical skills; (g) commitment to upholding confidentiality with fellow students in interpersonal and supervisory experiences and also with clients/supervisees in practicum and internship; (h) awareness of how to maintain appropriate interpersonal boundaries with faculty, fellow students, clients, trainees, and supervisees; and (i) the ability to interact appropriately and effectively with other students, faculty, and staff. Each year, advisers assess whether each student has met every disposition or whether it cannot be determined if they have met a specific disposition.

In reviewing this case, we consider students' dispositions in relation to their response in the course as well as their performance throughout their program of study. In addition, we need to clarify and prioritize salient issues. We also examine how the cultural backgrounds of Jessica, Veronica, and the students influence the response to this case. Finally, we consider how the *ACA Code of Ethics* (ACA, 2014), the ASCA School Counselor Professional Standards and Competencies (ASCA, 2019), the MSJCC (Ratts et al., 2016), and dispositions impact the response to this incident.

Actions and Outcomes

It is essential that Jessica and Veronica first process their reactions to the class in general, the cohort dynamic, and specific students in the context of their cultural identities (e.g., biases, assumptions, power, and privilege). Jessica and Veronica will want to integrate aspects of the safe and supportive schools model when considering the classroom climate. They will want to consider how to optimize engaging the class in a discussion while maintaining emotional safety and managing the classroom environment. As the lead instructor, Jessica will want to consult with other faculty in the department.

It is crucial to consider complex identities and the role of privilege and oppression in the class, with particular attention to Beatrice and Amy. Jessica and Veronica hold positions of power and privilege because of their status as instructors. Jessica also has privilege as a white counselor educator, and Veronica holds membership in both privileged and marginalized groups. Beatrice, an African American female student, is part of several marginalized groups. Amy, a white female student, holds membership in both privileged and marginalized groups. At the cohort level, the instructors want to address the rupture between the students of color and white students and race relationships in general given the political and social climate. It will be vital to highlight how classroom dynamics connect to students' advocacy work as future school counselors. Jessica and Veronica will also need to be mindful of how power and privilege impact their interactions with the class and implementation of the intervention. This is especially important because some students who identified as African American or Black expressed their frustration and disappointment at having to be the voice of Black people and their white peers appeared disinterested in interacting with them. Some white students also expressed hesitation about engaging in open dialogue about marginalized populations.

Beatrice's reaction to the video was passionate. She expressed her frustration in an open, engaged, and respectful manner. However, Amy's mental and physical disengagement from the discussion is most concerning. Her actions run counter to several dispositions the program considers essential for student success. Amy's actions may indicate a lack of integrity, self-awareness, sensitivity to individual differences and respect for diversity, and adherence to the *ACA Code of Ethics* (ACA, 2014) and an inability to accept and make use of feedback. Amy's actions can create more harm within the cohort if they are not addressed or it appears that the instructors are excusing or ignoring her behaviors.

Jessica decided to consult other faculty to determine whether Amy's behavior was an isolated incident or whether Amy consistently disengaged from class discussions, especially those related to multiculturalism. Reports from faculty were mixed. One faculty member reported that Amy was more reserved in class than other students but did not come across as disengaged or disrespectful. Another faculty member shared that Amy tended to be more disengaged when topics related to multiculturalism and social justice were discussed. He recalled a class session in which Amy walked out while several students of color were presenting on school counselors working with students who were undocumented. He did not think anything of it because it was not unusual for students to take breaks throughout the 3-hour class, but he noted that Amy did not participate in the discussion following the presentation. Both faculty members also reported an underlying tension in the class, and they observed students self-segregating. Based on this feedback, Jessica invited Amy to an individual meeting to discuss concerns related to her reaction to multicultural and social justice issues and her closed-off behavior in class.

Jessica and Veronica were concerned that the cohort rupture would impact how the group continued with internship, in which there would be more discussion of the MSJCC. They put aside course content to facilitate the final class session as a continued discussion of cultural climate. At the start of the class, Jessica and Veronica established ground rules for respectful dialogue and reviewed the *ACA Code of Ethics* (ACA, 2014), the ASCA School Counselor Professional Standards and Competencies (ASCA, 2019), and the MSJCC (Ratts et al., 2016).

Jessica used a fishbowl approach to facilitate a conversation about race relations, cohort dynamics, and work as a school counselor. Jessica asked for six volunteers to sit in the middle of the classroom and discuss the topics at hand. The group was mixed evenly with students of color and white students. The intervention also called for six observers of the discussion and seven observers of the intervention at large. The majority of class time was spent addressing unanswered questions and exploring ways to move forward as a cohort and as future school counselors. The last 20 minutes of the class were used to wrap up the intervention and express unanswered concerns before the students left their last class as a cohort.

Although there were still some unresolved issues within the cohort, the students were willing to address them overtly and engage in a productive discussion. In addition, Amy was open to meeting individually and listening to feedback, and she processed insecurities regarding her multicultural awareness. As the students progressed in their respective internship groups, they continued exploring their cultural heritage and the impact their cultural identities had on their colleagues and themselves.

Conclusion

This case documents intersecting identities of facilitators and students as well as the impact of sociopolitical climate on cohort dynamics and learning environment. Jessica and Veronica's multicultural and social justice counseling competencies were demonstrated in (a) their level of awareness of their own worldviews and those of their students, (b) their knowledge of how these dynamics impacted the classroom, (c) the interventions they used, and (d) their advocacy efforts at individual and systems levels. Their decision-making and intervention were guided by the *ACA Code of Ethics* (ACA, 2014), the ASCA School Counselor Professional Standards and Competencies (ASCA, 2019), the CACREP Standards (CACREP, 2016), and the MSJCC (Ratts et al., 2016). Although the incident was not fully resolved, students expressed growth following the cohort rupture. In addition, Jessica and Veronica assessed the students' professional dispositions and believed the cohort was ready to continue with internship, having a deeper understanding of multicultural awareness and interpersonal dynamics.

Reflection Questions

1. What are some additional issues that need to be considered in this case?
2. What additional issues would you consider in setting ground rules for the fishbowl exercise?

Critical Incident Response

Jonathan H. Ohrt and Kathryn P. Linich

The timing of this incident presents a significant challenge, as the end of the semester is typically focused on wrapping up content and processing learning and experiences. Nevertheless, the instructors made a sound decision to address cohort dynamics and concerns around multicultural and social justice counseling competencies. This response focuses on the initial conversation, cohort support, and programmatic implications.

Consistent with their constructivist, student-centered approach, the instructors did a good job facilitating open and honest discussion. To prepare for the conversation, they might have assigned some brief readings that address privilege, oppression, and experiences of students in counseling programs (e.g., Paone et al., 2019). The instructors could model disclosure and vulnerability by acknowledging their own biases and blind spots with the class (Pulliam et al., 2019). For example, the video likely included an effective intervention; however, Black students may have been frustrated by not learning from a Black counselor. The instructors could acknowledge that some curricula are still colonized, validating Black students' feelings of anger and frustration (Haskins et al., 2013). In the future, the instructors could further decolonize materials so students are able to hear Black, Indigenous, and people of color (BIPOC) perspectives in readings, case examples, and videos.

The instructors did well to honor the needs of the cohort and focus on unfinished business in the last class. This reinforced the expression of concerns as well as productive and honest discussion. Structuring the class around how to have a respectful and progressive discussion of multicultural issues provided a substantive opportunity for professional development, and these instructors made it clear to their students that they were invested. Having a safe and nonjudgmental environment in which to reflect on difficult topics aided Amy's growth and that of the cohort overall. The activity Jessica and Veronica used and other service-learning activities could be incorporated into the curriculum more regularly in other classes, such as classes on ethics, multicultural counseling, and group work (Langellier et al., 2020). Because the students were in a cohort, the instructors could have further developed a plan to continue to address unresolved issues as the students transitioned to the next internship.

Although this case is specific to a course, the cohort tension that emerged indicates that more systemic program dynamics are present. The instructors handled their concerns about Amy in a fair and ethical way through consultation with faculty and discussion. It could be helpful to review program policies and practices to ensure the perspectives of minoritized students are heard. For instance, program faculty members could develop an advisory committee. The program could also review all courses to ensure diversity concepts are reinforced and multicultural and social justice counseling competencies are included in coursework.

Finally, faculty members could engage in continuous professional development to increase their awareness of diversity in higher education and improve their ability to build relationships with BIPOC students (Haskins et al., 2013; Pulliam et al., 2019).

It appears that this concern has been simmering over the course of these students' graduate studies with no real outlet. The key to encouraging multicultural and social justice counseling competencies in all students is to integrate them into professional identity development early and often (Decker et al., 2016). The program may find ways to facilitate these conversations and integrate opportunities for advocacy from the first semester of classes, with continued check-ins throughout the course of the program. This would encourage students to have these conversations more openly and avoid a situation like the one discussed in this case. This could also be accomplished by assigning advocacy work, reflective exercises, experiential learning, and service learning (Decker et al., 2016; Langellier et al., 2020). Infusing social justice and advocacy into counseling courses could also help faculty notice discrepancies in development, such as the behaviors and beliefs demonstrated by Amy. In these ways, program faculty members can recognize and address student- and program-level concerns earlier and more proactively.

• • •

Chapter 9

I Need a New Partner: Addressing Cultural Encapsulation and Racism

LoriAnn Sykes Stretch and Denita N. Hudson

2014 *ACA Code of Ethics* Standards Addressed

- A.1.a. Primary Responsibility
- A.4.b. Personal Values
- C.5. Nondiscrimination
- F.7.c. Infusing Multicultural Issues/Diversity
- F.7.g. Student-to-Student Supervision and Instruction
- F.8.c. Self-Growth Experiences
- F.8.d. Addressing Personal Concerns
- F.9.b. Limitations
- F.11.b. Student Diversity
- F.11.c. Multicultural/Diversity Competence

• • •

Kayla, a white, 27-year-old, first-year graduate student in an online clinical mental health counseling program, was finishing up her first 21 credits. She was enrolled in the hybrid course Helping Relationship and Technique Development. The course required students to complete three live lab sessions supervised by a doctoral student and one week of lab sessions during a face-to-face residency. After Kayla's final live lab session before residency, she approached her doctoral lab supervisor, Amanda, and said she was "having trouble understanding my lab partner and relating to the challenges she is presenting in the live lab." Amanda noticed Kayla seemed irritated and anxious about her lab grade. She suggested Kayla continue practicing active listening and ensured her she would become more confident after working in person with her lab partner, Marisol. The night before her residency began, Kayla sent the following email:

> Hello Amanda,
>
> I am genuinely enjoying your supervision, and I have learned so much about being a counselor and the techniques counselors use to help their clients overcome their challenges. It seems a large part of my grades come from our live lab sessions and residency practice sessions. Although I am thrilled that so much of the course includes active participation and practice, I would like to request a new lab partner during residency. I am from a tiny town in Tennessee and will work with predominantly white females and their families. My community is not very diverse, yet I have still worked hard to respect other cultures and their values. However, I believe working with someone similar to the clients I will serve is more beneficial to the acquisition of skills and will better prepare me to work in my community.
>
> Working with Marisol, who is from Haiti, is too difficult for a counselor-in-training. I have trouble understanding her strong accent, and I cannot relate to the family dynamics she discusses in sessions. I appreciate you encouraging me to keep practicing my skills, but I do not believe my frustration and challenges are related to my abilities. I know I can succeed in lab and residency if I have a client who has a similar culture and background. I am sure you have had similar experiences when working with international students or students of color. Please consider my request; I believe it would benefit Marisol as well as myself.
>
> Thank you,
> Kayla

Amanda noted that Kayla did not include Professor Trimmel, the supervising faculty member, on her email. She forwarded the email to Professor Trimmel and requested a consultation. Amanda and Professor Trimmel met via Zoom that same day to discuss the situation. Professor Trimmel shared that Marisol had approached him about Kayla's performance during the lab sessions and Amanda's nonchalant response to her "racism." Professor Trimmel stated he was planning to discuss the situation at their scheduled supervision session before residency.

According to Professor Trimmel, Marisol reported that she had attempted to use her immigration story as her client problem. She discussed leaving her country and moving to the United States with her husband. At first she thought her topic was too tricky for Kayla, but she noticed Kayla did not attempt to listen or use her skills. Marisol stated that Kayla seemed disinterested and annoyed with her. Professor Trimmel reported he empathized with Marisol and asked her to continue to work with Kayla during residency so he would have the opportunity to observe the interactions. He explained she would have the opportunity to work with a second-year student (a "Res II Buddy") who would provide Kayla and Marisol with feedback and support during residency lab sessions. After the consultation with Professor Trimmel, Amanda responded to Kayla, stating that she would need to continue to work with Marisol at residency and that she, Amanda, would be there to support Kayla.

During their first practice session at residency, Kayla turned her chair slightly away from Marisol to face the Res II Buddy, a second-year African American student, and stated, "I cannot paraphrase what I do not understand." Her Res II Buddy suggested she summarize Marisol's experience. Marisol stated, "She does not seem to understand what I feel." Kayla countered, "How can I reflect feeling when that is not something I have experienced?" Kayla asked Amanda to help, stating the Res II Buddy and Marisol were "ganging up on me because I am white."

Amanda called a break and texted Professor Trimmel. She asked Marisol, Kayla, and the Res II Buddy to meet in the conference room after a 15-minute break. She reminded them about confidentiality agreements and said they would address the tension after the break.

Case Analysis and Discussion

Counselor education students must be prepared to address the needs of a diverse world (American Counseling Association [ACA], 2014; Council for Accreditation of Counseling and Related Educational Programs [CACREP], 2016). The Multicultural and Social Justice Counseling Competencies (MSJCC; Ratts et al., 2016) state that counselors are to explore intersections of counselor and client identities while developing knowledge and skills related to counselor self-awareness, client worldview, and the counseling relationship. Although faculty convey ethics codes and multicultural and social justice counseling competencies early in the matriculation process, the transition from cultural knowledge and awareness to clinical practice can be challenging for students and problematic for counselor educators to measure (Estrada & Rigali-Oiler, 2016). Recent literature recognizes the correlation between the teaching alliance in counselor education (specifically in multicultural learning environments) and student growth, safety confronting difficult subjects, and skills acquisition (Estrada & Rigali-Oiler, 2016). This case analysis considers three major areas: self and impact of self on others, curriculum and preparation, and supervision. For each area, we discuss key issues, action steps, and outcomes.

Self and Impact of Self on Others

A key concern is Kayla's use of intrapersonal communication. What is first an inner dialogue ("I cannot gain anything valuable from my experience with Marisol" or "Marisol's communication style prevents me from using good counseling skills") leads to a conscious decision to not fully engage in the process. Although Marisol is not officially her client, Kayla marginalizes Marisol and disrupts her development, a direct violation of *ACA Code of Ethics* (ACA, 2014) standards regarding primary responsibility (Standard A.1.a.) and nondiscrimination (Standard C.5.). Kayla's actions are also detrimental to her self-growth experience (Standard F.8.c.), which is essential to quality skill development. Kayla's ethnocentric cognitive processing has limited her ability to interact effectively with her peers and the faculty team (Jun, 2018).

Helping Kayla change her cognitive distortions will not be an easy task. Kayla has focused solely on the perceived negatives of her experience. The magnification of Marisol's accent and the minimization of Kayla's ability to empathize with her have only confirmed her belief that she is best suited to working with clients similar to her. If he does not attempt to disrupt Kayla's cognitive distortions and ethnocentric biases, Professor Trimmel will find himself in violation of ethical standards (ACA, 2014, Standard F.8.d.) and accreditation requirements for addressing competency concerns through remediation (CACREP, 2016, Section 1, Standard O).

The following action steps may assist Kayla in addressing her ethnocentric biases and cognitive distortions. Reinforcing appropriate intrapersonal communication and thinking styles can aid Kayla in becoming more reflective and attuned to internal verbalization (Estrada & Rigali-Oiler, 2016; Jun, 2018). In addition, Professor Trimmel's supervision and professional guidance are indispensable as Amanda assumes the professional role of teacher, supervisor, leader, and advocate in her work with Kayla. Amanda can facilitate Kayla's development of multicultural and social justice counseling competencies using the positive relationship they have developed during lab sessions.

Marisol could also benefit from Amanda's growth as a counselor educator. Marisol views Amanda as nonchalant in responding to the unjust treatment and oppression she has experienced. By neglecting Marisol's needs during this experience, Amanda's supervision has fallen short of CACREP Standards (CACREP, 2016) and the MSJCC regarding social impact on others and sources of discomfort (Ratts et al., 2016). Seward (2014) found that instructors who presented themselves as knowledgeable and facilitated open dialogue on cultural identity promoted more personal development than instructors who did not use cross-cultural teaching strategies. Similar actions could assist Marisol, Kayla, and Amanda in understanding one another's intersecting identities.

Jun (2018) offered several learning activities for changing intrapersonal communication and addressing cognitive distortions through uncensored writing activities. For example, Kayla could review recorded lab sessions and focus on describing her thoughts while Marisol is playing the client. This exercise would help Kayla recognize ineffective thinking styles, such as hierarchical thinking ("My needs are more important than yours") and linear thinking ("I have not been able to understand her, so I won't try"). Once Kayla has identified five to 10 cognitive distortions, she can begin to examine her interpersonal and nonverbal communication. Reflective exercises increase awareness and build empathy for the client (Ivers et al., 2016; Seward, 2014). Repeating the process and scrutinizing her verbal and nonverbal interactions (e.g., turning her chair) may assist Kayla in understanding Marisol's frustration. Then Amanda should process the impact of Kayla's thoughts on her interactions with peers and clients. Amanda would be able to assess Kayla's growth and remediation efforts while also assisting her in understanding how her actions violate the *ACA Code of Ethics* (ACA, 2014).

The outcome of these activities will largely depend on Kayla's ability to have a holistic view of self. It can take years of practice and self-reflection to change thinking styles. As a mentor, Amanda can assist Kayla in addressing negative aspects of herself as they relate to the course and skill development. Developing a teaching alliance with Marisol would also be important to her healing process. Professor Trimmel's follow-up is essential to ensuring standards are met and establishing a practice of continued monitoring as Kayla matriculates through the program.

Curriculum and Preparation

Counselor educators must prepare students to work effectively with "multicultural and pluralistic characteristics within and among diverse groups nationally and internationally" (CACREP, 2016, Section 2, Standard F.2.a.). After a year of coursework, Kayla does not appear to have any internalization of the importance of working with diverse groups or any knowledge of how to engage with individuals different from herself. The program has a responsibility to provide exposure to diverse clients throughout their training (ACA, 2014, Standards F.7.c., F.11.c.).

Culturally skilled counselors must seek out opportunities to understand and enhance their effectiveness in working with diverse populations (Ratts et al., 2016). Kayla felt justified in requesting a specific type of partner because she anticipated limiting her future practice to white females and their families. However, having earned a counseling degree indicates that an individual is qualified and capable of working with diverse populations (ACA, 2014, Standards A.4.b., C.4.). The specific training Kayla seeks is far too limited for a counseling degree and would result in a misrepresentation of her qualifications.

Atkins et al. (2017) found that white counselors can become multiculturally competent when they take time to listen, tolerate conflict, question (wonder), check for understanding, and take action. In this situation, Kayla is inhibiting her own growth by refusing to participate in this process. This calls into question the exposure to and opportunities for practice with a diverse clientele that Kayla has had to date in her coursework. In addition, Kayla requested a segregated training experience. Beyond the multitude of counseling standards and competencies that require a timely response to such a concern, the Civil Rights Act of 1964 prohibits segregation in educational settings. To assign lab partners based on race would be a direct violation of this law.

Programs must engage in ongoing systematic evaluation of program objectives and student learning (CACREP, 2016, Section 4, Standard A.1.), including students' ability to work with diverse clients. Programs have a responsibility to train students in the complexity of multiculturalism to ensure students can validate the experiences of their future clients (Duan & Brown, 2016). Kayla's program faculty need to examine the curriculum to determine whether current course materials prepare students to be effective with diverse groups. In particular, the faculty need to evaluate the diversity of clients in course material and opportunities for students to engage with diverse client material both in writing and via multimedia.

Kayla needs to understand the nature of the degree she is seeking. Her faculty adviser should meet with her to review the 2016 CACREP Standards (CACREP, 2016), the MSJCC (Ratts et al., 2016), and the *ACA Code of Ethics* (ACA, 2014). It would also be appropriate to introduce a formal remediation plan asking Kayla to write a reflection paper evaluating the course of training she is requesting and noting what standards and competencies are and are not met by her proposal. A review of the paper with her adviser would engage Kayla in a collaborative process focusing on student feedback and self-assessment. If Kayla's inability to demonstrate multicultural and social justice counseling competencies continues, the faculty would be obligated to escalate the remediation plan.

At the program level, these action steps will result in a more intentional approach to training students to "gain awareness, knowledge, and skills in the competencies of multicultural practice" (ACA, 2014, Standard F.11.c.). Ideally, the review of courses and assignments will result in a curriculum map that identifies where curricula address the MSJCC as well as an assessment plan that will determine when and how the program will assess students' dispositions, skills, and knowledge regarding the MSJCC and their ability to work with a broad range of clients (ACA, 2014; CACREP, 2016; Ratts et al., 2016). At a personal level, Kayla will better understand the scope of a counseling degree and the importance of honoring diversity as a core professional value.

Supervision

Another key issue relates to the supervision of the master's students and doctoral student in this program. Supervisors must address multicultural and social justice counseling competencies as part of the supervisory relationship (ACA, 2014, Standard F.2.b.) and the counseling relationship (ACA, 2014, Standard A.2.c.). Acknowledging cultural factors has a significant impact on client satisfaction, counselor credibility, and content of sessions

(Day-Vines et al., 2018). In this case, there does not appear to have been any conversation regarding cultural dynamics at the beginning of the skills lab.

Similarly, there is no indication that Professor Trimmel and Amanda have addressed the cultural dynamics of their supervisory relationship or that Amanda is prepared to address cultural dynamics in supervision. This unspoken dynamic is now inhibiting rather than enriching the experience of all involved. To date, Amanda has avoided dealing with this issue, as reflected in her communications with Kayla and her lack of response to Marisol. Although Kayla's desire to avoid diversity is overt, Amanda is demonstrating a passive avoidance that perpetuates Kayla's belief that culture does not need to be valued or discussed.

An additional concern is Professor Trimmel's failure to address the racism in a timely manner. Professor Trimmel did not reach out to Amanda after Marisol reported a very serious concern regarding Amanda's nonchalant response to Kayla's racism. As a counselor educator, Professor Trimmel has a duty to ensure that students' rights are not compromised (ACA, 2014, Standard F.7.g.). Specifically, he needs to mentor Amanda by role modeling discussions of racism and multiculturalism, demonstrating a timely response to concerns, and outlining a plan for development for all involved.

Professor Trimmel should be a cofacilitator of the meeting after the break with Amanda. Amanda has a working alliance with Kayla, which could be a core factor in Kayla developing self-awareness and cultural awareness (Ivers et al., 2017). During the meeting, Professor Trimmel needs to outline the professional dispositions, skills, and knowledge required of counselors. Then he needs to provide a supportive space for each party to share the impact of the situation and their desired outcomes. Next Amanda and Professor Trimmel should demonstrate how to discuss culture in a session. Finally, a plan of action needs to be developed that requires the graduate students to repeat the time lost in lab under the supervision of Professor Trimmel and Amanda. The plan should also include a reflective journal from each student, including the Res II Buddy and Amanda.

These action steps will result in several important outcomes. First, Amanda will receive training in gatekeeping, a strengths-based and reflective model of conflict resolution, and appropriate ways to address multiculturalism and diversity. Second, the graduate students will engage in multicultural skill building while being able to reflect on self and self in relation to others. Third, Marisol will feel validated. Although this one intervention may only start this lifelong process, the hope is that Kayla will develop multicultural and social justice counseling competencies and begin to internalize the professional value of embracing a multicultural approach (Atkins et al., 2017).

Conclusion

A key implication of this case is the importance of having a comprehensive curriculum that includes training in multiculturalism, cultural humility, and the ability to serve diverse populations. Another key implication is that counselor educators and counselor-educators-in-training must be able to address professional dispositions and engage procedures that support early remediation. Finally, all students involved need to be supported in their own cultural growth and feel safe to explore concerns with one another and their supervisors.

Reflection Questions

1. How effective do you believe the proposed steps will be in addressing Kayla's concerns? What are some additional options for addressing the issue?
2. What does Marisol need in this interaction? How might Professor Trimmel and Amanda attend to this?
3. How can counselor educators prepare doctoral students to respond to concerns related to counseling students' multicultural and social justice counseling competencies?

Critical Incident Response

Carlos P. Hipolito-Delgado

I find myself generally in agreement with the discussion and analysis in this case. Thus, I will focus on providing additional considerations or nuance in how to respond. Specifically, I will focus on the need to pay more attention to Marisol's educational needs and the possibility that Kayla is culturally encapsulated and in need of more authentic interactions with diverse communities.

My main concern is the focus on Kayla and her learning needs. As is often the case in graduate studies (Haskins et al., 2013), Marisol's main function is furthering the education of white counselors. I agree that Professor Trimmel should have been quicker to address Marisol's concerns. At a minimum, Professor Trimmel should have brought Marisol, Kayla, and Amanda together to discuss their issues. He might also address the larger class about the importance of dialogue and collaboration between partners. This more active approach goes beyond empathizing with Marisol to validate her experience and demonstrate commitment to her educational success.

Professor Trimmel's lack of action might be evidence of discomfort with difficult dialogues and the need to further understand privilege and cultural inclusion (Watt, 2007). Unfortunately, Professor Trimmel's lack of action in addressing Marisol's concerns might convey that he does not find them to be valid or worthy of his attention. This could lead Marisol to limit her participation and ultimately feel alienated from the program (Haskins et al., 2013).

I appreciate that the authors described the need to evaluate the counseling program's goals and outcomes related to multiculturalism. Although they described this in terms of ensuring opportunities for cross-cultural encounters, having a climate of assessment may also ensure that Marisol and other students of color are being educated in a program that includes and affirms students from marginalized backgrounds (Hipolito-Delgado et al., 2017). Although student diversity can add educational richness to a counseling program, this potential is lost if students of color are silenced and alienated (Hipolito-Delgado et al., 2017).

As the authors noted, Kayla is self-centered in her learning experience. Alas, Amanda reinforces this through her response to Kayla's email. Had Amanda instead met with both partners, she would have conveyed how she prioritized the educational needs of both students. As is the case with Professor Trimmel, it could be that Amanda is not comfortable having difficult dialogues about diversity and might need to reassess her cultural competence as a supervisor and future counselor educator.

Aside from being self-centered, it appears that Kayla is culturally encapsulated and unaware of other cultural perspectives (Wrenn, 1962). I agree that Kayla could benefit from more cross-cultural encounters. However, I differ with the authors on how said encounters should occur. The contact hypothesis holds that authentic, cooperative, nonhierarchical, cross-cultural interactions are necessary to overcome bias (DeRicco & Sciarra, 2005). Working with diverse clients might not be enough to foster Kayla's cultural understanding and cultural competence, as the counseling relationship can reinforce power dynamics with people of color being dependent on white helpers. Although being exposed to diverse clients during training is codified in the *ACA Code of Ethics* (ACA, 2014, Standards F.7.c., F.11.c.), counselors who lack cultural competence are likely to do more harm than good. Thus, I disagree with the idea of using culturally diverse clients to promote Kayla's cultural understanding.

Instead, I would look for opportunities for Kayla to work alongside members of diverse communities to develop an understanding of diversity and come to respect the humanity of those culturally different from herself. Hipolito-Delgado et al. (2016) found that white counselors who were allies of communities of color developed empathy by learning from those communities. These changes were due to positive experiences with communities of color and a personalized understanding of inequalities faced by them. Development can best be achieved through more personalized contact, perhaps in service learning or cultural immersion, with diverse communities. It would also be wise to foster Kayla's critical consciousness. A recognition of systems of oppression and how they rob the humanity of communities of color (Freire, 1970) might aid Kayla in questioning her part in these systems and how she can be an ally in the liberation of oppressed communities.

Balancing the needs of marginalized and privileged students can be challenging. Although the authors are to be commended for describing strategies to promote Kayla's growth, the needs of Marisol and other potential clients of color require more attention. In this response, I described interventions to affirm Marisol and promote the growth of Kayla in ways that are not at the expense of communities of color.

• • •

Chapter 10

Interacting With Me: Title IX and Faculty-Student Consensual Relationships

Imelda N. Bratton

2014 *ACA Code of Ethics* Standards Addressed

- F.10.a. Sexual or Romantic Relationships
- F.10.b. Sexual Harassment
- F.10.d. Nonacademic Relationships
- F.10.f. Extending Educator-Student Boundaries

• • •

Richard was a single, 56-year-old faculty member in a counselor education program at a midsize university. Richard held a doctoral degree in counselor education and was dually credentialed as a licensed professional counselor and certified school counselor. He had been employed by the university for 3 years and taught two doctoral-level courses per semester. Prior to working as a faculty member within higher education, Richard had gained extensive experience working as a career counselor in public elementary and secondary schools. Richard was well known for training mental health professionals in the application of career counseling theories in a variety of settings. He had published a textbook and numerous articles on the subject and was frequently sought out for consultation and continuing education.

Maya, a 49-year-old counselor education doctoral student, approached Richard to discuss the use of career inventories with clients. The pair met by videoconference, as they lived an hour away from each other and were never on campus at the same time. As with all student meetings, Richard prioritized establishing rapport with Maya. He took the time to tell her a bit about himself, both personally and professionally; Maya also described her professional experiences and aspirations.

Maya was a licensed professional counselor serving as clinical director at a community mental health center. Her agency had recently acquired a contract to use federal funding from the Local Workforce Investment Board. This contract would permit her agency to provide free educational and training opportunities and career counseling to members of the local community. Maya had some anxiety about taking over this contract because career counseling was new to her. She expressed great admiration for Richard's work and gratitude for his willingness to informally mentor her.

During the conversation, Maya disclosed that she had been in a tumultuous relationship for the past 3 years and was devastated as her fiancé had recently overdosed on opiates. After stabilizing, he had admitted himself into a 6-month inpatient treatment program. Maya reported that her fiancé made blaming and degrading statements such as "Of course I use drugs. It is the only way I can cope with being with someone like you." Richard expressed shock at Maya's recounting of recent interactions with her fiancé. She confirmed that these statements were in line with a long pattern of emotional abuse that had marked the duration of their relationship.

Maya had decided to take the 6-month rehabilitation period to work on herself as well. She had moved out of the condo she shared with her fiancé, as it was in his name. During this time she had also applied for and started the counselor education doctoral program. Maya stated that she was very pleased with her decision to pursue this degree, as she enjoyed attending classes and found it to be the only outlet that gave her meaning. She said she was attending weekly individual counseling sessions and found them to be very helpful. Richard thanked Maya for trusting him with such personal information. He also reinforced her decision to continue counseling. The two then discussed several validated open-access career counseling assessments Maya's agency might use with their contract and discussed best practices related to the same. The discussion ended with Richard advising Maya to contact him if she had other questions.

Maya contacted Richard via phone a few weeks later to ask whether he would help her with a career inventory she had recently purchased to use with clients. Richard had used the inventory in the past and knew it could sometimes be challenging to interpret the results. The pair set up three biweekly virtual meetings to discuss the inventory and its application across specialized populations.

At first Richard and Maya's conversations were focused on career counseling. But over time the conversations became less formal and took on a more friendly tone. The pair talked about life experiences, hobbies, fears, and dating in middle adulthood. Over the next few months they began to flirt with each other and extended their communication to texts and phone calls. They often sought dating advice from each other and even inquired about how their dates with other people had gone. Eventually Maya and Richard were speaking several times per week and considered themselves friends. Although Richard and Maya grew close, they never discussed a potential romantic relationship. They lived approximately 1 hour from each other, and both had transportation, yet they never met in person.

Soon Richard launched a complex new research study that required much of his time and effort. He spent several weeks completing an institutional review board application for the study and had minimal time for personal activities. One evening Maya called Richard and asked him why he was not speaking with her as frequently. She was upset and aggressive during their conversation. Maya began crying and indicated that she felt betrayed by Richard's absence, as he had "abandoned" their "relationship." Richard was surprised by Maya's anger, saying he did not understand what she meant. Maya launched into a series of expletives and accused Richard of breaking her trust and discarding her. Richard indicated he did not appreciate how Maya was speaking to him and said he needed to terminate the call. Before he had the opportunity to disconnect, Maya yelled, "I'll save you the trouble!" and hung up. Richard did not hear anything more from Maya.

The following week Richard received a phone call from the Title IX compliance officer at his university. The officer stated that Maya had filed a complaint against him for inappropriate behavior. Richard provided a written response to the Title IX compliance officer and participated in two interviews to provide information regarding the nature of their interactions; he did not consult with or hire an attorney throughout the investigation.

Case Analysis and Discussion

University settings are unique in that faculty are expected to be available for students throughout the school year. Students typically connect with faculty members who have similar interests or professional expertise. Close relationships are more common in doctoral programs, in which students begin to collaborate with professors to enrich and advance their skillset.

Title IX requires universities to establish and publish grievance procedures for complaints of discrimination based on sex (Office for Civil Rights, 2020, 2021). Procedures include the right for material to be presented by both the complainant and respondent. In addition, Title IX provides the right for an impartial investigation, equal opportunity, and an appeal process for the complainant and respondent in cases of sexual discrimination, including unwelcome sexual behavior, harassment, and the creation of a hostile work environment (Equal Employment Opportunity Commission, 2008). Sexual harassment may include quid pro quo harassment in which employment, grades, or other decisions are conditional on the fulfillment of unwanted sexual actions. Maya submitted a complaint that alleged Richard had an inappropriate relationship with her and sexually harassed her throughout their interactions. During the investigation, the Title IX compliance officer discovered several critical issues in the case that are described below. In addition, university policy and ethical considerations are addressed.

Title IX Investigation

Both Richard and Maya portrayed the relationship as one that evolved out of mutual interests, and they provided text messages, emails, and phone records that confirmed they had communicated almost daily over a 4-month period. The messages initially focused on professional topics, then gradually became more personal in nature. Communication ranged from discussions of daily events to discussions of their dates with others. Text messages included dating advice in relation to the people they were dating. At times, the written communication contained flirtatious content; both parties referenced their mutual attraction to each other, and text messages included several salacious sexual innuendos. Their written communication never specifically identified or referenced a relationship between the two parties. Richard and Maya had never met in person. No reference to or discussion of plans to meet was provided in the text messages.

As part of the investigation process, the Title IX compliance officer asked both parties to submit to two individual video interviews. This allowed him to clarify specific points so he could make an objective determination regarding whether university policies had been violated. The interviews with Richard also included a representative from the university's human resources office to ensure protocol was maintained throughout the interviews.

University Policy Regarding Personal Relationships With Students

The university's faculty handbook included a policy regarding consensual personal relationships with students. The policy acknowledged that relationships could occur between faculty members and students. Dual relationships of any type with undergraduate students were prohibited; however, dual relationships with graduate students were permissible. In addition, the policy specified that faculty should exercise caution, maintain professionalism, and avoid conflicts of interest if a relationship developed with a graduate student. Furthermore, a statement about the possibility of a power differential between faculty members and students was included. Exploitation of students was forbidden. Finally, faculty members were required to report any romantic or dating relationships to their direct supervisor.

Although universities cannot deviate from Title IX requirements, they are able to create their own policies regarding consensual relationships between faculty and students. Policies on consensual relationships can provide guidance for faculty members concerning what the university allows and prohibits. Clear, unambiguous policies can result in consistent action from the administration (Gerdes, 2004) and inform faculty of potential risks associated with faculty and student relationships (Mack, 1999). Policies can range from not addressing consensual relationships to prohibiting any such relationships between faculty members and students (Richards et al., 2014).

This university's policy on consensual relationships would be considered a limited ban policy because it prohibits consensual relationships in specific instances (Mack, 1999). There is a strong case for these types of policies in the literature (Jafar, 2003; McArthur, 2017; A. Rodriguez, 2019). Being able to be in a romantic relationship with another is a basic human right (A. Rodriguez, 2019). Richard and Maya were not in what would traditionally be considered a romantic relationship, but there was playful banter and flirtation over time. Maya never enrolled in a course with Richard as an instructor. Their interactions had a sexual tone at times, yet they were limited to text messages and phone calls, as the two did not meet face to face.

Complete ban policies prohibit any consensual relationships between faculty members and students (Mack, 1999). Supporters of these types of bans believe that relationships between faculty members and students cannot be consensual because of the power differential (Adam, 2019). Others (Bellas & Gossett, 2001) recommend a ban on relationships when faculty are direct teachers or current supervisors of students. This is a hybrid ban policy (Mack, 1999). In this case, Maya was not currently enrolled in a course with Richard, nor was she his supervisee. Maya approached Richard to discuss career interventions relating to her employment as a clinical counselor, which was unrelated to university coursework. The university had a limited ban policy and not a complete or hybrid ban policy in the current faculty handbook; therefore, the compliance officer determined that university policy had not been violated.

Richard received a letter from the Title IX compliance office regarding the outcome of the investigation. The university used the preponderance of evidence standard in Title IX (Office for Civil Rights, 2021) to indicate that sexual discrimination was not substantiated, and the case against Richard was dismissed. Maya did not request an appeal.

Ethical Considerations

Separate from university policy, the *ACA Code of Ethics* (American Counseling Association [ACA], 2014) provides guidance on relationships between faculty and students. Standard F.10.a. prohibits counselor educators from participating in romantic or sexual interactions with students "currently enrolled in a counseling or related program and over whom they have power and authority." Richard and Maya had what may be considered romantic interactions. Although part of this ethics code may have been defied, Richard was not acting in the role of her current professor or supervisor. In this instance, Richard did not have power or control over Maya.

The *ACA Code of Ethics* (ACA, 2014) prohibits counselor educators from exposing students to sexual harassment or tolerating the sexual harassment of students (Standard F.10.b.). Sexual harassment pertains to unwelcome sexual advances (Office for Civil Rights, 2021). The current situation did not have a quid pro quo element, as Richard did not require Maya to participate in flirtatious discussions in exchange for a grade or employment, and she appeared to engage readily.

Nonacademic relationships are discussed in Standard F.10.d. (ACA, 2014), which states counselor educators should "avoid nonacademic relationships" in which students could be harmed or that risk impacting students' experiences in training or grades. Maya initially approached Richard to discuss learning about career interventions. Their relationship developed quickly and led to flirtatious electronic interactions. The purpose of the discussions was related to Maya's outside employment and not directly to university requirements. As these discussions were not a requirement for a course, Maya's experiences in training or grades were not impacted.

Richard and Maya had recently undergone highly emotional experiences. Richard had recently divorced. Maya had ended a relationship with her significant other when he entered an addiction program. Both types of experiences may cause individuals to be in a vulnerable state, in which the potential for poor decision-making can increase.

Conclusion

Consensual relationships are not covered under Title IX and are not illegal. Universities set their own policies by which faculty are expected to abide. Policies regarding consensual relationships fall into a gray area that has not been extensively researched. The limited research available indicates that consensual relationships between graduate students and professors are not uncommon (McKay et al., 2007). Counselor educators should be aware of university policies and ethical responsibilities and implement a decision-making model to make an informed decision before considering or pursuing a consensual relationship with a student.

Reflection Questions

1. Do you agree or disagree with the claim that the relationship between Richard and Maya was not problematic because he was not currently her instructor or supervisor?
2. Even if permissible under university policy, what impacts might such faculty-student relationships have on the overall climate of a doctoral program?

Critical Incident Response

Shawn L. Spurgeon

The problematic situation between Richard and Maya highlights the potential for meaningful relationships between professors and students to expand beyond their boundaries. By its very nature, the counseling profession involves intimate relationships between individuals. Counselor training relationships have components that are similar in nature to those of therapeutic counseling relationships. For example, counselors have a fiduciary responsibility to act in the best interest of their clients. This includes being more aware of boundaries and values and having a deeper understanding of the self in relation to personal and professional values. In some ways, this responsibility extends to faculty members' relationships with students.

Counselor educators engage in meaningful interactions with students, and there is a level of intimacy associated with this work. Still, they need to take steps to ensure they are behaving in the most ethical manner possible. This case represents a good example of how boundary crossings can occur and highlights challenges counselor educators face. More specifically, it demonstrates the importance of self-awareness and commitment to professional responsibilities when working with students. Although the university cleared Richard of legal wrongdoing in terms of sexual harassment, he clearly violated his ethical responsibilities by engaging in an inappropriate personal relationship with a student.

This case response focuses on the lack of credible evidence of sexual harassment in the context of university policy regarding Richard and Maya's consensual relationship. Although their contact may not have violated university policy, Richard was clearly connecting with Maya as a student in the program. In this response, I provide pointed feedback on key aspects of this case. Specifically, counselor educators are responsible for maintaining appropriate relationships with their students. The *ACA Code of Ethics* (ACA, 2014) highlights several important responsibilities of counselor educators as professional evaluators and gatekeepers of the profession. Given this power differential, of which students are well aware, counselor educators have concrete responsibilities that guide how they interact with students.

The relationship between Richard and Maya certainly started in a professional manner. At some point, it dissolved into more personal discussions. This constitutes a boundary extension and does not fit the description of acceptable scenarios as outlined in Standard F.10.f. of the *ACA Code of Ethics* (ACA, 2014). In addition, the *Code* notes that counselor educators should take precautions regarding boundary extensions with students in a manner similar to what counselors do when they work with clients.

These precautions are important because the *ACA Code of Ethics* (ACA, 2014) requires counselor educators to be fair and honest in their assessment of students. Although Maya was not in one of Richard's classes at the time of the boundary crossing, there are broader implications that have not been considered. Richard could very well serve as her instructor at some point during her training. Given the small size of doctoral programs, it is presumable that he would be engaged in evaluating students in the program. Thus, he has a heightened responsibility to govern himself in a manner that does not demonstrate undue favoritism. Richard would have a very difficult time doing this given the relationship he had with Maya. Regardless of the physical distance from Maya and the virtual nature of their interaction, he was still in a position of power and needed to display an appropriate level of self-awareness when interacting with students. This is an aspirational aspect of ethical behavior and yet an important developmental component to remember when connecting with students.

In addition, other students in the program could be affected by this relationship. This relationship could negatively affect peers' ability to engage Maya or Richard in any type of academic, professional situation. For example, if Maya is not doing her part in a group project, it may be difficult for peers to voice concerns because of their awareness of this relationship. The ethical climate and reputation of the program could also be called into question by stakeholders. Richard's behavior violated the basic ethical principle of fairness in the counseling profession.

This relationship has broader implications in terms of Richard's colleagues. If they are aware of this relationship, it could affect the way they engage in their evaluation and gatekeeping role with Maya. For example, a junior faculty member might be less likely to provide negative feedback to Maya because of Richard's seniority in the program. In addition, the program would need to consider major shifts to accommodate the need to avoid contact between Richard and Maya. This would create additional complexity in the program. Given Richard's status in the program and in the community, this is a genuine concern for all faculty involved.

Standard F.10.d. of the *ACA Code of Ethics* (ACA, 2014) highlights the need for counselor educators to avoid nonprofessional relationships with students. Though there was no risk for Maya in terms of grades, Richard did not attend to every aspect of the nonprofessional relationships statute. More specifically, Richard needed to assess the veracity of such a relationship in terms of the potential risk for harm. Given Maya's emotional state and Richard's experience as a counselor educator, it is presumable that Richard understood Maya was in a vulnerable state related to the trauma she had experienced. A critical aspect of counselor educators' ethical responsibilities is assessing student growth. When Richard learned of her concerns, it was his ethical responsibility to consider supportive measures to enhance her learning and growth.

Instead of engaging in this level of ethical awareness, Richard chose to deepen the relationship by sharing his own personal challenges and triumphs with dating. This clearly goes beyond the scope of the professional relationship. Ethics codes clearly identify that mandates apply to both in-person and virtual relationships with students. It was not permissible for Richard to engage in flirtatious behavior and texts because he and Maya were not in the same space. Richard needed to be aware of this fact when he chose to engage in flirtatious texting.

The Healthcare Providers Service Organization counselor liability claim report (Healthcare Providers Service Organization, 2019) noted that sexual misconduct and allegations of multiple relationships with clients increased in 2018 and has done so over the past 5 years. These relationships increase the possibility of harm and create an aversive climate for individuals seeking help. Section F of the *ACA Code of Ethics* (ACA, 2014) notes that counselor educators have many of the same responsibilities with their students as counselors have with their clients. Counselor educators protect client welfare by monitoring student development and by evaluating student growth. How can Richard be a fair, evaluative person when his relationship extends beyond what is permissible?

Richard could have engaged an ethical decision-making model (EDMM) to navigate this situation. The first step of such a model requires counselor educators to determine the nature of the problem. If Richard had taken this step, he could have surmised that there were problematic boundary crossings inherent in the sharing of personal information. A key component of any EDMM is the consideration of virtues and values and their role in the dilemma (Kocet & Herlihy, 2014). If Richard had engaged in an EDMM, he may have better understood Maya's vulnerabilities, his responsibilities, and his commitment to fairness and justice in his role as counselor educator. Consultation is an essential step in any EDMM (Remley & Herlihy, 2020), and Richard needed to connect with another counselor educator to process his responses to Maya, express his concerns, and secure additional feedback for making an informed decision about his choices. Seeking consultation may have helped Richard better reflect on how his attention to Maya was different from his attention to other students in the program. In so doing, he may have identified the boundary violation and perhaps would have taken steps to address this potential problem.

• • •

Section 3
Instructor Preparedness

Chapter 11

Embracing the Digital World: Instructor Preparedness for Online Delivery

Olga R. Dietlin and Jenny L. Chien

2014 *ACA Code of Ethics* Standards Addressed

- F.7.a. Counselor Educators
- F.7.b. Counselor Educator Competence

• • •

Barb Pearson was a professor in a clinical mental health counseling program accredited by the Council for Accreditation of Counseling and Related Educational Programs (CACREP). She had been teaching for 20 years and had also maintained a successful private practice. Barb was well liked by her students and known for her warmth, humor, and charisma in the classroom. She taught a number of residential courses within the graduate program, her favorite being Counseling Skills and Techniques. Professor Pearson believed the development of counseling skills was imperative to successful practice. She enjoyed the interactive components of the course and the student engagement.

Recently, the dean had requested Professor Pearson teach the course online to meet the needs of students at a satellite location. When Professor Pearson was reluctant, the dean said, "Barb, this should be easy! Just take what you do and upload the content into the learning management system." Professor Pearson did not agree the task would be so easy. As a tenured faculty member, she could not help but wonder whether all the work would be worth it. She said to herself, "I've been successful teaching residentially. Why make changes at this point in my career?"

Professor Pearson's concerns grew as she reflected on the dean's request. She was reluctant to embrace technology associated with the online learning environment. She only used the learning management system to input student grades. Her use of other technological tools in the classroom was limited. She did not know what she did not know. How did students engage with the content? How did they interact with one another and with the faculty member? Would she be managing online discussion boards only? What sort of technical assistance would she have?

Barb was also concerned about the nature of the course being conducted online. Counseling Skills and Techniques was a prerequisite for practicum and key to evaluating students' professional dispositions. Barb wondered how she could assess student growth when she could not see students face to face and interact with them directly.

Moreover, Barb was a strong proponent of the pedagogy of care (Noddings, 2005) and core conditions for facilitative learning (C. Rogers & Freiberg, 1993), including congruence (realness or authenticity), acceptance, and empathy. She strived to develop caring relationships with her students. Barb struggled to see how she could convey such care online and build strong relationships. She perceived the online course environment as impersonal and detached.

Barb's final concern was that she simply would not enjoy teaching online. She thought about all she enjoyed about the residential format: rapport with students, the ability to engage them in the process, and the joy of watching them acquire new skills. Barb wondered whether being online would strip her course of everything she knew and loved.

Barb communicated her concerns to the dean, who recommended she consult with Professor Shanice George, a counseling faculty member who had been teaching for 5 years and had successfully developed and taught numerous online courses. Barb reached out to Shanice with apprehension but found her to be a passionate advocate for online education. Shanice encouraged Barb and addressed her concerns. She shared her student course evaluations; remarkably, Barb found them to be very positive, capturing appreciation for Shanice's caring and genuine personality, the learning experience, and personal growth.

Shanice connected Barb to integrated university resources in information technology, learning management support, and course design. Barb was relieved to know she would not be alone in course development. She was even more pleased to learn the importance of pedagogy in online education. Shanice shared her experiences combining her teaching style, counseling philosophy, and personality to be effective as an online educator. She showed Barb some of her assignments and demonstrated how she integrated interactive assignments, videoconferencing, and group projects into the material. Shanice concluded by sharing the importance of intentionality, authenticity, and community in online environments. Barb could hardly believe she had heard the words "intentionality," "authenticity," and "community" in reference to online courses. Shanice generously expressed a willingness to mentor Barb through the course development process and to help her build her online skillset. Hesitant, but with newfound curiosity, Barb considered embracing the digital world of graduate education.

Case Analysis and Discussion

The number of counselor education programs offered online is on the rise (Snow et al., 2018), reflecting a general trend in higher education: More than 30% of students were enrolled in at least one online course in 2016 (Seaman et al., 2018). Convenience and flexibility are the two main reasons why adult learners choose online platforms. Online learning can increase access to higher education for women and underrepresented racial minority students (Xu & Xu, 2019) who would otherwise not pursue it, and flexibility and convenience play a positive role in their pursuit of learning and academic performance (Kumi-Yeboah & Smith, 2016). Web-based learning will soon become common in residential settings, and expectations to teach online will increase for the majority of faculty (Anderson, 2020). It is only a matter of time before all counselor educators experience opportunities and challenges similar to those described for Professor Pearson.

The *ACA Code of Ethics* (American Counseling Association [ACA], 2014) emphasizes the importance of pedagogical mastery, professional knowledge, and ethical practice in "traditional, hybrid, and/or online formats" (Standard F.7.a.). It specifically includes the expectation that counselor educators "develop competence in the use of the technology" (Standard F.7.b.) in counselor education. Furthermore, the *ACA Code of Ethics* addresses the advancement of technology and directs counselors to "actively attempt to understand the evolving nature of the profession with regard to distance counseling, technology, and social media" (Section H, Introduction).

Although many counselor educators prefer traditional, face-to-face instruction (Murdock et al., 2012), the CACREP Standards (CACREP, 2016) encourage the integration of technology into counselor training and practice. Counselor educators need to be open to learning about and pursuing online modalities, carefully considering ethics guidelines and opportunities and limitations presented by the use of technology in counselor education (Murdock et al., 2012). Professor Pearson has three types of concerns about transitioning her residential class to an online setting: subject matter, pedagogical, and personal concerns. Although these concerns are overlapping and cannot be clearly distinguished from one another, it is helpful to address them separately.

Subject Matter Concerns

Professor Pearson's hesitation is a common response among counselor educators who emphasize skills and rely on in vivo observation of the development of microskills or empathy in students (Murdock et al., 2012). Although few researchers have investigated the effectiveness of web-based counseling skills courses, Murdock et al. (2012) found that students enrolled in online and traditional courses demonstrated similar levels of competence in starting a counseling session, developing an alliance, and conceptualizing the client's problem. Skill modeling and role-playing peer dyads (Murdock et al., 2012), video recordings and video chats (Jerry & Collins, 2005), and even three-dimensional virtual environments (Walker, 2009) can all enhance the experiential nature of courses. Online skills courses could offer added value by helping students be better prepared to establish online therapeutic relationships. Web-based alternatives for skill development in counselor education are unavoidable elements of the profession's future. They need to be explored with courage and curiosity.

Pedagogical Concerns

Professor Pearson's pedagogical framework of care (Noddings, 2005) and valuing of core conditions of education (J. L. Rogers, 2006) is a commendable and, we hope, common orientation among counselor educators. The transformative process of learning requires relationships (Barbeau & Mahfood, 2012). Professor Pearson's concerns about limitations of the online format in terms of launching, sustaining, and growing relationships are shared by many.

J. L. Rogers (2006) reflected on what mattered most in influencing his students' pursuit of deeper learning: "I have learned that a primary way for me to impact my students' search for meaning, purpose and values is by role-modeling authenticity" (p. 1). Defined as genuine expression of the self in the context of community and characterized by consistency among one's values and actions, authenticity has been recognized as an essential aspect of pedagogical mastery and a prerequisite for transformative learning (Barbeau & Mahfood, 2012; Cranton, 2016). Faculty authenticity is linked to students' motivation, engagement, and affect (Z. D. Johnson & Labelle, 2017). Students perceive their instructors to be authentic when teachers are approachable, passionate, attentive, capable, and knowledgeable (Dietlin et al., 2019). We echo Brené Brown's (2010) perspective on authenticity as a process of being and becoming rather than a static trait. In this light, Brown stressed the importance of a daily practice of "cultivating the courage to be imperfect, to set boundaries, and to allow ourselves to be vulnerable" (p. 50).

In a digital world, this struggle may include accepting the inability to control for technological glitches or finding one's voice in a course designed by another instructor. Practice does not make perfect; practice makes authentic. From our extensive experience as online counselor educators, we believe that authenticity can be lived out in the confines and freedoms of cyberspace. Faculty can create and cultivate caring environments in which community members are genuinely concerned about one another's well-being, are available to assist one another, and provide a safe place to express and resolve learning gaps. Dietlin et al. (2019) summarized several strategies for cultivating authenticity online: (a) maintain regular, consistent, and quality communication with students (Paquette, 2016); (b) provide meaningful formative feedback; (c) engage in synchronous interaction; (d) appropriately share parts of the self, admit mistakes, and acknowledge one's own limitations; (e) send weekly greetings; (f) address people by name; (g) learn to be curious and care about students holistically; (h) express care for and interest in others' ideas; and (i) provide a structure for student connections in the course. Care for course content and students can be expressed through carefully designed structure, realistic and balanced assignments, and clear expectations for student and faculty performance and interactions.

Expressions of empathy can also be intentionally conveyed in online environments. Fuller (2012) described eight themes for building empathetic learning environments, many of which overlap with recommendations for practicing authenticity. They are orienting students to what it takes to be successful online; using a synchronous connection; "using a conversational tone" (p. 43); thoughtfully facilitating discussions; practicing empathy; providing a consistent structure that minimizes navigation problems; communicating overtly regarding student progress; and making positive, personal connections at the beginning of class.

Personal Concerns

Despite overwhelming evidence of the continual growth of online courses, Educause found that only 9% of faculty members preferred a completely online environment to other teaching formats (as cited in Darby, 2019). It is safe to assume that the majority of academics may very well reflect Professor Pearson's ambivalence and hesitation to explore online learning. Being satisfied with what we do is an important aspect of our well-being. Yet it is important to carefully distinguish the perceived and actual limitations of online counselor education.

Pink (2009) proposed that among those engaged in primarily intellectual work, intrinsic motivation, engagement, and job satisfaction increase when the following factors are at play in the workplace: autonomy (the opportunity to be self-directed), mastery (the drive to become better at a task), and purpose (the desire to do work that is meaningful and important). Paradoxically, educators who are navigating the transition to online settings will initially experience dependence on instructional designers and support staff; ineptness at facilitating learning smoothly and congruently; and the mundaneness of asynchronous, automatic, and impersonal interaction. Yet autonomy, mastery, and purpose will increase with experience. In fact, new mastery and deeper purpose await counselor educators who explore online instruction with a student-centered, genuine, and committed approach. Gannon (2019) discussed how engagement with online instruction impacted how he taught in the traditional classroom, making his design, tone, and content more intentional and conducive to real learning.

Conclusion

We conclude this analysis with a reflection that corresponds to our development as online counselor educators. To the timid, the weary, or skeptics, we echo Gannon (2019):

> Teaching online helped me grasp all of that. Far more than simply "moving material" into a learning-management system (LMS) or some other digital space, teaching online—and doing it well—demands the type of critically reflective practice that can transform you into a better teacher overall. Whether or not you're in the same physical space as your students, you can still work at your craft and develop practices that make for successful teaching and learning in any medium. (para. 22)

Professor Pearson had several subject matter, pedagogical, and personal concerns when transitioning to an online delivery platform. Although these concerns are understandable, with courage, curiosity, and commitment to continued learning and authenticity, Professor Pearson and her future students may reap the rewards of participating in online education. We ask our students to engage in coursework with this same openness and vulnerability. As counselor educators, we must also be willing to model these values in both traditional and online learning communities.

Reflection Questions

1. How do faculty in online learning environments convey an authentic connection to course content and to students—individually and as a group?
2. Which of your concerns about teaching counseling online have been addressed in this chapter? Which concerns have not been addressed?

Critical Incident Response

Catherine Y. Chang and Erin C. M. Mason

As recognition of the viability and advantages of online education grows, counselor educators will increasingly be faced with the same dilemmas as Professor Pearson. Like many educators tasked with transitioning in-person courses to online formats, Professor Pearson initially approached this task with trepidation and reluctance. With support and education, she eventually embraced this challenge. The authors appropriately identified Professor Pearson's subject matter, pedagogical, and personal concerns.

Subject matter concerns were related to Professor Pearson's apprehension regarding moving a skills-based course to an online format. In a Delphi study by Swank and Houseknecht (2019), teaching experts identified knowledge of how to develop and teach online courses as an important teaching competency for counselor educators. Skills-based counseling courses typically require modeling and observations of verbal and nonverbal communication, so Professor Pearson's concerns are understandable. Although support for the efficacy of online counseling skills courses is limited in the literature, the authors provided a reasonable summary of the existing research on online learning. The authors also identified an additional benefit of online classes: preparing students for telemental health counseling sessions.

Pedagogical concerns included Professor Pearson's framework of care and the importance she placed on creating and maintaining authentic relationships with and among her students. The authors provided clear strategies for cultivating authenticity online (Dietlin et al., 2019). We agree that connections are critical to learning. Students want to feel connected to the instructor and their classmates, and faculty members are key to creating and maintaining that learning environment. In addition to the recommendations the authors provided, we highlight the importance of consistency within the course (e.g., post assignments on the same day each week), regular check-ins with students regarding how the class is going for them, and opportunities for small-group discussions during synchronous class sessions (Sheperis, Coker, et al., 2020). Instructors may also log into the class 15 minutes early to provide students the opportunity to connect and chat; this may help approximate the informal time students have with one another before and after class. Sheperis, Coker, et al. (2020) also cited the importance of connecting with students outside class time through video chats, telephone calls, and emails to foster and strengthen relationships.

Although a variety of teaching strategies can be effective, it is students' engagement with content that influences learning (K. A. Hunt et al., 2016). Engagement may also help with connectedness. When students feel connected to the content, they may also feel connected to one another and the instructor (Stone & Springer, 2019). Furthermore, complex nuances among multiple factors contribute positively to students' engagement in and satisfaction with online courses. These include five variables: accessibility, functionality, group discussion, students' communicationality, and technology aptitude (Purarjomandlangrudi & Chen, 2019, p. 11). Attending specifically to engagement could help Professor Pearson maintain her framework of care while also addressing her concerns about content.

One area of online learning the authors did not address is the importance of addressing the legal and ethical challenges of moving a course online. We direct you to Sheperis, Ordway, and Lamar (2020), who discussed vicarious liability, cybersecurity, licensure obligations, and gatekeeping concerns for online courses. It is important to attend to these considerations while simultaneously attending to content and engagement considerations.

As experienced counselor educators, we share Professor Pearson's concerns regarding moving counseling skills classes online. It is not unusual for us as counselor educators to become comfortable in the courses we teach and how we teach them, so the idea of moving our course online has us screaming, "No way! I have always taught this way, and my students love it!" or "Why change something that is working?" This case study reminds us that as we encourage our students to take risks and grow, we also need to challenge ourselves and actively engage in our pursuit of autonomy, mastery, and purpose. That path may just lead us to online education. Just as ongoing support from Professor George and university resources boosted Professor Pearson's self-efficacy around teaching online, we may also benefit from the support of colleagues and university resources.

• • •

Chapter 12

Does It Apply to Me? Instructor Competency to Teach Specialty Courses

Vaibhavee R. Agaskar and Jean Georgiou

2014 *ACA Code of Ethics* Standards Addressed

- F.7.a. Counselor Educators
- F.7.b. Counselor Educator Competence
- F.7.d. Integration of Study and Practice

• • •

Professor J. Soleman identified as a 29-year-old white, cisgender male of Jewish faith who was raised in an upper-middle-class family. He was a certified school counselor and second-year assistant professor in a midsize urban public university with a predominantly first-generation, ethnically diverse student body. The university offered a graduate program accredited by the Council for Accreditation of Counseling and Related Educational Programs (CACREP) with specializations in school counseling (SC); clinical mental health counseling (CMHC); and marriage, couple, and family counseling (MCFC). Faculty in this program valued combining students from different specialties, as they learned from others' experiences in courses. Thus, students from all specializations took courses together, except for mandatory courses for each specialty area.

Professor Soleman had completed his degrees in CACREP-accredited programs, and his own field experience was limited to school settings. He was not a licensed professional counselor (LPC) or an approved clinical supervisor. In addition, he had not taken any coursework in formal diagnosis and lacked experience in CMHC and MCFC. A last-minute influx of students and administrative policy to reduce adjunct costs had led the chair of Professor Soleman's department to reassign a course to a core faculty member. Professor Soleman was eager to help the department in this crisis, and the chair offered him a section of internship for CMHC and MCFC students as a last resort. Thereafter, the chair continued to offer internship courses to Professor Soleman.

Professor Soleman found himself in a quandary when he needed to provide examples relevant to CMHC and MCFC students. While supervising students, he also struggled with diagnosis, case conceptualization, and treatment options for clients with severe mental health issues. He worried about liability and risk management of clients with intense mental health needs because of his limited clinical experience and scope of practice. He had also been challenged by students' questions about the National Counselor Examination for Licensure and Certification and the trajectory of their careers after graduation. During internship courses, apprehensive students addressed him directly regarding his lack of credentials, experience, and professional identity. Professor Soleman himself understood the students' concerns. He too realized that although his competence in SC was very strong, he was not an expert on what he was teaching because the content focused on CMHC and MCFC. More recently, students had begun voicing their concerns regarding Professor Soleman's preparation and credentials to the department chair.

Case Analysis and Discussion

Teaching internship requires supervision training, experience, and professional identification as well as relevant clinical experience and credentials (American Counseling Association [ACA], 2014; CACREP, 2016). A key issue in this case is how Professor Soleman can offer guidance and supervision in settings in which he himself has no training and clinical experience. Specifically, how can CMHC and MCFC students look to Professor Soleman to assist them with laying a strong foundation of professional identity when he himself cannot identify as a counselor? This critical incident also raises questions regarding responsible gatekeeping.

Counselors should use an ethical decision-making model (EDMM) to guide their practice (ACA, 2014). We used Corey et al.'s (2019) practice-based model to understand the issues involved in this case and decide how to remediate the situation. In addition, we relied on our combined 40 years of clinical experience, our 15 years of teaching experience, and Kitchener's (1984) basic principles of ethics as the foundation for problem-solving.

The first step in using an EDMM is to identify the problem or dilemma. Professor Soleman realizes his limitations in offering clinical examples from diverse settings but has continued teaching internship courses because of financial constraints in the department. CMHC and MCFC students have begun to realize his inability to offer them supervision.

The second step is to identify the potential issues involved. First, the program may find itself in violation of the CACREP Standards (CACREP, 2016) and the *ACA Code of Ethics* (ACA, 2014) if Professor Soleman continues to teach CMHC and MCFC internship courses. Second, there may be a concern regarding self-awareness. Once students began questioning Professor Soleman's credentials and brought the issue to his attention, his limitations and lack of self-awareness were identified. Self-awareness is essential for counselors (Skovholt & Trotter-Mathison, 2016; Tobin et al., 2009) and should be used in conjunction with an EDMM to explore one's worldview and values as they affect decision-making (Evans et al., 2013).

In the third step, counselors consider ethics codes relevant to the dilemma. We reviewed the ethics codes of the American School Counselor Association, American Association for Marriage and Family Therapy, and ACA. Standard F.7.b. under

Responsibilities of Counselor Educators in the *ACA Code of Ethics* (ACA, 2014) applies to our case study. It states that counselor educators and supervisors need to teach within their subject matter expertise and domain. Standards F.7.a. and F.7.d. further emphasize clinical practice and its usefulness in extrapolating knowledge when teaching clinical courses.

Kitchener's (1984) five core principles (i.e., autonomy, justice, beneficence, nonmaleficence, and fidelity) can also guide how counselors resolve ethical dilemmas. Autonomy refers to respect for independence and self-determination. Beneficence involves a responsibility to promote well-being. In this case, Professor Soleman has limited effectiveness as a supervisor of CMHC and MCFC students, which likely restricts students' effectiveness with their clients. Nonmaleficence highlights the principle of doing no harm, which outweighs all other ethical principles. As mentioned previously, Professor Soleman's limited foundation in diagnosis and familiarity with community settings could negatively impact the care of vulnerable clients and leave students at risk for vicarious traumatization. Fidelity reflects loyalty, faithfulness, and the honoring of commitments. Professor Soleman's choice to supervise beyond his scope of practice raises questions regarding fidelity.

The fourth step involves knowing applicable laws and regulations. In addition to the aforementioned codes, the 2016 CACREP Standards (CACREP, 2016) set out the program's responsibility to offer a quality education. Section 3, Standard N, requires that "counselor education program faculty members serving as individual/triadic or group practicum/internship supervisors for students in entry-level programs have (1) relevant experience, (2) professional credentials, and (3) counseling supervision training and experience." Similarly, Section 1, Standard BB, clearly necessitates that "all core and non-core counselor education program faculty have relevant preparation and experience in relation to the courses they teach." Section 1, Standard X, requires core faculty strengthen their professional identity through membership in professional counseling organizations, the maintenance of certifications and licenses in their specialty areas, and sustained participation in professional development activities in research and service. It is evident that Professor Soleman's program is in direct violation of several 2016 CACREP Standards; the department chairperson needs to assign Professor Soleman courses based on his training, credentials, and expertise.

In the fifth step, the involved parties obtain consultation. Professor Soleman could begin by looking to his own department for peer support. Some universities provide junior faculty members with a mentor to offer guidance and support. The mentor could be a faculty member who is tenured and an LPC. Professor Soleman could also reach out to various professional associations. The Association for Counselor Education and Supervision (ACES), for example, offers a New Faculty Interest Network. This mentoring program for pretenure faculty provides general information, encouragement, and guidance. The New Faculty Interest Network often pairs novice pretenure professors with tenured professors willing to offer mentorship. Any or all guidance from veterans in the counseling field will allow Professor Soleman an opportunity to resolve this ethical issue. Finally, Professor Soleman could contact his local chapter of the American School Counselor Association to inquire about local peer supervision groups in which he may be able to network with other professionals. This will assist him in strengthening his own professional identity. Furthermore, Professor Soleman might engage in self-advocacy work with the head of his program to find a way to honor the accreditation body and spirit of teamwork in the department.

In the sixth step, the involved parties consider possible and probable courses of action. First, the counseling program could modify the program by offering different sections of internship based on students' specialization and faculty members' education, credentials, and clinical experience. For example, the program could implement a policy in which MCFC students enroll in internship with a faculty member credentialed as a licensed marriage and family therapist, CMHC students enroll in internship with a faculty member credentialed as an LPC, and SC students enroll in internship with a faculty member credentialed as a school counselor. Second, the department chair could hire adjuncts with expertise in various specializations offered by the department. This would allow faculty to teach courses within their scope of practice. Finally, the department could develop initiatives for faculty members interested in continuing education and efforts to secure licensure across specialty areas. Professor Soleman might also review the ACES Teaching Initiative Taskforce (2016) report and *Best Practices in Clinical Supervision* (ACES Supervision Taskforce, 2011) to assist him in becoming a better educator and supervisor.

The seventh step involves enumerating the consequences of various decisions. When internship courses are separated by specialization, students may miss being exposed to different professional roles and responsibilities and might not come to understand the benefits of teamwork across settings. They might also feel isolated, and they may lose the support of one another in the learning process. Furthermore, they might not be able to understand the importance of collaborating with other professionals. In contrast, separating students by specialization may enhance learning and foster professional identity when students learn from those with subject matter expertise. The department chair and faculty need to engage in a programmatic review to reform policies related to internship teaching qualifications and the sustainability of specialized internship sections. Special attention from the department chair will be important when looking to core faculty or adjuncts to teach internship courses to avoid future infractions.

Finally, the eighth step involves choosing what appears to be the best course of action. In this case, the department chair assigns Professor Soleman's section of internship to another professor with the necessary credentials and experience to teach this course. After careful consideration, Professor Soleman decides he could better serve students at his current university and would have more in common with students if he were an LPC. Under the guidance of his mentor, he prepares for licensure examinations and begins seeking the clinical experiences necessary for this licensure. In the end, the department chair adopts a policy regarding credentials necessary for teaching fieldwork courses. This policy reflects previous discussion that all professors who want to teach fieldwork courses to CMHC, MCFC, and SC students be licensed in the corresponding area. The department chair also looks into securing professional development funds so faculty can seek and maintain their licenses or certifications. The department also decides to explore specific modifications to the program to keep valuing connectedness across specialty areas in other core courses.

Conclusion

To strengthen professional identity and support the future of counseling, counselor education programs must ensure they are committed to being grounded in the CACREP Standards (CACREP, 2016) and the *ACA Code of Ethics* (ACA, 2014). Counselor educators with a strong professional identity naturally lead by example, assisting students in identifying their own professional counseling identity. It is unrealistic to expect students to identify with faculty members who are not familiar with their area of study. "If the new professional is not successfully integrated into the professional culture and does not develop a well-defined sense of identity, role confusion may result (Erikson, 1994; Studer, 2007), which may impair the counselor's ability to function ethically as a professional" (Gibson, Dollarhide, & Moss, 2010, p. 23).

Reflection Questions

1. How might Professor Soleman's cultural identities have played into his self-assessment of competence and his interactions with students?
2. How likely is it that counselor educators will have experience in all specialty areas? What steps could one take to increase one's familiarity with other settings?

Critical Incident Response

LoriAnn Sykes Stretch and Denita N. Hudson

Using an EDMM to address the department's dilemma helps to dissect and address Professor Soleman's actions. However, it would be negligent to ignore the influence of cultural dimensions and the department's responsibility to support a second-year faculty member in their program. Professor Soleman must reflect on the impacts of his whiteness, Jewish faith, and upper-middle-class status on his interactions with students. In addition, the department chair must identify faculty development needs and consider creative solutions to abide by CACREP Standards (CACREP, 2016) and the *ACA Code of Ethics* (ACA, 2014).

In developing cultural competency among counseling professionals, the Multicultural and Social Justice Counseling Competencies (Ratts et al., 2016) require self-awareness, understanding of oppression and privilege, and critical thinking skills. Professor Soleman should consider the impact of his intersecting cultural identities on his decision to teach an internship course outside his area of expertise. Professor Soleman did not appear to attend to his social identities, strengths, or limitations while providing supervision to culturally diverse students. His students could perceive his lack of knowledge as a lack of support, care, or concern for their development, thereby fostering cultural mistrust (Koch et al., 2018). Professor Soleman must view his actions through a multicultural lens, taking care to reflect on how his decisions have obstructed supervisory relationships with marginalized students and their clients. He should consider having a conversation with his students regarding his efforts to rectify his ethical challenges while also exploring the impact of cultural identities, power, and privilege on the internship experience.

From an administrative perspective, Professor Soleman is a second-year assistant professor who needs mentoring and leadership. It is surprising that Professor Soleman completed a CACREP-accredited doctoral program without acquiring knowledge and experience across multiple counseling settings (CACREP, 2016, Section 6, Standard B.1.f.). As evidenced in the EDMM, Professor Soleman should not have accepted the internship course without relevant "theoretical and pedagogical foundations" (ACA, 2014, Section F, Introduction) to teach all specializations represented in his section. More important, however, the department chair should not have assigned the course to him because Professor Soleman lacked "knowledge and competence" and did not have "current information" to support the students in his internship course (ACA, 2014, Standard F.7.b.).

A primary task of department chairs relates to faculty development, including mentoring and providing teaching support (Berdrow, 2010). Professor Soleman should have a professional development plan that identifies areas of growth in the core areas of his workload. If the department values cross-specialization training, the faculty as a whole should cross-train as much as possible to be able to provide a well-rounded education to students of all three specializations. This aligns with best practices for interdisciplinary training that moves beyond training silos (Atieno Okech & Geroski, 2015).

Team teaching may be a creative solution to the lack of faculty members who are knowledgeable across specializations. The department chair could have matched Professor Soleman, a school counselor, with a more senior faculty member who specializes in one or both of the other specializations. As a team, they could have alternated supervising students across two sections, cosupervised students, or split a section of students for half the workload credit. Splitting credits when team teaching may be an effective way of maximizing resources and capitalizing on faculty knowledge and experience while also cross-training faculty members. The team teaching model would provide students with support across specializations and also provide an opportunity for Professor Soleman to expand his competency while receiving mentorship from the senior faculty member with whom he is teaching and supervising (Lock et al., 2016).

• • •

Chapter 13

Something to Share: Promoting Unethical or Illegal Practice

Shawn L. Spurgeon

2014 *ACA Code of Ethics* Standards Addressed

- A.10.c. Establishing Fees
- A.10.e. Bartering
- C.2.e. Consultations on Ethical Obligations
- C.6.e. Contributing to the Public Good *(Pro Bono Publico)*
- F.7.e. Teaching Ethics

• • •

Professor Wright, an assistant professor in a program accredited by the Council for Accreditation of Counseling and Related Educational Programs, was licensed as a professional counselor and approved supervisor. Professor Wright had previously worked in private practice; however, she stopped that work because of responsibilities at the university. She had strong connections in the community and often attended seminars sponsored by the local professional counseling organization. She enjoyed the opportunity to network with professionals and shared this information with her students.

Professor Wright taught most of the core courses in the clinical mental health counseling (CMHC) program, and she focused on helping students develop assessment and evaluation skills for working with clients. Introduction to CMHC was a course designed to introduce salient aspects of mental health counseling. She used different types of delivery methods in this course, including small-group discussions and role play. One of her favorite methods was to invite former students to talk about their professional development and work in the community. She considered this to be integral to the course and valued the perspectives former students brought.

During Week 6, Professor Wright invited Mike to the class and asked him to talk about his development and growth after graduation. Mike, a white, cisgender male, was a licensed professional counselor working toward approval to serve as a clinical supervisor. Mike had graduated from the program 4 years ago. He had worked for an agency for 3 years, and 1 year ago he had joined a group practice that consisted of independent practitioners.

During his presentation, Mike talked about the important things he had learned during his training and how those things translated to his work at the agency. He told students that he had felt somewhat restricted by agency policies and procedures, and he mentioned that he had used his learning to develop his own approach in private practice. He saw 20 to 25 clients a week and noted that this was much more manageable than the 35 clients a week he had seen at the agency. He also highlighted his autonomy as an independent practitioner, noting that he enjoyed the freedom to shape his daily schedule and control his approach. Mike provided detailed information about the challenges of transitioning from trainee to agency work to private practice.

During question-and-answer time, a student asked Mike about strategies for dealing with managed care. Mike responded that he was a panel member on every major insurance company in the state, and he provided a detailed explanation about the process he had gone through to become a member of panels. He noted that insurance companies could be challenging because each company had a different set of standards they expected clinicians to follow, including for how to write case notes, which assessments to use, and how frequently to have a utilization review. He noted that his coworkers lamented dealing with managed care and provided concrete examples of times payment was delayed because the insurance company demanded information he did not want to provide.

Mike went on to say that he had developed a plan for dealing with minutiae created by managed care, especially for clients who were unable to afford his services. He told students that he provided a sliding scale for clients who were unable to afford his services or did not have insurance. He stated that because he was in private practice, he had the freedom to support clients in this manner. One student asked Mike what he did when a client had insurance but did not want to use it. Mike stated, "We process the relevant factors and create a plan for addressing the client's concern. If it is less expensive for the client to use my sliding scale, I have no problem offering this to them. It is my ethical responsibility."

Case Analysis and Discussion

This case provides an opportunity to examine the tenuous relationship between professional responsibilities and personal convictions. Such conflicts are often at the heart of ethical decision-making and can serve as a barometer for professional development and growth. I identify key issues, analyze and evaluate the incident, consider actions, and assess outcomes.

Key Issues

The critical incident highlights salient and critical issues that merit further evaluation. Issues related to Mike include his use of a sliding scale and his legal responsibilities to insurance companies. Issues related to Professor Wright include her responsibility to address salient concerns related to the sharing of ethical and legal information and the impact of ill-advised practice on counselor development. Special attention is given to their connection to the *ACA Code of Ethics* (American Counseling Association [ACA], 2014) and the existing literature related to each issue.

The Use of a Sliding Scale

Sliding scales have traditionally been used to support clients who may not have the financial means to pay for counseling services. Most recently, the focus has been on the relevance of reduced fees as they pertain to working with clients. Reduced fees represent a form of bartering, a method by which counselors exchange goods and services with clients to offset fees related to seeking help (Lane, 2012). Bartering for services is common practice in many professions. An important aspect of bartering in CMCH is that it may help diverse clients obtain counseling. Some clients come from impoverished backgrounds and are underinsured or cannot afford a company insurance plan. Given the disparity that sometimes exists between clients' ability to afford services and the cost of those services, bartering can serve as a bridge for work with indigent populations (Remley & Herlihy, 2020).

The *ACA Code of Ethics* (ACA, 2014) provides clear guidelines for counselors to attend to when considering reducing fees. Standard C.6.e. highlights the ethical responsibility of counselors to provide reduced fees to their clients. This includes free workshops or engagement in community events. Standard A.10.e. establishes provisions for bartering. The action must be initiated by the client, it must be an acceptable and established practice, and it must not be prohibitive for the client. These regulations ensure that counselors do not engage in exploitive behavior (Kaplan et al., 2017).

Mike's actions can be considered a form of bartering. Given that he is offering a sliding scale that reduces fees, he is trying to practice within his ethical responsibility. However, he also misses the mark. The action he takes is not initiated by clients; Mike stated that he engages in a discussion with clients to determine the best approach to paying for services. We do not know whether this form of bartering is accepted in the community, so this is another concern that merits further evaluation. Furthermore, we do not know whether this action benefits clients. Generally speaking, bartering for services is designed to reduce the financial burden for clients and thus create a less stressful environment (Zur, 2008). Counselors sometimes do things that are meant to be in clients' best interest without understanding clients' worldview; this is a form of the white savior complex and can be detrimental to the therapeutic relationship (Barden et al., 2017). Because Mike initiates this action, this could create discomfort for clients.

Responsibilities to the Insurance Company

Counselors who work with managed care need to be aware of their legal obligations to abide by established policies and procedures. The insurance industry has clearly delineated expectations and responsibilities for panel members. One such expectation is that each client serviced under their insurance policy will be treated with the same process. This includes adherence to procedures for accessing mental health benefits. Not following proper procedures creates problems for providers and consumers.

A major responsibility of clinicians who serve as providers is to avoid engaging in fraudulent practices. Insurance fraud occurs when individuals access some sort of benefit to which they are not entitled or do so in a way that is not in line with established rules and regulations (Lane, 2012). Premium diversion is the most common type of insurance fraud among mental health providers. Premium diversion occurs when mental health providers fail to send premiums to the insurance company and instead pocket the money for personal gain. Typically mental health providers create an avenue through which clients receive services and avoid the insurance company's additional costs in premiums. This also helps providers avoid procedures that can be tedious and challenging at times. For example, clients may pay an out-of-pocket premium to avoid receiving a diagnosis. The arrangement can help both client and counselor.

Mike may be engaging in premium diversion. He encourages his clients to avoid using their insurance and then offers them a reduced fee in lieu of using their insurance. He pockets the money from this reduced fee and does not notify the insurance company of his actions. Thus, he has diverted funds from the insurance company in violation of established policies and procedures. Mike may believe this helps his client because it is cost effective and less cumbersome; however, this is a form of premium aversion and is illegal.

Mike has an ethical responsibility to protect the welfare of his clients, and he argued that providing a sliding scale fee does that very thing. However, he has a greater responsibility to abide by the legal requirements of insurance companies. Section I of the *ACA Code of Ethics* (ACA, 2014) provides counselors with information on how to address conflicts between ethics and the law. We have a responsibility to be aware of our ethical obligations to our clients but to make sure we understand them within the context of legal constraints.

Actions Taken and Not Taken

There are several actions Professor Wright needs to take in this situation. The best possible approach would be to request a time to consult with Mike and use an ethical decision-making model as a road map for guiding the discussion. It would be important for Professor Wright to walk Mike through the decision-making process and to help him better understand the salient aspects of his choices. This may help Mike develop a clear understanding of what his actions mean for continued work as a counselor. As a result of this step, Mike could choose to remove himself from all insurance panels and only accept self-pay clients. Or he could affirm his commitment to his ethical responsibilities, even in the face of behavior that clearly violates legal statutes.

A licensed professional herself, Professor Wright now knows that Mike is engaging in an illegal practice. Thus, she has a responsibility to notify relevant parties about his behavior. This is a dilemma for Professor Wright because Mike is a former student she values. In addition, Professor Wright is well aware of the developmental challenges and growth he has experienced throughout his career. She knows that he is only 4 years into his career, and she would not want to jeopardize it or be a source of discontent for him. However, her professional responsibilities are important to her and are very critical to consider in this situation. Her action could result in Mike losing his license for a period of time or permanently. Also, he could be removed from insurance panels and find himself unable to work with insurance in the future.

There are additional steps Professor Wright can take both before and during a guest presentation that would help her better address situations like this. Given the importance of the development of cognitive complexity for counselors-in-training (Spurgeon, Woodside, et al., 2012; Wilkinson & Dewell, 2019), these procedures can serve as critical steps for deepening the development of her trainees.

Professor Wright could send guest speakers a brief synopsis or syllabus. This would help them shape presentations and provide a framework for better understanding course content and structure. In addition, she could request a vita or résumé to increase her awareness of the speaker's scope of work and have a better understanding of potential discussion points. She could then use this information to solicit student questions before the presentation. Professor Wright could provide this information to the guest speaker as a way of maintaining a connection with the course content. Finally, Professor Wright could provide the guest speaker with information about the development of the current students in the class. This is a critical aspect of the work of a counselor educator; increased awareness of student development is a foundational principle to which educators need to adhere (Spurgeon, Woodside, et al., 2012).

It is important for Professor Wright to continue to stay engaged throughout the presentation. For example, she could periodically connect Mike's work to course concepts. This would help students make connections between their understanding of CMHC and daily practice procedures. In addition, Professor Wright could encourage Mike to talk about his experiences as a counselor-in-training as a way of understanding the current thinking of the students. This approach would help Mike relate more directly to the students and enhance his efforts to connect his clinical work to the trainees' current knowledge acquisition.

An additional action is necessary at this point. Professor Wright needs to follow up with the students in her class. The students have been provided with inaccurate information regarding the ethical and legal ramifications of using sliding fee scales. They do not understand the inherent legal problems they could face if they chose to engage in these types of behaviors. Professor Wright needs to send an email immediately after class with a brief explanation, in the most positive form possible, of the inaccuracy of the information provided by the guest speaker. She also needs to begin the next class with detailed attention to the use of sliding fee scales in clinical practice, including both ethical and legal aspects. This information is essential to students' professional development and cannot be avoided.

Conclusion

This case was designed to show how common dilemmas faced in the counseling field may contradict best practices taught in the classroom. It highlights a common dilemma professional counselors face in their daily practice. The issues presented here speak to the complex nature of working with clients and reinforce the importance of attending to details related to ethics and the law during counselor training. The need for continued consultation and supervision cannot be overstated, especially when counselors are faced with these types of dilemmas.

Reflection Questions

1. What additional options did Professor Wright have for addressing the problematic nature of Mike's response to the question about managed care?
2. In what other ways might aspirational best practice and the daily practices of counselors conflict? How might counselor educators address them?

Critical Incident Response

Jacqueline M. Swank

This case focused on a guest speaker presenting information to a class that involved unethical and illegal practice. The instructor, Professor Wright, was in a difficult position and had a responsibility to address the situation with all stakeholders. In addition to taking the course of actions discussed in the analysis, Professor Wright should also discuss the situation with program faculty. This is important, as the situation may arise in other classes, and it is crucial that faculty members be prepared to address it.

In addition, it appears that Professor Wright struggled with how to respond to various aspects of the situation; consultation with other faculty may help further clarify the best course of action. The *ACA Code of Ethics* (ACA, 2014) includes consultation as an important step in addressing ethical dilemmas (Standard C.2.e.). Furthermore, discussion with faculty would provide an opportunity to consider whether they should invite Mike as a guest speaker in the future, as guest speakers and expert panel discussions are common within counseling courses. The counselor education faculty may consider developing a list of counseling providers, including alumni who are strong, ethical practitioners, to present in their courses. They may also develop a list of providers they are hesitant to invite, for various reasons, to reference in the future.

It is unclear why Professor Wright did not address Mike's statement during the class period when it occurred. There may not have been enough time left in class, Professor Wright could have felt awkward and unsure how to address it in the moment, or she may have thought it was more appropriate to address as she did through an email after class and a follow-up discussion in the next class. When having a guest speaker or panel discussion in class, faculty may consider planning the presentation or panel at the beginning of class to allow time at the end of class, after the guests have left, to process what was shared and ask follow-up questions. By planning Mike's presentation at the beginning of class, Professor Wright would have had the opportunity to address the problematic practice Mike referenced in the moment. This could have been helpful for students, as they may not have understood an email message. However, Professor Wight may also have needed some time to process the situation herself and decide how to approach it with students. Regardless, the crucial point is that Professor Wright addressed the concern with students.

The *ACA Code of Ethics* (ACA, 2014) outlines the counselor's responsibility to inform clients about fees and billing arrangements (Standard A.2.b.). Regarding Mike's approach to addressing fees with clients, it is important to discuss with students the fact that this topic should be included within the informed consent document and discussed at the beginning of the counseling relationship. It appears that Mike discussed client concerns first and then payment for services toward the end of the first session. This creates an awkward situation for both Mike and the client, as Mike will want to get paid for this first session; however, payment arrangements may not have been discussed yet. Outlining fees and methods of payment in the consent form clarifies this issue for all parties at the onset of counseling and provides them with an opportunity to discuss concerns related to payment, if needed, before moving forward with counseling.

Guest speakers can enhance classes by providing unique perspectives that are welcomed and appreciated by students. However, like any teaching strategy, they can present challenges at times for the instructor. Thoughtful, advanced planning, as discussed in this chapter, can reduce the likelihood of problematic situations occurring, but it does not prevent them. Thus, counselor educators should be prepared to address problematic statements made by guest presenters, as they are ultimately responsible for the content shared within their classes.

• • •

Resources

Barrio Minton, C. A., Gibson, D. M., & Wachter-Morris, C. A. (2016). *Evaluating student learning outcomes in counselor education*. American Counseling Association.

Herlihy, B., & Corey, G. (Eds.). (2015). *Boundary issues in counseling: Multiple roles and responsibilities* (3rd ed.). American Counseling Association.

Indiana University. (2020). *How to recognize plagiarism: Tutorials and tests*. https://plagiarism.iu.edu/certificationTests/

Malott, K. M., Hrindaya Hall, K., Sheely-Moore, A., Krell, M. M., & Cardaciotto, L. (2014). Evidence-based teaching in higher education: Application to counselor education. *Counselor Education and Supervision, 53*(4), 294–305. http://doi.org/dq53

McGhee, C., Baltrinic, E. R., Laux, J., Clark, M., Liu, Y., & Harmening, D. (2019). A phenomenological investigation of creative teaching in counselor education. *Counselor Education and Supervision, 58*(2), 127–140. http://doi.org/dq55

Moffatt, G. K. (2018, August 13). The hurting counselor. *Counseling Today*. https://ct.counseling.org/2018/08/the-hurting-counselor/

Moran, K., & Milsom, A. (2015). The flipped classroom in counselor education. *Counselor Education and Supervision, 54*(1), 32–43. http://doi.org/dq54

Turnitin.com Editors. (2016). *Infographic: The plagiarism spectrum*. https://www.turnitin.com/infographics/the-plagiarism-spectrum

Part II
Supervision

Section 1
Supervisee Dispositions and Behaviors 111

Section 2
Issues With Site Supervisors 143

Section 3
Doctoral Student Supervisors 167

Counseling supervision is a multifaceted process important for fostering counselor development and ensuring quality client care. Supervision may focus on a variety of topics related to clients, as well as counselor growth and development. In addition, the supervision process may involve multiple supervisors. The *ACA Code of Ethics* (American Counseling Association, 2014) includes ethical considerations related to counseling supervision. Also, the 2016 Council for Accreditation of Counseling and Related Educational Programs (CACREP) Standards (CACREP, 2016) outline counselor educators' responsibilities for providing counseling supervision for master's- and doctoral-level counseling students as well as identify supervision as a core domain for training counselor education and supervision doctoral students. Furthermore, the Association for Counselor Education and Supervision (ACES) *Best Practices in Clinical Supervision* (ACES Supervision Taskforce, 2011) provides guidelines for counseling supervision.

Counselor educators are responsible for overseeing students' clinical experiences and ensuring students develop the counseling competencies necessary to provide quality, ethical counseling services to clients. This includes establishing clinical placement sites, maintaining communication with site supervisors, and providing various types of supervision for students (e.g., individual, triadic, and/or group). Counselor educators who work with doctoral students also have the responsibility of ensuring these students develop counseling supervision competencies while providing quality, ethical counseling supervision to master's-level counseling students during counselor education internship experiences. In providing supervision and supervision of supervision, counselor educators may experience a variety of critical incidents involving supervisees, site supervisors, doctoral student supervisors, and the supervision process. This section encompasses nine chapters grouped within three primary areas: (a) supervisee dispositions and behaviors, (b) issues with site supervisors, and (c) doctoral student supervisors.

Supervisee Dispositions and Behaviors

Many supervisee dispositional and behavioral concerns present challenges for supervisors to address within supervision. There is not enough space in this section to address all these challenges, but we address four common concerns. The first relates to using a technique with limited training. Counseling students and new counselors may feel anxious and struggle with deciding what to do when they feel stuck in session or frustrated that a client is making slow or no perceived progress. Because all skills feel new at the beginning and require practice, supervisees may struggle to discern which skills are acceptable for growing competence and which must wait. In response, they may choose to integrate a technique that they read about briefly in a book or learned about in a brief presentation at a conference. This is concerning when the technique requires advanced training to facilitate effectively and inexperienced use may result in harm. "This Is Cool, Does It Work? Using a Technique With Limited Training" pertains to a master's student supervisee who feels overjoyed about having a breakthrough with a client after having attended just a short training on a highly specialized technique. The supervisee decided to use the technique after the faculty supervisor encouraged her to think outside the box when working with clients.

The second concern is supervisees refusing to work with clients who have different values and beliefs than themselves and consistently believing referral to be an acceptable solution for avoiding conflict. This may occur in the case of different political views, religious beliefs, or other values-based conflicts. "I Don't Believe in That: Addressing Counselors' Values Conflicts" pertains to master's student supervisees who struggle working with clients who identify as lesbian, gay, bisexual, transgender, queer, or intersex (LGBTQI+), stating it conflicts with their values and beliefs.

The third common concern relates to supervisees' unaddressed personal concerns and impairment. Counselors' personal concerns may arise when they are working with clients; when not addressed, these impairments may result in lack of effectiveness or harm to clients, which can manifest in multiple ways. In "I'm an Emotional Person: Determining Counselor Impairment," a master's student supervisee becomes emotional and cries frequently during client sessions. The supervisee eventually reveals unresolved trauma from childhood that is affecting her ability to work with clients.

The fourth issue that is especially problematic for counselors-in-training is reluctance or refusal to bring session recordings to supervision. This is problematic because supervisors may not have a clear understanding of client communications or counselor skills without being able to view a session. Supervisors are responsible for gatekeeping for the profession; not being able to review a supervisee's counseling skills makes this difficult. Furthermore, the 2016 CACREP Standards (CACREP, 2016) require supervisors to view recordings of counseling sessions or watch them live. "Don't Watch Me: Not Bringing Session Recordings to Supervision" focuses on a master's student supervisee who repeatedly refuses to bring a counseling session recording to supervision sessions, eventually revealing a concern with the placement and the student's lack of client contact.

Issues With Site Supervisors

Another area addressed in this section focuses on concerns related to site supervisors. Students may receive supervision from multiple types of supervisors, including counselor education faculty members, site supervisors, and sometimes doctoral students. Supervisees may also receive supervision from multiple individuals of one type, such as multiple faculty supervisors or multiple site supervisors. The existence of multiple supervisors increases the need for consistent, strong communication to ensure supervisees do not receive conflicting messages. "I'm Getting Different Messages: Incongruence Between Supervisors" focuses on a master's student supervisee who receives incongruent messages from site supervisors, which leads to confusion for the supervisee.

When establishing clinical placement sites for practicum and internship, it is important for counselor educators to vet sites to ensure quality learning experiences for students. Counselor educators can implement rigorous procedures to facilitate this process; however, problems can still arise with site supervisors. In "The Other Side: A Supervisor Presenting Differently to Students," a site supervisor presents well to faculty, but students report negative experiences with him.

Like any counselor, site supervisors may also struggle with their own personal concerns, which can affect the work they do with clients and the supervision they provide to students. Or supervisees may experience site supervisors differently than faculty because of their frequent contact with them. When supervisors present problematic behavior, supervisees might be reluctant to share this with faculty because they do not want to get their site supervisor in trouble or to jeopardize their clinical placement. In "To Tell or Not to Tell: Site Supervisor Impairment," a master's-level supervisee reports to a faculty supervisor that a site supervisor appears to be impaired.

Doctoral Student Supervisors

Having doctoral student supervisors adds another layer of complexity to the supervision process. In addition, doctoral students are in the process of learning to be supervisors and may struggle with providing supervision competently and confidently. This can be particularly difficult when working with challenging supervisees. In "Biased: A Doctoral Student Supervisor's Struggle With a Supervisee's Lack of Awareness," a doctoral student supervisor of color has strong reactions to a supervisee's lack of awareness of biases and white savior attitudes.

Doctoral student supervisors may also struggle with maintaining boundaries with supervisees. This may be particularly challenging when they have multiple relationships with master's student supervisees related to contact in other courses or interactions outside the academic program. "I'm Attracted to My Supervisee: A Doctoral Student Supervisor's Struggle" focuses on a doctoral student supervisor's attraction to his supervisee. Thus, this domain addresses common critical incidents regarding multiple areas of supervision.

Section 1
Supervisee Dispositions and Behaviors

Chapter 14

This Is Cool, Does It Work? Using a Technique With Limited Training

W. Bradley McKibben

2014 *ACA Code of Ethics* Standards Addressed

- C.2.a. Boundaries of Competence
- C.2.b. New Specialty Areas of Practice
- C.2.f. Continuing Education
- F.1.a. Client Welfare
- F.6.b. Gatekeeping and Remediation
- F.9.a. Evaluation of Students

• • •

Camila was a master's-level counseling student completing her internship at an outpatient community mental health center. Her faculty supervisor, Joan, recognized that Camila had been making progress in developing her counseling skills (e.g., reflections). As Camila built her caseload, Joan encouraged her to "think outside the box" and to more intentionally conceptualize her client's needs and her therapeutic approach using counseling theory.

During individual supervision, Camila shared that, in the spirit of thinking outside the box, she had recently attended a 50-minute, online webinar about prolonged exposure (PE) therapy. Camila said, "It was only an introduction to PE, but it has changed the way I think about counseling and will be helpful for my clients with trauma histories!" She shared that she had ordered several books and workbooks on PE immediately after attending the webinar, and she intended to use these resources with her clients. She also shared that the day after attending the webinar she had had a counseling session with one of her clients who had a history of trauma stemming from physical and sexual abuse throughout childhood and early adulthood. She stated, "I felt like I hadn't been getting anywhere with this client in our previous three sessions, and I wasn't really sure where to go with her, so I figured why not use PE? The client had an incredible breakthrough! It was amazing to see all the emotions coming forward as she talked about her trauma."

Case Analysis and Discussion

Supervisees can process only about three points of feedback in a given supervision session, and at least one should be connected to their own learning goals for supervision (Borders & Brown, 2005). Therefore, the primary challenge for Joan is to triage the key points and offer focused feedback so Camila can hear, process, and attend to the most important feedback. The discrimination model (DM; Bernard, 1979) offers Joan a concrete, tangible method of organizing and prioritizing feedback for Camila. The DM (as modified by Lanning, 1986) offers four focus areas for supervision. *Counseling performance skills* refer to helping skills, theory-based techniques, procedural skills, and issue-specific skills (Borders & Brown, 2005). *Cognitive counseling skills* refer to case conceptualization skills, the development and testing of hypotheses about client issues, and the integration of counseling theory. *Self-awareness* includes personal experiences or factors (e.g., background, culture) of the counselor that could influence their work with a client (e.g., countertransference). Self-awareness also includes the counselor's therapeutic style or approach. *Professional behaviors* involve ethical, legal, and professional issues, both generally and in session. Although counseling performance skills tend to be the most discrete and concrete areas for feedback, this particular case raises issues of professional behaviors, self-awareness, and cognitive counseling skills. Thus, these three areas are the primary focus of this analysis.

The DM (Bernard, 1979) includes three roles (i.e., teacher, counselor, consultant) from which the supervisor can address the four feedback areas. In the teacher role, the supervisor instructs, demonstrates, or models for the supervisee how to do something. In the counselor role, the supervisor assists the supervisee in recognizing and addressing personal issues, including blind spots and reactions to a client or supervisor. In the consultant role, the supervisor provides support and collaboration when a supervisee is able to work independently. Given that Camila is a new counselor developmentally speaking, the teacher and counselor roles will be most helpful for Joan to assume.

Professional Behaviors

A salient concern in Camila's case relates to professional behavior, in particular ethical considerations (e.g., counselor competence, client welfare). The *ACA Code of Ethics* (American Counseling Association [ACA], 2014, Standard F.1.a.) and the Association for Counselor Education and Supervision *Best Practices in Clinical Supervision* (Borders et al., 2012) note that clinical supervisors monitor supervisee service delivery and professional development and protect client welfare and safety. The *ACA Code of Ethics* (ACA, 2014) requires counselors to practice within the boundaries of their competence (Standard C.2.a.), take steps to gain competence in new specialty areas before practicing in them (Standard C.2.b.), and seek continuing education to maintain competence (Standard C.2.f.).

Camila attempted PE, an intensive, trauma-focused treatment approach, with limited training and no supervised practice in it. The University of Pennsylvania's

Center for the Treatment and Study of Anxiety (n.d.) specifies that before using PE, practitioners need to be certified in it, which requires attending an intensive 4-day workshop, completing at least two PE cases under a certified PE consultant, and being recommended for certification by their PE consultant. In addition to the lack of certification, Camila's limited, yet emerging, counseling skills further limited her competence with the approach and with in-depth trauma work. In using PE, she arguably exceeded the scope of her competence as an intern.

In addition to assessing competence, Joan needs to determine whether the client was harmed. Based on Camila's initial report, it does not appear that harm occurred; however, Joan should inquire further to be certain (e.g., through additional conversation with Camila, by reviewing the session recording if possible, by consulting with the site supervisor). Joan might also consider making a site visit to observe Camila's work with this client live, if possible, or request that the site supervisor observe Camila's sessions. If harm did occur, then Joan needs to work with Camila and the site supervisor to mitigate the issue. Joan may consider formal remediation (e.g., ACA, 2014, Standards F.6.b., F.9.a.) in line with the counseling program's publicly stated policies (e.g., 2016 Council for Accreditation of Counseling and Related Educational Programs [CACREP] Standards, Section 1, Standards N, O; CACREP, 2016) to provide Camila with fair due process while also ensuring the safety of Camila's clients. Any formal remediation should include clear feedback on what the deficiencies are, what needs to be done to address the concerns (i.e., what Camila needs to do to successfully complete remediation), what supports are available to Camila, and what the next steps are if remediation is unsuccessful.

If harm did not occur, it is still important to discuss with Camila the idea of practicing within the scope of her competence. The training required to provide PE, coupled with the client's trauma history, warrants supervisory intervention. In general, it is helpful for supervisors to allow supervisees to identify their own struggles, explore their difficulties nonjudgmentally, and work together to create a plan for change (Neufeldt, 2007). This could prove difficult for Camila because she likely perceives the PE session as a success and believes she heeded Joan's prior feedback of practicing from theory. Difficult feedback is often easier for supervisees to hear and digest when it is delivered behaviorally and concisely (McKibben, Borders, & Wahesh, 2019). Framing this feedback in the context of Camila's learning goals for supervision may also be helpful.

Joan might also use the DM counselor role to process reactions Camila might have to the corrective feedback. She might expect Camila to say, "You told me to use theory, and I did, and now you're saying I did something wrong and I'm not competent to do it?" In such an instance, it is important to validate the frustration or confusion Camila is experiencing and to invite her to process these feelings. Joan might consider acknowledging that her prior feedback was vague as a way to connect with Camila and encourage her to express her feelings. The supervisory relationship is a key agent of supervisee growth and development (Ladany et al., 1999; Tangen & Borders, 2016). Therefore, Joan needs to ensure the relationship with Camila is preserved and lean into it to create a safe place for Camila to feel and express vulnerability and frustration. When personal reactions like this emerge, the supervisor needs to attend to them so both parties can return to collaboratively working on the supervisee's growth as a counselor.

Self-Awareness

In addition to the professional behavior displayed in this case is the extent to which Camila recognizes the limits of her own preparedness for, and competence with, intensive trauma work. Camila's decision to use PE with limited planning or thought about whether she was ready could signal a barrier to her self-awareness of her limits as a counselor. Limited self-awareness is fairly common among beginning counselors. According to the integrated developmental model (Stoltenberg et al., 1998), beginning counselors (i.e., those at Level 1) tend to be black-and-white thinkers, are concerned with right and wrong ways of providing counseling, and are fairly limited in self-awareness and intentionality. The transition to Level 2, which often occurs around graduation and the transition to post-master's professional practice (Borders & Brown, 2005), is marked by increases in self-awareness, intentionality of interventions, and flexibility in thinking about self and clients.

Camila recently started her internship, which would suggest Level 1 development. Consistent with this level, Camila may have perceived using PE as a correct intervention, given she was not sure what else to do and her supervisor had encouraged her to integrate theory. With so many aspects of the client and the counseling sessions to attend to, it is possible that Camila did not pause and self-evaluate her readiness to work with the client's complex trauma story.

Cognitive Counseling Skills

Beginning counselors often struggle with what to do and where to go in session. In response, they may seek intervention ideas, worksheets, or other therapeutic techniques to have something to cling to in session. This is not inherently bad; however, developmentally speaking, supervisees may not have a clear understanding of the goal of the intervention or how it fits into a treatment plan. Camila's case highlights this developmental gap, which is expected as a supervisee works to shift from a conceptual understanding of counseling theory to application.

Neufeldt (2007) provided several supervisory intervention strategies for addressing cognitive counseling skills from the DM teacher role. To help her develop a theory-based perspective of the client, Joan could ask Camila to generate ideas about the client's in-session behaviors and then to hone in on a hypothesis about the client. Joan might then ask Camila to identify interventions that would substantiate her hypothesis. Note that Joan may need to provide some structure if Camila cannot identify interventions. Joan might also explore with Camila the potential outcomes of using the interventions with the client. This process helps the supervisee begin to practice intentionality by conceptualizing what is happening with the client and why, then using an approach based on an informed hypothesis about the client and their needs.

The supervisor may also discuss evidence-based practice (EBP) with Camila. Wachter Morris et al. (2018) noted that EBP involves the intersection of empirically supported treatments, clinician expertise and judgment, and client factors (e.g., needs, goals, preferences, culture). PE is based in empirically validated approaches (e.g., behavior therapy [systematic desensitization, imaginal flooding], cognitive behavior therapy [cognitive reappraisal]) and has a solid research base (e.g., McLean & Foa, 2011; Powers et al., 2010), but Camila needs to also consider her own expertise and judgment and client factors in deciding whether to use PE.

By developing her conceptual skills, Camila can begin to develop an intentional approach to counseling.

Joan needs to scaffold conversations about theory, case conceptualization, and EBP to Camila's developmental level as a counselor. For example, Camila might be able to describe PE and some of the research supporting it, but Joan would expect her to have some difficulty with the nuances of explaining how and why PE works and why and how it is or is not appropriate for her client. When Camila gets stuck in this process, Joan can help her fill in the gaps, perhaps by explaining the meaning behind an intervention or describing components of counseling theory to help her think through case conceptualization.

Regarding diversity, Camila's work with her client, and the supervisory feedback surrounding it, should be culturally contextualized. At the counseling level, Camila's use of PE should be explored in light of the client's cultural background and norms around trauma. For example, PE is based on in vivo exposure, which involves reexperiencing trauma memories and narratives. Camila needs to ensure that it is culturally appropriate to speak about trauma directly with a client before using the intervention. At the supervisory level, Joan must be aware of, and responsive to, cultural similarities or differences that might influence the supervisory process. For example, Wind et al. (2021) found female supervisees may view the supervisor as holding more power in goal setting and case conceptualization, both of which were discussed in this case. A feminist-based supervisory approach in which Camila and Joan's intersecting social identities are recognized and respected, and in which a relationship is founded on mutual respect and appropriate sharing of power, may promote an open learning environment in which Camila and Joan can work together to help Camila improve as a counselor (see McKibben, Cook, & Fickling, 2019).

Actions and Outcomes

In this case, Joan began by exploring whether any harm had occurred for the client. Because she learned of Camila's session during supervision, she asked Camila to process how the PE session had gone and how the client had responded, which allowed Joan to assess whether harm may have occurred. Joan also learned that Camila had audio recorded the counseling session, which Joan listened to after supervision. Feeling comfortable that the client was not harmed, Joan broached the topic of confidence by owning her prior feedback to Camila and how it may have affected this situation. Joan stated, "I told you to start using more theory-based interventions, and I recognize that is what you did here. But I'm also wondering about your readiness to use an intervention like PE with a client who has a significant trauma history." This approach validated Camila while also introducing a discussion of Camila practicing within the scope of her competence. Joan brought up the three components of EBP, which allowed Camila to see that she had not considered factors of the client in her decision-making but rather her own feelings of being stuck. From here, Joan and Camila refocused on the client's goals for counseling and talked through therapeutic strategies to address these goals.

It is not uncommon for supervisors to encounter supervisees who attempt treatment interventions without clearly understanding how to implement them or why they are choosing them. When counselors are new and likely focused on right or wrong ways to do counseling, supervisors encouraging them to think outside the box could result in them doing what Camila did: She got stuck, tried to "unstick" herself, and did not discern the blurred boundaries of competence and risk. Thus, supervisors must evaluate supervisees' developmental abilities and scaffold feedback. Telling supervisees to be more intentional and to use theory may not be enough to move them forward in their development.

Conclusion

Though not uncommon, this case serves as a reminder that not all "let's see if this works" situations are created equal. The intent of a therapeutic intervention does not always match the outcome. An intern who uses a self-esteem worksheet they found on the internet without clearly understanding what they are trying to accomplish may be similar to Camila in terms of cognitive counseling skills and self-awareness, but the risk to the client may differ because of the intensity of the treatment approach and the client's trauma history. Thus, supervisors must evaluate each "let's see if this works" instance with attention to client welfare and counselor competence. The counselor needs a safe space to develop skill and intentionality, whereas the client needs to be protected from potential harm, even from a well-intended intervention.

Reflection Questions

1. Would you have approached supervision any differently with Camila? If so, how?
2. What might Joan do in supervision moving forward with Camila to continue to foster her growth and development?

Critical Incident Response

Jane M. Webber

Supervisors have unique responsibilities with internship students. In addition to teacher and counselor supervisory roles, Joan may use structuring, encouragement, coaching, or mentoring to help expand Camila's skills and manage her motivation and enthusiasm to think outside the box (Hersey et al., 2012). The author appropriately selected the DM, referenced an integrative developmental lens, and prioritized ethical concerns to do no harm and to counsel within the scope of practice and training. Developmental supervision is framed around differing individual needs from beginning to master counselor and supervision styles, support, and directedness for each level.

Level 1 supervisors and supervisees are concerned with doing the right thing, and Joan struggled to give clear feedback (McNeil & Stoltenberg, 2015). Level 1 supervisees often perceive feedback as a directive, and Camila complied with Joan's feedback by attending a webinar that changed her views, a sign of growth. She increased her knowledge to think outside the box and expand her approach. Although Joan acknowledged the lack of clarity around her feedback, Camila, with little structure or mentoring, tried a treatment that bypassed ethical, conceptualization, and self-reflective processes and potentially put her client at risk.

The author placed the burden of responsibility and consequences for ethical breaches on Camila. It is unknown what element of PE Camila used in session. The client was not harmed and may have made gains in treatment. I agree with the recommendation for more scaffolding in supervising Camila. Because the client had a history of abuse, trauma-informed supervision should have begun prior to Camila's first counseling session. Joan could identify potential treatment concerns and coach Camila with trauma-informed interventions within her scope of practice to pace the process. "The supervisor, during this transition time, will watch carefully to ensure the supervisee does not attempt to progress too far too quickly" (Aasheim, 2012, p. 43).

Integrating a trauma-informed developmental approach into the DM can normalize Camila's Level 1 needs and reactions by increasing structure and space for personalization and self-reflection. For example, Camila can replay her decision to use PE. Joan can teach Camila coping skills to brake before accelerating her interventions in session as a self-monitoring tool (Rothschild, 2000).

The first 3 weeks of supervision are not discussed. Joan should review them in supervision of supervision or in consultation to be aware of transference or countertransference. Although Joan's level of supervision and experience providing counseling supervision related to working with clients who have experienced trauma is not known, Level 2 supervisors may demonstrate confusion rather than clarity in feedback or focus on supervisees' weaknesses instead of their strengths (McNeil & Stoltenberg, 2015). The use of a feminist supervision approach could shift Joan's singular, directive feedback toward collaborative and shared decision-making with Camila. Although the need for trauma-informed counseling and supervision is not addressed, the author stresses the importance of culturally informed trauma counseling.

A single type of trauma treatment is not for everyone. Camila must collaborate with her client on the treatment plan and work toward the client's goals. New counselors without strong trauma-informed training and supervision often push for a recounting of story details. Traumatologists with increased somatic and neurological knowledge concur that not all trauma survivors want or need to retell their story to recover. Clients may instead learn to cope and live healthy lives without the risk of retraumatization and pain (Gentry, 2016; Rothschild, 2000).

Even with training and adherence to protocol, flooding and exposure trauma treatments can lead to hyperarousal, abreaction, and retraumatization (Shapiro, 2010). Camila's frustration with the lack of progress is a common reaction among Level 1 supervisees, who may unintentionally force the therapeutic process before the client is ready, risking retraumatization and other serious responses (e.g., flashbacks and suicidal ideation). Although her behavior may have been an unintentional slip, Joan must address this with Camille to prevent any further risk to the client, and a remediation plan should document this required action. Teaching clients emotional regulation to help them remain within their window of tolerance during counseling and explaining treatment options and risks to clients are prerequisites to using any intervention. Camila and Joan, as well as everyone in their department, would benefit from training in trauma-informed care.

Many counseling professionals have experienced trauma. Camila and Joan's avoidance of trauma during supervision could reflect their own trauma histories or vicarious traumatization. Joan should monitor Camila's potential for countertransference and address challenges and risks for vicarious traumatization by providing psychoeducation, monitoring the delivery of trauma interventions, observing signs of vicarious traumatization, and teaching Camila self-regulation and self-care (Berger & Quiros, 2014).

• • •

Chapter 15

I Don't Believe in That: Addressing Counselors' Values Conflicts

Anita A. Neuer Colburn

2014 *ACA Code of Ethics* Standards Addressed

- A.4.a. Avoiding Harm
- A.4.b. Personal Values
- A.7.a. Advocacy
- A.11.b. Values Within Termination and Referral
- C.1. Knowledge of and Compliance With Standards
- C.2.a. Boundaries of Competence
- C.2.e. Consultations on Ethical Obligations
- C.5. Nondiscrimination
- F.1.a. Client Welfare
- F.4.c. Standards for Supervisees
- F.5.a. Ethical Responsibilities
- F.6.b. Gatekeeping and Remediation
- I.1.a. Knowledge
- I.1.b. Ethical Decision Making

• • •

Amanda, a cisgender white female, was a core faculty member of a secular counseling program providing triadic internship supervision. Jesse was a cisgender white male counseling student in internship who introduced himself as a Christian who was pursuing his master's in counseling in response to his "calling." Felicity was a Black cisgender female who was placed at an addictions facility for her internship. Felicity reported that she faithfully attended church every week and that it was a source of comfort and centering for her. Amanda wanted to form a strong supervisory working alliance; therefore, she disclosed that she was also a woman of faith.

Because both supervisees had mentioned religious beliefs, Amanda wanted to ensure that they were keenly aware of the *ACA Code of Ethics* (American Counseling Association [ACA], 2014), specifically the parameters related to a counselor's values (Standards A.4.b., A.11.b.). She also wanted both students to review the Association for Spiritual, Ethical, and Religious Values in Counseling (ASERVIC) Competencies for Addressing Spiritual and Religious Issues in Counseling (ASERVIC, 2009). When they discussed these in session, both Jesse and Felicity appeared to understand that even though they both endorsed religious values, they were not supposed to impose them on a client. When asked what imposing these values might look like, Felicity responded, "It would be wrong for me to advise a client to pray more about their problem, right?" Jesse offered, "We probably should not do that, and we have to let them believe what they want about God, even though we all know people are going to continue having problems if they don't yield to God's power." Amanda noted a sense of rigidity in Jesse's response but chose not to address it. During the rest of the session, Amanda focused on ASERVIC (2009) Competency 8 related to counselors using spiritual or religious concepts consistent with clients' perspectives and/or acceptable to them and *ACA Code of Ethics* (ACA, 2014) standards related to counselors being aware of their beliefs and values and not imposing them on their clients (Standard A.4.b.) and not harming clients (Standard A.4.a.).

When they met for supervision in Week 2, Jesse reported feeling relieved that he had a few client referrals so he could build his caseload but stated that he could not take one of them. When Amanda encouraged Jesse to share more, he reported that Andrew, a white cisgender gay male, had been referred for depression, but Jesse was fairly confident he would not be able to help him. Amanda reminded Jesse that he had worked with depression before. In fact, his practicum evaluation indicated that his site supervisor had been impressed with his ability to help clients feel comfortable exploring their depression. Jesse then reported that working with this client went against his Christian identity. He stated that if he helped him, it meant he agreed with his sexual orientation, and he did not. Amanda shared that she could see the conflict Jesse was experiencing. He was aware of the *ACA Code of Ethics* (ACA, 2014) related to imposing values yet felt incongruent about working with Andrew because he disagreed with the client's sexual orientation. Felicity shared that she understood the difficulty and that it would also probably be a struggle for her. Amanda asked Jesse whether he was aware of ACA Standard A.11.b., which related to counselors not referring clients based solely on counselors' own values and beliefs and highlighted the importance of instead seeking training in areas in which they were at risk for imposing their values. She also reminded him that clients, in particular marginalized clients, report feeling rejected when they are referred to other counselors. Jesse replied, "What am I supposed to do? I thought we were supposed to be congruent. How am I supposed to go against God?"

Case Analysis and Discussion

Whitman and Bidell (2014) advised educators and supervisors to help students experiencing religion-based values conflicts recognize the difference between altering their behavior and losing their faith. They also emphasized supporting them through the potential grief that might arise from the deconstruction of faith, referring them to counselors who are skilled in working with religion-based values conflicts, and connecting them with religious leaders who can help them navigate the transformation of their beliefs. Similarly, Ametrano (2014) urged educators to provide space and support as students learn to tolerate the ambiguity they feel as they reflect on any differences between their personal and professional values.

In addition to the *ACA Code of Ethics* (ACA, 2014) and the ASERVIC (2009) Competencies for Addressing Spiritual and Religious Issues in Counseling, appropriate analysis would include also reviewing the Association for Multicultural Counseling and Development Multicultural and Social Justice Counseling Competencies (Ratts et al., 2015) and the Society for Sexual, Affectional, Intersex, and Gender Expansive Identities (formerly the Association for Lesbian, Gay, Bisexual and Transgender Issues in Counseling) Competencies for Counseling With Lesbian, Gay, Bisexual, Queer, Questioning, Intersex, and Ally Individuals (Harper et al., 2013). The notion of privilege and marginalization in the counselor-client dyad is foundational to the Multicultural and Social Justice Counseling Competencies and to competent clinical work. Jesse was privileged as a straight white Christian man, and as the counselor he held additional power in his relationship with Andrew. Although white and male, Andrew was marginalized as a gay man, as his sexual orientation was his prevailing characteristic from Jesse's perspective. Amanda held supervisory power in her relationship with Jesse while also holding marginalized status as a female. Jesse may have felt safe expressing his bias against Andrew because Amanda had disclosed her own religious beliefs.

Multiple ethical issues are relevant in this case. The Preamble to the *ACA Code of Ethics* (ACA, 2014) outlines the importance of honoring diversity, embracing a multicultural approach, supporting the worth and dignity of people within their cultural contexts, and promoting social justice. Jesse was also in violation of the ethical principles of nonmaleficence (referral could harm Andrew), beneficence (withholding treatment demonstrates a lack of support for the good of the client), and justice (Jesse was helping only some clients with depression). Applicable specific ethical standards include A.4.a. (Avoiding Harm), A.4.b. (Personal Values), A.7.a. (Advocacy), and A.11.b. (Values Within Termination and Referral). Jesse was also bound to Standards C.1. (Knowledge of and Compliance With Standards), C.2.a. (Boundaries of Competence), C.2.e. (Consultations on Ethical Obligations), and C.5. (Nondiscrimination). Lack of knowledge of the *Code* is not a defense for nonadherence (Standard I.1.a.), and counselors must use an ethical decision-making model (Standard I.1.b.) when experiencing an ethical dilemma.

In accordance with the *ACA Code of Ethics* (ACA, 2014), supervisors monitor client welfare (Standard F.1.a.) and ensure supervisees follow the *Code* (Standards F.4.c., F.5.a.). Supervisors also act as gatekeepers for the profession by recommending the remediation or dismissal of student supervisees who are unable to demonstrate an ability to provide services to diverse clients (Standard F.6.b.). Amanda should inform Jesse of his ethical responsibility related to Andrew. She should also discuss ethical decision-making models with her supervisees, challenging them to choose one and use it to resolve this and other ethical dilemmas. According to the Association for Counselor Education and Supervision (ACES) *Best Practices in Clinical Supervision* (ACES Supervision Taskforce, 2011), Amanda should provide direct feedback and recommend alternative behaviors (3.b.iii.). She must also be mindful of her responsibility to build and safeguard a healthy supervisory relationship (Section 5), concurrently addressing cultural factors and values. Amanda decided to consider various approaches to resolving values conflicts.

Handelsman et al. (2005) adapted Berry's (2003) model of acculturation to create the ethical acculturation model, defining *ethical acculturation* as a process during which students use adaptation strategies to navigate differences between their own moral traditions and concepts and those of the profession. Confronted with such a difference, Jesse appeared to be ill prepared to navigate the ethical dilemma, which highlights the importance of embedding multiculturalism throughout the curriculum (Whitman & Bidell, 2014). Amanda could help Jesse understand that being empathic and judgmental at the same time is virtually impossible. She might invite Jesse to consider how his religious values are congruent with the professional value of affirmation (Handelsman et al., 2005). Kocet and Herlihy (2014) introduced ethical bracketing, or the ability to separate personal and professional values to provide ethical counseling to all clients. Amanda could assist Jesse in using ethical bracketing by having him consult codes of ethics and competencies more thoroughly, engage in additional training, and identify ways to maintain his own beliefs while still providing effective counseling.

Fallon et al. (2013) professed the utility of critical thinking, noting that people with fundamentalist religious beliefs may struggle with viewing critical thinking strategies as credible and may be skeptical about the critical thinking process. Ultimately Amanda avoided imposing her own values, and those of the profession, onto Jesse. Instead, she took a more affirming stance, honoring his values by offering nonjudgmental observations and asking challenging questions. Minnix (2018) created the relational equilibrium model, defining *relational equilibrium* as the ability to balance connection with others and God. In the relational equilibrium model, attitudes of less or more lesbian, gay, bisexual, and transgender (LGBT) affirmation and Christian beliefs inhibiting or supporting LGBT affirmation work together to balance threats to and stabilizers of relational equilibrium. Minnix discovered that when Christians learned sexual orientation was not a choice, they did not view same-sex attraction as a sin and therefore no longer viewed LGBT affirmation as conflicting with their relationship with God. Jesse resisted "going against God"; thus, providing him with etiological information may have been helpful.

Actions and Outcomes

Amanda was keenly aware that pushing Jesse into immediate ethical compliance could severely damage the supervisory working alliance (Whitman & Bidell, 2014). She decided to use culturally affirmative remediation (J. S. Rose et al., 2019). In culturally affirmative remediation, the supervisor (a) assesses the supervisee's level of proficiency or deficiency regarding LGBT information, (b) provides resources to remediate any deficiency, (c) collaborates with the supervisee to develop a culturally affirming remediation plan, and (d) implements the plan with formal and informal competency measures. Amanda determined that Jesse was deficient in several areas, including (a) lack of awareness of how his bias could be harmful, (b) lack of knowledge of LGBT populations, (c) lack of understanding of the *ACA Code of Ethics* (ACA, 2014), and (d) lack of understanding that a counselor can endorse professional values without agreeing with a client's beliefs or actions. She used the supervisory working alliance to obtain a commitment from Jesse that he would work with Andrew while they continued working on a plan to resolve the conflict.

Amanda provided Killermann's (2012) list of heterosexual privileges and Project Implicit's (2011) Sexuality Implicit Association Test to help her supervisees develop self-awareness of their attitudes toward the LGBT population. She referred Jesse and Felicity to the Frequently Asked Questions section of the Queer Café (2017) website, which provides historical and etiological information along with information about religion and myths and biases about the LGBT community. Jesse and Felicity reported feeling embarrassed to learn how much privilege they enjoyed because they were straight. They were especially surprised to learn that being gay was not a choice. Felicity noted, "How can being gay be a sin if the person is born that way?"

In keeping with culturally affirmative remediation (J. S. Rose et al., 2019), Amanda facilitated what she termed a "values reconciliation plan." Jesse agreed to continue learning more about the LGBT population and engaging in in-depth reading of the *ACA Code of Ethics* (ACA, 2014) so he would better understand counseling values. He agreed to revisit the values conflict as frequently as necessary until it was resolved. In preparation for their next meeting, Amanda asked Jesse and Felicity to assess their competency for counseling with LGBT individuals (Harper et al., 2013). With their permission, she invited Randall, a program graduate, to join them for the next supervision session. Randall was a Black cisgender gay man who identified as Christian. He shared the pain he had endured as a result of being judged and rejected by his former church "friends" and the devastation he had experienced when a counselor had told him he could not help him and referred him to someone else.

As their internships progressed, both supervisees had more client referrals for people identifying as gay or lesbian. They shared that their ongoing internal struggle was dissipating but still there. Both reported being equipped to provide services and aware of their ethical obligations not to impose their values on clients. They continued processing their feelings and experiences in supervision and appeared more comfortable as they gained experience.

Conclusion

Amanda helped foster the growth and development of her supervisees through the integration of several resources, including ethics codes, models, competencies, and supervisory best practices. Supervisors are encouraged to use these resources when assisting supervisees to navigate ethical dilemmas. Thus, supervisors provide support to supervisees to promote the provision of quality care to clients.

Reflection Questions

1. How can supervisors support supervisees in being congruent and ethical when supervisees disagree with something related to a client?
2. How can supervisors mentor supervisees in ethical compliance and professional competency without imposing their own values on them?

Critical Incident Response

W. Bradley McKibben

In this critical incident, the core issue defined by the author is a values conflict for Jesse; namely, his religious values conflicted with a marginalized identity of the client, Andrew. It is important to note that Jesse did not just have a values conflict; he also intended to act in a way that affirmed his own values over the needs and preferences of the client. A situation like this can be tough for a counselor educator and/or clinical supervisor. The author offered a solid approach to working with a supervisee like Jesse.

As the author pointed out, Jesse's initial plan to refuse to counsel Andrew was in violation of the *ACA Code of Ethics* (ACA, 2014, Standard A.11.b.). Ethics are not values neutral, and neither are the counseling profession and *ACA Code of Ethics*. Indeed, the *Code* specifies five professional values in its Preamble: human development, diversity and multiculturalism, social justice, the therapeutic relationship, and competent and ethical practice. These professional values guide the *Code* and define what the counseling profession views as necessary and acceptable behaviors for counselors. Thus, when we evaluate Jesse's initial decision as unethical, we do so because it conflicts with the values and behaviors esteemed by the counseling profession. One could argue that professional ethics in the *ACA Code of Ethics* (ACA, 2014) do not exist to force counselors to conform to a certain worldview. They exist to protect the public and to ensure that counselors prioritize clients' needs and best interests over their own (Kaplan, 2014), as in essentially all helping and medical professions. Previous court decisions have affirmed the right of the counseling profession and of counselor education programs to uphold and enforce a code of ethics grounded in such professional values (e.g., *Ward v. Polite*, 2012; *Ward v. Wilbanks*, 2010).

Several court cases that have stemmed from situations just like this critical incident have important implications for counselor education. In *Ward v. Wilbanks* (2010), a practicum student who held a position similar to Jesse indicated she could not affirm a gay client's identity and asked about referring the client. Ward underwent a disciplinary review and ultimately was dismissed from the program. Ward sued the university, but the court upheld the university's decision and dismissed the case. However, the Sixth Circuit Court of Appeals overturned the initial ruling and ordered Ward's case reopened (*Ward v. Polite*, 2012); the case was later settled. It is important to note that the Sixth Circuit Court's opinion affirmed universities' ability to set and enforce reasonable curriculum standards and antidiscrimination policies. The court noted that Ward had made several statements throughout her program about not wishing to affirm same-sex identities, but no remediation had occurred prior to her dismissal in practicum. The court also noted that the program did not have a policy in place for referring clients.

It is critical for counselor educators to have clearly stated, readily accessible programmatic policies in place around ethical practice within a counseling program. A student handbook is an ideal place to state such policies. The courts have consistently upheld that counselor education programs have the freedom as academic units to set and enforce expectations for professional/competent practice, but students should be aware of the expectations as well as the consequences of not meeting them (e.g., remediation procedures, due process and review, dismissal). Counselor educators may consider having the university's legal counsel review policies and provide feedback as well as consult with them regarding legal and ethical dilemmas, as Wheeler and Bertram (2019) emphasized the importance of legal consultation in making ethical decisions. In Jesse's case, it is important that Amanda's remedial approach be consistent with programmatic remediation policies while also being honed to Jesse's areas for growth. Finally, responding to students' problematic behaviors, values conflicts, or ethical concerns cannot wait until practicum or internship if such issues emerge earlier in the program. There is no evidence of this with Jesse, but had Jesse expressed an intent to not counsel a gay client in a class prior to practicum, for example, then faculty would have needed to address this concern as soon as they became aware of it.

Having policies leads to another consideration in clinical supervision: supervisory informed consent. *Best Practices in Clinical Supervision* (ACES Supervision Taskforce, 2011) states that supervisors provide supervisees with written informed consent (e.g., a professional disclosure statement; 7.a.i.) and policies and procedures related to due process rights (7.a.vi.). A disclosure statement would detail Amanda's supervisory qualifications and approach, ethical considerations, expectations of supervisees, evaluation processes, and fees (Borders & Brown, 2005). Supervisors should review student handbook policies (or whatever programmatic policies are published), including any dispositions, behaviors, or evaluative components relevant to practicum and internship, with supervisees at the outset of the supervisory relationship. In this case, Amanda, the supervisor, did well to address ethics codes and ASERVIC competencies from the outset of supervision as a means of clearly outlining expectations she could then refer back to as the process with Jesse unfolded. As supervision progresses, providing constructive—and in this case remedial—feedback that is concrete, behavioral, and grounded in supervisees' learning goals can help supervisees better grasp what is expected of them and what they need to do. In sum, supervisors must provide initial and ongoing supervisory informed consent to supervisees.

• • •

Chapter 16

I'm an Emotional Person: Determining Counselor Impairment

Jane M. Webber

2014 *ACA Code of Ethics* Standards Addressed

- A.1.a. Primary Responsibility
- A.2.c. Developmental and Cultural Sensitivity
- A.4.b. Personal Values
- A.6.b. Extending Counseling Boundaries
- A.6.c. Documenting Boundary Extensions
- C.2.d. Monitor Effectiveness
- C.2.g. Impairment
- F.1.a. Client Welfare
- F.4.a. Informed Consent for Supervision
- F.5.b. Impairment
- F.6.a. Evaluation
- F.8.d. Addressing Personal Concerns

• • •

Tanya, a 25-year-old cisgender Latina master's student, lived with her 10-year-old daughter and mother. She worked as a bilingual case manager in a community agency where she was also completing her counseling internship. Tanya was an advocate for her clients, in particular young Latina mothers who were also survivors of sexual abuse. Tanya's colleagues admired her for rocking a crying baby to sleep while counseling the baby's mother.

The site supervisor, Jamal, was a 63-year-old cisgender African American male who had practiced as a counselor for 32 years and as a clinical supervisor for 8 years in the same agency. He often brought his three young grandchildren to the agency to promote a family-friendly environment, and Tanya enjoyed caring for them between sessions. He praised Tanya's commitment to underage mothers and her willingness to work additional hours. Jamal's individual supervision sessions with Tanya often ended early because of client crises and emergencies. He shared two concerns with her university supervisor: (a) the potential for burnout due to her intense schedule of work and internship; and (b) Tanya's deep expression of emotion with clients, which might be a sign of compassion fatigue (CF) and unresolved personal issues.

Janette, Tanya's university supervisor, was a 36-year-old Latina and an advocate for children in foster care. Tanya babysat Janette's two adopted children (5 years and 8 months) and brought her daughter to Janette's apartment to help. This was Janette's first year as a faculty member and university supervisor, and their individual supervision sessions often digressed to conversations about their children. During group supervision, Janette observed Tanya become emotionally distressed (e.g., tear up) while she listened to cases of sexually abused young women and discussed her clients. When Janette heard Tanya's voice crack on her first audio recording in individual supervision, Tanya defended herself, saying she had become "a little overemotional." Janette expressed concern about Tanya's crying and its potential effect on clients and told Tanya to bring a video recording to her next individual supervision session.

Tanya did not bring a video for 3 weeks until Janette warned her she might not complete internship and graduate if she did not present a recorded session. Janette and Tanya watched the session together, seeing her cry as the client handed her tissues, provided words of support and empathy, and hugged Tanya. Tanya welled up as Janette questioned her competence and readiness to graduate and stated, "I'm an emotional person. The tears are from the real me, and I can't stop them." Janette broached her impairment as a counselor, proposing that Tanya take a leave of absence "to pull herself together." Tanya pleaded, "I have to help my clients. I am the only one who can save them."

Janette consulted with Jamal about Tanya's emotional distress as a possible sign of incompetence and impairment. Jamal had some training in trauma-informed care and secondary traumatic stress (STS), and the next day he asked Tanya how she was feeling, stating he was worried about her. She began to cry, and he queried in a nonjudgmental, normalizing tone: "Tanya, what happened to you?" Sobbing, Tanya disclosed that her uncle had raped her when she was 15 and her grandmother had taken guardianship of her baby, raising Tanya's daughter as her own until Tanya finished high school. Tanya had lied to the program about her age (saying she was 35) to protect her daughter from shame and stigma as she also protected underage mothers.

Case Analysis and Discussion

Effective supervision in this case requires the development of a safe, trusting relationship with Tanya so she can explore her intersecting roles and concerns as a counselor, student, mother, trauma survivor, and "savior." Unaware of Tanya's traumatic experiences of rape and separation from her child, Janette related to her on a surface level rather than seeing Tanya through the lens of her traumatic history. Therefore, she had missed opportunities in individual supervision to broach

Tanya's trauma issues. Three key supervision questions emerge in Tanya's case: Is Tanya an impaired counselor? Is she a competent counselor ready to graduate? What triggers Tanya's emotional distress and crying? To process these questions, I examine four ethical and professional supervision issues in this analysis: (a) counselor-client boundaries, (b) countertransference and identification with clients, (c) trauma history, and (d) intense emotionality and crying. In terms of the *ACA Code of Ethics* (American Counseling Association [ACA], 2014), critical issues relate to the well-being of Tanya's clients and possible counselor impairment (Standards A.1.a., C.2.g.).

Tanya was responsible for monitoring her performance and seeking assistance from her supervisors and peers before her problems could affect client care (ACA, 2014, Standards C.2.d., F.5.b.). Tanya's secrecy and feelings of blame, guilt, and shame held her back from sharing her traumatic history with Janette. Tanya was unable to reflect on the potential for countertransference issues, creating concern in monitoring her effectiveness (Standard C.2.d.) and impairment (Standard C.2.g.). Therefore, her supervisors were unaware of key triggers (e.g., overidentifying with client problems, needing to care for children, meeting clients outside the agency, crying, and reversing roles in sessions). Her commitment to promoting her clients' well-being was genuine, but she may have guided clients toward goals related to her own trauma and belief that she alone could save them, creating concern regarding the ethical principles of autonomy, beneficence, and nonmaleficence (ACA, 2014). Her sobbing reversed the roles, and her clients provided her with support and entered Tanya's personal space to hug her.

Tanya's overinvolvement and deep attachments with her clients led to concerns with boundaries (ACA, 2014, Standard A.6.b.) because she met them in unsupervised home sessions after work hours, a violation of their informed consent and her internship contract. Tanya continually sought comfort and connection with the children of clients and supervisors, in particular infants. She also provided childcare to her clients and supervisors, which served both their personal needs and hers and extended the client and supervisory relationships beyond professional boundaries (ACA, 2014, Standards F.3.a., A.6.b.). Tanya's fluid boundaries in her relationships with clients and their children paralleled those with her supervisors' families and were supported by the supervisors. In a study by Burns (2019) that examined perceptions of ethical boundary crossing among 224 graduate students, counselor educators' hiring a student to babysit was rated "moderately unethical" and "completely inappropriate for a counselor educator to engage in" (Burns, 2019, pp. 61, 65). Tanya's secrecy about her own trauma clouded her self-monitoring and ethical decision-making, and she did not take precautions to ensure the well-being of her clients. Tanya did not consult with her supervisors, change informed consent, or document the rationale and potential benefits and consequences of the way she interacted with her clients and their children (ACA, 2014, Standards A.6.b., A.6.c.).

Trauma triggers and emotional reactions frequently pushed Tanya outside the window of tolerance, overwhelming her ability to make objective, ethical decisions and giving her clients the impression that her personal values and goals reflected agency and counselor ethics (ACA, 2014, Standard A.4.b.). Baum (2016) emphasized counselors addressing their potential savior complexes and setting boundaries and achievable goals with clients. Maintaining boundaries strengthens counselor and client roles, especially with interns and new, inexperienced counselors who often feel they need to save their clients. Tanya continuously advocated on behalf of underage mothers in her overlapping roles as agency case manager and master's-level intern. As an unlicensed master's intern, Tanya could see clients only under supervision at her site.

Janette focused on Tanya's crying as a skills issue, ascribing her emotionality to incompetent counseling behavior. Janette did not treat all individuals as if they had experienced trauma, which is a trauma-informed principle (Trauma-Informed Community Network, 2018). Thus, she did not recognize signs of CF, STS, or a traumatic history. Examining crying as an emotional marker in 684 psychologists and psychology trainees, Blume-Marcovici et al. (2013) found that 72% had cried in sessions and only did so in 7% of their overall sessions. Nearly half (46%) indicated their crying had a positive effect on the therapeutic relationship, 53% reported no real effect, and less than 1% reported a negative effect. In a subgroup of 411 participants who reported crying, 73% indicated the client was also crying and 81% had no regrets about crying (Blume-Marcovici et al., 2015). Of the reported tearing up, 89% was instantaneous to less than 1 minute in duration. Most therapists (77%) reported their tears were not related to personal issues, whereas 16% reported they were related. Most therapists also reported their crying was related to client situations (e.g., grief, trauma, termination) and they had felt sadness (75%) or been emotionally touched (63%), and they thought their clients' emotions had included sadness (59%), loss (38%), and being emotionally touched (31%; Blume-Marcovici et al., 2015). In comparison, Tanya teared up or cried with trauma-affected clients during much of her work, a sign of CF and STS and reactions to trauma triggers.

Janette labeled Tanya's crying responses as unhealthy expressions of emotion that negatively affected clients, breaches of boundaries, and signs of incompetence and impairment. Tanya believed her crying was a spontaneous process that communicated deep feelings to the client without using words. For the majority of therapists, crying is a natural human reaction (Blume-Marcovici et al., 2015; Collier, 2016). Janette had no training or experience in trauma-informed supervision, whereas Jamal had years of experience working with trauma survivors. Thus, his nonblaming query "What happened to you?" offered a safe space for Tanya to disclose her trauma. Jamal recognized that Tanya's crying was an emotional reaction to her clients' trauma, which also triggered her own trauma. Viewed through a trauma-informed lens, Tanya's crying showed empathy for clients and served as a coping mechanism that reduced the traumatic stress she absorbed listening to their stories. Tanya may also have cried for herself; she should monitor triggers for such intense expression of empathy to respond appropriately (Rothschild, 2017).

Tanya demonstrated several strengths that were overshadowed by boundary crossings and slips of unethical behavior. She lived in the Latina culture and understood family-of-origin issues. She was a native Spanish speaker who shifted to counseling in Spanish to be culturally appropriate for her clients (ACA, 2014, Standard A.2.c.). Tanya perceived her work with young mothers outside the agency as essential to their therapy and overidentified with them because she too had been raped as a teenager and her child was the result of the sexual assault. Her savior complex brought empathy and insight to counseling, but her trauma could have influenced clients and ultimately affected her graduation and her job (ACA, 2014, Standard F.8.d.).

Actions and Outcomes

Tanya's disclosure to Jamal resulted in her new perception that he did not judge or blame her for her secrecy about the rape, thus strengthening trust in their relationship. Tanya shared this insight with Janette, who sought her own consultation and training in trauma-informed care. Their individual supervision sessions became less threatening and more empowering for Tanya, who no longer feared Janette's possible judging of the rape and pregnancy. When she completed the Adverse Childhood Experiences survey in university group supervision, Tanya's score was 6, which indicates high risk for later physical and mental health problems. As she learned the effects of adverse childhood experiences, Tanya recognized the effects of trauma in her life and in the lives of her clients.

In supervision, Jamal focused on empowering Tanya to strengthen her boundaries with clients, use appropriate adaptive coping strategies, prioritize self-care, and join him in relation-based reflective supervision to increase her awareness of her feelings about clients (Trauma-Informed Community Network, 2018). Tanya did not completely stop crying in sessions, but she became aware of her triggers and how to manage their intensity. She also learned to manage somatic reactions to stay within the window of tolerance during sessions, using coping strategies developed in personal counseling (e.g., diaphragmatic breathing, mindfulness, self-place anchoring, and self-rescue grounding; Rothschild, 2000, 2017). Tanya also learned to self-monitor her distress by taking note of her subjective units of distress (Wolpe, 1969) and checking in with colleagues about her reactions rather than isolating herself from others.

Given Tanya's multiple intersections as a Latina woman, trauma survivor, mother, and bilingual counselor working with clients with rape trauma, Janette and Jamal collaborated to use a flexible supervision framework that integrated elements of several approaches, including the discrimination model (Bernard & Goodyear, 2019), the integrated developmental model (Stoltenberg & McNeill, 2010), narrative supervision (White & Epston, 1990), and trauma-informed supervision (Knight, 2018; Substance Abuse and Mental Health Services Administration, 2014). Considering the discrimination model, the supervisor, using the counselor role, focused on Tanya's feelings and affective reactions to her traumatized clients as well as referral to trauma-informed counseling. Jamal encouraged Tanya to share her personal reactions to clients' trauma, normalizing and validating her responses rather than focusing only on her trauma or the clients' problems (Baum, 2016).

By using the teacher role, the supervisor equipped Tanya with knowledge of the effects of trauma on the brain and body and the effect of CF and STS on "heroic treaters" (Cerny, 1995). This required Janette to learn about trauma-informed supervision through trainings and in a supervision-of-supervision group and to share her new knowledge with her interns in group supervision. Baum (2016) reported that supervisors may not have an understanding of trauma therapy. This was true for Janette, and therefore she consulted more frequently with Jamal about Tanya's work with clients with severe trauma while she also pursued professional development.

The integrated developmental model is used to provide greater structure and supervisory direction for Level 1 supervisees. Tanya was encouraged to write down questions and challenges each day to present during individual supervision. Her questions reflected a lack of familiarity with the *ACA Code of Ethics* (ACA, 2014), which Janette also addressed in supervision. In narrative supervision conversations, Tanya shared her successes and sparkling moments that increased her sense of empowerment (White & Epston, 1990). Grounded in trauma-informed supervision, Tanya came to understand chronic crying to be her body's inadequate adaptive defense and coping mechanism to manage overwhelming feelings about clients' trauma and the signs and effects of CF and STS (Substance Abuse and Mental Health Services Administration, 2014). With her greater transparency in supervision, her supervisors monitored signs of CF, STS, and burnout; assigned her more diverse clients without histories of sexual abuse or trauma; and increased break times rather than adding more clients.

Tanya developed a self-care plan using mindfulness, exercise, socialization, and parent-child play times (ACA, 2014, Section C, Introduction). In her own counseling, she realized that because she protected her secrets, she had no friends and had unintentionally used her clients as friends while disclosing too much personal information. Thus, she began attending counseling program events when she would have previously gone to clients' homes.

Conclusion

Individuals may enter the counseling profession deeply affected by personal traumatic events with the goal of saving others who have had similar traumatic experiences. Counselors, including counselors-in-training, have an ethical responsibility to be aware of personal concerns, in particular trauma, that may affect their ability to provide counseling to clients and seek their own personal counseling when needed (ACA, 2014, Standard C.2.g.). Without self-awareness, counselors like Tanya may experience CF, STS, and burnout that can lead to impairment.

Reflection Questions

1. What strategies might you use to explore countertransference with Tanya?
2. Was it inappropriate for Jamal and Janette to have Tanya watch their grandchildren and children?

Critical Incident Response

Anita A. Neuer Colburn

The supervisors' collaboration in support of Tanya is integral to this case. Supervisees may receive conflicting messages when working with multiple supervisors. Supervisees may also choose not to disclose things to all supervisors (Cook et al., 2018). When multiple supervisors work together, everyone gains an understanding of the supervisee's strengths and struggles.

The author highlighted the importance of using a trauma-informed lens to assess supervisee development. Counselors with their own unresolved trauma are at risk for impairment, and it is incumbent on supervisors to help mitigate impairment (Jones & Branco, 2020). Supervisors must also focus on supervisee development and client welfare (Bernard & Goodyear, 2019). Tanya received help from her counselor, and she is now able to see the connection between unresolved trauma and her functioning, which may help her notice this in her clients.

Both supervisors provided poor modeling of boundaries. Because of power dynamics, supervisors should be clear about relationship boundaries to avoid negatively affecting the supervisory working alliance (Hooley, 2019). Jamal praised Tanya for caring for his children between sessions. Similarly, Janette had Tanya babysitting her children with no noted discussion about multiple relationships in supervision. Each supervisor had a responsibility to discuss with Tanya her role as a babysitter and their roles as supervisors of her clinical work. It is not uncommon for supervisory relationships to gradually become more collegial, but because the supervisor is in the position of power, any boundary extensions should be discussed to avoid possible harm to the supervisee. For example, if Tanya decides she no longer wishes to babysit, she might not feel free to express this out of fear of supervisory retaliation.

Both supervisors also neglected to provide regular supervision, potentially increasing the risk for harm to Tanya's clients (ACA, 2014, Standard F.1.a.). Jamal ended sessions early, and Janette spent supervision time talking about their children. Supervisors are responsible for providing informed consent to supervisees regarding the nature of the supervisory relationship, including the frequency and length of meetings and provisions for rescheduling supervision meetings (ACA, 2014, Standard F.4.a.; Bernard & Goodyear, 2019). It is the supervisor's responsibility to set the agenda for supervision meetings and to tend to the quality of the supervisory relationship, the functioning of the supervisee, and client welfare (Bernard & Goodyear, 2019). Because the supervisory relationship is central to the outcomes of supervision, personal discussions (e.g., discussions about children) are not completely inappropriate. However, having such conversations to the exclusion of appropriate clinical supervision is unprofessional and unethical (Hooley, 2019).

The supervisors' actions could have communicated to Tanya that her caring nature and the relationships she has with them are more important than her continued development of counseling skills. Tanya may have internalized the idea that her caring disposition is the most important gift she has, and this could have resulted in her hiding her counseling strengths and struggles. Because of the supervisors' actions and Tanya's own unresolved trauma, Tanya is not reporting everything she should be in supervision, and supervisee nondisclosure can put both supervisees and clients at risk (Cook et al., 2018). Both Jamal and Janette are responsible for providing ongoing formative feedback regarding Tanya's professional development and clinical skills (ACA, 2014, Standard F.6.a.). This could be accomplished through a written clinical skill assessment form that is discussed at the beginning of supervision and used to self-assess and set goals. The list could then be revisited periodically by the supervisor and supervisee. Using the form would increase the likelihood that all aspects of Tanya's development would be examined.

Janette is new to supervision and developing her own supervision style. She appears to lean into personal relationship to the exclusion of honoring her identity as an evaluator, which could be why she interpreted the observed impairment as possible incompetence. Supervisors must establish trusting relationships with their supervisees while maintaining healthy enough detachment to ensure their role as evaluator is not confounded (Hooley, 2019). As a new counselor educator and supervisor, Janette may benefit from working with one supervision model and seeking supervision of her supervision. For example, even if Janette did not know about trauma-informed supervision, if she was using the discrimination model of supervision (Bernard & Goodyear, 2019), she may have learned of Tanya's earlier trauma by endorsing the supervision role of counselor when working with Tanya on personalization skills.

Jamal's use of relation-based reflective supervision demonstrates appropriate intentionality and sensitivity to Tanya's needs. Being referred to trauma-informed counseling gives Tanya an opportunity to resolve her traumatic memories and equips her to see her clients and their issues more objectively. In addition to the importance of using a trauma-informed lens, this case demonstrates the importance of supervisor training and boundaries in supervision.

• • •

Chapter 17

Don't Watch Me: Not Bringing Session Recordings to Supervision

Devika Dibya Choudhuri

2014 *ACA Code of Ethics* Standards Addressed

- A.4.a. Avoiding Harm
- A.4.b. Personal Values
- C.2.d. Monitor Effectiveness
- C.6.d. Exploitation of Others
- D.1.b. Forming Relationships
- D.1.i. Protection From Punitive Action
- F.1.a. Client Welfare
- F.2.b. Multicultural Issues/Diversity in Supervision
- F.4.c. Standards for Supervisees
- F.5.a. Ethical Responsibilities
- F.6.a. Evaluation
- F.6.b. Gatekeeping and Remediation
- F.7.e. Teaching Ethics
- F.7.i. Field Placements
- F.9.b. Limitations

• • •

Sandy Nowak, a Polish American cisgender woman, was in her late 30s. She had entered a clinical mental health counseling program to pursue a career change after initially acquiring a business degree and working in human resources for a large company. For her internship placement she selected Rescue Legion (RL), a community agency that specialized in working with clients who were homeless and chronically mentally ill. Her faculty adviser, Professor Creighton, a middle-aged Scottish

American cisgender man, had concerns because RL was known for providing case management rather than counseling. However, Sandy assured him that the agency contact, Carla, who would be her site supervisor, had arranged for her to maintain an ongoing client load and record sessions. Carla, an Italian American cisgender woman in her late 30s, had the necessary qualifications (a master's in social work) to be a site supervisor. Therefore, after Carla signed the university internship site agreement form, Sandy transitioned to working part time at her human resources job and started her internship at RL for 15 hours a week. She also had weekly group supervision on campus with her peers.

Sandy's faculty supervisor, Professor Saleh, an Arab American cisgender woman in her early 40s, had worked at the university for 10 years. Professor Saleh had had Sandy as a student in the diagnosis course and remembered that Sandy was relatively effective with concrete information but less comfortable with ambiguous situations. In group supervision, Sandy was positive about her experience and, unlike her peers, asserted her ease in adjusting to her site.

By the third week of group supervision, Sandy had not signed up to do a case presentation, nor had she talked about her cases, except for characterizing the client population as "dirty and smelly." She stated, "They'll never get a job without a bath!" When Professor Saleh followed up with her, Sandy had varying reasons for not discussing her cases or showing a session recording. She initially reported that she did not have any clients. Later she reported that Carla had the recordings and she "forgot to get them." When pressed again, Sandy stated that she did not like to be watched and felt too nervous to show a recording in group supervision. Professor Saleh found it worrisome that Sandy consistently left group supervision in a hurry before Professor Saleh had a chance to talk with her, and she had not turned in her weekly logs for countersigning.

In the fourth week, Professor Saleh asked Sandy to meet with her individually and to bring a set of recordings from her client sessions. Sandy came to the meeting and stated she did not have the recordings because Carla would not let them leave the agency. Professor Saleh offered to call Carla. She stated they could also watch them when she came for a site visit in a few weeks. Sandy displayed shock and agitation about the site visit and asked why she was being harassed. Professor Saleh was surprised and asked whether there was a problem with their supervisory relationship. She stated, "I get the sense you think I am singling you out. A midterm site visit, signed weekly logs, and a midterm evaluation are required for internship. Is this an issue between us or with the site and you? Would you like me to bring someone else in if you feel uncomfortable with me?"

Sandy hesitated and then disclosed she had not seen any clients and had only shadowed case management sessions. Professor Saleh responded, "I can call Carla and intervene. I'm here to help navigate concerns with sites." Sandy insisted she could manage the situation and was confident she would start seeing clients soon. Troubled, Professor Saleh consulted with Professor Creighton. He validated her concerns and advised her to contact Carla. He stated, "They knew each other prior to her internship. I remember Carla writing one of Sandy's recommendation letters for admission." Professor Saleh called Carla to schedule the site visit and check in. Carla asserted that there was no need for a site visit because she was happy with Sandy's work. Professor Saleh persisted, saying, "In the site agreement form you signed, it specified that Sandy's weekly logs countersigned by you, a site visit, and midterm and end-of-term evaluations were program requirements. Faculty are gatekeepers for the profession and verify to the state that Sandy has met the requirements for a limited license when she graduates." Carla stated that she would need to consult with her superiors at RL about this and abruptly hung up. Professor Saleh met with Professor Creighton again to discuss what had happened. Meanwhile, Sandy missed the next group supervision session and did not respond to Professor Saleh's email to check in about her absence.

Professor Creighton shared with Professor Saleh that the company that employed Sandy heavily funded RL. Deeply concerned, he and Professor Saleh scheduled an informal review with Sandy based on the program's student review policy. At the meeting, Sandy disclosed that she had arranged with Carla to do her internship at RL in return for promising funding to RL. She had not been working with clients and had no recordings. Carla was reluctant to jeopardize her own license by signing off on false hours and would not comply with the request. Sandy did not see what was wrong with this arrangement because no clients had been harmed, and she thought the internship requirement was irrelevant for her as she planned to be a coach, not a counselor. She stated, "All that stuff about helping is fine, but this is the real world. I might work for an employee assistance program but not with homeless losers! I can't believe Carla backed out. She will have a big problem when RL doesn't get the money!" Professors Creighton and Saleh stared at Sandy speechlessly, then at each other in dismay.

Case Analysis and Discussion

According to the *ACA Code of Ethics* (American Counseling Association [ACA], 2014), it is crucial that counselor education programs infuse ethical and professional development into every course (Standard F.7.e.). Given the humanistic focus of many counseling programs, educators often view student concerns as lack of understanding, impairment due to life stressors, co-occurring mental illness or substance abuse, or lack of academic preparedness or necessary skills rather than deception stemming from amoral or unethical stances (Pope et al., 2006). In this case, there are three predominant areas of concern related to the *ACA Code of Ethics*: (a) professional responsibility (Section C); (b) relationships with other professionals (Section D); and (c) supervision, training, and teaching (Section F). At the core of this case is (a) whether the counseling program did its due diligence in training Sandy to consider ethical concerns and monitoring her adherence to the ethical values of the profession, (b) whether Sandy's placement should have been approved, and (c) whether Sandy was appropriately monitored and supervised by Carla and Professor Saleh to ensure no harm came to clients.

As a social worker, Carla should follow the National Association of Social Workers (NASW) *Code of Ethics* (NASW, 2017). By agreeing to work with Sandy as an intern at RL and by signing the supervision contract without actually assigning her responsibilities, she encouraged unethical conduct (NASW, 2017). She also failed to evaluate Sandy based on the internship criteria (NASW, 2017, Standard 3.03). Regardless of whether the program had failed to outline Carla's responsibilities as a site supervisor (ACA, 2014, Standard F.7.i.), Carla signed the site agreement form, and that put her license in jeopardy. Although she may have thought she had a commitment to ensure continued funding for the agency and felt pressured to maintain it, she valued the interests of her employer over ethical practice (NASW, 2017, Standard 3.09). Though she refused to falsify documents by signing off on fabricated weekly logs, Carla did not uphold the integrity of the social work profession or its high standards of practice and ethics (NASW, 2017, Standard 5.01). If Professor Saleh had not pushed for a site visit and signed logs and reminded Carla about the professional ethics of gatekeeping, it is unclear whether Carla would have allowed Sandy to continue to deceive the program.

According to the *ACA Code of Ethics* (ACA, 2014), Professor Saleh was responsible for monitoring Sandy's internship, her performance and development, and the well-being of her clients (Standard F.1.a.). Faculty supervisors often must rely on the site supervisor in checking the accuracy of documentation, as their primary focus is on the professional development of the counselor-in-training. This gatekeeping function is essential for field supervisors (Center for Substance Abuse Treatment, 2009). Many beginning supervisees are reluctant to share recorded client sessions during supervision, a disinclination often shared by site supervisors who are understandably busy. However, Bahrick (1990) found that in a good supervisory working alliance, in which anxiety should be low, there is less of a chance that recording reluctance is linked to anxiety.

Given her previous positive relationship with Sandy, Professor Saleh had no reason to suspect Sandy was anxious about self-disclosure, a common issue with beginning interns who are anxious about sharing their performance with an unknown supervisor (Stoltenberg & McNeill, 2010). Professor Saleh assessed Sandy's lack of recordings as problematic and a sign that something was amiss at her site. As the on-campus supervisor, she could not oversee Sandy's work as closely as Carla could, and she seemed to have appropriately given Sandy time to get acclimated to her site. It was Professor Saleh's responsibility to inform Sandy of the internship requirements (ACA, 2014, Standard F.6.a.) and her professional and ethical responsibilities (Standard F.4.c.). She also needed to hold Sandy accountable and help her become aware of impairments and limitations that could impede her work as a counselor (ACA, 2014, Standard F.6.b.). Bernard and Goodyear (2019) described the supervisory relationship as one with temporary inequality between a beginning or junior member of the profession and a senior member, in which the senior individual reviews, monitors, and evaluates the professional functioning of the junior individual to enhance their development and serve as a gatekeeper for the profession in protecting client welfare. Professor Saleh also assessed the multicultural considerations in supervision (ACA, 2014, Standard F.2.b.), being aware of the possible effect of her visibly minoritized religious and ethnic identities on majority students and having the social management skills to work through their possible discomfort. Professor Saleh ascertained that the self of the supervisor was not the reason for Sandy's resistance to disclosure.

When Professor Saleh did not get a satisfactory response from Sandy, she consulted with Professor Creighton (ACA, 2014, Standards C.2.e., F.6.b.), a colleague with knowledge of the supervisee. As Sandy's faculty adviser, he had approved her placement and could have been remiss in not ascertaining the suitability of the site but rather just taking Sandy's word for it (ACA, 2014, Standard F.7.i.). However, in line with the 2016 Council for Accreditation of Counseling and Related Educational Programs (CACREP) Standards (CACREP, 2016), Carla was a qualified site supervisor (Section 3, Standard P) and RL met the criteria for an internship site (Section 3,

Standard J). Both Sandy and Carla signed the internship agreement (CACREP, 2016, Section 3, Standard R), so there were no concerns at that time.

There is some question about how Sandy got to internship without concerns having been identified earlier in the program, especially during practicum. Concerns over her academic work may not have become apparent, or there may have been limited opportunities for assessing students on their professional dispositions at earlier points in the program. If the latter is true, it is a failure to evaluate students on an ongoing basis, provide feedback, and if necessary address the inability of some students to achieve clinical, ethical, and/or professional competency by remediation or dismissal (ACA, 2014, Standard F.9.b.). It is apparent that Professors Creighton and Saleh took their responsibilities seriously enough to intervene. They followed due process as outlined in their student and program policies and met with Sandy before she continued for more than 5 weeks at the site (ACA, 2014, Standard F.6.b.).

Ethical violations become predictable when self-serving motivations are the cause of deviations from standard practice (Keith-Spiegel, 2014). Sandy's sense of being virtuous, given her ability to disburse company funds as donations to nonprofits, may have allowed her to justify her later dishonesty (Merritt et al., 2010). This self-serving unscrupulousness runs counter to the developmental approach that counselor educators often take to impairment, which implicitly assumes the possibility of remediation or rehabilitation. According to the *ACA Code of Ethics* (ACA, 2014, Section C, Introduction), counselors aim for authentic, clear, and truthful communication in their interactions with other professionals and the public. They promote access to counseling services for all while practicing with cultural competency and professionalism and without discrimination.

Students and supervisees have a responsibility to abide by the *ACA Code of Ethics* (ACA, 2014, Standard F.5.a.). In analyzing the concerns in this case, one issue is Sandy's entering a profession to which she had little commitment. D. F. Baker (2017) discussed the need to teach empathy and ethics in business, but these values are less rigorous than in counseling. This is exemplified by Sandy's lack of concern about getting Carla to give her an internship placement (ACA, 2014, Standard D.1.b.). Sandy appears to have exploited the agency's dependence on her company for her own personal gain (ACA, 2014, Standard C.6.d.). Carla did not provide supervisory oversight of Sandy's internship (ACA, 2014, Standard C.2.d.) and failed to describe her work or provide any documentation. Sandy also failed to uphold the professional and ethical responsibilities of her service to the agency and with Carla. Her comments at the informal review meeting indicate she may act vengefully against Carla for failing to cover her deception (ACA, 2014, Standard D.1.i.). Sandy appears to have progressed in the program without having examined her discriminatory attitudes toward the marginalized client populations of homeless and mentally ill persons (ACA, 2014, Standard A.4.b.). Her refusal to view their struggles with compassion reflects an imposition of values that will likely have harmful consequences for her future clients (ACA, 2014, Standard A.4.a.).

Actions and Outcomes

Following the informal review, Professors Creighton and Saleh recommended Sandy have a formal review meeting. Made aware of the seriousness of her actions, Sandy came to the meeting with much contrition. She reported feeling overwhelmed by working full time while also being a full-time graduate student. Her employer had denied her sabbatical and did not allow her to work part time. She believed the professors would not understand this because they did not know what it was like to work in the real world. She stated, "I'm going to get a 50% bonus at the end of the year for all the work I've done on layoffs. I can't quit now."

Once informed of her dismissal from the program, Sandy grieved the matter with the dean. She argued she should get some recompense for the academic credits she had paid for because she would not be eligible for licensure and she was experiencing emotional devastation from having been dismissed at the end of the program. Although the dean supported the program's decision, Sandy hired an attorney and the matter went to the provost. Eventually she was awarded a master's degree in independent studies after completing a thesis. Sandy faced no repercussions for her actions at work, and because the standards of practice in coaching are voluntary rather than a legal requirement, Sandy may decide to pursue her goal of becoming a coach (International Coaching Federation, 2015). Nevertheless, Professors Creighton and Saleh, along with other faculty, fulfilled their responsibility as gatekeepers for the counseling profession.

Conclusion

Avarice, greed, expediency, and a blindness to everything except what benefits the self can occur among mental health professionals (Koocher & Keith-Spiegel, 2016). Thus, gatekeeping is crucial. Effective supervision requires access to factual documentation rather than reliance on self-report (Milne, 2016). Self-report is dependent on supervisees' memory and perception, which are subjective. Monitoring client outcomes is also necessary in supervision (Swift et al., 2015). Furthermore, effective supervision includes encouraging autonomy and discussion (Ladany et al., 2012). According to Topor et al. (2018), reviewing session recordings allows supervisors to allay anxiety in their supervisees. Supervisors should be cautious about assigning motives too early or pathologizing supervisee resistance; however, they are responsible for holding supervisees accountable for discussing cases and showing session recordings so they can monitor supervisee development and ensure client welfare.

Reflection Questions

1. Would you have done anything differently had you been in Professor Creighton's or Professor Saleh's position? If so, what?
2. Should the faculty have intervened earlier in the program? If so, what action should have been taken?

Critical Incident Response

Gülşah Kemer

In Sandy's case, Professor Saleh addressed her gatekeeping responsibility as the faculty supervisor. Based on Sandy's defense in the formal hearing, her dismissal from the program appears to be the correct decision. Professor Saleh's work with Professor Creighton (the faculty adviser) and attempts to collaborate with Carla (the site supervisor) were also critical in this due process. Even though it is difficult to recognize when students intentionally attempt to deceive programs and faculty, it may be important to discuss certain systemic considerations of this case further, if it is possible to do so, to identify similar cases before they progress to the level Sandy's case did.

In this case, one main question was whether Sandy's perspectives and dispositions could have been assessed earlier in the program. I agree that counseling program faculty often recognize each student's unique pace in developing professional competencies. Therefore, the struggles of counseling students may not be so visible in their academic work, and faculty's concerns about students may not rise to the level of urgent action in the earlier stages of their program. In addition to focusing on each counselor trainee's unique developmental pace, it is important to understand how the program conducts student screening procedures and uses the recently integrated CACREP (2016) key performance indicators and key professional dispositions. Counseling program faculty may only be formally reviewing students who do poorly in their program. Sandy's case reminds us of the necessity of regular screening of all students for faculty to have an awareness of how each student is doing, in particular the ones they advise and teach.

The next area to consider is how aware Professor Creighton was of Sandy's performance and progress in the program. Professor Creighton was initially concerned that RL was known for providing more case management than counseling but still relied on Sandy's verbal assurance she would get the necessary counseling experience at this site. The counseling program does not appear to have a clinical coordinator who is responsible for practicum and internship site placements. Being responsible for approving Sandy's internship site, Professor Creighton may have considered different aspects of this placement prior to making his decision. First, it would have been critical to consider Sandy's clinical abilities based on her practicum performance when deciding whether RL would be a good fit for her strengths and growth areas. Second, Professor Creighton knew that the company Sandy worked for heavily funded RL but seemed to underestimate this potential conflict of interest. In addition, Sandy's background in business (a well-defined discipline), the fact that RL offered more case management than counseling, and the fact that Carla was from a professional background other than counseling could all have been important informants of Professor Creighton's approval of the site. RL's service activities and Carla's professional background may be a good match for Sandy's preference for concrete work, but could her professional experiences at RL stretch her understanding of multiple perspectives? Yet it is also debatable how much these areas were exclusively Professor Creighton's responsibility as a faculty adviser. Ultimately, the counseling program was responsible for assigning interns who were competent enough to serve vulnerable populations at sites like RL.

Sandy's case also may point to potential concerns about communication between faculty and supervisors working with counselor trainees in the program. From her diagnosis course, Professor Saleh was aware of the salience of Sandy's concrete developmental orientation over formal and dialectical orientations as a counselor trainee (Rigazio-DiGilio et al., 1997), which could have created challenges to Sandy working with diverse clients (e.g., homeless individuals). However, it is not clear whether Sandy's practicum supervisor(s) had access to this information to inform their supervision with her or whether Sandy's practicum performance informed Professor Saleh's internship supervision. In addition to evaluation, Professor Saleh may have focused on certain best practices in clinical supervision to create continuation from previous semesters (Borders et al., 2014). For example, she may have worked with Sandy to develop goals based on the characteristics of her placement site and clients as well as received feedback from previous and current supervisors. Similarly, when Sandy appeared inconsistent in her reasoning about not completing supervision expectations and made judgmental comments about her clients in supervision, and because Carla was not responsive, Professor Saleh may have considered contacting the practicum supervisor(s) or reviewing her practicum evaluations to support her conceptualization of Sandy. Finally, Professor Saleh may also have used Sandy's judgmental comments as opportunities to engage supervisees in offering peer feedback in group supervision to observe Sandy's responsiveness and increase awareness of diversity and advocacy considerations in counseling and supervision practices.

In conclusion, because she engaged in unethical behavior during her internship, Sandy was removed from her program. Although Professor Saleh acted promptly and accurately in terms of her gatekeeping responsibility, her integration of best practices in the first 5 weeks of supervision is not clear. In addition, the counseling program faculty as a whole were just as responsible as Sandy's immediate supervisors for screening her (and other counselor trainees') performance throughout the program to facilitate professional development and ensure client welfare. Therefore, in the future, counseling faculty in this program may review and consider using the programmatic procedures discussed here to attend to similar cases earlier than they did in this case.

• • •

Section 2
Issues With Site Supervisors

Chapter 18

I'm Getting Different Messages: Incongruence Between Supervisors

Joel F. Diambra

2014 *ACA Code of Ethics* Standards Addressed

- A.1.a. Primary Responsibility
- A.1.b. Records and Documentation
- A.1.c. Counseling Plans
- A.4.b. Personal Values
- C.2.e. Consultations on Ethical Obligations
- D.1.a. Different Approaches
- F.1.a. Client Welfare
- F.2.a. Supervisor Preparation
- F.2.b. Multicultural Issues/Diversity in Supervision
- F.4.a. Informed Consent for Supervision
- F.5.a. Ethical Responsibilities
- F.7.a. Counselor Educators
- F.7.i. Field Placements
- F.9.a. Evaluation of Students
- F.11.c. Multicultural/Diversity Competence

• • •

Blanca was a 52-year-old female university supervisor who identified as Hispanic. She had her doctorate and was a licensed professional counselor. Paul was a new agency program director who was licensed as a drug and alcohol counselor. He identified as a 31-year-old white male and considered himself to be in lifelong recovery. Blanca had a long-standing professional connection with Justin, the site supervisor, who identified as a 46-year-old Black male. He had his licensed drug and alcohol counselor and licensed professional counselor credentials and was not in recovery. Leslee was an internship student who identified as a 25-year-old white lesbian female.

The counseling program had a 6-year history of placing students at Waxturn County Drug and Alcohol Recovery Program (WCDARP). Within the past 3 months, WCDARP had hired Paul. Blanca conducted an orientation with Paul within his first month. She informed Paul that all agency personnel providing site supervision had to meet licensure requirements, and she gave him a university form to collect these data. She also shared that Justin had to complete an online supervision training, provided by the university, within the next 2 weeks. Blanca reviewed the internship requirements and provided Paul with a handbook with all required documents.

Shortly after orientation, Blanca learned that Paul was providing supervision to Leslee following meetings with Justin and without consulting him. This had resulted in Leslee receiving conflicting expectations, information, and treatment suggestions and modalities. Paul had also neglected to submit his credentials and complete the online training. In addition, he demanded Leslee work full time through the semester and holiday breaks, as expected of any full-time employee, regardless of whether a continuity plan was developed and agreed on by WCDARP and Blanca. When communicating with Blanca through email, Paul excluded Justin and Leslee. Paul's increased level of direct supervision, hourly demands, and incommodious communication patterns created confusion for Leslee, Justin, and Blanca. Despite Blanca's attempts to clarify expectations through a string of detailed group emails, each of these issues remained unresolved.

Case Analysis and Discussion

The priority here is to ensure Leslee has a quality internship experience. This experience should provide maximum opportunity for growth and development as a counselor through experiences with adequate supervision. There are three key issues: (a) ensuring intern wellness and safety in the face of conflicting supervision and demands to work through semester and holiday breaks without obtaining a continuity agreement, (b) obtaining required written agreements and credential documentation, and (c) facilitating communication regarding expectations.

Culture, values, and diversity are also important supervision issues. Garrett et al. (2001) encouraged supervisors to be attentive and responsive while appreciating opportunities that arise to address diversity. Gatmon et al. (2011) recommended supervisors consider cultural variables (e.g., ethnicity, gender, sexual orientation). In addition, Luke et al. (2013a) infused action steps with attention to culture into the ethical decision-making process. Toporek et al. (2011) also encouraged supervisors to consider diversity, values, and cultural issues as they relate to counseling. Along with cultural considerations, Forester-Miller and Davis's (2016) seven-step ethical decision-making model is used to guide the discussion of this case.

Step 1: Identify the Problem

Forester-Miller and Davis (2016) identified three actions in this initial step of the model: (a) identify facts and distinguish them from conjecture; (b) determine the spotlight of the problem, prioritizing ethical, legal, professional, or clinical foci; and (c) secure legal input when needed. Blanca realizes all involved are making assumptions and may be experiencing a clash of cultures: different roles and values (e.g., power, minority vs. majority identities) and contrasting work environments and expectations (i.e., a counseling agency vs. academia). Leslee is likely confused and wondering whether the feedback from Paul or Justin is more important and accurate. She may suspect Paul does not believe she is adequately skilled given his harsh criticism in supervision. Although it has not been discussed much, she is comfortable with her sexual identity and knows it is common knowledge. She wonders whether her sexual identity is bothersome to Paul and a reason for his behavior. Justin may hypothesize that Paul does not trust his supervision style or ability. He has not communicated with Paul about this concern. He believes their tension is based on interpersonal style and workplace adjustment, and he wonders whether his race and experience are troublesome or threatening to Paul.

Along with these individual differences, the cultures of WCDARP and the university are different. WCDARP is a for-profit business with an emphasis on generating billable hours, and their busiest periods typically coincide with the university's breaks. In contrast, the university believes quality education is paramount and breaks are important for student wellness. Blanca realizes Paul is doing his best to acclimate to a new setting, is overwhelmed consuming new information and implementing new policies, and has not had the time to complete the required documentation. She wonders whether her orientation may have been ill timed given his recent arrival.

Step 2: Apply the *ACA Code of Ethics*

There do not appear to be any breaches of state law in this case; however, there are relevant *ACA Code of Ethics* (American Counseling Association [ACA], 2014) standards. A counselor's primary objective is to ensure dignity and promote client welfare (Standard A.1.a.). Because Leslee is feeling unsettled and receiving contradictory supervision, it is wise to check on her dignity and welfare and that of her clients during university supervision. In addition, counselors maintain the documentation necessary to provide professional services (Standard A.1.b.). This prompts Blanca to consider Paul's missing documentation and how this is a poor example for Leslee.

Section C of the *ACA Code of Ethics* (ACA, 2014) emphasizes counselors having open and honest communication with professionals and the public. This implies the importance of conversations about cultural context. Given their power differential and different interpersonal styles, if Leslee communicates directly with Paul regarding her concerns she could put her internship at risk. Paul may think Leslee is manipulating the situation (e.g., trying to avoid internship during semester breaks). This could escalate and lead to Paul treating Leslee disrespectfully or terminating her internship. As a precaution, Leslee should consult with others regarding her ethical obligations (Standard C.2.e.). She wisely seeks consultation from Justin and Blanca. Justin refers her to Blanca, and Blanca indicates she will contact Paul. Client welfare takes precedent, and Leslee is also responsible in part for sifting through multiple perspectives, clarifying roles and obligations, and resolving inconsistencies to provide the best client services. Blanca has a corresponding responsibility to ensure client and supervisee welfare and safety. In addition, Section D of the *ACA Code of Ethics* focuses on professional relationships. Leslee and Blanca should be respectful of the different theoretically and empirically based approaches offered in separate supervision sessions (Standard D.1.a.).

Section F of the *ACA Code of Ethics* (ACA, 2014) prompts Blanca to ensure client and supervisee welfare (Standard F.1.a.). Conflicting supervision has diminished Leslee's self-confidence, affecting her work with clients. Leslee's professional growth and development are being stymied because of conflicting input; therefore, Blanca has an obligation to step in and address the situation. Blanca must also ensure that Paul is qualified to provide supervision and that he provides his credentials (Standard F.2.a.). Blanca can also ask Paul to provide Leslee with informed consent, policies, and procedures related to supervision (Standard F.4.a.). Finally, supervisees are responsible for knowing and following the *ACA Code of Ethics* (Standard F.5.a.). This suggests Leslee shares in the responsibility for resolving this situation. Counselor educators act ethically, serve as role models, develop and enforce policies, and provide assistance with field experiences (Standards F.7.a., F.7.i.). Blanca is obligated to ensure internship supervisors are properly credentialed and to inform Justin (and Paul) of their obligations related to their roles (i.e., providing proof of qualifications, completing internship documents; Standard F.7.i.). Thus, the ethical standards provide direction for Blanca and the other stakeholders.

Step 3: Determine the Nature and Dimensions of the Dilemma

Blanca considers four foundational principles of professional ethical behavior (autonomy, justice, beneficence, and nonmaleficence) and Kitchener's (1984) fifth principle (fidelity). Although autonomy is important, Paul has verbally agreed to enter into this internship relationship with all parties. Justice is a factor in whether Leslee should be treated differently than other students. Beneficence involves Leslee's responsibility to sustain client welfare and to do good. Given Paul has made no formal or serious complaints regarding Leslee's performance, her continuing to provide services to clients would contribute to their betterment and likely not cause harm. Nonmaleficence, or the principle to do no harm, ensures Blanca resists acting in a manner that could cause clients harm. Neglecting the situation in the hope that it will all work out could cause harm to clients and Leslee. In contrast, demanding Paul be in immediate compliance (i.e., by providing proof of credentials and signing required documents) could incite malice. Blanca could first review the expectations shared in the initial orientation meeting, ensure all parties have a mutual understanding, and offer an action plan. Fidelity involves honoring commitments. Leslee has committed to providing a therapeutic relationship for her clients. Paul has verbally committed to providing an internship site and ongoing supervision to Leslee. Fulfilling these obligations is paramount.

Step 4: Generate Potential Courses of Action

Two extreme considerations are terminating or continuing the internship at WCDARP. Terminating the internship would have dire consequences and likely violate ethics codes and ethical principles. Continuing the internship would mean accomplishing several tasks: (a) obtaining Paul's credentials and qualifications, (b) getting documents signed, and (c) discussing site supervision delivery and related diversity and cross-cultural variables.

Blanca considers two options to secure Paul's qualifications. She can locate his state licensure and supervision status on verification websites or a copy of his résumé online, or she can request these documents from Paul again. Regarding documentation, Blanca may (a) not require signed documents, (b) require Paul's signature, or (c) ask him to allow Justin to sign the documents. Options for site supervision include (a) both Paul and Justin, (b) Paul only, and (c) Justin only. Regarding cultural considerations, Blanca identifies she could either have or avoid the conversation. As a final action, Blanca shares her plan with another colleague who teaches the course on ethics and professional orientation. They agree that she has considered all options.

Step 5: Consider Potential Consequences

This step requires dismissing options that lead to undesired outcomes or problematic consequences and considering options that have the best chance of accomplishing identified priorities. In this case, terminating the internship would be premature and unsuitable because it would prevent the addressing of miscommunication and likely create tension for remaining interns. It would also require Leslee to secure another internship site and mean abandoning clients, disrupting services, and increasing the counselor-to-client ratio for counselors at WCDARP.

Three options remain for continuing the internship. Blanca could search for Paul's credentials online, which may be successful. She could ask him again, which may invoke appreciation, lead to a neutral reaction, or increase tension and result in all, partial, or no proof of qualifications. The manner used to request the information may determine the outcome. Requiring no signed documentation would not be an ethical option. Having a meeting at the site with Paul and Justin may be effective for obtaining Paul's signature or his agreement to allow Justin to sign.

Blanca believes continued supervision by both Paul and Justin will likely continue to cause confusion and stress for Leslee. Although she does not rule it out, she knows that for efficiency and clarity most sites have one direct supervisor who also has direct contact with clients. Finally, regarding diversity, she recognizes there is something attractive about not hashing out differences but knows that neglecting them is not ethical or helpful because it means the related problems and challenges will continue. Postponing the conversation models neglect to Leslee and the agency staff. Having dialogue will clarify perspectives, allow for empathy across all parties, and model healthy communication.

Step 6: Evaluate the Selected Course of Action

Next Blanca needs to evaluate her plan by considering three litmus tests identified by Stadler (1986): justice, publicity, and universality. Justice suggests a person will treat others in the same manner they would like to be treated. Blanca identifies that she would treat Paul respectfully by considering he might be feeling overwhelmed and communicating with him again to reiterate the information. She reflects on reversing roles and feels comfortable knowing someone would give her a second chance by reviewing the process, expectations, timelines, and requirements. Publicity helps provide an outside, public perspective and creates a check and balance should others judge the course of action. Blanca has eliminated strategies that might be viewed as harsh or spiteful. Although her plan may be perceived as directive or manipulative, she is confident it has the best likelihood of resulting in clarification for all parties and ensuring the welfare of Leslee and her clients. Universality is the notion that Blanca would recommend the same course of action to a peer. Given the rationale she identifies when reviewing for justice and publicity, Blanca determines she would suggest the same plan to a colleague.

Step 7: Implement the Course of Action

Blanca supports continuing the internship by devoting 2 hours to seeking Paul's qualifications online and contacts Paul and Justin to request a meeting. In the email, she informs Paul that most sites have one direct site supervisor, and she provides an agenda for the meeting that includes (a) credentials (i.e., what she does not find online), (b) signatures, (c) assigned site supervisor, and (d) the influences of diversity and culture on the internship experience. In the meeting, Paul provides proof of his credentials and apologizes for not doing so sooner. He reports he misunderstood the expectations, thinking the university expected Leslee to receive supervision by an administrator and a counselor. Justin indicates that Paul assigned him to supervise Leslee and that Paul would oversee his work. Paul then asks for clarity about Leslee continuing at the site between semesters. Blanca explains that the Council for Accreditation of Counseling and Related Educational Programs requires ongoing university oversight and supervision during breaks and the university requires a continuity agreement. Paul expresses his hope for Leslee to continue at a reduced schedule during breaks if university supervision is available.

Blanca comments that Paul's request for clarification of the different work culture expectations (i.e., academic vs. agency) is thoughtful and culturally astute. She suggests that other cultural considerations be explored (i.e., professional disciplines, personal values and identities). She starts by sharing a personal story about being a Hispanic woman in the counseling field. This leads to a group discussion in which Blanca prompts each person to share positive and challenging experiences, and then she shifts the discussion to focus on the ups and downs experienced in internship. Although the tone of the conversation becomes more somber, they share relevant examples, some uncomfortable. Blanca facilitates the conversation so false assumptions are addressed and clarified and apologies are offered and accepted. The team resolves to consider cultural variables in future supervision and counseling at WCDARP.

Blanca sends a follow-up email to the team requesting input regarding the current supervision process and suggestions for improving future internship orientation efforts. Blanca closely monitors Leslee's weekly counseling tapes, assessing for client care, safety, and welfare. She also checks in with Leslee each week during class, specifically assessing supervision quality and tension related to culture or values to ensure Leslee's safety and well-being. Furthermore, Blanca reviews Justin's evaluations of Leslee and her site evaluation.

Conclusion

Establishing and sustaining effective communication across university and agency settings is challenging and time consuming, especially when various helping professionals and diverse personal perspectives and identities are involved. However, effective communication is crucial to helping ensure a positive internship experience for students. The *ACA Code of Ethics* (ACA, 2014) and ethical decision-making models can assist with this process.

Reflection Questions

1. What additional steps could Blanca take to ensure Leslee's safety and wellness?
2. If you were Blanca, would you have addressed this situation differently? If so, how?

Critical Incident Response

Heather J. Ambrose

Misunderstandings can occur between universities and training sites. If left unattended to, they can cause harm to internship students, clients, and the relationship between the university and the training site. To ensure a quality internship experience, clear communication of expectations and requirements is paramount.

There could be cultural differences among Paul, Justin, and Leslee as well as between the agency and the university. The *ACA Code of Ethics* (ACA, 2014) states the importance of supervisors being aware of potential multicultural issues and diversity in supervisory relationships (Standard F.2.b.). Blanca needs to examine the possible cultural issues that might be interfering with communication among Paul, Justin, and Leslee and between Paul and Blanca. Understanding these communication issues will help Blanca determine how to address them using cultural humility (S. Shaw, 2016). Cultural issues potentially affecting the work environment at WCDARP include ethnicity, race, gender identity, and sexual orientation. It is not known whether Paul has training in creating and supporting a culturally diverse workplace. Hiemstra et al. (2017) examined psychological predictors of support for cultural diversity at work and found that diversity-related behaviors among employees are influenced by people in positions of power. If Paul is not demonstrating cultural competence and cultural humility with his employees, it is likely his employees are not demonstrating these skills with him and one another. Although it is possible that Justin and Leslee would like to promote cultural diversity at the agency, they may feel inhibited because of a lack of social norms created by Paul to reflect cultural diversity.

There is also a potential cultural difference between the agency and the university. Whereas the university may expect adherence to and compliance with policies and procedures because of accreditation standards, the agency may not have firm guidelines. Paul is also new to the role of program director; thus, he is likely learning the agency's functioning and culture. Blanca and Paul may also need to establish trust with each other. Getting off on the right foot entails being open to influence from culturally dissimilar partners (Saef et al., 2019). In addition, it is important for Blanca and Paul to understand the expectations and requirements of each entity.

The *ACA Code of Ethics* (ACA, 2014) outlines the importance of counselors and clients developing counseling plans together that offer a "reasonable promise of success" (Standard A.1.c.). The conflicting messages from Paul and Justin regarding client treatment might also make it difficult for Leslee to create treatment plans. Another potential ethical issue involves Leslee's internship evaluation. The *Code* states counselor educators should clearly communicate students' expected clinical competencies (Standard F.9.a.). However, because of the mixed messages she is receiving from Paul and Justin regarding her clinical abilities, and from Paul regarding work expectations, Leslee could be experiencing dissonance around expectations for her. Leslee might also be afraid to express her concerns because, as a student intern, she does not have much power. Supervisory relationships are inherently hierarchical because of their evaluative nature (Bernard & Goodyear, 2019). It will be important for Blanca to reinforce with Paul and Justin the clinical skills Leslee is expected to demonstrate. Finally, the *Code* states counselor educators continually discuss and demonstrate multicultural and diversity competence in supervision (Standard F.11.c.). Not only will it be imperative for Blanca to have discussions with Leslee regarding the diversity of her clients, but it will be important for Blanca to discuss diversity issues affecting Leslee's supervisory relationships with Justin, Paul, and Leslee herself. This will promote Leslee's development of multicultural competency.

Another concern is whether Leslee is being treated differently than other interns. Leslee has stated her sexual orientation is not a secret. A question is whether Paul is discriminating against Leslee based on her sexual orientation. If Leslee is being treated differently, Blanca is responsible for discussing this with Paul. It might also be necessary to explore Blanca's concern regarding potential violation of the *ACA Code of Ethics* (ACA, 2014), which states counselors are aware of their own values and avoid imposing them on and discriminating against others (Standard A.4.b.). Although this standard applies to client welfare, it could also apply to the supervisory relationship. Counselor educators must model ethical decision-making for their students, which involves upholding the principle of nonmaleficence. It is hoped that if the ethics code and the mandate of doing no harm are addressed, Leslee will receive equal treatment, which relates to the principle of justice (Remley & Herlihy, 2020).

Communication is key in resolving misunderstanding. It is important to use an ethical decision-making model and the *ACA Code of Ethics* (ACA, 2014) to address discrepancies between supervisors. As counselor educators and supervisors, we must work for the betterment of students and their clients.

• • •

Chapter 19

The Other Side: A Supervisor Presenting Differently to Students

Derrick A. Paladino and Leigh D. DeLorenzi

2014 *ACA Code of Ethics* Standards Addressed

- F.1.a. Client Welfare
- F.2.b. Multicultural Issues/Diversity in Supervision
- F.7.i. Field Placements

• • •

Fatima was a 31-year-old, third-year counseling student in internship. She was an international student from Lebanon and had worked as a nurse in her native country before coming to the United States. She believed her prior work experience in health care made her a good fit for an internship at an inpatient psychiatric hospital. The site supervisor, Matt, was 44 years old and a graduate of Fatima's counseling program. He had maintained a positive working alliance with the program faculty for more than 15 years. The site had a reputation as both challenging and rewarding. In written evaluations of the site, previous internship students had described such strengths as "ample client contact" and "great exposure to complex client presentations" and such weaknesses as "unstructured (sometimes chaotic) atmosphere" and "staff shortages."

Early in the internship semester, the faculty supervisor, Professor Rowan Gabe, made a site visit to review the internship policies and discuss early impressions of Fatima. Matt reported Fatima worked hard, was comfortable working with challenging clients, and was the last to leave each day.

One month after starting her internship, Fatima was noticeably withdrawn during group supervision class (e.g., keeping to herself, not sharing about her site experience). Her peers noticed the shift in her demeanor and checked in with her. Fatima stated, "I'm feeling exhausted; I have been working long hours at my site without breaks. Everyone is overwhelmed because of the staffing shortages. The fatigue is catching up to me. Last night I fell asleep in my car at a stoplight. I don't know what to do. I don't want to complain to my site supervisor because I don't want him to think I'm unprofessional or I can't do my job. I'll do my best to push forward."

Fatima's peers and Professor Gabe discussed their concerns that she was not taking breaks for her basic needs, agreed it was unsustainable, and outlined the various threats to her personal safety and client welfare if unaddressed. Fatima was coached on solutions that involved open, professional communication with her site supervisor to ask for appropriately scheduled breaks to meet her basic needs. The following day, Fatima emailed Professor Gabe to report the discussion with Matt had gone well and she felt relieved she had asked for help.

Two weeks later, Fatima called Professor Gabe in tears. She stated, "A few minutes ago, Matt screamed at me. I felt extremely intimidated and embarrassed by his words and behavior as people in the hallway heard it. He accused me of missing sessions with my clients. I was taking my agreed-on 45-minute lunch break. I tried to remind him of our conversation, but he then accused me of taking advantage of my colleagues and neglecting my responsibilities." She further disclosed, "I was afraid to tell you that Matt has not been at the site in almost 10 days and I have not received weekly supervision since I started my practicum." Professor Gabe inquired why Fatima had felt afraid to share this, and she reported, "Matt is so intimidating; I thought he would retaliate against me if he knew I told you. He brags about getting people fired who make him angry. He told me I was a 'broke, clueless intern that didn't know anything.'"

Professor Gabe called an emergency meeting with Fatima and the faculty placement coordinator to discuss a course of action. After discussing options, Fatima expressed an interest in talking to Matt, in the presence of a colleague witness, about how the encounter had made her feel threatened. Professor Gabe suggested he attend the meeting with her. Fatima responded that she did not want faculty to intervene yet because she was convinced Matt would retaliate not only against her but against her colleagues as well, as she had seen this occur in the past.

Case Analysis and Discussion

When examining this case study, it is vital to explore key issues and potential responses through multicultural, sociocultural, historical, and ecological lenses. Any supervisor would be remiss not to consider Fatima's gender, racial and ethnic background, and culture while examining her experience and the potential response by the counseling program. For example, the historical oppression of women (i.e., Fatima's male supervisor) and the current U.S. rhetoric around international students (i.e., what happens to her student visa status if she does not complete her internship and graduate on time) might affect Fatima's perception of her ability and willingness to advocate for herself. A supervisor using the multicultural orientation model (Owen et al., 2011) may elicit meaningful conversations with greater awareness on both sides of the supervisory relationship. This model allows supervisors and counselors to connect with supervisees and clients, respectively, through three interconnected areas: cultural humility, cultural opportunity, and cultural comfort (Owen, 2013; Owen et al., 2011). In addition, Ancis and Marshall (2010) found that when supervisors introduced conversations on cultural influence into the supervisory relationship their openness, acceptance, and flexibility had a positive effect on both the supervisory relationship and clinical relationships.

The *ACA Code of Ethics* (American Counseling Association [ACA], 2014) requires supervisors to address multicultural considerations in supervision (Standard F.2.b.). Though multicultural concerns were not explicitly identified in this case, all site and faculty supervisors who hold privilege or majority status (i.e., are male, white, straight, Christian, of a higher socioeconomic status, able bodied) should have an understanding of how they may be viewed as representatives of societal oppressors or of the power they innately hold as a result of one or more of their identities. This extends beyond the power associated with having supervisor status. For example, Fatima stated she avoided drawing attention to her missed weekly site supervision sessions because she feared Matt would somehow retaliate against her or her peers. If Fatima's behavior is examined through a sociocultural lens, it can be understood as a power differential reaction to her supervisor lashing out. This is concerning because tension in the supervisory relationship can lead to greater avoidance of help seeking when supervisees experience complicated client matters, which poses a threat to client welfare (Grant et al., 2012; Kozlowska et al., 1997; Ladany et al., 1997).

It is also important to consider the contractual language of the clinical site placement agreement. Clinical site placement agreements provide detailed expectations for students, faculty, site supervisors, and the clinical site. Having a contract that outlines the role and responsibilities of all parties aligns with the *ACA Code of Ethics* (ACA, 2014, Standard F.7.i.). In this case, when Matt signed the agreement, he acknowledged understanding his responsibilities, which included immediately informing the faculty supervisor about concerns regarding students. However, Matt did not communicate with Professor Gabe once concerns arose regarding Fatima's performance. Because Matt informed Fatima about her poor performance, he also would be expected to contact Professor Gabe. Honest and consistent communication between site and faculty supervisors is important for promoting a positive experience for all stakeholders. Furthermore, Matt's failure to abide by the signed placement agreement to provide weekly supervision to Fatima was also a threat to client safety and welfare (ACA, 2014, Standard F.1.a.).

Matt's interpersonal behavior is another area of concern, as it was unprofessional and caused Fatima to feel threatened and embarrassed. Scholars describe characteristics of problematic supervision as unprofessional confrontation, criticism, blaming, confusing supervisor agendas, and instructive rather than interactive learning processes (Grant et al., 2012; Ladany, 2004; Ratliff et al., 2000). This type of supervisory working alliance has the potential to negatively affect a supervisee's clinical self-efficacy, with the development of perceived credibility of the supervisor and lack of faith in the supervisee (Morrison & Lent, 2018). In addition, it violates the *ACA Code of Ethics* (ACA, 2014), which requires supervisors to have respectful and meaningful relationships with supervisees (Section F). Although the supervisory relationship is intended to enhance safety and support for counseling trainees and their clients, researchers have found some supervisees report experiencing harm in supervision (Ellis, 2006; Grant et al., 2012; Ramos-Sánchez et al., 2002). Bad or harmful supervision equates to a betrayal of trust (Wong et al., 2013). In contrast, effective supervision develops from a trusting, safe, egalitarian relationship in which a supervisee can receive timely and constructive feedback (Degges et al., 2013).

Actions and Outcomes

In developing a course of action, the program faculty should create, gather, and maintain documentation regarding Fatima's experiences at the site. It is important to consider multiple perspectives prior to making decisions about how to proceed. The faculty should also discuss the issue as a unit to explore various perspectives and courses of action. Professor Gabe, Fatima, and the clinical placement coordinator may also begin exploring alternative placement sites. However, switching placements in the middle of the semester is not always a seamless process, and the transition could create costly delays for Fatima (e.g., falling behind in required clinical hours).

In exploring possible options, the program may decide to confront the site supervisor and consider removing Fatima from the site. Having a formal meeting with Matt provides him with information about the concerns and gives him an opportunity to discuss his perspective on them. Faculty should acknowledge concerns related to the placement contract as well as the *ACA Code of Ethics* (ACA, 2014). Following the meeting, faculty may decide to allow Fatima to continue at the site, if they are comfortable doing so, while warning Matt that continued reports of such behavior will result in Fatima being removed and reassigned. Another option is to honor Fatima's request not to intervene until she receives a new placement, at which time the faculty can pull Fatima from the site, ensuring she has enough time to terminate with her clients. Faculty can then, if deemed appropriate, choose to remove this site as an option for future practicum and internship students. If they elect this option, they should send a formal letter of concern describing student and faculty concerns to Matt, along with the related ethical concerns and reports of concerning interpersonal professional conduct with supervisees. A final option is to allow Fatima to stay at her site until she completes the internship. If this is the ultimate decision, faculty may consider scheduling more frequent site visits as check-ins. During these meetings, Professor Gabe can inquire about weekly supervision sessions. He can also reference logs that report Fatima's weekly supervision hours as well as remind Matt that weekly individual supervision is a requirement specified in the site placement contract. This method of intervening, although more indirect, can communicate to the site supervisor that the faculty are monitoring student progress closely, which may deter him from missing weekly supervision sessions in the future. After Fatima completes her training at the site, the faculty should still provide Matt with a formal letter of concern referencing the site evaluations and listing ethical concerns. The faculty can then decide whether to continue to place students at the site.

To reach an outcome, the faculty supervisor, Professor Gabe, and the clinical placement coordinator first consulted with their department's core faculty during a faculty meeting to discuss possible options. All faculty agreed that each student at this site should be asked for their perspective and experiences of the site and site supervisor. Professor Gabe and the clinical coordinator met separately with the three students who had been placed at the site, and all expressed concern regarding the power and control dynamics there. The students also agreed that individual supervision was not happening, which was a breach of the clinical site placement agreement.

Professor Gabe then scheduled a site visit. On arriving at the site, he observed Matt speaking unprofessionally to an intern when he told her to "shut the door and try not to screw everything up." In their meeting, Professor Gabe began by asking Matt how he thought things were going. Next Professor Gabe discussed the concerns of the faculty, including the argument reported by Fatima, the lack of supervision, and Matt's unprofessional tone with the interns. Matt listened intently and verbally acknowledged that he knew things needed improvement and that his "stress from being understaffed" was contributing to his short temper. They agreed on an action plan that involved consistent supervision of the interns and weekly check-ins with Professor Gabe. Finally, Professor Gabe reminded Matt that site evaluations were reviewed at the end of each placement and any future intern placement at the site would be contingent on whether he met the agreed-on expectations listed in the placement agreement.

Subsequently, the interns (including Fatima) reported supervision was proceeding regularly as required per the clinical site agreement. In addition, Matt apologized verbally to them for his unprofessional tone. Yet despite these improvements, the site evaluations were overwhelmingly negative, and the department's core faculty unanimously decided not to send students to the site during the next round of intern placements.

Conclusion

The case of Fatima focuses on a deteriorating supervisory relationship and its effects on an intern. As a result of Matt's unprofessional behavior and disregard of the site agreement, Fatima experienced fear, intimidation, exhaustion, and powerlessness. Supporting Fatima and understanding any sociocultural influence is paramount, as is ensuring the site is an appropriate environment for Fatima to continue to see clients. Finally, it is vital to understand the full scope of this issue prior to making any formal response. Faculty supervisors are strongly encouraged to consult; consider ethical standards and gatekeeping guidelines; and review all agreements between the site, student intern, and counseling program during this process.

Reflection Questions

1. What multicultural and social justice issues are relevant in this case?
2. If you were Professor Gabe, would you have responded differently? If so, how?

Critical Incident Response

David Julius Ford Jr.

In the case analysis, the authors discussed the importance of considering culture in the supervisory relationship. Cultural broaching is an aspect of addressing culture that needs further attention in this case. Broaching culture in the supervisory relationship facilitates growth in cultural responsiveness in the supervisor and supervisee, enhances client care, and strengthens the supervisory relationship (K. M. King & Jones, 2018). It is an appropriate intervention for Matt to use with Fatima and other supervisees to strengthen the supervisory relationship and model broaching behavior for supervisees to use with clients. Supervisors can use cultural broaching to acknowledge the relevance of cultural identities and invite supervisees to dialogue (Jones et al., 2019). Fatima was afraid to address her concerns with Matt. If Matt had broached culture at the beginning of and throughout the supervisory relationship, Fatima may have been empowered to be more open in communicating with him.

The Multicultural and Social Justice Counseling Competencies (Ratts et al., 2016) provide a foundation to integrate culturally responsive counseling into clinical supervision (Fickling et al., 2019). Matt needs to be aware of his own culture, biases, and judgments as well as how they may affect his relationship with Fatima. He also needs to broach a conversation with Fatima about her cultural identity and worldview. Doing so would help Matt understand her worldview and the influence it has on the supervisory relationship. It would also enable Matt to be more attuned to his and Fatima's cultural identities and how they influence supervision and to provide culturally responsive supervision.

Matt also needs to address his burnout. He admits to being overworked because the site is short staffed, and this has led to him lashing out and not providing adequate supervision for Fatima. The *ACA Code of Ethics* (ACA, 2014) addresses counselor impairment and the importance of self-care (Section C, Introduction). Matt's burnout has led to him being an impaired supervisor in that he is not providing Fatima with proper supervision and is speaking to the supervisees in an unprofessional tone. Matt's supervisors would need to provide him with a professional development plan that includes self-care. He could also model the importance of self-care for Fatima.

Per the 2016 Council for Accreditation of Counseling and Related Educational Programs (CACREP) Standards (CACREP, 2016), counseling program faculty should provide orientation, consultation, and professional development opportunities for site supervisors. This orientation strengthens the relationship between program faculty and site supervisors and facilitates ongoing communication. Fatima's program faculty should provide training related to culturally responsive supervision using cultural broaching, the Multicultural and Social Justice Counseling Competencies, and the multicultural orientation model as a framework. Another aspect of professional development is promoting self-care among site supervisors.

Fatima might feel uncomfortable continuing to receive supervision from Matt, and yet the program faculty did not ask her thoughts and feelings about this before deciding to have him remain as her supervisor. The program faculty could have consulted with Fatima and given her options about continuing at the site or moving to another site to continue her field placement. This conversation would have empowered her as a supervisee and respected her autonomy. She may feel powerless in her relationship with Matt, and the actions of the faculty reinforced her lack of power. Her feeling of powerlessness is concerning because it may negatively affect her continued work with Matt as a supervisor and her work with clients. Thus, this case emphasizes the importance of the supervisory relationship; cultural broaching; self-care; and communication between the counseling program, site supervisor, and student supervisees.

• • •

Chapter 20

To Tell or Not to Tell: Site Supervisor Impairment

Heather J. Ambrose

2014 *ACA Code of Ethics* Standards Addressed

- A.4.a. Avoiding Harm
- C.2.d. Monitor Effectiveness
- C.2.g. Impairment
- F.1.a. Client Welfare
- F.3.a. Extending Conventional Supervisory Relationships

• • •

Professor Jones, a 46-year-old white female, was the faculty supervisor of Carolyn, a 28-year-old white female student in a master's-level counseling program. Carolyn told Professor Jones she wanted to discuss something that was happening at her site, but she was hesitant because she did not want to get her site supervisor, Ms. Anderson, a 53-year-old white female, in trouble. The supervisee believed Ms. Anderson was engaging in questionable or unethical activities.

Carolyn explained that Ms. Anderson had changed her behavior over the past few weeks after her mother had died suddenly from a medical incident. In recent individual supervision sessions, Ms. Anderson had frequently discussed her difficulty coping with her grief and processed previous issues she had had with her mother. Ms. Anderson told Carolyn she was unable to say goodbye to her mother and was therefore unable to make peace with her regarding some issues in their relationship. Carolyn informed Professor Jones that she felt uncomfortable knowing so much about Ms. Anderson's personal life. She also believed Ms. Anderson was drinking while at work. She suspected this because she noticed a difference in Ms. Anderson's behavior throughout the day. In the mornings Ms. Anderson seemed depressed but was also alert and could have a coherent conversation. However, as the day progressed she became less coherent and often slurred her speech. She also had difficulty following conversations and providing feedback.

The previous week Carolyn met with a teenager who revealed she was being abused by her stepfather. Carolyn went to Ms. Anderson's office to confirm she needed to make a report to child protective services and to seek support in discussing this with her teenage client. Ms. Anderson was passed out at her desk and could not be roused, and Carolyn also thought she smelled alcohol on her. Carolyn was distraught and found one of the other clinicians in the office to consult with about the case. She informed the other clinician that Ms. Anderson was coping with a crisis of her own and could not be reached for consultation.

Carolyn received support from the other clinician and followed through with discussing the report with the client. Then she made the report to child protective services. Carolyn, under the guidance of the other clinician, found a safe place for her teenage client to go after the session. At the end of the day when Ms. Anderson was leaving the office, Carolyn asked her whether she was OK and told her she had tried to consult with her about a case, but she was unresponsive. Ms. Anderson stated she had not been getting enough sleep and decided to take a nap between client sessions. She apologized for being in such a deep state of sleep that she could not respond to her.

Carolyn reported being concerned about Ms. Anderson because she was still engaging in clinical work. Carolyn wondered whether Ms. Anderson could be effective with her clients. She did not think the clinical director of the agency knew what was going on because the director tended to take a hands-off approach with her senior clinical staff. Carolyn was unsure what she should do regarding the situation. She was concerned about the level of care Ms. Anderson's clients were receiving. She was also concerned about the supervision and training she herself was receiving—or more appropriately not receiving—from Ms. Anderson. However, Carolyn reported she liked Ms. Anderson and had learned a lot from her before her mother had died. Carolyn was also aware that Ms. Anderson was single and struggling financially with having to pay for her mother's funeral expenses among other things. Carolyn did not want to get Ms. Anderson fired, but she was also concerned about her behavior.

Case Analysis and Discussion

There are many issues in this case. Carolyn was in a very difficult position. As a master's-level counseling student, she did not have much power or the ability to advocate for herself or Ms. Anderson. Therefore, it was essential for Professor Jones to address this situation with empathy and care for Carolyn while considering Carolyn's needs, Ms. Anderson's clients, and the program.

Key issues in this case include ethical and legal issues surrounding the supervisory relationship between Carolyn and Ms. Anderson; Ms. Anderson's ability to provide competent supervision; ethical and legal issues associated with Carolyn's clients; and actions the program needed to take to protect Carolyn, her clients, and the program now that Professor Jones was aware of what was happening at the site. It is imperative that counselor educators model ethical decision-making for students in addition to upholding the primary mandate of nonmaleficence, or doing no harm to those they serve (Remley & Herlihy, 2020), which is outlined as a key professional value in the *ACA Code of Ethics* (American Counseling Association [ACA], 2014). Upholding the mandate of nonmaleficence with students becomes more complicated when outside agencies are involved. Counselor educators should consider systemic effects and repercussions when making ethical and legal decisions regarding the education of a student and protection of the general public (Hansell, 2017).

The first critical incident associated with the case is that Ms. Anderson was having Carolyn serve in the role of her personal therapist. Carolyn stated that many of her individual supervision sessions were spent processing Ms. Anderson's grief and the difficulties she had had with her mother. According to the *ACA Code of Ethics* (ACA, 2014), counseling supervisors are required to clearly define what the supervisory relationship looks like and maintain professional and ethical relationships with their supervisees (Standard F.3.a.). By having Carolyn serve as her own personal therapist, Ms. Anderson was violating this standard. The supervisory relationship is inherently hierarchical in nature because of the evaluative component of supervision (Bernard & Goodyear, 2019). Carolyn may have felt uncomfortable telling Ms. Anderson that she could not act as her counselor because of the power differential in their relationship. It is possible that Ms. Anderson did not recognize that talking about her personal issues with her supervisee was an ethical violation (Strandberg, 2015). However, in the case of graduate-level training, establishing and maintaining clear boundaries is essential because of the supervisor's role as evaluator (Strandberg, 2015).

The second critical incident associated with the case study is impairment. Carolyn reported that Ms. Anderson appeared to be drinking while at work and mentioned several signs to support this claim. According to the *ACA Code of Ethics* (ACA, 2014), counselors continually monitor themselves for any kind of physical, mental, or emotional problems that could contribute to their becoming professionally impaired (Standard C.2.g.). Counselors should refrain from providing services to clients while impaired. Carolyn stated that Ms. Anderson was continuing to see clients. Although there is nothing specific to the impairment of a supervisor in the *ACA Code of Ethics*, it could be surmised that this standard of monitoring one's own self for possible impairment should also be applied to clinical supervisors.

Ms. Anderson's behaviors related to her suspected drinking while at work led to the third critical incident. This incident involved Ms. Anderson not being able to provide supervision to Carolyn during an emergency. This directly relates to the *ACA Code of Ethics* (ACA, 2014), which states supervisors are to monitor counseling services provided by supervisees (Standard F.1.a.). This includes being available to supervisees for consultation during crisis and emergency situations. Because Ms. Anderson was passed out at her desk and unable to be roused, she was not available to provide supervision to Carolyn during a session that involved making an abuse report to child protective services. This incident could have led Carolyn to withhold important future information from both Ms. Anderson and Professor Jones. Cook et al. (2018) found supervisees did not disclose that site supervisors were not helpful during a time of need because they did not want to upset their site supervisors or rupture their supervisory relationship.

The case also presents a legal issue related to vicarious liability, which is based on the legal principle of *respondeat superior*. According to this doctrine, a person who has authority or control over another person, in this case Ms. Anderson, can be held legally liable for any damages caused to a client because of negligence on the part of a subordinate, in this case Carolyn (Simon & Swerdlik, 2017). Fortunately for everyone involved, Carolyn was aware of her responsibility to consult with Ms. Anderson or another qualified colleague regarding the situation. The supervisee was adhering to the *ACA Code of Ethics* (ACA, 2014).

Vicarious liability is also an issue for Professor Jones in this case, because a faculty supervisor often has administrative control in working with the supervisee (Harvey & Struzziero, 2008). Clinical supervisors are legally and ethically responsible for their supervisees. If Carolyn had lacked the knowledge or foresight to consult with another colleague regarding the best course of action for her teenage client, she may have decided not to report the disclosure or not to follow up with the client, which may have resulted in the client experiencing harm. If this had happened, Professor Jones could have been held liable for the harm caused to Carolyn's client, because the harm would have occurred within the course and scope of the supervisory relationship (Simon & Swerdlik, 2017).

The ethnic and cultural backgrounds of the individuals involved in this case are similar. However, it is important to discuss potential multicultural variables and influences, as they affect counseling and supervision. Researchers have found that when multicultural variables are addressed in clinical supervision, supervisees feel more satisfied with supervision and report having a deeper working alliance with their supervisors (Y. Chan, 2019). In addition, Y. Chan (2019) found that when supervisors addressed multicultural variables in supervision, supervisees viewed supervisors as more competent. The counseling profession has made great strides in moving beyond its monocultural origins (P. A. Hays, 2016). The shift to addressing multicultural and social justice issues enhances counselors' work with clients from diverse populations (Ratts et al., 2016). Continuing to explore diversity issues beyond race assists in moving the counseling profession forward in a positive direction (Dworkin & Pope, 2012).

Actions and Outcomes

Professor Jones thanked Carolyn for alerting her to the issues at the site. She reinforced with Carolyn that she was acting in a professional and ethical manner and that steps would be taken to assist her and Ms. Anderson with the issues presented. Professor Jones met with the chair of the counseling program and other program faculty members to discuss a potential course of action. All agreed that Carolyn needed to be protected as much as possible in this situation.

The faculty decided that Professor Jones and Carolyn would make an appointment to meet with the clinical director of the agency. The meeting was scheduled to alert the clinical director of the issues with Ms. Anderson and for Professor Jones to advocate on behalf of Carolyn and Ms. Anderson. Professor Jones wanted to ensure Ms. Anderson received fair treatment while also ensuring Carolyn would be able to continue working at the site with another supervisor. Professor Jones decided not to go directly to Ms. Anderson to discuss the concerns presented because she did not want Ms. Anderson to potentially retaliate against Carolyn for disclosing what had occurred at the site. Professor Jones had a good relationship with the clinical director of the site and believed the situation could be addressed with empathy, compassion, and understanding.

The clinical director was surprised to learn what had transpired with Ms. Anderson over the past few weeks. However, she also stated that she too had been concerned about how Ms. Anderson was functioning at work. Professor Jones expressed her desire for Ms. Anderson to be given assistance with her drinking and grief issues while remaining adamant that Ms. Anderson should not continue to supervise Carolyn or see clients during this time. The clinical director agreed and appointed a different supervisor for Carolyn. Ms. Anderson took a leave of absence to work through her own personal concerns. She returned to the site 2 months later and was able to resume her supervision duties with Carolyn. They were able to rebuild their supervisory relationship, and Carolyn expressed her gratitude to Professor Jones for the way she addressed the situation.

Conclusion

This case highlights the complexities involved in providing clinical supervision to master's-level counseling students. If a faculty supervisor is not diligent, issues that occur at clinical sites off campus can go undetected and can also pose potential ethical and legal issues for the faculty supervisor, the supervisee(s), the clinical site, and the counseling program. It is important for counselor educators serving in the role of clinical supervisors to receive ongoing training in clinical supervision. It is also important for faculty supervisors to build strong relationships with their students and site supervisors, which will aid in addressing issues in a professional and ethical manner.

Reflection Questions

1. Should Professor Jones have met with Ms. Anderson before meeting with the clinical director? Why or why not?
2. Do you agree with the decision to have Ms. Anderson continue to supervise Carolyn when she returned? Why or why not?

Critical Incident Response

Derrick A. Paladino

This case is about compassion and ethics. Empathically and logically, one's heart goes out to Ms. Anderson as she struggles, as an only child, with the sudden loss of her mother and the financial responsibilities that accompany it. It is understandable that this experience would affect her emotionality, impact her everyday functioning, and introduce new coping mechanisms and struggles into her life. Complicated grief can introduce an inability to stop thinking about the loss and cause a heightened state of bereavement (Duffey et al., 2020). With any case issue, one must remember that clinicians are human too.

The author identified failures in maintaining a professional supervisory relationship, self-monitoring for signs of impairment, and providing consistent and timely monitoring of Carolyn's clinical work as critical ethical issues, and there are additional ethical considerations to discuss regarding the case. For example, the site's clinical director disclosed previous concern for Ms. Anderson's functioning. According to the *ACA Code of Ethics* (ACA, 2014), colleagues and supervisors are to be held accountable when witnessing impairment (Standard C.2.g.). Therefore, if the clinical director had knowledge of Ms. Anderson's behavior but allowed it to continue sans consultation and intervention to prevent harm to her clients, she would have been violating the ethics code. In addition, counselors are responsible for monitoring their clinical effectiveness and applying remediation as needed (Standard C.2.d.). Also, Standard A.4.a. requires counselors to avoid harming trainees and clients; this addresses both Ms. Anderson's clients and Carolyn. Ms. Anderson's diminished emotional regulation and functioning may harm her clients through mismanagement of clinical treatment, harm Carolyn and Carolyn's clients through poor guidance of cases, and increase discomfort in supervision because of power differentials in the relationship.

In responding to the ethical dilemma, Professor Jones went directly to the clinical director after meeting with Carolyn, thus bypassing Ms. Anderson. Typically the faculty supervisor would have an initial discussion with the clinician who is exhibiting the unethical behavior prior to going to the clinical director, but there is not always one right way in ethical decision-making. Professor Jones's decision to shield Carolyn from retaliation by the site supervisor is wise, as it protects Carolyn and ensures that any remediation of unethical behavior does not solely rest on Ms. Anderson. It also reduces potential issues around the power differential, such as supervisor error and misuse of power (De Stefano et al., 2017).

In reviewing this case, one would be remiss not to note that this scenario plays out seamlessly because of preexisting successful relationships. Four relationships made this happen:

1. A supervisory relationship between Carolyn and Professor Jones in which Carolyn was comfortable enough to share her experience with Ms. Anderson
2. A solid relationship between Professor Jones and the clinical director that allowed for easier communication with the site along with the communication of compassion for Ms. Anderson's situation
3. A supportive relationship between the site and Ms. Anderson in which the site offered a 2-month leave of absence
4. A good relationship between Carolyn and Ms. Anderson that allowed them to return to a supervisory relationship after Ms. Anderson's 2-month leave of absence

Strong relationships can assist with reducing power differentials and increasing response to ethical behavior.

One final issue to note is Carolyn's return to supervision with Ms. Anderson after her 2-month leave of absence. Professor Jones and the clinical director should carefully examine this situation before implementation and monitor it afterward. Given the information provided in this case, I would suggest that Carolyn remain with her interim supervisor for a few reasons. First, it is probable that Ms. Anderson will discuss what happened with Carolyn. Even if this discussion is minimal, it could still put Carolyn in a difficult and uncomfortable position. Second, Ms. Anderson may modify her supervisory methods (consciously or unconsciously) knowing that Carolyn reported her behaviors. Third, Carolyn will have fostered a new relationship with her interim supervisor over the 2 months. Even though Carolyn knows Ms. Anderson well, they will still need to rebuild trust, and that takes time away from case management. Finally, the faculty supervisor should consider scheduling additional meetings with the clinical director about reintegrating Ms. Anderson as Carolyn's supervisor, suggest creating a new supervision contract or revising the current one to further protect Carolyn and make sure Carolyn has the ability to choose to stay with her interim supervisor if desired. Thus, the faculty supervisor must remain focused on what is in the best interest of Carolyn as well as her clients.

• • •

Section 3
Doctoral Student Supervisors

Chapter 21

Biased: A Doctoral Student Supervisor's Struggle With a Supervisee's Lack of Awareness

Gülşah Kemer

2014 *ACA Code of Ethics* Standards Addressed

- A.4.b. Personal Values
- C.2.a. Boundaries of Competence
- F.2.b. Multicultural Issues/Diversity in Supervision

• • •

Jennifer was a 29-year-old, Black, able-bodied doctoral student who identified as bisexual and from a middle-class family. She described herself as a socially liberal Christian. Because she had started her doctoral studies immediately after completing her master's program, Jennifer's counseling experience was limited to what she had done in her master's program. It was her first semester providing supervision. In supervision of supervision (SOS) with Professor Austin, a 45-year-old Black male, Jennifer discussed a concern with her supervisee, Lindsay, a 28-year-old, single, cisgender, white, able-bodied practicum student. Lindsay described herself as a Christian, middle-class, heterosexual female. Her client, Tanesha, was a single, Black mother in her 30s with two children, the youngest with special needs. As a middle-class woman who worked full time, Tanesha had difficulty taking time off work for her child's doctor appointments and navigating the demands of raising two children with different abilities. Having divorced her children's father (Ryan) and received full custody the previous year, Tanesha did not want to ask him for help. She felt guilty about the divorce, as she was not able to give equal attention to her children.

Lindsay teared up in supervision a few times when discussing Tanesha's challenges. She told Jennifer, "Helping Tanesha and her children may be my calling.

I know I can help." Lindsay presented her plan for the upcoming sessions as listening to Tanesha, understanding her circumstances, helping her manage current stress, and determining her resources. Following the next session, Lindsay submitted the recording for supervision. Watching the tape while preparing for supervision, Jennifer experienced frustration with Lindsay, as she observed her engaging in advice giving that did not appear to be aligned with Tanesha's wishes. For example, Lindsay was selective about attending to Tanesha's challenges and helplessness while highlighting silver linings in her situation (e.g., "You seem to be feeling inadequate as a mother, but I am hearing that at least you and Kate [the older child] are able bodied, so you both can attend to Sally [the younger child]") as well as encouraging Tanesha to ask Ryan for help (e.g., "It seems that, at least until you have a plan, you can ask Ryan for help. Your children may also benefit from connecting with their father while you receive the support you need.").

During SOS, Jennifer presented discomfort with Lindsay's assertion that she knew what was best for Tanesha despite observing Lindsay's positive intentions to alleviate Tanesha's stress. Jennifer also wondered whether Lindsay's comfort in offering advice might have been based on some multicultural dynamics, such as a white savior complex. Jennifer thought Lindsay appeared to have a hierarchical perspective, as if she were able to provide direction for Tanesha's life in hopes of saving her and her children. However, Jennifer could not point out a solid behavior that directly exemplified a white savior complex. She was torn between her intuition and her observations because she had not experienced any multicultural challenges with Lindsay in supervision as a supervisor of color. She left SOS with a plan to point out Lindsay's engagement in advice giving and to explore potential challenges with multicultural competency with Lindsay.

In supervision, Jennifer asked Lindsay to tell her about the session. Lindsay reported, "This was one of my best sessions. I feel good about my work with her. I think I helped her gain broader perspectives." This was clearly different from what Jennifer had observed in the recording. Jennifer showed a segment from Lindsay's session in which she was asking intentional questions to obtain certain answers and asked what Lindsay was seeing. Lindsay responded, "I am reflecting the feeling of inadequacy as a mother, which led to feelings of helplessness and hopelessness, so I was showing empathy." Jennifer also asked Lindsay whether cultural differences between her and Tanesha may have influenced counseling and the relationship. Lindsay expressed confidence in her multicultural competencies, stating she had extensive volunteer experience in youth shelters with many Black girls. Jennifer discussed the differences between sympathy and empathy. However, she was not sure how to present her perceptions of Lindsay's white savior attitudes, as Jennifer herself was struggling to identify concrete examples.

Case Analysis and Discussion

In this case, along with processing sympathy versus empathy, Jennifer needs to attend to Lindsay's multicultural competencies. It is also important to consider the identities of the client, supervisee, and supervisor. Kemer (2020) presented a brief data-driven supervision model: (a) assessment of the supervisee's personal and professional characteristics and development, (b) supervisor self-assessment and reflection, (c) the supervisory relationship, (d) conceptualization and interventions of supervision, and (e) administrative and logistical aspects of supervision. The first four of these areas are considered in this case analysis.

In terms of the assessment of supervisees' personal and professional characteristics and development, personal and professional growth is often intertwined. Although it is crucial for supervisors to set clear boundaries and not become supervisees' counselors, supervisors cannot ignore this interconnection between personal and professional development. According to the integrated developmental model (Stoltenberg & McNeill, 2010), Lindsay demonstrates characteristics of a Level 1 counselor trainee, as evidenced by her high motivation and self-focus as well as her limited awareness of self in relation to the client. Giving herself a pat on the back for her best session, Lindsay needs positive feedback and little to no direct confrontation. Jennifer's focus must be on Lindsay's ability to work within the client's frame of reference and ethical practice. According to the *ACA Code of Ethics* (American Counseling Association [ACA], 2014), Lindsay appears to be breaching ethical boundaries by imposing her perspectives and values onto Tanesha (Standard A.4.b.). This is particularly evident when she is searching for specific answers, engaging in advice giving, and encouraging Tanesha to behave in certain ways. Feelings of inadequacy, helplessness, and hopelessness appear to be more Lindsay's interpretations than Tanesha's presented experiences. Also, despite Tanesha's unwillingness to interact with Ryan, Lindsay recommends she do so. By stating the children "may also benefit from connecting with their father," Lindsay presents her parenting values as a solution for Tanesha.

The *ACA Code of Ethics* (ACA, 2014) emphasizes the importance of counselors obtaining knowledge, awareness, and skills to be culturally competent to work with diverse populations (Standard C.2.a.). Beyond engaging in advice giving, Lindsay does not seem to focus on Tanesha's personal experience, not only as a parent of a child with disabilities but also as a Black woman. Lindsay's inclination to push her views onto Tanesha might be related to her preconceived stereotypes of Black women. Examining the perceptions of 435 undergraduate students, Rosenthal and Lobel (2016) found perceptions of a Black pregnant woman included not having the father involved and needing public assistance. To better understand Lindsay's case, we may need to assess her personal identity development as a white person.

According to Helms's white identity development model (Helms, 1992), white people pass through six stages on a continuum of developing an antiracist identity. Helms described a white savior complex in the pseudoindependence stage, in which white individuals attempt to help members of marginalized racial groups fit in to white culture and act white to prevent discrimination. Lindsay perceives Tanesha as inadequate and helpless and feels a "calling" to help her. This perception seems to include a narrow understanding of Tanesha's concerns mainly based on Lindsay's views, not Tanesha's expressions. In her conceptualization of Tanesha, Lindsay seems to have jumped to conclusions and solutions. As a result, she thinks she is empathizing and doing a good job with Tanesha but does not recognize she might be part of a systemic problem, reflected in the minimal attention she gives to Tanesha's own resources. Perhaps she is endorsing solutions from a white frame of reference and promoting whiteness rather than truly observing and honoring the client's background as a person of color (Helms, 1992). It is also critical to highlight the fact that Lindsay is most likely unaware of these thought processes and actions while operating from a prominent feeling of responsibility (her "calling").

Regarding supervisor self-assessment and reflection, it is important for Jennifer to reflect on her personal reactions in relation to supervising Lindsay as she counsels Tanesha. Jennifer shares common identities with Lindsay (e.g., generation, religiosity) and the client (e.g., Blackness). Some of these identities help Jennifer empathize with and feel connected to both women, in some cases maybe Tanesha more than Lindsay. The most salient of these identities is both Jennifer's and Tanesha's Blackness. Therefore, it is helpful to explore the possible connection between Jennifer's discomfort and frustration and her observations and perceptions of Lindsay's attitudes toward her Black client. In SOS, Professor Austin may ask the following of Jennifer: "What is coming up for you personally?" "Is countertransference happening in supervision?" "How much do you (over)identify with the client?" "Is any vicarious trauma being triggered in you while you observe Lindsay interact with the client?"

Similar to Lindsay, Jennifer may also benefit from reflecting on her own identity development as a Black person. In his Black racial identity development model, Cross (1991) described five stages African Americans pass through to develop an understanding of their identity. Despite not being able to specifically point out Lindsay's white savior attitudes, Jennifer seems to perceive Lindsay's solutions as being centered around a white person's frame of reference rather than the client's frame of reference as a Black person. Jennifer may be in the encounter stage, and reflecting on her identity development could inform her personal awareness as well as her supervisory work.

In her most recent supervision session, Jennifer focused on developing Lindsay's understanding of empathy versus sympathy and did not go deeper into multicultural dynamics. In SOS, Professor Austin may ask Jennifer the following: "What kept you from examining Lindsay's potential white savior attitudes toward her client?" "What do you know about the white savior complex?" "What are your thoughts and feelings toward raising this concern with Lindsay? Do you have any reservations about doing it (e.g., not knowing how to present the topic, fear of losing control, fear or damaging the relationship)?" As a Black supervisor, Jennifer has not observed savior attitudes from Lindsay in their supervision sessions, and this is not an easy topic for Jennifer (a Black supervisor) to broach with Lindsay (a white supervisee) without tension. Jennifer may think it is not her job as a Black person to give feedback on white savior attitudes to a white person. However, as the party liable for the supervisee's growth as a counselor and the client's welfare, Jennifer must address this issue with Lindsay. According to the *ACA Code of Ethics* (ACA, 2014), supervisors are responsible for discussing diversity in supervision (Standard F.2.b.). A critical factor to consider is perhaps whether Jennifer addressed multicultural differences between herself and Lindsay at the beginning of the supervisory relationship. Broaching cultural differences early in supervision may facilitate revisiting multicultural dimensions of counseling and supervision (Borders et al., 2014; Jones et al., 2019).

In relation to the supervisory relationship, Jennifer's experience of Lindsay as a person and a supervisee appears to be positive. Lindsay presents as an open, responsive, and invested counselor trainee, which are supervisors' descriptions of easy (good) supervisees (Kemer & Borders, 2017; Norem et al., 2006). Examining expert supervisors' priorities with supervisees, Kemer et al. (2017) found that supervisors reported prioritizing assessment of their easy supervisees' personal and professional qualities while focusing on the supervisory relationship with their challenging supervisees. However, Jennifer may want to attend to both priority areas, in particular her experience of Lindsay's receptivity to supervision and response to feedback as well as intentional collaborations with Lindsay. Jennifer's approach to this critical event will affect the supervisory relationship.

Jennifer may continue to reflect on her potential countertransference, which, if it has not already, could influence her supervisory work and relationship with Lindsay. Examining expert supervisors' experiences with supervisees, Kemer et al. (2017) found that experts reported the need to reflect on their own contribution to challenging supervisory relationship incidents. Through SOS, Jennifer may explore her productive and unproductive responses in supervision to support positive supervision outcomes.

Actions and Outcomes

As described above, Jennifer assessed Lindsay's personal and professional development, engaged in self-assessment and reflection, and considered the supervisory relationship, which provided a foundation for conceptualizing supervision and implementing interventions. In exploring Lindsay's awareness, Jennifer noticed Lindsay was invested in creating change for Tanesha. However, she was not aware of how she was pushing her values on Tanesha, which indicated multicultural insensitivity and incompetency and was a breach of the *ACA Code of Ethics* (ACA, 2014). Lindsay's work could have unintentionally led to outcomes not determined by the client, which may have led to harm (nonmaleficence; Kitchener, 1984). Jennifer conveyed these concerns to Lindsay by showing segments of sessions in which she was searching for answers and giving advice. In addition, using Socratic questioning (Overholser, 1991), Jennifer asked "what" and "how" questions to help Lindsay reflect on her work with Tanesha (e.g., "What was the reason you asked this question?" "How do you think this response attends to what the client presented?") and on being a white counselor working with a Black client (e.g., "How does this interpretation reflect Tanesha's point of view?" "What may Tanesha be perceiving in the interpretation?"). The use of interpersonal process recall (Kagan, 1976) also helped Lindsay explore potential unstated agendas, cognitive examination, expectations, and mutual perceptions (Bernard & Goodyear, 2019). To offer more direct reflective observations to expedite Lindsay's processing of her internal realities, Jennifer used the thinking-aloud approach (Borders & Brown, 2005). Focusing on Lindsay's reflective process created a safe space for Lindsay to explore possible biases behind her counseling behaviors. Jennifer also used the thinking-aloud approach to identify and process the potential meaning of Lindsay's expressions and responses representing white savior attitudes.

Self-disclosure and immediacy may enhance the supervisory working alliance. Jennifer disclosed her personal experience of Lindsay in the counseling videos. She used the counselor and teacher roles with a focus on Lindsay's conceptualization and personalization skills (discrimination model; Bernard, 1979). Jennifer explored how Lindsay's perspectives and biases may have hindered a robust conceptualization of the client's concerns, the setting up of client-driven goals, and the use of interventions to meet the goals. In addition, through intentional supervisory work, Jennifer helped Lindsay develop a better understanding of her role as a counselor and enhance her counseling with Tanesha. Lindsay was then able to create a parallel process in counseling to dialogue with Tanesha and increase the client's awareness of resources. This promoted the use of Tanesha's own solutions that were compatible with her life stressors and experiences and relevant to her cultural background.

The course of action helped facilitate positive supervision and counseling outcomes. Regarding supervision, Lindsay developed an awareness of her own—as well as Tanesha's—multicultural identities and increased her knowledge and practices relevant to developing cultural competence and not imposing her personal values on others (ACA, 2014, Standards A.4.b., C.2.a.). Jennifer reflected on her own awareness and developed an understanding of the role of her own multicultural identities in supervision. She also practiced supervisory skills and interventions to address Lindsay's developmental needs by discussing cultural diversity (ACA, 2014, Standard F.2.b.). Regarding counseling, Lindsay focused on Tanesha's frame of reference, in particular her needs and perspectives, which enhanced the therapeutic alliance and helped Tanesha develop coping skills and use personal resources compatible with her cultural background.

Conclusion

Counseling and supervision are multicultural. A white savior complex can be a subtle concern that supervisors should assess and address with diligence and sensitivity. This involves focusing on supervisees' development of multicultural awareness and competencies, encouraging supervisors to reflect on their own values and identities, and supporting multicultural supervision practices. These approaches help promote effective supervision and counseling outcomes.

Reflection Questions

1. What are Lindsay's strengths and areas for growth as a counselor-in-training?
2. What other strategies may Jennifer use with Lindsay to foster her growth and development?

Critical Incident Response

Joel F. Diambra

The case highlights intersectionality and the challenges of bias, potential bias, racial identity development, white savior attitudes, and countertransference. The author identified Lindsay as breaching ethical boundaries by unknowingly imposing her views onto her client. This seems plausible given Lindsay's early stage of counseling development (i.e., she is a practicum student) and her statements about counseling Tanesha being her "calling." Viewing client issues from limited perspectives primes the counselor to miss elements of client identity and experience. When this occurs, effective counseling is seldom accomplished (Ali & Lee, 2019).

Because Lindsay's white race and Christian identity afford her power and privilege in her broader culture, she may be blind to how her status influences her perspective on Tanesha's circumstances, causing her to neglect addressing these issues in counseling. Hook et al. (2016) found that the most frequent racial microaggression the majority of clients identified experiencing was their counselor's failure to address cultural issues because of a lack of awareness or denial of prejudice and stereotypes. Clients connected fewer microaggressions to the counselor when they perceived the counselor as demonstrating cultural humility (Hook et al., 2016). Addressing Lindsay's multicultural competence, beginning with cultural awareness and humility, appears to be an appropriate starting point for Jennifer.

Ali and Lee (2019) provided three creative instructional strategies (i.e., abacus, flower of life, and pieces of me) that Jennifer could adapt for supervision to help Lindsay explore intersectionality; address privilege, power, and bias; and increase her multicultural competency. Ali and Lee provided thorough explanations of these creative self-reflective instructional activities, but one adaptation is offered here. Jennifer could use an abacus to help illustrate the fact that people experience marginalization and privilege on a continuum, not dichotomously. By assigning relevant aspects of Lindsay's cultural identity (status, race) to each abacus row, and assigning one end as marginalized and the other as privileged, Jennifer could prompt Lindsay to move the beads along each row to indicate her experiences related to her cultural identities. Then Jennifer could ask Lindsay to consider different contexts (e.g., geographic location) for each identity and adjust the beads. Once Lindsay has recognized her own positionalities and the influence of context, Jennifer could prompt Lindsay to repeat the process related to Tanesha. Discussion regarding similarities and differences indicated by moving the beads may illuminate perceived privilege, marginalization, and intersectionality for both counselor and client. To lessen conjecture, Lindsay could ask Tanesha to complete a similar process with the abacus.

This case grounds itself in supervision and developmental theories and models from which to consider client, counselor, and doctoral supervisor viewpoints. Doing so suggests the importance of using existing frameworks to consider and problem solve complex situations, perspectives, and context. Although not mentioned in the case, Lindsay will soon be required to develop and apply a personal theory to her counseling practice. Spruill and Benshoff (2011) indicated this is vital for fledging counselors-in-training. Professor Austin and Jennifer's application of existing developmental and supervision models to better understand circumstances and relationships demonstrates sound practice and provides an exemplary learning model for Lindsay. As supervision continues, Jennifer could inform Lindsay about the models and framework she is using, provide examples of how theory informs supervisory action steps, and assist Lindsay in identifying counseling theory and applying tenets to her work with Tanesha.

Other identities indicated or implied are sexual orientation, age, sex, class, parenthood, and marital status. Although Jennifer focused on Lindsay's lack of client and cultural awareness, it might be prudent to explore these other identities—and Lindsay's reasons for attending to or neglecting them in the counseling relationship—when Lindsay becomes more culturally aware. Attending to these potential areas of bias promotes self-awareness and professional growth.

In line with the idea that knowledge is socially constructed and there is opportunity for growth even for the faculty supervisor (Owens & Neale-McFall, 2014), Professor Austin's role is that of a fellow learner rather than an all-knowing authority. He has occasion to reflect on and consider his perspectives and influence based on his own identities and experiences. Additional considerations may include Professor Austin's racial identity development, professional development, age, and sex (as the only male). This multitiered case elucidates the intricacies involved in navigating effective and ethical supervision when addressing bias.

• • •

Chapter 22

I'm Attracted to My Supervisee: A Doctoral Student Supervisor's Struggle

David Julius Ford Jr. and Matthew Tirrell

2014 *ACA Code of Ethics* Standards Addressed

- F.1.a. Client Welfare
- F.2.b. Multicultural Issues/Diversity in Supervision
- F.3.c. Sexual Harassment
- F.3.d. Friends or Family Members

• • •

Andrew was a 40-year-old queer-identified white man pursuing his doctorate in counselor education. He was licensed and had 10 years of counseling experience. He advocated for members of the lesbian, gay, bisexual, transgender, and queer (LGBTQ+) community and considered himself an ally of queer and trans people of color and of other Black and Brown communities. He had been diagnosed with HIV and provided pro bono counseling services to the local AIDS Care Organization (ACO).

For his supervision internship, Andrew worked with five master's-level counseling students. He had two pairs for triadic supervision and the remaining student for individual supervision. His individual supervisee, James, was a 26-year-old queer-identified Black man. James had been placed at the ACO for his internship, where he had also completed his practicum. Like Andrew, James was HIV positive. Andrew had worked with James at the ACO during his practicum but had not disclosed his relationship with him to his faculty supervisor. Andrew scheduled weekly supervision sessions with James at his in-home private practice.

James was assigned to work with Eric, a 25-year-old queer-identified Black man. Eric had been "poz" (the term Eric used to mean HIV positive) since he was 16 years old and had been in and out of counseling since then. Once his parents had found out he was gay and HIV positive, they had kicked him out of the house and he had become a "survival gay." He was homeless and started having survival sex with older men. When he was 18 years old, he had been sexually assaulted by a guy he had met on Grindr (a social media site for gay, bisexual, trans, and queer people). Since the incident, he had seen several counselors, all of whom had been queer-identified white men. When he came to the ACO, he stated he preferred a queer-identified Black man for his counselor, and the site director assigned him to James. Eric disclosed to James that his previous counselors had never understood him and had never seen him as a Black man.

James broached culture early in his work with Eric and approached counseling from a developmental perspective. He was well versed in integrating the Multicultural and Social Justice Counseling Competencies (Ratts et al., 2016) into counseling and assessed Eric's racial identity development using William Cross's theory of nigresence (Vandiver et al., 2001). In supervision, Andrew told James he was impressed with the way he integrated culture into his work with Eric. He then stated, "You are good looking and smart. You're becoming an excellent counselor!"

During his fifth supervision session with Andrew, James expressed concerns about Eric. He believed Eric was developing feelings for him and had heard Eric making sexually suggestive comments about him. He was no longer comfortable seeing Eric for counseling but was reluctant to refer him because there was not another Black therapist working at the ACO. Andrew leaned over and started to rub James's leg to comfort him as he was talking. James started to cry and stated he had a passion for working with clients like Eric and really wanted to make a difference. He did not want to do anything wrong and bring shame to the profession. Andrew told James that attraction between clients and counselors happened all the time and that he could not abandon Eric. Andrew instructed James to gently confront Eric in the next session.

James came to the next supervision session and stated, at Andrew's request, that he had told Eric what he had noticed and wondered whether Eric was developing an attraction toward him. Eric had immediately started crying and admitted he was attracted to James, was always falling for the wrong guys, and was always getting his heart broken and getting abandoned. He had told James he was just like every other man, judging him and abandoning him. Before James could respond, Eric had cursed at him and stormed out of the office.

James became tearful while talking about the session. Again, Andrew rubbed James's leg to comfort him. While James was talking, Andrew made comments such as "I can see how Eric would be attracted to you. You're a handsome guy." Andrew then attempted to hug James, but James moved back. Andrew noticed James's discomfort and stated, "I like to hug; there is nothing wrong with us hugging." James expressed his discomfort to Andrew, and Andrew apologized and suggested ending the session.

Andrew had supervision of supervision with Professor Harris, his faculty supervisor, immediately after his session with James. In the session, Andrew revealed what had happened during the supervision session, stating he was physically attracted to James and that he also had had a collegial relationship with him prior to starting supervision with him. He then discussed what had transpired in James's session with Eric and his session with James.

Case Analysis and Discussion

When Andrew received his supervision caseload and saw that James was one of his supervisees, he should have told Professor Harris about their previous professional relationship. According to the *ACA Code of Ethics* (American Counseling Association [ACA], 2014), supervisors should avoid engaging in supervisory relationships with persons with whom they cannot remain objective (Standard F.3.d.). James and Andrew had a previous collegial relationship, and the impetus was on Andrew to inform his faculty supervisor. Andrew was also responsible for the welfare of James's clients. The *ACA Code of Ethics* mandates that supervisors monitor services provided by their supervisees for the sake of their clients (Standard F.1.a.). Andrew instructed James to address Eric's assumed attraction without guiding him on how to do this ethically, which violated Andrew's ethical duty to Eric. Andrew's attraction to James appeared to impair his objectivity when working with him. He also touched James without his permission when rubbing his leg and giving him a hug, which could be viewed as sexual harassment because of the sexual undertones, violating the *ACA Code of Ethics* (ACA, 2014, Standard F.3.c.). Of counselor liability claims in 2019, 43.9% were related to inappropriate sexual or romantic interactions (CNA & Healthcare Providers Service Organization, 2019).

By the time Andrew informed Professor Harris about his past collegial relationship with James and what had occurred during supervision, Eric had already experienced harm, and James had experienced ineffective supervision and sexual harassment. Andrew engaged in multiple ethical violations in supervising James. Professor Harris needed to address the ethical concerns related to Andrew's behaviors, support James in his development as a counselor while also assisting him in working through his experience with James and potential sexual harassment/Title IX violations, and ensure Eric received quality counseling. If James moved forward with reporting sexual harassment, Andrew could experience consequences at the university regarding the pursuit of his degree as well as consequences from the licensure board, which could include a suspension of his license.

Andrew failed to address multicultural considerations in supervision, a mandate in the *ACA Code of Ethics* (ACA, 2014, Standard F.2.b.). In addition, according to the Multicultural and Social Justice Counseling Competencies (Ratts et al., 2016), counselors must consider the client's worldview. The supervisor not only assists the supervisee in considering the client's worldview but also considers the supervisee's worldview and how it affects the client-counselor relationship and the supervisee-supervisor relationship. In this case, Andrew could have empowered James to approach the most recent session with Eric from a more culturally affirming stance. Had Andrew considered James's and Eric's worldviews, he would have given more guidance to James when addressing Eric's feelings. With Andrew's assistance, James could have shown acceptance and understanding toward Eric, being careful not to alienate him and not to allow Eric to misperceive any rejection as being based on his identity as a queer Black man who was HIV positive. Eric's frustration regarding the confrontation may have resulted from his perception of being stigmatized as hypersexual because he was a queer-identified Black man.

White counselors-in-training struggle with bringing up racial issues with clients (Day-Vines et al., 2018). Andrew exhibited this struggle in supervision by not broaching race within the supervisory relationship with James. Because Andrew was white and James and Eric were Black, Andrew's level of racial self-awareness may have affected the quality of supervision. According to Bernard and Goodyear (2019), it is better when supervisors are further along in their racial identity development than their supervisees or clients. Andrew appeared to be at a less advanced stage of racial identity development than either James or Eric, which contributed to James receiving incomplete and insufficient supervision and Eric receiving inadequate, culturally bereft treatment. As the supervisor, Andrew was responsible for encouraging James to continually engage in cultural self-awareness and assessment. In a parallel process, if James and Eric had been at different stages of racial identity development, such as Eric being further along in his racial identity than James, Eric would have been likely to receive culturally unresponsive treatment.

Andrew did not adhere to the Association for Counselor Education and Supervision (ACES) *Best Practices in Clinical Supervision* (ACES Supervision Taskforce, 2011), which recommends supervisors gather feedback from various sources, including the site supervisor (3.c.i.). Andrew should have collaborated with James's site supervisor in providing feedback. In addition, *Best Practices in Clinical Supervision* instructs the supervisor to create a safe environment that fosters mutual trust (5.b.i.). Andrew did not provide a safe environment for James to process his feelings and concerns. Andrew also violated several best practices indicated in Section 6 regarding diversity and advocacy. He did not broach culture at the onset of the supervisory relationship and did not integrate cultural and advocacy competencies into supervision (6.a.i., 6.a.ii.). Furthermore, Andrew did not model the interventions suggested in 6.b. to encourage the supervisee to integrate diversity and advocacy into his interventions. This would have given James the tools to advocate for Eric in a culturally responsive manner. Moreover, Andrew prioritized his own needs, instead of those of the supervisee and the client (7.b.v.). Furthermore, he failed to consider the power differential between the supervisor and the supervisee as well as between the supervisee and the client (7.d.ii.). Andrew was responsible for attending to power issues with James to prevent harmful nonsexual and sexual relationships. He should have also modeled this behavior for James so James could address the power differential with Eric.

Andrew did not establish appropriate professional boundaries and should have been intentional about not engaging in multiple relationships with James (ACES Supervision Taskforce, 2011, 5.c.iii.). Andrew's compliments regarding James's looks, his rubbing of James's leg, and his attempt to hug him were all boundary violations. Andrew also knew James before they started supervision. Once Andrew knew that he had been assigned James as a supervisee, he should have informed Professor Harris of their previous relationship so James could have been assigned to another supervisor or, if they had to work together, Professor Harris could have monitored the relationship while supervising Andrew. Andrew's modeling of appropriate boundaries in supervision could have helped James set appropriate boundaries with Eric. Had proper boundaries been in place, James could have worked through Eric's transference with him and his countertransference with Eric. Transference and countertransference are normal in the counseling relationship and in the supervisory relationship and sometimes create a parallel process. Morrissey and Tribe (2001) posited that parallel process has origins in transference and countertransference that should be addressed in supervision when observed. In addition, client attraction to counselors is common, and counselors-in-training should learn how to address it through supervision and training experiences (Meier & Davis, 2011). Andrew did not provide these training experiences because of his own countertransference with James.

Actions and Outcomes

Ultimately, Professor Harris was responsible for Eric's well-being, as per the 2016 Council for Accreditation of Counseling and Related Educational Programs (CACREP) Standards (CACREP, 2016), counselor educators are required to support and consult with site supervisors (Section 3, Standard Q). Professor Harris discussed the situation first with the clinical placement coordinator and then with faculty in the counselor education program, and they identified action steps to address the situation. To ensure Eric continued to receive adequate care and James continued to receive adequate supervision, Professor Harris met with Angela, James's site supervisor, to discuss what had occurred between James and Eric. They discussed a plan for Eric's care and James's continued development. Professor Harris also met with Andrew to inform him that he would no longer be supervising James; Professor Harris would become James's university supervisor. Professor Harris then met with James to process the situation that had occurred with Andrew and shared that he (Professor Harris) would be James's new supervisor. Professor Harris and Angela then met with James to discuss a plan for Eric as well as a plan for James's continued development as a counselor.

Because Andrew's actions constituted a Title IX violation, a report needed to be made to the Title IX office at the university. Professor Harris discussed this with James, and because James was uncomfortable making the report, Professor Harris made the report. According to Tillman et al. (2014), faculty may report Title IX violations without the victim's wishes if university policy directs them to take this action. They further stated that counselor educators must be aware that although Title IX may not require faculty to report an incident, university policy might require a report. Professor Harris consulted the department leadership regarding the steps required in making a Title IX violation report. Per university policy, he informed the university Title IX coordinator of the situation, which initiated an investigation. The university conducted an initial investigation into the allegations by interviewing James, Andrew, and Professor Harris. The university concluded the allegations had merit and suspended Andrew from the program pending further investigation.

Professor Harris also made a report to the state's counseling licensure board. The licensure board ruled that Andrew had violated ethical standards related to multiple relationships, sexual harassment of supervisees, and multicultural issues/diversity in supervision. As a result, the board suspended Andrew's license for 3 years and noted that once his license was reinstated, he would be on probation for another 2 years. Because Andrew was an active member of ACA, Professor Harris made a report to the ACA Ethics Committee. The Committee found Andrew in violation and suspended his membership for 4 years. Andrew was also required to complete a remediation plan before his membership would be reinstated.

Conclusion

The supervisor's role is to equip the counselor with tools to address transference and countertransference and to model this behavior in supervision. The supervisor must also attend to cultural variables and set professional boundaries. Attraction may occur in the supervisory or counseling relationship, and it is important to be aware of it and seek supervision when it occurs. Communication and transparency are crucial within supervision and supervision of supervision to foster supervisor and supervisee development and quality client care.

Reflection Questions

1. How might Andrew have broached culture with James? How might James have broached culture with Eric?
2. Is there anything you would have done differently had you been Professor Harris? If so, what?

Critical Incident Response

Devika Dibya Choudhuri

The transferential and countertransferential attraction counselors may experience with clients and vice versa is familiar to many supervisors. In addition to the issues addressed by the authors, some other areas are offered here for consideration. Andrew accrues the most penalties, which is appropriate because his ethical violations were the most egregious, but he also appears to be the sole recipient of consequences. Hagler (2020) discussed the importance of LGBQ-affirming supervision for a queer-identified trainee and of respect and understanding for one's identities. I propose an alternative understanding of events from the perspective of affirmative supervision (Halpert et al., 2007).

When Andrew and James first met they were providing counseling at the site, Andrew pro bono as part of his service commitment and James as part of his practicum. To inform Professor Harris of his prior relationship with James might have outed James as both queer and HIV positive given the site. In a small local queer community, members know one another in multiple ways (Perlstein, 2009) and outing is egregious. In addition, disclosing someone's HIV-positive status is sometimes unlawful as well as many times unethical, in particular given the high possibility of stigma and discrimination (Lambda Legal, n.d.).

We are unaware whether Andrew broached the subject of his feelings for James in supervision with Professor Harris or he did not feel safe doing so. Heterosexism and cultural ignorance in supervision of LGBQ supervisees results in decreased frequency and depth of disclosure and a weaker working alliance (Hagler, 2020). The supervision process needs to encourage a supervisory alliance that conveys acceptance, respect, and support as well as discussions of power dynamics and diversity (Halpert et al., 2007). Given Andrew's and James's relative ages, common identification as queer males, and HIV-positive status, a supervisor should expect boundary crossings and address them early, acknowledging the slippery slope from a strong sense of empathy and alignment to an innocent hug to more violations (Perlstein, 2009). Andrew is criticized for not exploring racial identity development with James; however, it is unclear whether in his own supervision he was encouraged to address sexual identity development regarding James or with James about Eric.

In contemplating the triadic nature of Andrew, James, and Eric's intersecting identities, a supervisor might note that after the initial intervention, the triangle of rescuer (Andrew)/persecutor (James)/victim (Eric) cycled to Andrew becoming the persecutor, James becoming the victim, and Eric disappearing. The problem is not Andrew having feelings for James but his inability to process them safely so as not to blur boundaries and cause emotional invasions that are both sexually and racially charged. With affirmative supervision, Andrew may have felt culturally competent enough to challenge James's overly protective and nurturing stance toward Eric and not violate boundaries.

The assumption in the case analysis was that when Eric responded with anger at being confronted, having a better prepared counselor would have resulted in a different outcome. However, Eric's trauma history shows he felt uncomfortable with intimacy and the safety he felt with James as his first queer Black male therapist was a trigger to feel abandoned, whereupon he left first. The dynamics of not taking queer Black men seriously enough to respect their resilience plays out in casting James and Eric as passive victims, one to be rescued by Professor Harris and one by Angela.

The Title IX, state counseling licensure board, and ACA Ethics Committee reports made by Professor Harris discounted James's perspectives and protected James, ensuring his victim status. This resulted in Andrew being suspended from the doctoral program, having his license suspended, and finding his career and education at a standstill. Given he is HIV positive, if he has no ability to finance his health care because of his license suspension, and no access to university health care because of his program suspension, this is very close to mortal jeopardy. Neither the Title IX office, state licensure board, nor ACA Ethics Committee appears to have considered Andrew's marginalized and vulnerable statuses, and to some extent this is based on what testimony and views the reporting faculty presented and the extent to which Andrew was encouraged to advocate for himself. To Andrew's credit, he made full disclosure of his transgressions when he realized where he had fallen and accepted the consequences. I suggest that Andrew could have faced developmentally appropriate consequences as a student-learner in which he had to take additional coursework or attend workshops on racial and sexual identity development and supervisory ethics and it was recommended he seek counseling for his own poor boundaries before being allowed to supervise again. There is no indication that he behaved unethically as a counselor, so suspending his license was extremely punitive. James was ill served by not receiving any educative work to address the boundary crossings when they first occurred, with both Andrew as well as Eric.

Neither James nor Andrew was allowed to explore the complexities of what occurred in a mediated conversation between queer HIV-positive men, and reparation could be neither made nor accepted to facilitate healing. The counseling program also does not appear to have been well served by the disposition of this case, as candid revelations of values, desires, or marginalized statuses appear to not bring repair, reducing the likelihood of future disclosures.

• • •

Part III
Research and Scholarship

Section 1
Collaboration and Authorship 187

Section 2
Client Interest and Well-Being 209

Section 3
The Publication Process 229

Research and scholarship are crucial for advancing the counseling profession, and professional counseling organizations have emphasized the importance of rigor and ethics in research. The *ACA Code of Ethics* (American Counseling Association, 2014) has an entire section focused on research and publication (Section G). In addition, the 2016 Council for Accreditation of Counseling and Related Educational Programs (CACREP) Standards (CACREP, 2016) outline research and scholarship as one of five core areas for doctoral programs. Moreover, the Association for Counselor Education and Supervision Guidelines for Research Mentorship (Borders et al., 2012) focus on various areas related to research mentorship. Furthermore, the *Publication Manual of the American Psychological Association* (American Psychological Association, 2020) provides guidelines for the writing and publishing processes.

Counselor educators must conduct and engage in rigorous, ethical counseling research and scholarship while also teaching, modeling, and mentoring doctoral students to do the same. The research and scholarship practices in which doctoral students engage are likely to inform the practices they will use after they graduate in their own work as researchers, teachers, and mentors. Thus, it is crucial to instill ethical research and writing practices into doctoral students. There are multiple ethical considerations related to these processes. This section includes nine chapters within three areas of common research concerns: (a) collaboration and authorship, (b) client interest and well-being, and (c) the publication process.

Collaboration and Authorship

Collaboration is common within research and writing. Consistent, clear communication is crucial to helping facilitate a positive experience for all collaborators. Faculty members should take the initiative to model this process, mentoring students in how to facilitate it on their own in the future. When faculty members neglect to model this process, challenges related to ownership of ideas and authorship may rise. Doctoral students and junior faculty members may struggle with initiating conversations because of power differentials within collaborative relationships. The first two chapters in this section focus on critical incidents related to receiving credit for scholarly work. In the first chapter, "That's My Idea: Taking Someone Else's Work as Their Own," a junior faculty member and a senior faculty member who served on her dissertation committee navigate challenges regarding acknowledging the scholarly work of others and plagiarism. The second chapter, "Who to Include: A Case of Contested Authorship," pertains to what constitutes authorship in the context of collaborations between faculty members and paid graduate assistants.

Research collaboration may also include working with an interdisciplinary team on grant proposals, as funders often like a team of experts from different disciplines. This may present challenges as scholars from different disciplines view topics or issues differently, emphasizing the importance of open communication. In "Is This How It's Supposed to Be? Collaboration Gone Wrong," an interdisciplinary research team must consider professional values and navigate philosophical differences.

Client Interest and Well-Being

Conducting research with people involves considering what is in the best interest of the participants. This begins with the conceptualization of the study and continues throughout the project. Institutional review boards (IRBs) review research protocols to protect client welfare, and approval is generally required for researchers employed by institutions of higher education. Many organizations have similar processes involving research oversight and compliance. IRBs may request revisions to study protocols that researchers might be reluctant to make because of the effects on their study. In some cases, researchers may also believe changes may negatively affect the participants. "I Need Your Approval, but I Don't Want to Do That: Getting IRB Approval" pertains to researchers navigating IRB feedback that may negatively affect the feasibility of their study.

Recruitment and selection of participants may also be difficult for researchers. They can be particularly challenging when populations are small and researchers have difficulty obtaining enough participants. Further complications may arise when researchers have preexisting relationships with members of the population that present a conflict of interest or boundary issues. In "Should He Be Included? I Know His Sister," a researcher navigates a preexisting relationship with the family member of a potential research participant.

Researchers must ensure they are not compromising the well-being of their participants to complete their projects. This can be challenging when researchers experience pressure to produce research and complications change the focus or direction of projects. Several factors may complicate this process, especially when one is working with marginalized populations or wait-list control groups. In "Do We Stop the Study? Best for the Client vs. Best for Research," a researcher must navigate participants in a wait-list control group withdrawing from a study.

The Publication Process

The publication process is complex, with multiple components. Researchers often struggle with deciding whether they can publish multiple manuscripts from a single data set. Pressure to publish as much as possible and to work smarter may lead researchers to want to get multiple publications from their data. However, there are critical areas to consider when deciding whether the data can be split for multiple publications. "A Little Bit Here, a Little Bit There: The Least Publishable Unit" pertains to ethical decision-making related to dividing data from a single study to generate multiple publications.

Another common concern related to the publication process is publishing research after realizing similar research has already been published. Counselor education doctoral students and new counselor educators may become discouraged when they see research published on similar topics and wonder whether they can still publish their work. "It's Already Published: Can I Still Submit My Manuscript?" focuses on a researcher discovering an existing article similar to her dissertation study and determining whether her work can still be published.

The final common concern discussed in this section relates to addressing editorial feedback. Scholars may struggle with deciding how to address reviewer feedback, in particular when they think it compromises their work or presents it inaccurately. The pressure to publish compounds this difficulty, as authors may wonder whether their manuscript will be rejected if they do not follow the recommendations of the reviewers. In "Do I Compromise to Get Published? Responding to Reviewers' Feedback," researchers receive a rewrite and resubmit decision from a prestigious journal, but the requested revisions potentially compromise the integrity of the study. Thus, the chapters in this section address common critical incidents experienced by scholars related to multiple aspects of research.

Section 1
Collaboration and Authorship

Chapter 23

That's My Idea: Taking Someone Else's Work as Their Own

Melissa Luke and Sherrie L. Bruner

2014 *ACA Code of Ethics* Standards Addressed

- G.5.e. Agreement of Contributors

• • •

Professor Ani Jamison was a third-year, pretenure counselor educator. She had graduated with distinction from a top-tier research institution. Professor Jamison was a student member of two separate research teams, one run by nationally renowned counselor education professor Erich Doci, whose Career Exploration lab had more than $2.3 million in external funding. The other research team, which was studying the education of linguistically diverse and racially underrepresented students, was headed by tenured associate professor Ezekiel Pratt. Through her research team collaborations, Professor Jamison had coauthored five articles prior to graduation and developed an emergent expertise in the intersection of career development and racial identity development in linguistically diverse adolescents. She had published her dissertation on this topic in a top-tier, high-impact counseling journal.

Professor Jamison served as an editorial board member for the journal in which her dissertation article had been published. In addition, she had recently delivered a presentation at a state-level education conference focused primarily on her dissertation research. The session had been recorded and was saved on the association's website as a webinar. Participants could pay a fee to view it for continuing education credit. In the presentation, Professor Jamison discussed a novel conceptual framework she had developed through which to understand prior theory and research in the career development of linguistically diverse and racially underrepresented adolescents. She used data from her own dissertation (but not included in her previous publication) to illustrate and translate the framework. Several times within the presentation, Professor Jamison noted her intention to develop a manuscript that introduced her framework and used the data from her dissertation to illustrate practice implications for counselors and other educational professionals working with linguistically diverse and racially underrepresented adolescents. She was confident this would add to the literature and improve services to students.

Professor Jamison was in disbelief when she opened an email from the journal for which she served as an editorial board member and was asked to review a manuscript that put forth a conceptual framework remarkably similar to her own but did not credit the work she had independently developed and included in her recent presentation. Not only did the manuscript reference the same literature—including references to her own work, some of which involved as of yet unpublished data from her dissertation—but there were even a few places in which entire sentences were the same. As the manuscript under review was deidentified, Professor Jamison could not discern who had authored it; however, it included several references attributed to the deidentified "Author." After carefully analyzing the material attributed to "Author," Professor Jamison had a deep concern that the author was Professor Pratt or someone who worked in his lab. Struggling to make sense of what she perceived as a theft of her framework and the intellectual ideas discussed in her dissertation—and the further possibility of interpersonal betrayal—Professor Jamison decided to reach out to Professor Pratt in hopes of receiving clarification. Soon after leaving a voicemail message explaining the situation as professionally as she could from her perspective, Professor Jamison received the following texts from Professor Pratt: *I'm sole manuscript author; Considered inviting, but already have P-T in bag; I M going up 4 full; and you don't own lit; Recuse self from review & I'll disregard webinar wo me; That's my idea.*

Case Analysis and Discussion

Scholars across disciplines share concerns about academic integrity broadly and note the necessity of inculcating professional norms for conduct around research and publication more specifically (Eggert, 2011). The counseling literature centers the socialization processes involved in teaching, modeling, and influencing research practice through mentorship (Borders et al., 2012, 2019). Over the past decade, there has been an increase in attention in the counseling literature on authorship integrity, ethics, and decision-making (R. Foster & Ray, 2012; Swank et al., 2019, 2020; Wester, 2011).

The *ACA Code of Ethics* (American Counseling Association [ACA], 2014) has a section expressly focused on research and publication (Section G). Furthermore, Wester's (2011) step-by-step overview of publishing ethical research recognizes five principles to consider across four areas of research practice. On a related note, the Association for Counselor Education and Supervision Guidelines for Research Mentorship (Borders et al., 2012) and the Research Competencies Scale (Swank & Lambie, 2016) identify a range of strategies for developing researchers and conducting ethical research. Taken collectively, this literature helps provide an intentional and scaffolded approach to research and publication ethics and arguably aims to prevent ethical breaches, research misconduct, and authorship abuse and challenges. Nonetheless, counseling researchers should be prepared to use best practices when navigating ethical dilemmas.

Best practices in ethical decision-making involve the use of an ethical decision-making model. In general, ethical decision-making models provide structured frameworks through which counselors can explore the varied dimensions of a problem, engage resources and consultation, articulate possible courses of action and consequences, and ultimately decide on and document a course of action. Although there are numerous ethical decision-making models, we recommend starting with the intercultural model of ethical decision-making (IMED; Luke et al., 2013a, 2013b), a contextual ethical decision-making model that uniquely addresses not only the culture and worldview of the people involved but also the organizational context, and then synthesizing R. Foster and Ray's (2012) ethical decision-making model to determine authorship credit (EDMDAC). Our rationale for synthesizing these two models is that the IMED provides a seven-step linear structure for action that can incorporate the four phases of an authorship decision-making process as outlined in the EDMDAC (see Worksheet 23.1).

Actions and Outcomes

The first step of the IMED requires counselors to recognize that an ethical dilemma exists and to acknowledge the potential that cultural factors are embedded within that ethical dilemma. Research suggests that as many as 50% of counselors-in-training do not identify ethical dilemmas when they are introduced (Luke et al., 2013b); therefore, Professor Jamison's recognition of the dilemma is an important first step. In the social sciences it is generally accepted that authorship is determined based on who has "provided substantial assistance" (Wester, 2011, p. 305) and is based on contribution rather than seniority, role, or position (Eggert, 2011; Swank et al., 2019). Nonetheless, the misuse of positionality for authorship remains a problem (Gaughan & Bozeman, 2016), perhaps in part because many individuals do not re-

WORKSHEET 23.1

Synthesis of the Ethical Decision-Making Model to Determine Authorship Credit and the Intercultural Model of Ethical Decision-Making

Instructions: Use this worksheet as a guide throughout the writing process to determine proper author credit. Consider each step and make relevent notes at each stage, revisiting the stages if necessary throughout the writing process.

	Stage			
Step	Development of Idea	Literature Review and Research	Manuscript Writing	Revision and Editing
1. Become aware of cultural worldview factors present in the ethical dilemma				
2. Identify relevant cultural worldview factors				
3. Identify relevant institutional or organizational policies and procedures				
4. Identify and consult with cultural, institutional, and professional experts				
5. List potential actions and their consequences				
6. Analyze the relationship(s) between potential actions and relevant cultural worldview factors				
7. Select, document, and evaluate actions in light of relevant cultural worldview factors				

port the issue when it happens (American Psychological Association, 2015; Sandler & Russell, 2005). It is clear that Professor Jamison recognizes an ethical dilemma, and in this particular case clear power and cultural differences between Professors Jamison and Pratt have likely contributed to the dilemma.

As per the first phase of the EDMDAC, it is important to first consider conversations that may have occurred previously between Professors Jamison and Pratt when Professor Jamison was a student. The *ACA Code of Ethics* (ACA, 2014) requires individuals conducting joint research to discuss task assignment and authorship or acknowledgment credit at the beginning of the project (Standard G.5.e.). R. Foster and Ray (2012) emphasized the importance of initial and ongoing conversations about authorship. In this particular situation, Professor Jamison could refer to the EDMDAC to better understand the types of contributions that might earn authorship and the processes that may help clarify her, as well as Professor Pratt's, contribution. Furthermore, Eggert (2011) proposed a taxonomy and ranking system for each author across publication-related tasks. Thus, there is shared understanding that engaging in conversations regarding authorship from the initial project development through the assignment of tasks and editing and revision can help ensure collaborators receive appropriate credit for their work through authorship (Borders et al., 2012; Eggert, 2011).

In this case, unfortunately, there is evidence of a fracture in the open and continued communication about contribution between Professors Jamison and Pratt. In retrospect, Professor Jamison may be able to identify opportunities when she could have intervened to facilitate this communication; however, many authors have indicated the role of power in the broaching of these conversations (Gaughan & Bozeman, 2016) and emphasized the importance of those with power broaching these topics early and often (Borders et al., 2012). In this particular case, it is important to consider how Professor Jamison's initial role as a student and her current role as an untenured faculty member in conjunction with her gender, racial, and disciplinary identities might affect the ways in which she may have been able to broach this subject and advocate for herself in this process with an older, male, faculty member who had been her supervisor in a research lab and committee member on her dissertation. Ultimately, it is important to note that while working through the IMED, more information may be needed about potential initial conversations or ongoing check-ins that could have been initiated by Professor Pratt. Such interactions undoubtedly have the potential to align with cultural worldview factors, as described in the IMED, and may have decreased the likelihood of issues and provided clarity regarding expectations for both Professor Pratt and Professor Jamison.

Next the IMED calls for identification of the cultural worldview factors that influence both Professor Jamison and Professor Pratt. Professor Jamison's prior accomplishments include earning a National Board for Certified Counselors Minority Fellowship and being selected as a prestigious Holmes Scholar. These recognitions suggest that in addition to being female, Professor Jamison may hold other marginalized identities. In addition, Professor Jamison was a student at the time the collaboration began and now is an untenured faculty member with a limited research profile. In contrast, Professor Pratt is described as a male tenured associate professor with an established research profile in one of the areas informing the publication. In addition, not only was Professor Pratt the head of a research team on which Professor Jamison worked as a doctoral student, but he also appears to have been a committee member of her dissertation, and his recent texts suggest that he may be experiencing pressure related to his own promotion. These factors place Professor Jamison in an extremely vulnerable position across each phase of the EDMDAC as she navigates this ethical dilemma. Researchers suggest that research mentors can significantly influence a new counselor educator's research productivity in positive and negative ways, and Professor Pratt's lack of intentionality is especially concerning given the significant power he holds as a tenured research mentor (Borders et al., 2011, 2019).

As per the IMED, Professor Jamison must also consider the contextual circumstances involved in the situation and then align these with the potential cultural and worldview issues. The scholarship in question was part of Professor Jamison's dissertation, and in addition to having shared this document and publicly defended this work she previously presented on the work in the professional webinar that is currently archived online, which creates a documentation trail. Alternatively, the case suggests Professor Pratt has a long-standing track record of research in one of the conceptual areas involved in the manuscript. We have little information about how Professor Jamison's work with Professor Pratt, and his mentorship, may have informed her development of the conceptual framework. It would be important for Professor Jamison to consider ways in which Professor Pratt may have informed her work while maintaining her own ownership, especially in light of Professor Pratt's suggestion that she overlooked him in presenting her webinar.

Although ideal practice would have included documentation of this, it is unclear what, if any, evidence exists regarding the level of Professor Pratt's contribution. Therefore, it is important to use the ethical decision-making model to consider authorship of both the webinar presented by Professor Jamison and the manuscript submitted by Professor Pratt. It appears Professor Jamison thinks she has been aggrieved by Professor Pratt, and she may be wondering whether she is the first student researcher with this experience or she is misreading the circumstance. Because it is common for individuals who experience authorship disputes not to report them, it is possible that this is not the first time Professor Pratt has misused student research (Sandler & Russell, 2005). Professor Jamison is likely to consider the effect of following up on this issue for her own benefit but may also consider the effect her vulnerability may have on other individuals who have been or are in similar positions.

The next step in the IMED is to examine relevant ethics codes and institutional policies. In this case, not only should Professor Jamison review the *ACA Code of Ethics* (ACA, 2014) but she will also want to examine documentation and procedures related to research conduct and authorship at her doctoral institution as well as at the organization through which she delivered the webinar and the journal to which Professor Pratt submitted the manuscript. The *ACA Code of Ethics* is clear that research collaborators should agree regarding authorship (Standard G.5.e.), and scholars provide some recommendations for authors (i.e., Wester, 2011). In this case, it appears that the *Code* may not have been followed because there was no conversation about authorship with Professor Jamison prior to publication. Professor Jamison should also consult any relevant university or journal policies that may be applicable in this situation. When individuals are paid for their work on a project, it can also be important to consider which part of a contribution is paid or unpaid. In some situations, there are exceptions to traditional authorship frameworks when work is paid and thus is considered "works for hire" (Mawdsley, 2009, p. 263).

After identifying the problem and reviewing relevant information, the IMED signifies the importance of Professor Jamison considering consultation with trusted mentors and experts in her field to assist in understanding the issues and context, including the cultural worldview factors. Only after doing so, and in this case examining the dilemma across the four phases of the EDMDAC, should she begin to identify potential courses of action. As with any situation, there are potential risks and benefits to any action taken by Professor Jamison. Some junior scholars may be hesitant to proceed with formal action for fear of repercussions, but some researchers suggest that individuals who report authorship issues—even those who experience negative consequences—would make the same decision again. If Professors Jamison and Pratt work at the same university, there may be a mediation office or ombudsperson that could provide initial guidance for Professor Jamison. Professor Jamison may decide that she wishes to pursue allegations of plagiarism at the university level, although research suggests that pursuing action through official university channels can be time consuming (Fox & Beall, 2014), and given that academia reflects power and privilege structures found in society at large the grievance system may inadvertently favor Professor Pratt and others with similar identities and social locations. Professor Jamison may also consider reporting the issue to the journal in question, although it is important to recognize the limited liability of journals in the publishing process. Nevertheless, it is possible that reporting the incident might lead to retraction of the article, appropriate credit for Professor Jamison, or sanctions against future publication in the journal or its affiliates (Fox & Beall, 2014).

We recommend that prior to taking action Professor Jamison understand the institution's and journal's policies on what constitutes plagiarism and that she be prepared to provide documentation that could support her claim (Fox & Beall, 2014). Given the current reliance on indemnity clauses within publication outlets, it is possible that Professor Pratt will be required to defend himself against any allegations made by Professor Jamison, which would give him significant motivation to deny the allegations (Mock et al., 2010). This seems especially likely in this case given the veiled threats in Professor Pratt's text responses. Still, given the information available in the case itself, we recommend that Professor Jamison consider pursuing journal and institutional options for protecting her work. As noted in the IMED, Professor Jamison should document her decision-making process and the selected course of action, and then monitor and evaluate the outcomes. In this instance, we would anticipate that the dilemma may not be immediately resolved and that adequate resolution may require more comprehensive discussions across identified stakeholders, which in this case includes both Professor Jamison and Professor Pratt and potentially their academic institutions, their professional organizations, and the journal in question.

Conclusion

We have used the case of Ani Jamison to demonstrate how responsible authorship and ethical publication practices involve an iterative process. This process proactively begins prior to and extends beyond the termination of the project itself. Thus, we recommend all authors consider their publications and collaborations through an ethical decision-making lens.

Reflection Questions

1. What would you have done if you were Professor Jamison?
2. How might your perspective change if you were hearing this story from a character other than Professor Jamison?

Critical Incident Response

Richard E. Watts and
Jacqueline M. Swank

This case focuses on a senior faculty member (Professor Pratt) taking a previous student's work (dissertation) as his own without giving the former student (Professor Jamison) credit. Issues relevant to the case include plagiarism, power differential and misuse of power, integrity in authorship integrity, and veracity. This response focuses on some additional areas to consider in analyzing the case and preventing and addressing authorship conflicts.

There are many unknown factors in this case, including the extent of Professor Pratt's involvement in Professor Jamison's dissertation, whether they previously discussed authorship credit on publications resulting from her dissertation, whether Professor Pratt was a coauthor on Professor Jamison's published article related to her dissertation, and whether Professor Pratt reviewed Professor Jamison's webinar and obtained the idea for the conceptual framework from it or developed this idea from working with Professor Jamison and having access to her dissertation. However, what appears to be clear is that Professor Pratt plagiarized Professor Jamison's dissertation by including complete sentences from it in his article as well as including her unpublished data without acknowledging her work. He may also have plagiarized content from the webinar, as the conceptual framework he discussed was similar to what she independently developed and included in the presentation. Watts (2015) noted that it is important to remember that plagiarism pertains to both verbal and written communication of ideas and words. Therefore, even if Professor Jamison only verbally discussed the idea of the conceptual framework with Professor Pratt, he would still need to cite her as a personal communication.

It is only by chance that Professor Jamison became aware of Professor Pratt's manuscript, and she has been unsuccessful in facilitating a conversation with him about it, as he appears to be dismissive of her concerns. Given the challenges with attempting to communicate with Professor Pratt, she may want to involve another person, such as a mentor or a trusted colleague, to help facilitate the conversation. Depending on their relationship, her dissertation chair might be an ideal person to help facilitate the conversation, being a mentor to Professor Jamison, knowing Professor Pratt, and having knowledge of Professor Jamison's dissertation process. Professor Jamison appears to plan to continue writing and publishing on a research line related to her dissertation, and it is unclear how much involvement Professor Pratt had in coconstructing ideas related to this research line. Thus, in addition to discussing the current article it is important for Professors Jamison and Pratt to discuss their previous collaborations to determine authorship credit on projects as well as discuss moving forward with their distinct lines of research to hopefully avoid continued ethical dilemmas regarding authorship credit on future publications.

This case also brings up the broader critical issue of sharing ideas publicly before publishing them. Fortunately, in this case, the organization recorded and published the webinar on its website, so Professor Jamison's ideas were published in some form (although not in print). However, this is not always the case, in particular when scholars present at conferences. Scholars should consider whether they want to share their ideas in presentations before publishing them, even when the presentations are recorded. When deciding to share their ideas, scholars should explicitly state during the presentation the importance of others citing their work if they use content from the presentation. They may also provide a suggested citation as a footnote on handouts.

Regarding dissertations, universities may allow doctoral students to decide whether they want to have their dissertation publicly available and, if so, the time frame for releasing it to the public. Students may consider holding their dissertation for a year or two before making it accessible to the public to provide adequate time to publish an article on their work. It is crucial for doctoral mentors to help guide students in this process, as students may never consider the possibility of someone taking their ideas as their own.

Unfortunately, scholars cannot prevent others from plagiarizing their work; however, they can take steps to help protect their work and receive credit for their ideas. They can also take action when they have knowledge of plagiarism. This can be an uncomfortable process, but ethical dilemmas are often uncomfortable to some degree, and this does not mean counseling scholars shy away from addressing them. Scholars, especially those new to the field, should seek out support from trusted mentors when they need advocates or assistance navigating this process.

• • •

Chapter 24

Who to Include: A Case of Contested Authorship

A. Stephen Lenz, Diana Camilo, and Megan Speciale

2014 *ACA Code of Ethics* Standards Addressed

- G.5.d. Contributors
- G.5.e. Agreement of Contributors

• • •

Mena was a 28-year-old Mexican American woman in the third year of her counselor education and supervision doctoral program at Southern State University (SSU). She was enrolled in classes full time and employed by the SSU Counseling Department as a research assistant (RA). Mena and her adviser, Professor Campbell, had known each other for almost 5 years. Before entering the doctoral program, Mena had completed her master's degree in counseling at SSU, and Professor Campbell had been her instructor for several courses. Because of her strong performance in class, he had invited her to serve as his RA in her final semester. Professor Campbell had provided a positive letter of reference for her doctoral application and advocated for her admission into the program. After she was accepted, he selected her to be his doctoral advisee given their previous positive work experiences and shared research interests.

In her initial advising meetings with Professor Campbell, Mena shared that she was a first-generation college student and was actively searching for additional assistantships within the department to offset the cost of attending graduate school full time. Professor Campbell helped Mena secure an RA position in the department for 10 hours a week to provide logistical research support for his active research projects. Although Professor Campbell did not specify the exact nature of "logistical research support," Mena showed great enthusiasm for the research projects and regularly contributed hours beyond what was stipulated in her RA contract to complete the tasks assigned to her. Her assistantship duties were mostly administrative in nature; however, Mena also regularly engaged in in-depth discussions of each of the research projects with Professor Campbell and his research team and thus assumed she would be included as an author on publications.

After a year of working with Professor Campbell, Mena was transferred to working with Professor May, another professor in the counseling department. Professor May provided detailed contribution agreements to Mena for each study she was asked to support in her role as an RA. When she discovered she was not being invited for authorship, Mena approached Professor May to discuss potential opportunities for authorship and was informed that logistical support was traditionally not eligible for authorship. Concerned, Mena reached out to Professor Campbell for confirmation that she would be included as an author on the studies she had contributed to as his RA. He informed her she would not be an author. A manuscript developed from one of the studies was published a couple months later and Mena was not on the author list or cited in the acknowledgments; however, two other departmental RAs whose job responsibilities were similar to hers were included as authors. Mena observed that both of these students were male.

In her new RA position, Mena was tasked with managing Professor May's doctoral research lab. Over 6 months, several students from the counseling department expressed concern about feeling pressure from faculty to perform research and teaching support above and beyond what was outlined in their contracts. In addition, two students in the lab privately shared with Mena that they had also worked with Professor Campbell on a research study and had been denied authorship. Mena observed that these two students were also female and first-generation college students. With this realization, Mena was compelled to file an ethics complaint with the SSU Ethics and Compliance Office (ECO) to call attention to what she perceived as a pattern of violations of professional ethics. In the complaint, she reported she had been denied authorship on a manuscript that was based on work she had completed under the supervision of her adviser, Professor Campbell. Mena stated that in her role as departmental RA she had provided substantial intellectual contributions to the research study and did not receive recognition for her work. She also reported that this was a common experience among students within her department and provided specific examples in her report.

In his initial response to the ECO committee, Professor Campbell explained Mena had been hired as an RA to perform logistical duties, including filing, printing and copying, and basic data entry for several of his projects. He reported that authorship had not been discussed, stating it was uncommon for departmental RAs to receive authorship for performing logistical duties. Professor Campbell reported that Mena had not contributed to planning or implementing the research project or writing the manuscript, and his only conversations with Mena about the project had been related to mentoring her. Professor Campbell reported that because Mena had discontinued her work on the research project after being transferred to another professor, he had not shared with her that the manuscript was being submitted for publication.

Case Analysis and Discussion

Regarding diversity and power dynamics, the Association for Counselor Education and Supervision (ACES) Guidelines for Research Mentorship (Borders et al., 2012) highlight the need for mentors' awareness and acknowledgment of multicultural and power dynamics within the mentor-mentee relationship. There are numerous power differentials inherent to Mena and Professor Campbell's relationship. Mena is a first-generation Latina college student who is being advised by Professor Campbell, a white, male counselor educator. Chung et al. (2007) advised that even informal mentoring relationships begin with an invitation to mentees to participate in a dialogue about the goals of mentorship and the expectations of each member. Through this conversation, members collaboratively define the parameters of the mentoring relationship, including strategies for navigating unequal power dynamics and cultural differences within the working alliance. Having this discussion would have provided Mena a pathway for clarifying her authorship agreement with Professor Campbell as her RA responsibilities started to surpass those initially outlined. It is important to note that as the mentoring relationship evolves, there is a continued need for clear discussion regarding shifting power dynamics (Chung et al., 2007) that may influence personal and professional well-being and respecting the rights of all parties.

In terms of ethical counseling, the *ACA Code of Ethics* (American Counseling Association [ACA], 2014) requires counselors to acknowledge the efforts of individuals who contribute to the development of a research project through authorship, acknowledgment, or other means (Standard G.5.d.). Even if they are not included as authors, individuals who make minor technical contributions can be acknowledged in introductory statements or notes. The *Code* also requires that counselors discuss task allocation and acknowledgment of contributors before beginning a joint research project (Standard G.5.e.). Although the *Code* does not outline the scope of minor technical duties, any discussions Professor Campbell and Mena had regarding publication agreements would have warranted clarification of the logistical duties Mena engaged in as an RA. As the nature of the formal complaint is to call attention to a pattern of violations of professional ethics, the language within the *ACA Code of Ethics* may warrant a review of Professor Campbell and the department's practices regarding faculty-student working agreements.

Regarding best practices for research mentorship, the ACES Guidelines for Research Mentorship (Borders et al., 2012) specify that a mentor respects efforts through authorship or acknowledgment related to a research project (2.b.). Accordingly, mentees discuss expected project outcomes and any related rights to ownership among a team of scholars (6.b.). Although the ACES Guidelines do not stipulate what constitutes authorship versus acknowledgment, the shared responsibility of the mentor and mentee to have conversations together regarding expectations, collaboration, and roles early in the mentoring relationship (3.c., 6.a.) should deter potential conflicts. The ACES Guidelines indicate that mentees communicate their needs from the mentor (6.a.) and periodically renegotiate changes in the mentoring relationship (6.c.). From this perspective, the mentor and mentee share responsibility to outline research activity and authorship agreements. Professor Campbell and Mena may have been best served by outlining project aims, mentee goals and needs, credit for contributions, and possible mentor-mentee renegotiations early in the project.

The *Publication Manual of the American Psychological Association* (American Psychological Association [APA], 2020) also addresses authorship. Specifically, APA suggests that authorship is reserved for individuals whose contributions to and responsibility for a published work are substantial. This position allows individuals who complete substantial activities other than writing to be included within author bylines. APA publication guidelines also indicate that minor contributions (e.g., participant recruitment, data collection and entry, statistical consultation) do not constitute consideration for authorship. However, the APA guidelines acknowledge that meaningful combinations of these tasks may warrant a contributor's designation as an author, but at a minimum individuals who make contributions should receive acknowledgment within the author's note. Based on the APA guidelines, Mena's data entry activities alone did not constitute a substantial contribution and thus may not warrant author status unless they were coupled with other meaningful activities.

The Consortia Advancing Standards in Research Administration Information addresses issues inherent within traditional views of authorship through the use of the Contributor Roles Taxonomy (CRediT). Through a shift in perspective from authorship to contributorship, CRediT provides a framework for promoting visibility by acknowledging the diverse range of valuable inputs that are required to produce scholarly outputs (Holcombe, 2019). CRediT allows for contributions that extend beyond writing, such as conceptualization, data curation, formal analysis, and project management (Allen et al., 2019). Based on the number and extent of roles, individuals are acknowledged for their contributions to scholarly outputs in more even-handed and transparent ways. In Mena's case, CRediT would provide a framework for acknowledging her role in supporting data curation, which would result in a nuanced degree of credit-based authorship positioning.

Although journal editors are not expected to scrutinize the author listing of each submission, the Committee on Publication Ethics provides some guidance and support for taking reasonable actions after identifying a ghost author who has met the eligibility requirements for contributor-based authorship yet was excluded from the author list in published materials (Albert & Wager, 2003; Wager, 2013). When poor authorship practices lead to authorship disputes or the identification of ghost authorship, editors have some remedial injunctions available for consideration. First, Committee on Publication Ethics guidelines advocate for editors to recommend a missing author be added to the publication. Second, editors can request written agreement for the inclusion of the missing contributor from all authors. Third, editors can consider sending a letter of disappointment over the dispute to the lead author and sending a copy to the head of research compliance at this author's institution. Fourth, in extreme instances of negligence, editors may choose to ban a lead author or authorship team from publishing in the journal in the future. Finally, editors should revisit the journal's published policies for authorship inclusion to identify any ambiguities that may contribute to similar issues in the future. In the event that the journal editor identified and confirmed Mena as a ghost author, it would be reasonable practice to provide a corrigendum to correct the electronic version of the published manuscript.

Regarding legal considerations, copyright law of the United States and related laws contained in Title 17 of the *United States Code* provide language that protects authors whose works advance sciences and useful arts. However, authors and contributors are not always considered as such based on legal standing. Instead, the "work made for hire" doctrine can situate employers, funding agencies, or commissioning parties as the initial copyright owners of creative works. In instances of judicial injunction, there are generally two categories of remedies: equitable remedies and remedies at law (Gomez-Arostegui, 2008). In Mena's case, an equitable remedy may involve the nonjudicial inclusion of her on the authorship team. By contrast, a remedy at law may include compensation for damages associated with lost wages within the job market. However, in either case, legal remedies to authorship disputes may tend toward fruitless in the absence of a clear preponderance of evidence, malicious intent to exclude, or related harmful effects.

Actions and Outcomes

A review of Mena's case and related key issues by the SSU ECO committee suggested that a number of ambiguous or unacknowledged power, cultural, and professional dynamics had converged to create a difficult situation that could have been avoided. The ECO committee suggested that mitigation of Mena's situation from critical status would not necessarily have been defined by authorship alone but by increased clarity around the functional relationship among her activities, their perceived value within the broader department culture, and expected outputs. The ECO committee's analyses suggested that although Professor Campbell may not have operated outside the authorship guidelines described by APA (2020), his actions were inconsistent with the ACES Guidelines for Research Mentorship (Borders et al., 2012) and the *ACA Code of Ethics* (ACA, 2014). They determined it was probable that Mena's department culture—which was characterized by obfuscation of student-faculty interactions at best and inequitable distributions of opportunities at worst—had the potential to transfer poor mentoring practices across generations of counselor educators, which can be deleterious to the academic climate and students' sense of agency and meaning. The ECO committee determined that Mena's scenario may have been avoided by any combination of reasonable activities, such as discussing roles and expectations early and often (Borders et al., 2012), developing a clearly worded authorship agreement early in the process (see Flamez et al., 2017), or using a model-based decision-making process (Swank et al., 2019). These recommendations were submitted to Professor Campbell and Professor May's department head, who was requested to respond to the ECO committee, the dean of students, and the provost in writing with a course of action depicting what actions would be taken to mitigate similar occurrences in the future.

The department head sought feedback from faculty, students, and colleagues and situated those perspectives within the context of the ECO disposition. The formal response indicated that Mena had completed all activities, while using department equipment and facilities, within the boundaries of her weekly assistantship hours and that an article correction would not be requested from the journal editor. The department head acknowledged that although Mena's experience had been the status quo within faculty and department cultures, it may not have been best practice for student engagement or professional mentoring. The department hired a consultant to provide a 2-hour training for all students and faculty related to contemporary trends and ethical and legal considerations in authorship. In addition, a standard form for authorship agreements would be developed and required for all faculty work with students, regardless of its association with an assistantship. Thus, although Mena's experience did not result in her receiving authorship on the publication related to her complaint, her self-advocacy and the resounding affirmation of shortcomings in faculty-student relations prompted important changes in department culture that had the potential to increase equity moving forward.

Conclusion

The issue of ambiguous authorship credit has complicated the developmental experiences of many emerging and established scholars with unfortunate implications for equitable professional empowerment and career-sustaining self-concept. However, it does not have to be this way. Regardless of your position along the continuum from acknowledging meaningful contributions in footnotes to adopting the CRediT model, the most important positions to take are those of transparency, equity, and fidelity. We are counselors, and our profession is centered on relational experiences that are developmental and generative across the life span. Let us commit to authorship experiences that bear those values as well.

Reflection Questions

1. What are your views of the power dynamics in this case?
2. How might this case influence how you negotiate authorship inclusion or position in the future?

Critical Incident Response

Sherrie L. Bruner and Melissa Luke

The case of Mena provides an opportunity to reflect on and enact policies and procedures to support clarity in authorship decisions. The authors acknowledged the shared responsibility for conversations around research mentorship and provided concrete options for policy development (ACA, 2014; APA, 2020; Borders et al., 2012). Although either party in the relationship might introduce these conversations, it is important for mentors to recognize the power dynamics inherent in mentee-mentor relationships (Borders et al., 2012). This is especially important to consider given that Mena identifies as a female, first-generation, Mexican American student, all identities frequently exploited in research settings (Gaughan & Bozeman, 2016). Thus, students may not feel empowered to initiate conversations. It is important for faculty to model and provide a space in which open and honest dialogue about issues such as authorship can occur.

This case also offers meaningful opportunities for the development of Mena's professional identity as a mentor and researcher beyond the immediate issue of authorship. For example, because neither the department nor Mena's faculty appear to have attended to the conceptualization of graduate assistantships or the facilitation of professional identity, important opportunities were missed. Although faculty often have the freedom to assign tasks, graduate assistantships can socialize advanced students into academia and intentionally assist students in developing their professional identities alongside research and teaching skills (Nettles & Millett, 2006). In addition, graduate assistantships can play a meaningful role in developing connection to a program, an important component of persistence for graduate students (Gardner & Barnes, 2007; Kim & Otts, 2010). In the case of Mena, a negative experience could contribute to faltering progress within her graduate program. With that in mind, it is important for departments and mentors to conceptualize this issue more broadly than around authorship alone. Thus, the department should consider clarifying its practices around mentoring doctoral students. For example, in addition to encouraging faculty to participate in diversity, equity, accessibility, and inclusion training that centers on these issues in higher education, the department could engage in an equity audit that examines data including but not limited to student assistantships, identity, and authorship opportunities for the purpose of developing more equitable systemic procedures.

Finally, it is concerning that Mena was denied authorship but two other individuals with similar contributions were included as authors. Broderick and Casadevall (2019) found that there continues to be a difference in authorship position and attribution based on gender. An examination of departmental practices through a filter of culture (e.g., equity audit) may reveal additional instances in which inequity has occurred related to authorship credit as well as more broadly. Although it may be appropriate to extend traditional taxonomies of authorship when mentoring emerging researchers, consideration should be given to the reasons for and equity of these extensions and their use examined through an ethical decision-making model (Luke & Bruner, 2022). We recommend that similar to incrementally increasing expectations for performance across counseling, teaching, or supervision faculty should adjust expectations of what constitutes authorship developmentally: Authorship agreement for master's students may be predicated on literature review support or data gathering, whereas early doctoral students may complete these tasks while also coding or writing. Authorship agreements with advanced doctoral students could reflect the development of conceptual, methodological, and technical skills, with expectations for greater contribution and more independence in their work.

Procedures for facilitating conversations about authorship early and often reflect best practice in mentoring (see Luke & Bruner, 2022). Although departmental implementation of a taxonomy to scaffold authorship discussions could have protected Mena and created more opportunities for faculty to have identified and addressed differing perspectives during the authorship process, individual faculty can formally both implement and document these procedures on their own. Introducing students to this expectation would normalize the discussion and provide students with an opportunity to request such a discussion consistent with department policy if the topic is not broached by the faculty member. On a related note, important information about systemic inequity can become evident when a department commits to ongoing use of equity audits to improve its own policies and procedures.

• • •

Chapter 25

Is This How It's Supposed to Be? Collaboration Gone Wrong

Erik M. Hines and Paul C. Harris

2014 *ACA Code of Ethics* Standards Addressed

- C.5. Nondiscrimination
- D.1.c. Interdisciplinary Teamwork

• • •

Professor Balial was an African American, male, school counselor educator with a research interest in creating access and opportunity for underrepresented students to pursue degrees and careers in science, technology, engineering, and mathematics (STEM). The associate dean for engineering undergraduate studies and diversity at Technical University asked him whether he was interested in collaborating with a team of faculty from various STEM programs at the university, including science education (teacher education), biology, chemical engineering, and mechanical engineering. The team included three white individuals (two males and one female), one Indian male, and one Asian female. The group planned to apply for a national federal grant worth $3 million over 4 years.

Professor Balial joined the team, and during their first meeting the faculty discussed their common research interests and their approach to research. Most of the STEM faculty had a research paradigm that aligned with the hard sciences and had a quantitative focus. However, Professor Balial preferred a mixed-methods approach. When discussing research ideas and strategies for assisting underrepresented students, most faculty talked about the population from a deficit perspective. For example, one of the collaborators questioned whether students of color had the capacity to do well in STEM courses. Professor Balial was concerned about the colleague's cultural competency and educated him about the lack of resources these students had in their schools to attain the education needed to achieve high performance in the STEM fields.

The team decided to focus the proposal on increasing the number of students from underrepresented groups pursuing undergraduate degrees in the STEM fields. They planned to create a training program for college instructors and K–12 educators focused on ways to prepare underrepresented groups for STEM majors in higher education. They also planned to work with middle and high school educators and mentoring programs for underrepresented students. As the group continued to meet, Professor Balial noticed that some of the collaborators continued to question the intellectual capability of students rather than viewing the system as the genesis of the problem.

Professor Balial recommended, as part of the proposal, for the team to conduct focus groups with students at Technical University and high schools to obtain their perspectives on choosing STEM degrees and the barriers that may inhibit underrepresented students from pursuing these degrees. He also noted the importance of interviewing school counselors to understand their perspectives on these students not pursuing STEM degrees and recommendations for assisting them. Other team members responded with resistance to having focus groups, stating the team had sufficient data already to make decisions and qualitative data would not make a valuable contribution.

Professor Balial struggled to work with the group because of the lack of cultural responsiveness and the opposition to obtaining qualitative data to inform decisions. He believed it was important to hear the voices of underrepresented students because they were not in a position of power to make decisions. In addition, he was a person of color and could relate to the student population.

Case Analysis and Discussion

A need exists for women, people of color, and people from lower socioeconomic backgrounds in STEM fields (Hutton, 2019). Although this may be widely recognized, people may have difficulty understanding and developing cultural competence. An important aspect of cultural competence is recognizing that we all have blind spots in areas of knowledge and expertise but we may not be aware of them. When we work with a diverse team, in which others have different lived experiences and perspectives, we increase the likelihood of becoming aware of our blind spots. However, if we choose to ignore or deny the voices and perspectives of others, our blind spots remain and we continue to privilege our own voices while marginalizing others. This results in inadequate expression of those voices within research data. It may also contribute to difficulty recruiting and retaining underrepresented students in doctoral programs, in particular in STEM fields (Okahana et al., 2018). Views like those of Professor Balial's colleagues related to the capacity of underrepresented groups can permeate to such a degree that fewer of these students matriculate to graduate school, and the students who do may experience similar ideologies that cause unnecessary challenges. Biased views of underrepresented populations influence research, policy, and practice. Assenting verbally to the importance of cultural competence but not naming privilege and racism as sources of observed disparity is particularly harmful to underrepresented populations (Chun & Evans, 2016). This appears to be consistent with the actions of Professor Balial's colleagues despite his advocacy.

When discussing the best strategy for supporting underrepresented students, most team members talked about this population from a deficit perspective. In addition, some members believed some students of color did not have the capacity to do well in the STEM fields. Professor Balial immediately corrected his colleagues and reminded them that some students may not have had equal access to the resources needed to prepare them for STEM classes. This does not mean students of color are not capable, nor does it mean they should be viewed as less than their peers. Students of color and underrepresented students often experience inequities related to access to a rigorous quality education (Hines et al., 2019). Regarding cultural competency, the *ACA Code of Ethics* (American Counseling Association [ACA], 2014) mandates that counselors (in this case counselor educators) not discriminate against research participants or individuals from diverse backgrounds (Standard C.5.). This standard relates to Professor Balial discussing cultural competency with his colleagues and educating them on the complexities students of color experience related to the STEM fields. Educators need to be aware of their biases and to consider them prior to making decisions about how to properly serve students, especially students of color. Training in cultural competence is important across universities because diversity among faculty and students optimizes learning for everyone (Kruse et al., 2018). Professor Balial's team members muted his voice and experience and chose to privilege the voice of the majority. Professor Balial believed the lack of cultural competence and the bias against qualitative research had a role in their decision not to consider his suggestions. Often students of color are viewed from a deficit- rather than strengths-based model (Hines et al., 2015). In addition, some scholars view qualitative research as lacking the rigor of traditional scientific research (Sandelowski, 1986). Ignoring Professor Balial's recommendations may limit the data. To help prevent this situation, team members should intentionally immerse themselves in other cultures to develop openness to other perspectives, as the understanding and embracing of other cultures results from intentional endeavors (Szucs et al., 2019). In other words, the research team can resolve biases and beliefs about certain populations by engaging in immersion experiences.

Lack of openness to diverse voices is a form of microaggression and white privilege (Acuff, 2018). This may have negatively affected Professor Balial (e.g., leading him to question his sense of self-efficacy and contribution). Professor Balial knew the team wanted to work together based on expertise; however, cultural competency was a barrier to all of them working together effectively. When researchers work on interdisciplinary teams, they can expect some friction based on different motives, experiences, and expertise. The *ACA Code of Ethics* (ACA, 2014) addresses the importance of counselors focusing on what is best for the client (in this case research participants) when working on an interdisciplinary team (Standard D.1.c.). Although this standard is related to clinical work and not research specifically, it could be applied to working as a member of a research team to advocate for what is best for a clinical research participant. One benefit of interdisciplinary teams is that their research is comprehensive and culturally responsible. In addition, external funders prefer it when researchers work in an interdisciplinary capacity. When researchers work in silos, they may not get the expertise from other researchers needed to execute a comprehensive research study.

Regarding research methodology, Professor Balial believed quantitative data alone would not comprehensively capture students' experiences; therefore, qualitative data collection was also needed in the project. Professor Balial advocated for using a mixed-methods approach to understand the participants' experiences with barriers to accessing the STEM curriculum. He asserted that a mixed-methods approach to understanding the complexities of this research was supported in the literature. A mixed-methods approach has several advantages, such as helping researchers understand the contradiction in both methodologies and creating a rich, inclusive study (Wisdom & Creswell, 2013). Exploring experiences (qualitative) and examining constructs (e.g., intelligence, poverty, and race; quantitative) with underrepresented students and students of color in STEM as they transition to college would give the researchers a comprehensive understanding of this topic. This is crucial, as the findings will guide the development of guidelines for supporting underrepresented students in pursuing STEM fields.

Actions and Outcomes

Professor Balial experienced a challenging choice: either to leave the team or to stay on the project to ensure the story of the participants was complete and presented ethically. He decided to remain a member of the team to help ensure underrepresented groups were treated well, in accordance with ethics guidelines. He believed the study was needed and wanted to ensure no harm or misrepresentation came to the participants.

Professor Balial used data and relationship building to help his colleagues see the value in hearing from underrepresented students. This included adding data to the grant proposal and getting to know his colleagues on the research team. Over time, Professor Bilal gradually got his colleagues to understand his point of view as he continued to advocate for a mixed-methods design and the population involved in the study as well as share his experiences as an African American male.

When working in interdisciplinary teams, researchers must assert their expertise. Every team member has a role in the project and research process, and it is important that researchers work collaboratively and use ethical standards to guide their actions. The research team eventually agreed to use a mixed-methods approach to highlight the experiences of underrepresented students (qualitative) while examining the effectiveness of the training program (quantitative). Although the study was not funded because the grantor desired collaboration among multiple institutions, Professor Balial felt satisfied he had educated his colleagues about the population and looked forward to future collaborations with the team.

Conclusion

Collaboration is important in seeking external funding, and compromise is an essential component of this process. Counseling researchers should stay committed to their ethical beliefs when they encounter barriers or resistance while collaborating with others. They may use data, advocacy, and relationship building, as discussed in this case, to successfully navigate working on interdisciplinary teams.

Reflection Questions

1. What other strategies might Professor Balial have used in working with the research team to address ethical issues involving underserved or diverse communities in research?
2. What suggestions do you have for successfully navigating interdisciplinary collaborations?

Critical Incident Response

Jesse Fox

This case raises fundamental questions regarding the nature of epistemology and the philosophy of science, questions that have potentially powerful implications for the lives of people. Counseling is an applied social science. It is important to note that counseling research is part of a rich strain of intellectual inquiry that makes use of diverse epistemological perspectives to develop new knowledge, guiding decision-making and evidence-based practices. Though all researchers embrace epistemologies in their work, they are not always actively thought through, especially when interdisciplinary teams may draw from diverse perspectives.

Professor Balial's colleagues likely approached their work as scientists by embracing many assumptions of positivism or postpositivism (Heppner et al., 2016). Partially products of the European Enlightenment, positivism and postpositivism formed the intellectual basis through which the STEM fields developed (Grassie, 2010). Positivism stresses that knowledge can and should be empirically verified and that personal and cultural assumptions are irrelevant to the pursuit of science. One principle of positivism that appears especially relevant in this case is that researcher biases and preconceived notions of truth are not relevant to science. The life experience of the researcher(s), or the participants in research for that matter, is not important in positivism. The reason it is unimportant is that positivism contends that knowledge can be developed and truth known without the influence of the researcher's bias through the scientific method.

Professor Balial's approach to research emphasizes different assumptions from those of his STEM colleagues. Constructivist and critical epistemologies recognize the influence of the knower in the scientific process and do not view knowledge as something that is devoid of subjectivity. Subjectivity is inevitable, and there is no objective reality. Rather than naively attempting to eradicate researcher bias from the scientific process, constructivist and postcritical epistemologies reveal how biases influence the development of research questions, methods of collecting and analyzing data, and the interpretation of findings and their implications. Instead of attempting to arrive at the truth about something, constructivists and critical scholars emphasize the constructions of knowledge, which can be "simple or complex, naïve or sophisticated, uninformed or informed, but they cannot be proven true or false" (Heppner et al., 2016, p. 12). These epistemologies also assume social constructions are embedded in power structures that legitimize their validity, resulting in the oppression of those on the margins of society.

It is a misconception that science, and by extension the methodologies of science, is uniform and shares a common set of assumptions. Science, in common parlance, is often presumed and presented as the pursuit of empirical knowledge detached from the person of the investigator through the so-called scientific method. This version, the hypothetical-deductive method, begins with the researcher formulating a problem, then drawing on a theory to explain the problem, developing hypotheses, and collecting and analyzing data that support or refute the hypotheses (Heppner et al., 2016). However, philosophers of science have rejected this version of the scientific method for the reasons portrayed in this case. It accounts for nothing, for instance, of the messiness of scientific debate; the community of peers through which science is conducted; the sociohistorical influences on the way in which a problem is viewed; or the pragmatic implications of truth claims, which scientists then disseminate to the broader society (Grassie, 2010).

Professor Balial's concerns that implicit biases and lack of cultural competence were influencing the direction the research team took appear well warranted. History reveals that researchers' cultural biases and prejudices can influence the pursuit of science. One example is the eugenics movement in the United States and Europe. Eugenics, the prevailing view of the intellectual elite during the 19th and 20th centuries, held as fact that Blacks and other outgroups, such as Jews, were genetically and therefore intellectually inferior to whites (History.com Editors, 2017). In this case, it is difficult not to see the residue of scientific racism that was common in eugenics at work in Professor Balial's colleagues (Sue et al., 2019). Thus, it is clear that Professor Balial's advocacy required courage, and without it the team may have persisted in their cultural blindness. His actions are an example of the unique role and contribution counselors have in interdisciplinary research teams.

Practically speaking, when engaging in interdisciplinary work, researchers should consider beginning their work together by discussing how they view the process of conducting research. Actively raising questions about epistemology early on may help acknowledge and address blind spots among team members before they become problematic. Examining assumptions is an important step in the research process. This requires openness to dialogue, something all research team members need to commit to cultivating. It may also require researchers to expand their epistemologies to be more inclusive of other ways of knowing.

This case points to the critical need to include the perspective of the oppressed to correct simplified definitions of what makes science science. This includes questioning the supposed consensus regarding the uniformity of methodology, misguided uses of data, and pluralistic assumptions and lived experiences that form the background of scientific inquiries. Science is conducted best when diverse perspectives are brought together to expand the perspective on how research problems are framed and what tools are available to address them.

• • •

Section 2
Client Interest and Well-Being

Chapter 26

I Need Your Approval, but I Don't Want to Do That: Getting IRB Approval

Sam Steen and Shekila Melchior

2014 *ACA Code of Ethics* Standards Addressed

- G.1.a. Conducting Research
- G.1.b. Confidentiality in Research
- G.2.a. Informed Consent in Research

• • •

Juanita and Cathy, who identified as Black women, were school counselor educators at a local university. They planned to collaborate with a school district to address achievement gaps by examining the growth of Black and Brown children who were differently abled and then offering interventions. Many of the children needing the additional support were from low-income communities. The main goal of the research was to examine the effectiveness of small-group counseling interventions on students' academic and social skills following intentional interactions with peers. Master's-level students would lead groups as part of their advanced school counseling course that focused on teaching students to create interventions to use within a comprehensive developmental school counseling program. The school counselor educators decided to use the Achieving Success Everyday group counseling model (Steen et al., 2014), a group counseling intervention focused on academic and social-emotional development. Participants would be evaluated using the following measures: (a) Learning Behaviors Related to School Achievement (Myrick, 2003), (b) grade point average, and (c) student reflections through the Critical Incident Questionnaire (Bloch et al., 1979). In addition, group leaders would complete the Critical Incident Questionnaire as a self-assessment.

The researchers submitted an application to the university institutional review board (IRB) and received several requested revisions, three of which posed challenges for the researchers. The first item involved participant selection. The IRB requested the researchers be the sole recruiters and selectors of the K–12 student participants. The researchers' most salient relationships were with the school counselors; therefore, they had planned to have them help recruit the student participants.

The second requested IRB revision that posed a challenge had to do with the confidentiality of students related to identifying the location of the interventions. Because of the structure of the school district and the specific schools targeted, the researchers were unable to confirm in advance where the small-group interventions would convene at each school. The researchers would decide on the locations for the interventions on a weekly basis based on the unique needs of the schools.

Finally, the IRB wanted the researchers to modify the informed consent by including more details about the study to encompass the expected outcomes, the content of the group intervention, and the criteria used to select participants (academic and behavioral difficulties). The researchers were reluctant to share these details, as they believed this information could potentially be misunderstood or even considered discriminatory, in particular because the study focused on vulnerable populations, including children with disabilities. Moreover, these details could also compromise the study by providing too much information about the focus of the study to participants. These critical descriptions could potentially influence the students' desire to participate, their response to assessments, and their level of participation.

Case Analysis and Discussion

It is crucial the researchers address the three concerns identified by the university IRB, as they need IRB approval before they can conduct their study. Following institutional regulations is an ethical standard for conducting research identified within the *ACA Code of Ethics* (American Counseling Association [ACA], 2014, Standard G.1.a.). In addition, the IRB concerns become clearer when contextualized within basic ethical criteria (e.g., respect, beneficence, and justice) presented to protect students. Respect focuses on treating people as able to make their own decisions and protecting them if they have less autonomy (Robinson & Curry, 2009). Beneficence aims to minimize risk and maximize possible benefits and students' best interests. Justice focuses on who benefits and who bears the burden, or who is potentially at risk in the research study (Robinson & Curry, 2009). In the current case, Juanita and Cathy view responsible participant selection as allowing individuals who already have prior relationships with the students to do the recruitment. At the same time, having the stakeholders involved in recruitment might be an undue burden. The researchers need to explore this in advance to make an informed decision. An explanation to the university IRB can help provide justification for the recruitment decisions.

Confidentiality in research is a counseling ethical standard (ACA, 2014, Standard G.1.b.). The researchers cannot confirm the location of the sessions in advance; however, they can provide the IRB with options for the location. Having a plan to maintain confidentiality is also important to help prevent the consequences of a breach in confidentiality (Macpherson, 2001). Although it is difficult to maintain confidentiality about who is participating in a study within a school setting, as it is likely students will see other students meeting with counselors for the research study, the researchers and study personnel should still strive to maintain the confidentiality of research participants.

Informed consent is the final area of concern, with the IRB wanting Juanita and Cathy to provide more details about the study. Topics to include in the informed consent are purpose, procedures, risks and benefits, alternative procedures, statements about asking questions, and permission to leave the study at any time. The consent form should provide enough information for participants to make an informed decision without being misleading or misunderstood (Wester, 2011). The *ACA Code of Ethics* (ACA, 2014, Standard G.2.a.) describes the language to include in the informed consent. The students themselves are not old enough to provide consent. Therefore, the parents must have enough information to make an informed decision on behalf of their children. After receiving the parents' permission, the researchers could also ask the students to provide verbal or written assent. Thus, it is also important to explain the study to the students on a level they are able to understand and with the inclusion of sufficient details.

Regarding multicultural considerations, the American School Counselor Association (ASCA) provides support for protecting vulnerable populations, including the minors with disabilities in this study. ASCA has addressed the inadequate services children with disabilities have historically received and ways in which school counselors can provide equitable services to all students (ASCA, 2016b). In an effort to provide equitable services for this population, the researchers purposefully want to include children who are differently abled; however, the need to provide additional information about this in the consent form might compromise the students' desire to participate or their willingness to be authentic as well as their parents' desire to have their children participate.

Actions and Outcomes

To address the first concern, Juanita and Cathy offered an alternative to the participant selection process. The researchers proposed to the IRB that they work with school counselors in the identified schools to obtain a list of eligible K–12 students to use in recruiting participants for the study. Juanita and Cathy, with the help of the school counselors, would then select as many students as possible at each school to participate in the group intervention. The researchers decided to work in concert with the school counselors to avoid any barriers to engaging students in the future. The researchers submitted a note to the IRB emphasizing the importance of collaboration and the need for stakeholder influence in participant selection.

In regard to the second concern, Juanita and Cathy worked with school administrators and school counselors to identify three classrooms or meeting spaces at each of the school sites in which to offer the intervention. They confirmed that the three locations within each school were confidential spaces. The researchers provided this information to the IRB for approval.

Regarding the final IRB concern, Juanita and Cathy modified the protocol to include (a) the overall anticipated outcomes of the study written generally (e.g., "gain personal insight," "identify strengths and areas for improvement"), (b) specific topics addressed in the intervention (e.g., goal setting, resiliency, communication skills), and (c) the process that would be used to recruit participants (i.e., teacher recommendation). Within the consent form, Juanita and Cathy provided brief information about the content of the group curriculum and the recruitment process. The researchers provided only general selection criteria to the IRB and in the parental consent form (e.g., students identified as potentially benefiting from the intervention). Juanita and Cathy believed that providing some general information highlighting the benefits of participating and limiting the focus on deficits (e.g., achievement gaps) would decrease the likelihood that students and their parents would be offended by or misunderstand the criteria for selection. The IRB approved the study with these revisions.

Conclusion

This case illustrates the importance of considering strategies to satisfy IRB requests while also focusing on not compromising the integrity of a research study. Researchers may have to alter some aspects of their study to obtain IRB approval. However, providing a strong rationale for the research methods may help researchers collaborate with the IRB to identify solutions to obtain IRB approval without compromising the research aims. Thus, it is helpful for researchers to establish and maintain a strong working relationship with the IRB at their institution.

Reflection Questions

1. What are some strategies researchers may use to address disagreements with IRB recommendations?
2. Is there anything you would do differently from Juanita and Cathy in designing this research study?

Critical Incident Response

Diandra J. Prescod

In a statement provided in response to racial unrest, ASCA (2020) discussed school counselors' duty to recognize signs of racism and bias (e.g., achievement gaps, self-destructive behavior). To acknowledge these issues in schools and be part of school leadership, school counselors must form quality relationships with students, staff, and administrators. Black students are more likely than white students to say their school counselor was the person who urged them to think about postsecondary education (Cholewa et al., 2018). The Education Trust (2019) reported that 38 states were not adequately serving students of color and/or students in low-income families. In addition, C. A. Rose and Gage (2017) stated that students who are differently abled are bullied at disproportionate rates than their peers. Direct student services offered by school counselors include creating positive relationships with students, displaying empathy, and communicating appropriately (ASCA, 2020).

Keeping these points in mind, Juanita and Cathy wanted to approach their study with care and intentionality. Involving school counselors who have prior relationships with students shows a level of intentionality that should exist in all types of research. The IRB made a relevant point in considering confidentiality. The alternative posed to address the IRB feedback still allows the counselors to be part of the process but gives more responsibility for recruitment to the researchers. This keeps the researchers at the forefront of recruitment efforts and separates the counselors from that process. This change prioritizes participants' confidentiality and provides an opportunity for future research and engagement.

Determining the study or intervention location can be a complicated aspect of research. Whether conducting research virtually, in a higher education setting, in a public or private business, in an agency, or in a K–12 school district, researchers must keep the best interest of their potential participants in mind. Business buildings, schools, and institutions of higher education are all different, and finding a designated space for group counseling and other activities may be difficult. Juanita and Cathy identified three available spaces for the intervention, which is helpful, as flexibility is important in the research process. Maintaining confidentiality is also important in conducting research (ACA, 2014, Standard G.1.b.), and there could be a breach if individuals who are not participating in the intervention know the location. After using a location, researchers may discover there is too much noise or interruption and use a different space. Choosing a safe and private location may take time but could help provide a smooth process.

Researchers have not always been mindful of engaging in ethical work and protecting participants. For example, in the early 1970s the public learned that, for the past approximately 40 years, the government had been conducting research that allowed hundreds of Black men with syphilis to go untreated so scientists could study the disease (CDC, 2020). In addition, without her knowledge or consent, medical researchers in the 1950s used Henrietta Lacks's cancer cells to make large strides in cancer research; her cells are still used today (Johns Hopkins Medicine, 2020). These historical events continue to affect research, as many Black individuals do not trust researchers and choose not to participate in studies (Scharff et al., 2010). The *ACA Code of Ethics* (ACA, 2014) states researchers should do no harm to study participants, obtain their consent, and inform them of the details of the study (Standards G.1.e., G.2.a., G.2.g.).

The ASCA Ethical Standards for School Counselors (ASCA, 2016a) outline the importance of parents and guardians being aware of interventions involving their children. These adults have the right to decide whether they want their children to participate in research. As stated earlier, differently abled students are bullied more than their peers (C. A. Rose & Gage, 2017), and parents and guardians may be more sensitive to the effects of an intervention like the one in this case. The researchers could also include their contact information and allow parents and guardians to reach out if they have any questions. Furthermore, choosing to highlight benefits rather than deficits could increase the potential for continued participation in programs and interventions. Thus, researchers use care in designing their studies to promote participation and the best interest of their participants as well as to comply with IRB guidelines to ensure ethical research.

• • •

Chapter 27

Should He Be Included? I Know His Sister

Elizabeth A. Prosek

2014 *ACA Code of Ethics* Standards Addressed

- G.1.a. Conducting Research
- G.1.e. Precautions to Avoid Injury
- G.2.a. Informed Consent in Research
- G.2.b. Student/Supervisee Participation
- G.3.b. Relationships With Research Participants
- G.4.d. Identity of Participants

• • •

Angélica was a third-year doctoral student in a counselor education program. Her program was housed within the College of Education of a well-respected Tier 1 research institution. The university was geographically isolated in a small town and provided most of the employment and community resources there. As an international student, Angélica immersed herself in campus organizations with others who shared her identity. She was an active member of the Mexican American Student Association (MASA); during her undergraduate studies at a previous university, she had served as president of the organization at that school. As a doctoral student, her role with MASA had shifted to supporting undergraduate students in leadership positions. Participating in the organization brought Angélica joy, and she often mentored other international students, specifically those who shared her Mexican heritage.

Recently, Angélica had successfully proposed her dissertation, a qualitative investigation of the lived experiences of international students from Mexico earning their master's degrees at research-intensive American universities.

She had proposed using a phenomenological design to capture the essence of a shared experience among participants. Her projected data collection procedure included eight individual interviews and a focus group with five to six participants. Angélica had received approval from her institutional review board (IRB) to conduct the study, including posting advertising materials across campus and online via social media. Although Angélica hoped to capture face-to-face interviews with students on her own campus, she also wanted the opportunity to include participants from other universities. She posted an advertisement on her Facebook account as well as on the newsfeeds of organizations of Mexican students at comparable Tier 1 research universities. Because she had successfully secured a research grant from a division of the American Counseling Association (ACA), she was able to offer individual interview participants a $50 gift card as compensation for their time and focus group participants a $30 gift card as compensation. To screen participants for eligibility, Angélica had interested individuals complete an online survey, and then she contacted those who were eligible to schedule an interview. The online survey included the written informed consent for her research project as well as questions on key demographics that indicated eligibility (e.g., seeking a master's degree, being an international student from Mexico). The survey also clarified that the gift card compensation would be provided after the interview was completed. Finally, the survey allowed potential participants to choose a pseudonym to protect their identity from the beginning of the study.

Angélica was elated to receive several survey responses within a few days of her initial recruitment efforts. She began calling students who were eligible for the study to review the informed consent and schedule an interview. Most of the eligible participants were female; therefore, Angélica was relieved to see at least one male student had qualified. Mario was his chosen pseudonym. She called Mario, who happened to be a student at her university, reviewed the consent, and scheduled his individual interview for the following week. As they ended their phone call he expressed excitement about participating in the study: "I am really looking forward to it. It sounded like a great study. I knew I wanted to participate as soon as my sister told me about it. You know her from MASA—Citlali. She is the vice president." Angélica politely ended the phone call.

Angélica knew Citlali fairly well, and she had been the one who had encouraged Citlali to run for vice president. Over the past 2 years, Angélica had informally mentored Citlali as she had transitioned to the university as a freshman and struggled with big class sizes and loneliness. Angélica now recollected Citlali's excitement earlier this year when her older brother had decided to attend the university for his master's degree. He did not participate in MASA, and Angélica had never met him.

Angélica's eagerness for her scheduled interviews quickly dissipated as she contemplated the reality of her interview with the only male participant thus far. She started to doubt whether she could even interview Mario, given her relationship with Citlali. Although she did not know him or his real name, he was aware of Angélica and Citlali's relationship. In fact, it was Citlali who had happily shared the advertisement with him, seeing it as an opportunity for him to earn $50 while also helping her friend Angélica connect with potential participants for her study. From Citlali's perspective, it was a win-win situation. Angélica was keenly aware that she had less than a week to determine whether she could move forward with Mario's interview.

Case Analysis and Discussion

Similar to when counselors experience ethical dilemmas in clinical practice, researchers presented with a challenge can follow a decision-making protocol. Angélica had to contemplate the key issues in her dilemma, consult ethics-related resources, and determine her outcome. She was aware that as a doctoral student, her research was done under the supervision of her dissertation chair, who could serve as an important consultant.

Before taking any action, Angélica needed to clearly identify key issues in her research dilemma. Her main concern was whether it would be ethical to interview Mario given her preexisting relationship with his sister, Citlali. Her initial response to the situation included both emotional and cognitive reactions. For example, Angélica experienced a sense of urgency to retain Mario in the study because thus far he was her only male participant. In addition, she was having an emotional response because Mario had expressed interest in the study and she worried about disappointing him after scheduling the interview. Cognitively speaking, Angélica was aware that research was different from counseling; therefore, the ethics guiding multiple relationships were inherently different to some extent. However, she was unsure how the ethics code differed for the two domains.

The *ACA Code of Ethics* (ACA, 2014) includes a subsection devoted to research considerations (Section G: Research and Publication). Angélica carefully read the section to determine whether it included information about multiple relationships. Unfortunately, the answer was not clear on initial review. Although there was an ethical standard prohibiting sexual or romantic relationships with participants in research (Standard G.3.b.), there was no standard addressing nonsexual relationships or relationships with participants' family members. Angélica's emotional response to include Mario because he was excited to participate felt confirmed when she read that researchers are to take reasonable action to honor their commitment to participants (Standard G.2.f.). By allowing Mario to participate, she would be honoring her commitment to interview him. As Angélica carefully reviewed details on informed consent (Standard G.2.a.), she contemplated whether she had clearly explained the limitations to confidentiality to Mario during their phone call. She wondered whether he understood his interview was confidential and she would do her best to protect his identity (Standard G.4.d.). In a phenomenological design, the researcher uses direct quotes from participants in the findings section. Angélica became acutely aware that the informed consent document did not specify the use of direct participant quotes in the manuscript for publication. In addition, some things were unknown to Angélica in the situation. For example, she was unsure about Mario and Citlali's sibling relationship and whether Citlali would be able to easily identify him if she read the article after publication. If Citlali could identify him in the publication, would that cause undue emotional or social harm to Mario (Standard G.1.e.)?

Angélica considered other situations in research in which the principal investigator knows the participants. For example, faculty members conduct research in their classrooms with undergraduate and graduate students. The prevalence of this research is such that the *ACA Code of Ethics* (ACA, 2014) has a specific ethical standard for ensuring students or supervisees are not coerced to participate (Standard G.2.b.). Although in her situation there was no power differential in the relationships, the essence was the same. How could she be sure Mario fully understood the possible outcomes of his participation, especially in terms of her limited ability to protect his identity? How could she be sure Citlali had not coerced him to participate in her effort to help a friend? Finally, Angélica read that counseling researchers are to follow their institution's regulations for research (Standard G.1.a.); therefore, she decided to investigate the resources on her university's IRB webpage.

Among her university's resources was the *Belmont Report* (National Commission for the Protection of Human Subjects of Biomedical and Behavioral Research, 1979), which sounded vaguely familiar to Angélica from her human subjects training 2 years ago. The three principles in the report were respect for persons, beneficence, and justice. The first two resonated with her and overlapped with what she had already considered with the professional ethical standards (ACA, 2014). She wanted to respect Mario's autonomy to be a participant but also felt obligated to ensure his participation would not cause him any undue harm. However, Angélica had yet to consider the principle of justice as it related to her dilemma. Researchers are to avoid denying participation to an eligible participant without good reason (National Commission for the Protection of Human Subjects of Biomedical and Behavioral Research, 1979). Angélica had circled back to her original concern: Was her preexisting relationship with Citlali a good enough reason to remove Mario from the study?

Reflecting on the principle of justice, Angélica was aware she could not ignore her own identity as an international student in a graduate program. From her own experience, she was aware that earning money while on a student visa presented a significant challenge. Although $50 did not seem like a lot of money, she knew it could buy groceries for a week or pay a monthly utility bill. Previous researchers have found that Latino college students often find creative means of supporting themselves financially during their studies (Abrica & Martinez, 2016). It did not feel just to deem Mario ineligible and block his access to the compensation. More significantly, it did not feel just to disallow him the opportunity to share his perspective.

Angélica had been drawn to a phenomenological design for her dissertation because it offered participants, in particular marginalized populations, a direct voice in research (D. G. Hays & Singh, 2012). The Association for Assessment and Research in Counseling developed the Standards for Multicultural Research (O'Hara et al., 2016) to empower researchers to be culturally responsive in their goals and research designs. Angélica had referenced the standards when developing her study. In particular, her vision for the study aligned with the key standards that researchers challenge power and privilege, address cultural validity, and recruit diverse participants (O'Hara et al., 2016). Angélica wanted her sample to be representative of within-groups diversity, which included Mario. Angélica was deeply connected to her dissertation study and wanted to represent the voices of students who identified as international students from Mexico. Her desire to include Mario's perceptions may have been rooted in collectivist values as she sought to support the greater good in her outcome. Researchers found international counseling students reported the influence of collectivism when negotiating an ethical dilemma (Karaman et al., 2018).

Actions and Outcomes

Angélica met with her dissertation chair to inform her of the potential dilemma and three possible actions. She was hopeful the consultation would result in a viable solution. The first option was to call Mario and remove him from the study, citing the relationship with Citlali as the concerning factor. In this case, Angélica considered the preexisting relationship with Citlali too great of a risk to Mario's confidentiality or too much of a potential distraction in the interview process. She believed protecting Mario's identity was too important to risk harming him. He would not receive the $50 compensation.

The second option was to call Mario and request that he join the focus group rather than take part in an individual interview. In this case, Angélica could diffuse the potential distraction of her preexisting relationship with his sister because there would be five other participants in the room. His identity could be further protected if, on writing her findings, Angélica referenced focus group member quotes generically (i.e., by focus group participant) rather than with a chosen pseudonym. She could also choose to present the demographics of the group members collectively. However, this would not necessarily fully protect his identity if he remained the only male participant in the study. In this case, he would receive the $30 gift card compensation.

The third option involved Angélica meeting with Mario to conduct the scheduled interview. In her review of informed consent, before she began recording the interview, Angélica would discuss with Mario his increased potential risk of being identifiable in the study. She would also reinforce his autonomy to share information about his participation with his sister, although she herself would not disclose any information to Citlali. She could discuss with him ways in which she could further protect his identity in the findings. For example, Mario could review the transcript and highlight portions of the text he perceived would be too revealing. Angélica could then avoid using the highlighted text as direct quotes in the findings, but his perspective would still be included in the overall coding of themes during data analysis. Furthermore, Angélica could slightly alter how his demographics were presented in the manuscript, which could only work if at least one other male participant joined the study. In this case, Mario would receive the $50 compensation.

Angélica's dissertation chair, Professor Ruiz, was pleased she had carefully considered several options for how to proceed. In particular, Professor Ruiz appreciated the second and third options because they allowed Mario more control over his decision to participate. Professor Ruiz encouraged Angélica to call Mario and be transparent about the preexisting relationship with Citlali. Angélica could explain the differences between being a participant in a focus group and having an individual interview. She could also relay some of the ways she could potentially adapt his data to further protect his identity. Angélica could also reiterate that it was his choice how much, if anything, he disclosed to Citlali about his participation. Finally, Angélica could allow Mario time to consider his options (including his right to withdraw from the study at any time) and let her know how he wanted to proceed with the study.

Angélica decided to take action by calling Mario and offering him choices. Her decision was rooted in the principle of respect for persons (National Commission for the Protection of Human Subjects of Biomedical and Behavioral Research, 1979). She appreciated that she would be able to honor Mario's autonomy while doing her due diligence as a researcher to explain the risks and benefits of his continued participation. If Mario decided to withdraw from the study, she would respect his decision. After consulting with Professor Ruiz, Angélica felt less anxious about potentially losing her only male participant. She had only recently started recruitment, and even if data collection took a little longer, she believed the time was worth the outcome.

Conclusion

Like counselors, counseling researchers need to consider how preexisting relationships can affect research participants and the potential outcomes of a study. When making decisions regarding multiple relationships with participants, it behooves counseling researchers to put the welfare of the participants at the forefront, prioritizing minimizing harm, in alignment with ethical research with human subjects. In addition, counseling researchers may use consultation as a means to be reflective in their ethical decision-making process.

Reflection Questions

1. How, if at all, does Angélica's ethnicity support her role as a researcher? In contrast, what ethical challenges, if any, does her ethnic identity pose for her researcher role?
2. Identifiable disclosures are a concern in the reporting of qualitative research findings. What other strategies can counseling researchers use to protect their participants' identities?

Critical Incident Response

Sam Steen and Shekila Melchior

Angélica, a third-year doctoral student in a counselor education program, was unintentionally involved in dual relationships with Citlali, who was the sibling of Mario, the potential sole male participant in her study. After consulting with her adviser and exploring the *ACA Code of Ethics* (ACA, 2014) and her university's IRB website, Angélica decided to take action by calling Mario and offering him choices for his potential participation. This appears to be a good course of action. There are also additional factors to consider regarding the principle of justice and support for allowing Mario to participate despite the potential risk for breaching confidentiality. First, the experiences of Mexican male students are understudied because Latino youth in the United States drop out of school at substantially higher rates than other groups (Chapman et al., 2010). Second, the experiences of Mexican males are important, and Mario's involvement could highlight areas for research regarding misogyny and toxic masculinity for Mexican men on predominantly white campuses (Martinez, 2019). Third, snowball sampling involves using individual study participants to help with the recruitment of other participants. Angélica could have considered asking Mario to engage in snowballing by encouraging other Mexican males to participate. This method of recruitment inherently has the potential to involve dual or multiple relationships; however, it is very useful, especially for difficult-to-reach racial groups (Sadler et al., 2010). Similarly, when recruitment for a particular demographic occurs within a small community or a unique sample group, there is greater risk for a dual relationship. Angélica could have explored with Mario how they both have navigated balancing multiple relationships in other situations, given that Mexican families are often characterized as collectivist (Lam et al., 2012). An exploration of how to balance multiple overlapping relationships within Mexican communities—on college campuses and elsewhere—could be integrated into the research to possibly further strengthen the study.

Regarding recruitment, Angélica could have been more patient with the process of obtaining participants. Recruiting participants from marginalized populations requires effort and time. In addition, she could be more intentional infusing culture into the research design. There are other cultural considerations for Mario beyond compensation, considering his status as an international student from Mexico. A researcher would not want to imply that financial incentives are unique to international students, as this could be considered a microaggression. The benefit of including voices that have traditionally not been heard in research is more valuable than the limited funds available to participants. Angélica wanted to include Mario's perceptions because she valued collectivism. Therefore, it would have been appropriate to take a collective approach to all aspects of the planning and implementation of the research from the onset. Moreover, Angélica only consulted with her adviser. Although it is important that she discussed the situation with her adviser, she could also have consulted with a member of the IRB, as this could have provided additional suggestions for addressing the situation. Angélica could have consulted with the other participants in the same way she planned to consult with Mario to help inform the process used to recruit other Mexican students attending similar universities. Although Angélica did not know the other participants, she could have drawn from their relationships (e.g., using snowball sampling) to ensure more targeted representation of participants.

This chapter described a decision-making process used to address dual relationships experienced by a researcher. When recruiting participants from a community they are involved or connected with, researchers have an increased likelihood of experiencing dual relationships with the participants or their families. Thus, while seeking to obtain a strong sample for a study, researchers should consider what is in the best interest of potential participants during recruitment and throughout the research process when dual relationships exist.

• • •

Chapter 28

Do We Stop the Study? Best for the Client vs. Best for Research

Diandra J. Prescod

2014 *ACA Code of Ethics* Standards Addressed

- G.1.e. Precautions to Avoid Injury
- G.2.a. Informed Consent in Research
- G.2.d. Confidentiality of Information
- G.4.d. Identity of Participants

• • •

Professor Natasha K. Dixon, an experienced associate professor of color, used a randomized controlled trial to examine differences in job satisfaction among tenure-track faculty members (assistant professors) of color in counselor education. Participants were required to have been in a tenure-track position for at least 1 year to be eligible to participate in the study. Random assignment occurred before baseline assessments and interviews, and an attempt was made to assign the same number of participants to each group. Participants were informed of their random assignment through the mail. Group A consisted of the wait-list control group participants, and Group B consisted of the experimental group.

Both groups completed pre-, mid-, and postassessments of career self-efficacy and job satisfaction over the course of one academic year. Preassessment occurred during the first 2 weeks of the fall semester, midassessment took place during the 2-week period before the winter holiday season, and the postassessment was administered during the last week of the spring semester. Participants were not all employed by the same university; therefore, depending on the start date of the semester at each university, participants completed assessments over approximately 2 weeks. Participants provided demographic information and completed assessments via an online survey portal. At the end of the academic year, Professor Dixon planned to interview participants from both groups virtually to discuss their experiences during the academic year.

Group B received virtual support and access to webinars throughout the fall semester. Webinars included topics such as (a) research, (b) teaching, (c) service, (d) supervision, and (e) grant writing. Research webinars focused on publishing a dissertation, developing a research agenda, and publishing on a consistent basis. Teaching webinars focused on teaching strategies, coinstruction, and articulating scholarship of teaching and learning. Service to the department, university, and profession were topics included in the service webinars. Finally, supervision webinars focused on tips for supervising master's and doctoral students, and grant-writing webinars encompassed information on securing external funding to support research. In addition, participants assigned to Group B had the opportunity to schedule 60-minute, one-on-one mentoring sessions once a month with an associate professor or professor of color in counselor education. To ensure the quality and consistency of the intervention, webinar facilitators and faculty mentors received training on providing webinars and mentoring people of color in higher education, then met for 30 minutes once a month. In addition, experts in the field evaluated the webinar content prior to implementation to ensure accuracy. The plan was for the wait-list control group (Group A) to receive the intervention following the end of the study.

Participants represented tenure-track faculty from various institutions, and the group sizes were nearly equal, with 17 participants in the wait-list control group and 19 in the experimental group. However, by the midpoint of the study, five participants from the wait-list control group had decided to withdraw from the study; three did not complete the midassessment, and two had decided not to continue for fear of confidentiality being breached. There were then 12 participants left in Group A and 19 in Group B.

Participants had contacted Professor Dixon to discuss their decisions or thoughts about withdrawing from the study. She believed that because the counselor education field was small, and even smaller for people of color, participants viewed it as respectful and necessary to contact her instead of dropping out of the study without notice. She conversed with participants about their concerns without trying to convince or coerce them into remaining in the study. With two more people in Group A thinking about leaving the study, Professor Dixon was worried about the declining number in the wait-list control group.

Case Analysis and Discussion

When considering research design, researchers may use various types of control groups (Kinser & Robins, 2013; Schwartz et al., 1997). Four types of control groups discussed in the social sciences literature are the (a) usual care control, (b) wait-list control, (c) active control, and (d) dismantling/add-on control (Kinser & Robins, 2013). Participants in the usual care group receive the typical or standard care with nothing additional. The wait-list control group receives the standard care at the beginning of the experiment and then the intervention later. The active control group receives a type of intervention (different from that in the experimental group) that may also be effective. Finally, the dismantling/add-on group receives small portions of the intervention in an attempt to find the pieces of the intervention that are most effective.

Although randomized controlled trials can be difficult to implement, use of this design reduces selection bias. Within randomized controlled trials, it is important to consider internal and external validity. When there is high internal validity, differences between groups can be attributed to the intervention, which was the mentorship and webinars for tenure-track faculty members in this study. Bias and random error are two threats to internal validity (Houser, 2020; Spieth et al., 2016). When examining bias, we need to be clear about whether we are discussing attrition, selection, performance, or detection bias. Because the study used randomization, Professor Dixon controlled for selection bias. It would also have been appropriate for Professor Dixon to focus on attrition bias, or participants dropping out, as participants were withdrawing from the wait-list control group. Whether participants withdraw their informed consent, decide to discontinue for personal reasons, or stop engaging in the study, attrition bias can affect the results of a study (Spieth et al., 2016). In addition, performance bias, or not abiding by study protocol, would apply to this case because some participants had not completed all required tasks. Participants who fear their confidentiality being breached should have an opportunity to speak to the researcher before deciding to drop out of the study. Explaining the study in more detail, reviewing the informed consent again, or allowing the participant to choose a different pseudonym could be ways to lower dropout rates.

Scholars have focused on increasing the participation of people of color in health research (Watson et al., 2016); however, a mistrust of research remains prevalent in this community, regardless of prior research participation (Scharff et al., 2010). In addition, although Professor Dixon was a person of color, the results would be available for the public to access and read. The majority of counselor educators are white, and although it is necessary to publish research studies like this, participants may be hesitant to engage in research for fear of judgment or negative career consequences.

The *ACA Code of Ethics* (American Counseling Association, 2014) states that counselor researchers are responsible for the welfare of their participants and take precautions to avoid causing them harm (Standard G.1.e.). In addition, regarding informed consent (Standard G.2.a.), the *Code* requires researchers to inform participants about the study and instruct them that they are allowed to withdraw at any time. Informed consent also provides participants with information about potential risks and limits of confidentiality. Furthermore, researchers are required to keep information about participants confidential (Standard G.2.d.), which may be challenging in this study because counselor educators of color are a small group within counselor education.

According to the National Center for Education Statistics (2019), 13% of assistant professors identify as Black or Hispanic, with Black and Hispanic women accounting for 4% and 3% of the total, respectively. In addition, approximately 11% of associate professors and 7% of professors are Black or Hispanic (National Center for Education Statistics, 2019), and these percentages have not increased much in recent years (Davis & Fry, 2019). Furthermore, college students in the United States are twice as likely as faculty to be Black and 4 times more likely to be Hispanic. Thus, diversity is increasing at a faster rate among college students than faculty (Davis & Fry, 2019). Because the percentages of Black and Hispanic/Latinx faculty are small, individuals may be reluctant to participate in studies for fear of having their identities exposed. Researchers have an ethical responsibility to protect the identity of participants and prevent harm when discussing research results (American Counseling Association, 2014, Standard G.4.d.). In the case presented here, participants may be particularly sensitive to issues of confidentiality. Thus, it is crucial for Professor Dixon to discuss these concerns.

Counselor educators of color encounter various challenges and have similar experiences. Whether working through stress to continue toward tenure and promotion or finding a way to navigate microaggressions (Bradley & Holcomb-McCoy, 2011; Salazar, 2009), faculty of color have daily experiences that exceed their job responsibilities. They may feel pressure to work twice as hard as others to be seen as equal, strong, and legitimate scholars. Because there are fewer faculty of color in comparison to the majority, this group also experiences increased pressure to meet the needs of students of color through mentoring, research, and role modeling (Rucks-Ahidiana, 2019), as Black students report feelings of isolation (Haskins et al., 2013) and disrespect from faculty members (Henfield et al., 2013). Faculty of color also report racism from colleagues as a major challenge (Bradley & Holcomb-McCoy, 2011). In the midst of navigating challenges, both students and faculty of color in counselor education report mentorship as an important factor in their success (Bradley & Holcomb-McCoy, 2011; Zeligman et al., 2015). Thus, for faculty in Professor Dixon's control group, having to wait until the academic year is over to access mentoring and support is frustrating, because although these are services they should already receive without being in the intervention, the reality is that they may not be receiving them at their institutions.

Actions and Outcomes

Some participants in the control group contacted Professor Dixon to report they no longer wanted to participate. As a first step, Professor Dixon met with individuals one-on-one as they communicated their desire to leave the study. Reasons for leaving the study included disappointment over not being in the experimental group, decreased job satisfaction, and burnout. Participants stated they had joined the study to receive support and thought it was not fair for them not to receive the same benefits as the experimental group.

After obtaining a true understanding of the concerns of the participants, Professor Dixon brainstormed ways to continue the study to allow those in the wait-list control group to participate without compromising their well-being and the integrity of the study. Allowing Group A access to one-on-one mentoring sessions with an associate professor or professor of color in counselor education once a month was one potential solution to provide support to the wait-list control group. However, this change would result in no longer having a wait-list control group and instead having a dismantling/add-on control group. Group A would not have access to the full intervention; however, they would have access to mentorship after only a few weeks of being in the study. Mentorship is a meaningful experience for faculty of color (Bradley & Holcomb-McCoy, 2011; Dancy & Gaetane, 2014; Zeligman et al., 2015); therefore, this change may motivate the control group participants to continue in the study. However, mentorship was also a crucial construct being examined in the study, and this change would alter the design of the study.

Before implementing this change, Professor Dixon discussed the idea with the mentors in the study, as the change would require more time from the tenured faculty members and she did not want the mentors to experience burnout. She also considered giving the wait-list control group access to the webinars instead of mentorship. However, after listening to the participants' concerns and struggles, Professor Dixon decided that one-on-one mentorship would be more meaningful, and with the commitment of the mentors, she changed the study design. As a result of these changes, the individuals who originally wanted to leave the study decided to continue; thus, Professor Dixon was able to complete the study with nearly equal groups. Although she had to manage missing data for some individuals who did not complete all required assessments, Professor Dixon completed the study with publishable data and meaningful results.

Conclusion

In conducting research, it is important to balance what is best for the research project with what is in the best interest of the participants. It is unethical to conduct research that compromises the well-being and welfare of research participants. Thus, researchers may have to revise their research design to be able to continue with a research project while prioritizing participant well-being.

Reflection Questions

1. What other changes could Professor Dixon have made to the wait-list control group to increase the retention of participants?
2. What would you have done in Professor Dixon's position if you had experienced this dilemma?

Critical Incident Response

Kelly L. Wester

Ethical decision-making occurs at all stages of research, from designing the study to data analysis and dissemination (Wester, 2011). Although the *Belmont Report* (National Commission for the Protection of Human Subjects of Biomedical and Behavioral Research, 1979) was developed to provide researchers with guidelines to ensure respect, beneficence, and justice for participants, federal guidelines may not provide all the answers about conducting research with individuals with social vulnerabilities (Fisher, 1997). Ethical decisions are typically based in morality, which is embedded in the researcher-participant connection (Fisher, 1997). This means researchers need to consider respect for persons, justice, and beneficence based on participant needs and views. Professor Dixon did this in having conversations with participants about the possibility of withdrawing. A researcher should never force a participant to provide reasons for withdrawing from a study; however, in this case, participants reached out to Professor Dixon to discuss these reasons. This allowed Professor Dixon to gain a better understanding of the experiences and perceptions of participants, which assisted her in making the decision to alter the research study design to include an add-on control group rather than a wait-list control group. Although Professor Dixon could have responded in many possible ways to participants withdrawing from the study, she took a relational perspective (Fisher, 1997), listening to participants and adjusting the methodology as needed to ensure that participants' cost-benefit ratio was considered, with their costs minimized.

Although the decisions Professor Dixon made were ethical, some additional considerations can be made regarding the research process in this case—more specifically, the consent form. In this example, the participants who were withdrawing had two main concerns: (a) a desire to receive the intervention (i.e., videos, mentoring) and (b) a fear that confidentiality would be breached. An important component of research is individuals' ability to make an informed decision about participating in a research study. Making an informed decision requires having adequate information about the study and understanding it. This information is usually provided in the informed consent document. However, most participants do not read or recall information in the informed consent document (Douglas et al., 2020; McNutt et al., 2008).

One of the least read sections of the consent form is the confidentiality/anonymity section, with 80% of participants not reading or recalling information from this section (Douglas et al., 2020). However, one of the most read sections of the consent form is the procedures section (which is read by approximately 60% of participants). This information seems pertinent to the current situation, as approximately 20% of the participants in Professor Dixon's study considered withdrawing (40% of the wait-list control group). The participants in this study may not have been fully clear on the procedures (i.e., that wait-list participants would be able to receive the videos and mentoring only at the completion of the study) or on how information would remain confidential. The concern about confidentiality is something to consider in terms of what the participants may or may not have read or understood from the informed consent document. As stated by Douglas et al. (2020), "Failures of the informed consent process do not just pose potential ethical problems: they also may hinder or invalidate experimental manipulations" (p. 2). This applies to this case, given the ethical decision that Professor Dixon needed to (and did) make considering the effect of the study on research participants; however, the changes she made also affect the potential conclusions she can draw from her altered study. Even if she had decided to keep her study as is, which would have resulted in 40% of her wait-list control group withdrawing from the study, her results would still have been compromised, given that participants who complete treatment and provide data differ from participants who do not complete treatment and all assessments (de Beurs et al., 2018). Ensuring participants read and understand the informed consent document is an ethical responsibility of the researcher and aligns with the ethical principles of respect, beneficence, and justice. Professor Dixon upheld these principles by listening to her participants, understanding their concerns, and making a decision to alter her methodology. Ethical responsibility (i.e., protecting participant welfare) takes precedence over scientific responsibility (i.e., providing answers).

• • •

Section 3
The Publication Process

Chapter 29
A Little Bit Here, a Little Bit There: The Least Publishable Unit

Kelly L. Wester

2014 *ACA Code of Ethics* Standards Addressed

- G.4. Reporting Results
- G.5.c. Acknowledging Previous Work
- G.5.g. Duplicate Submissions

• • •

Data collection was complete. Liam and Emma had designed a quasi-experimental single-group pretest/posttest study in which they had tested the effect of a mindfulness group intervention on self-reported depressive symptoms in adults within a local outpatient mental health agency. According to the literature, and their own clinical experience, depression never existed in isolation. Therefore, they also had clients report their trauma history on the Adverse Childhood Experiences survey as well as anxiety symptoms and experiences of interpersonal support on various psychometrically sound measures at both pretest and posttest. To get a large enough sample to provide sufficient statistical power, they provided the manualized mindfulness group intervention three times, with 12 to 16 clients per group (for a total sample of 55 clients).

Now that data collection was finalized, Liam and Emma worked on analyzing and disseminating the results. Liam was excited about the possibilities for various publications. He told Emma they could get seven publications out of this data set. He listed the possible publications with research questions (including variables) and samples as seen in Table 29.1.

Emma was excited about the possibility of so many publications coming from the study, given the amount of time and energy they had put into the study and

TABLE 29.1

Possible Publications

Manuscript No. and Research Question	Dependent Variable	Independent Variable	Sample *n*
1. Does a mindfulness group intervention decrease self-reported depression?	Depressive symptoms	Pretest and posttest comparison	55
2. Does a mindfulness group intervention decrease symptoms of anxiety?	Anxiety	Pretest and posttest comparison	55
3. Does a history of trauma mediate the effect of a mindfulness group intervention on symptoms of depression and anxiety?	Anxiety, depression	History of trauma Pretest and posttest comparison	55
4. Does a mindfulness group intervention have differing effects on depressive symptoms among males and females?	Depression	Self-reported biological sex Pretest and posttest comparison	55
5. Is a history of trauma related to experiences of depression?	Depression	History of trauma	55
6. Does interpersonal support moderate the relationship between a history of trauma and depression in males?	Depression	History of trauma Interpersonal support	20
7. Does interpersonal support moderate the relationship between a history of trauma and depression in females?	Depression	History of trauma Interpersonal support	35

knowing that next year she would be putting her promotion and tenure materials in for consideration to move from assistant to associate professor. The more publications she had, in particular intervention-based research, the better off she would be when it came to earning promotion and tenure. Liam stated researchers typically did not conduct a study and produce only one article from it; various manuscripts were feasible given they would be answering different research questions and producing the manuscripts for different audiences across different journals within and outside the field.

Case Analysis and Discussion

The requirement within academia to publish or perish is a pressure many researchers within university and college institutions experience (Eagan & Garvey, 2015). This pressure also exists within for-profit institutions, such as among manufacturers of medication (Spielmans et al., 2009), and among other researchers who have a need or desire to increase their publication counts or increase exposure to their research findings. However, publishing separate yet similar findings can be unethical and is considered questionable research practice (Wester, 2011). Splitting the results of one study to produce multiple publishable papers is redundant publication, also known as *salami slicing* (Smart, 2017). Salami slicing involves dividing the results of one study into the least publishable units, which results in various manuscripts that overlap in hypotheses, sample characteristics, methodology, results, or conclusions (Abraham, 2000; Wester, 2011). Salami slicing consists of asking research questions that overlap and are not fully differentiated among multiple articles. It can also entail splitting a data set into smaller subgroups while still asking similar or overlapping questions.

The seven publications Liam outlined with Emma overlap in many areas, including asking the same question multiple times with slight shifts in the dependent variable (Manuscripts 1 and 2), adding covariates or moderating variables (Manuscripts 1 and 2 compared to 3 or 4), and splitting the data set into smaller groups while continuing to ask the same or similar research questions (Manuscripts 6 and 7). Some people may argue that each research question is different. For example, the research question from Manuscript 1 asks about the effect of the group on depression, whereas the research question from Manuscript 2 asks about the effect on anxiety. Simplistically they are different, with different outcome variables; however, both questions could be answered simultaneously and with coherence in the same manuscript. Similarly, a covariate is easily added (e.g., trauma added to Manuscript 3 as a mediator in the question in Manuscript 1), allowing for a more complete model to test given Liam and Emma indicated the literature on depression never exists in isolation.

The *ACA Code of Ethics* (American Counseling Association [ACA], 2014) mentions that counselors are encouraged to contribute to the knowledge base of the profession and that they are not to engage in fraudulent research or distort or misrepresent data (Standard G.4.). Although Liam and Emma were not creating fraudulent research by publishing in the least publishable unit—which would go beyond questionable research practices to research misconduct—they were beginning to distort and misrepresent their data, resulting in misleading findings for the profession and the public. Publishing in the least publishable unit, or salami slicing or redundant publication, gives more credibility to the findings than is warranted. For example, if knowing a mindfulness group intervention is truly effective for treating depression, having this reported in one publication from one study is helpful and adds to the knowledge base. However, having this reported across five articles enhances the credibility of the finding, resulting in the perspective that a mindfulness group intervention was effective in five different studies. If this was the result of five different studies (with different samples and different groups conducted), then yes, this is a helpful, potentially evidence-based practice. However, having five articles based solely on one study exaggerates the research results and threatens to skew the evidence base for client care (D. Jackson, 2013). Ultimately, publishing the same results repeatedly, or overlapping results from a single study, overloads the field with irrelevant information (Abraham, 2000). This creates misleading evidence by inflating the actual results from one study and ultimately deviates from the *ACA Code of Ethics* (ACA, 2014). The *Code* addresses duplicate submissions by requiring counselors to obtain permission from the original publisher before publishing a work with a substantial amount of content from the previous work (Standard G.5.g.).

Although to some, multiple publications may still be enticing, researchers need to consider that splitting a data set into smaller parts can also decrease statistical power, which ultimately affects the results. Although this may not be the case with larger samples, in the case of Liam and Emma's study with a total sample of 55 participants splitting the data set into males versus females (20 participants vs. 35) begins to decrease the statistical power. This could result in Type II error (not finding statistical significance when it may in fact exist). However, conducting multiple analyses (whether for the same article or different articles) increases the chance of Type I error (finding statistical significance when it does not exist) given the typical p value of .05. Another reason to not split a data set into smaller units is that it could lead to misleading results (because of Type II error) about populations or groups who may already be marginalized, resulting in false findings about the helpfulness (or lack thereof) of a treatment.

In addition, a question needs to be asked to better understand why Liam and Emma were separating groups (e.g., Manuscripts 6 and 7 for females and males) in the first place to be analyzed in separate manuscripts. Although researchers can separate samples into male and female groups, caution should be used when separating groups, and separations should be based on existing literature (Else-Quest & Hyde, 2016). Warner and Shields (2013) suggested that when researchers divide out groups of individuals based on various identities, or examine interactive effects of social categories or identities (e.g., gender, race, religion, class, sexual orientation), they should have literature to support the rationale for the analysis and the division of groups.

As noted, producing redundant articles from a single research project misleads reviewers, editors, and readers by giving the findings undue significance. For example, researchers who examined the effect of medication on depression published multiple articles from a single study (i.e., one article was published after 8 weeks of a 12-week trial, and another article was published at the conclusion of the 12-week trial; see Spielmans et al., 2009, for a review). The fact that a minimum of two publications came from the same study could result in readers believing the medication may be more important than it really is. In fact, the researchers could have succinctly answered their research questions within the same manuscript, revealing the influence of the medication across time within the treatment group.

Does this mean only one manuscript should come from a study or data set? No. There are circumstances and times when it makes sense, and is ethical, to produce multiple manuscripts. Many authors have suggested valid reasons for producing more than one manuscript from a study (D. Jackson, 2013; Norman, 2014; Smart, 2017). For example, the research questions answered in different manuscripts need to be truly different, ensuring each slice addresses a distinct, socially valid question. In addition, there are times when multiple works are produced to reach different audiences. Liam and Emma discussed this, with the idea that some manuscripts might go to different journals with audiences that are interested in different foci. However, one needs to consider what constitutes different audiences. Are the audiences within the same discipline, and although the works are in different journals, the audiences would be able to easily access all of them? Or are the audiences within completely different professional fields, and would they be less likely to access the other journals? Regardless of whether the audiences are different, if similar articles are produced for the sake of different audiences, or there is lengthier discussion of a finding or theme that emerged, each article that is sliced from the data set needs to cross-reference and acknowledge the other articles published from it, which authors can do within articles (ACA, 2014, Standard G.5.c.; Smart, 2017) and within cover letters to editors (D. Jackson, 2013; Norman, 2014). The Committee on Publication Ethics (2020) states that redundant publication occurs when a significant amount of the same data is presented in multiple works without referencing the other works.

Walter (1999) provided five strategies to guide authors in deciding whether they should publish redundant manuscripts, or salami slice from one study. Walter suggested results should generally be presented in the fewest possible papers with as little similarity between the papers as possible (not what Liam and Emma were planning to do with their seven manuscripts). Walter also indicated that if multiple papers are required, authors need to disclose to the editors the previously published work and the potential overlap that may exist (or not) across the papers. In addition, according to ACA (2014) and the Committee on Publication Ethics (2020), authors need to indicate in each manuscript studies that are linked or relevant to one another. Finally, editors need to consider the unique contribution of the paper to the journal, and ultimately to the wider discipline, so they do not publish a redundant paper simply because it may attract readers and researchers to the journal.

Actions and Outcomes

After consulting with a mentor about the publications they could potentially develop from the study, Liam and Emma decided the research questions they had noted for the seven different publications equated to salami slicing the data. Therefore, they decided to produce two publications from the existing data. The first would present findings from the pretest only as a cross-sectional study. This publication would answer the research questions "What is the relationship of a history of trauma (Adverse Childhood Experiences survey scores) on symptoms of anxiety and depression in clients?" and "Does perceived interpersonal support moderate the impact of trauma on depression and anxiety?" The second publication would be based on the findings of the quasi-experimental study with the mindfulness group intervention. In this second publication, Liam and Emma would answer the following research questions: "Does a mindfulness group intervention decrease self-reported depression and anxiety?" and "Does trauma or interpersonal support mediate the effect of a mindfulness group intervention on symptoms of depression and anxiety?"

Although Liam and Emma wanted to examine these research questions separately for males and females, as they had initially proposed doing within their seven publications, they recognized they did not have a large enough sample size for either biological sex to provide sufficient statistical power. An inadequate sample size increases the possibility of Type II error. Therefore, Liam and Emma planned to continue collecting data to increase the samples of males and females to further examine similarities or differences among these clients.

Conclusion

Researchers need to consider the most appropriate publications based on their study and data. The identification of appropriate publications should not be based on the quantity of publications desired or the length of time it took to collect data. Instead, it should be based on how many different research questions emerge from the study—questions that do not produce similar findings for the same or different populations—as well as how easily the findings can be combined into one coherent manuscript. Researchers should ask themselves the following: If the findings appear in different manuscripts, does this mislead the profession and the public about the importance of the results? If the answer is yes or maybe, then reducing the number of manuscripts submitted and combining research questions into fewer manuscripts may be the best ethical decision.

Reflection Questions

1. If more than one publication can come from a single study, what do you believe should constitute a least publishable unit?
2. How might publishing multiple publications from a study influence what mental health professionals consider evidence-based practice? How might it influence client intervention and treatment?

Critical Incident Response

Erik M. Hines and Paul C. Harris

Many faculty endure stress related to striving to earn promotion and tenure in academia (Eagan & Garvey, 2015). Matthew (2016) reported that additional layers of identity compound this stress, especially for racial minorities. Faculty members of color going up for tenure are judged by higher or shifting standards compared to their white colleagues (Matthew, 2016). The present case raises important ethical questions and concerns related to publishing, specifically salami slicing, which is unethical because

> it wastes resources (reviewers' time, journal space, etc.), creates a disjointed literature (forcing readers to go on scavenger hunts to find essential information), and dilutes an important currency of academia (inflating the curriculum vitae of some and risking the possibility that rewards will flow to those who "play the game" rather than to those who contribute most effectively). (Eva, 2017, p. 456)

The author discussed the negative implications of salami slicing, including decreased statistical power, exaggerated results, and misled reviewers and editors. In addition, the author noted the circumstances in which producing multiple papers from a data set is appropriate and useful. Although this chapter focuses on salami slicing as it relates to quantitative data, it is important to acknowledge that this may also occur with qualitative data, though sometimes it may be harder to detect (Janghorban & Azarkish, 2019). An example of salami slicing within qualitative research might be a researcher using different approaches to analyze the same qualitative data multiple times. The threat to publication ethics is just as serious in qualitative research, even though it is less explored than in quantitative research (Janghorban & Azarkish, 2019). The reasons why a researcher may produce multiple articles from one data set vary as well. For example, how might it be appropriate to split the data in a qualitative data set to delve more deeply into the lived experiences of the participants? In education, the lived experiences of racial minorities continue to be of great importance given the gaps in academic success that persist between Black and white students. Having different papers emerge from one study might allow the space to explore the multifaceted reality of racism in schools and the effects it has on students from historically underserved populations. For example, if data are collected from Black male student athletes about their lived K–12 educational experiences, many themes can emerge that can potentially warrant different papers. What are the societal influences on their athletic identity? What were their perceptions of their teachers and counselors, and how did those interactions influence their college choice process?

Researchers must be ethical in writing and publishing. In particular, they should produce articles that accurately reflect their data. Instead of salami slicing or using data multiple times to misrepresent or misinterpret a research project, researchers should conduct additional research if they want to produce several publications. Research and subsequent publication should be conducted ethically, accurately reflect the data, and contribute to the literature in the field.

• • •

Chapter 30

It's Already Published: Can I Still Submit My Manuscript?

Richard E. Watts, Jo Lauren Weaver, and Jacqueline M. Swank

2014 *ACA Code of Ethics* Standards Addressed

- G.5.b. Plagiarism
- G.5.c. Acknowledging Previous Work

• • •

Sarai was a 34-year-old cisgender Indo-American female. In the spring of the previous year, Sarai had defended her dissertation, interviewed for several counselor education faculty positions, secured a tenure-track assistant faculty position, and graduated. In the summer, she had taught multiple courses as an adjunct faculty member for her former counseling program, found a new apartment, and moved to a new city. She had also planned to develop a manuscript based on her dissertation during the summer. However, her schedule had become crowded, and she had not had the time to work on it before the start of the fall semester.

Being a new assistant professor, Sarai was busy and unable to start working on the manuscript from her dissertation until more than a year later. She was excited to begin transforming her dissertation into a publishable manuscript, as she had planned for this to jumpstart her research agenda. One of her first tasks was to search for any new publications to add to her literature review. Although she assumed she might find a few research publications somewhat related to her dissertation, Sarai was confident there would be no research articles closely related to her study because of her unique topic: experiences of school counselors working with first-generation Indo-American students. To her dismay, however, she discovered a newly published research article that was very similar to her dissertation topic.

In the recent study, the authors, Kennedy and Watson, had also interviewed school counselors about their experiences working with first-generation Indo-American students. Both studies had been conducted in the northeastern region of the United States with primarily white counselors working with Indo-American students. The researchers in both studies had used a phenomenological approach to analyze the data. Their findings included similar themes of cultural barriers, burnout, and political climate. At first glance these studies might have appeared identical, but on closer inspection there were notable differences.

Regarding participants, their ages and years of experience as a school counselor varied in each study. Sarai had a wide age range of participants with various years of experience, whereas Kennedy and Watson had interviewed mostly younger, new counselors who had been working fewer than 5 years. In addition, regarding design, Sarai's study used transcendental phenomenology, whereas the other study used a hermeneutical phenomenological approach. Although some of their findings were similar, the researchers had also found unique themes in each study. For example, in Sarai's study a theme of familial connection was present that was not in the other study. Another major difference concerned the identity of the researchers. Sarai identified as an Indo-American woman, whereas Kennedy and Watson identified as white females. Yet Sarai did not think these differences would be enough to distinguish her study, and she worried she would be accused of plagiarism. Disheartened, Sarai believed she could no longer publish her dissertation data. She decided to seek counsel from Professor Thomas, her dissertation chair. In an email to him, Sarai stated that she had found a recently published article on the same topic as her dissertation with similar findings and asked, "Does this mean that, given the similarity of our topics, my research cannot be published?"

Case Analysis and Discussion

Sarai is a new assistant professor who planned for her dissertation study to be the impetus of her research agenda. She has a dilemma: whether she can submit her dissertation study for publication because a similar study has recently been published. Sarai must outline the key issues in her dilemma, refer to ethics guidelines regarding research and publication, and decide whether to submit her manuscript to be considered for publication.

Sarai's first step in her decision-making process is to identify and analyze the key issues of her dilemma. Sarai is concerned that her study is too similar to the recently published study. Although there is overlap between Sarai's dissertation and the previous study, there are also some significant differences. For example, the positionality of the researchers is different, as Sarai identifies as an Indo-American (the population of study) whereas Kennedy and Watson do not share this identity with the participants. In qualitative research, the researcher is the instrument; thus, the findings are reflective and interpretive of the researcher's background, including their history, culture, and personal experiences (Marshall & Rossman, 2015; Ravitch & Mittenfelner Carl, 2016). The researcher's positionality shapes the study from the choice of research question(s) to data collection, analysis, and the researcher's overall expectations for the study (Creswell & Poth, 2018). Hence, Sarai's shared identity with her participants is an important and defining factor in her study, although both studies bring unique and diverse perspectives to the topic.

It is also important for Sarai to remember that there are many ways to investigate a single research topic. Having multiple studies on a research topic expands knowledge and understanding in the field. The American Psychological Association (2020) discusses the replication of an existing study as an ethical and acceptable practice in research that is designed to build on previous research to provide further evidence to support or refute previous findings. Although Sarai's study is not a replication study, support for this type of research provides evidence that she should still be able to publish her work. In addition, the purpose of science is to develop a knowledge base that helps us understand the world (Goodstein, 2011), and Sarai's findings contribute to further understanding the phenomenon under study.

Another issue relates to Sarai's concern that her study could be considered plagiarism or she could be perceived as stealing another researcher's idea. The *ACA Code of Ethics* (American Counseling Association, 2014) has a section focused on research and publication (Section G). The standard on plagiarism (Standard G.5.b.) focuses on giving credit to others for their work instead of misleading others into believing that it is one's own work. Sarai can assure herself that she did not plagiarize because she conducted her study without knowledge of the other people's work. Citing the recently published work gives the researchers credit for their work, and discussing similarities and differences between it and her own study can further distinguish Sarai's work as a unique, valuable contribution to the existing body of literature. This is also related to acknowledging previous work in publications (Standard G.5.c.). In addition, in publishing qualitative research studies, B. Hunt (2011) emphasized the importance of the literature review in providing support for conducting a study. Sarai could explore how the recent publication may provide support for her study. In addition, Hunt discussed the importance of researchers explaining why they chose a particular approach. Sarai can discuss the approach used in the previous study and the rationale for the approach she used in her study. Thus, it is crucial that Sarai cite the recently published article to engage in ethical conduct as a scholar and to follow best practices for writing qualitative research articles instead of choosing to leave out the study out of fear that it may affect the likelihood of her study being published.

Actions and Outcomes

Sarai and Professor Thomas reviewed the similarities and differences between the published study and her own manuscript. They concluded that Sarai needed to include the new study in the literature review of her manuscript, including a discussion of its strengths and limitations as well as its methodological differences (i.e., participant demographics, qualitative approach). She also needed to consider how the recent publication supported the rationale for her study. In addition, in the Discussion section of her manuscript, Sarai needed to compare her findings to those of the recent publication. This included identifying and explaining areas of agreement and differences as well as implications for practice and future research. In presenting all these points in her manuscript, Sarai would demonstrate the uniqueness and usefulness of her study.

After Sarai completed the revisions based on her discussion with Professor Thomas, they then discussed academic journals that might be a good fit to publish her work. This included reviewing the aims and scopes of various journals as well as the author guidelines. Professor Thomas shared that if she decided to submit her manuscript to the same journal that had recently published Kennedy and Watson's article, she should discuss in the cover letter how her manuscript made a unique contribution. He added that even if Sarai were able to make a clear case for her manuscript being published in the same journal, some journal editors preferred not to accept manuscripts on similar topics in chronological proximity. After considering this information, Sarai decided to submit the manuscript to a different journal that seemed to align well with the focus of her article. She carefully read the author guidelines and formatted the manuscript to fit the requirements.

After submitting the manuscript for consideration, Sarai found the contact information (i.e., email) of the first author of the recent research article. She sent an email introducing herself and discussing their similar research interest, including their article and information about her dissertation and recently submitted manuscript. Sarai asked whether they wanted to meet to further discuss their mutual interest, as limited research was available on the topic. As a new faculty member, Sarai wanted to network with other academics to learn from their experiences, brainstorm new ideas for research, and explore possible collaboration on future research projects. Kennedy and Watson welcomed a meeting with Sarai, and the group explored the possibility of future collaborative projects. Sarai felt relieved and excited to have her dissertation manuscript submitted for review and to have the opportunity to explore future collaborations with researchers who shared her research interest.

Conclusion

Sarai's dilemma presents the inevitable overlap of research. As a new professional, it can be intimidating and discouraging to see previously published studies on a similar topic, yet it is important to remember that two studies are rarely identical. A similar study may have important differences as well as further expand on knowledge of the topic by supporting or refuting previous findings. Thus, it is crucial to view the contribution each new study can make to the field while also acknowledging and critiquing previous research.

Reflection Questions

1. How might Sarai have further distinguished her study from existing research?
2. What are your thoughts about contacting the author of a study that is similar to yours?
3. What are the benefits and challenges of having multiple studies on a similar research topic?

Critical Incident Response

Elizabeth A. Prosek

Sarai experiences a full range of emotions on realizing her study greatly resembles more recently published research. After she is able to conceptualize how her situation differs from plagiarism and recognize that multiple perspectives on the same topic are essential in research, she may consider how the scope of her study can be underscored in her manuscript. As the authors noted, a distinguishing element of Sarai's work compared to the other study is her identity as the researcher. The foundation of qualitative research includes the researcher as a tool (D. G. Hays & Singh, 2012). Sarai can develop her Method section to highlight her philosophical paradigm and her identities in the design and interpretation. Prosek and Gibson (2021) suggested that authors emphasize the positionality of the research team in the Method section of the manuscript, given that context for interpretation is a hallmark of qualitative research. Much of the rigor in qualitative analysis is embedded in how the research team conceptualized and made meaning from the data during analysis. Sarai's concentrated efforts to describe her process may help illuminate the depths and potential uniqueness of her study. As additional context she could include the time frame of the data collection, which may increase the dependability of her findings. Thorough descriptions of the research team's process and trustworthiness are crucial in lived experience research, such as phenomenology (Prosek & Gibson, 2021).

Although B. Hunt (2011) asserted that recent literature can guide the researcher's choices in a current study, in Sarai's situation Kennedy and Watson did not necessarily inform her design. Sarai had completed her project in its entirety prior to discovering Kennedy and Watson's work. Therefore, it may be that references to Kennedy and Watson's results are more applicable in Sarai's Discussion and Implications sections. Giordano et al. (2021) purported that authors should compare and contrast current findings with previous research that builds toward implications. For Sarai, highlighting how her study is different from Kennedy and Watson's study may add new knowledge to the body of literature, which she can highlight in the Implications section. In this way, Sarai is sure to demonstrate the social validity of her study (Wester, 2011), which further differentiates it from previous studies.

Another topic related to this ethical dilemma in academia warrants further discussion: the format of the dissertation. Like other recent graduates of doctoral programs, Sarai struggles to submit a manuscript from her dissertation in a timely manner. A manuscript-style dissertation format promotes more efficient submission than a traditional dissertation style. For example, Broome (2018) described replacing the Method and Results chapters of the dissertation with two data-driven manuscripts derived from the dissertation study. Other programs may choose to follow a traditional chapter model and simply add a chapter for the manuscript. Freeman (2018) used an ethnographic framework to describe a dissertation manuscript process, noting a potential barrier could be lack of familiarity with the format among committee members. However, if the program formalizes a manuscript-style dissertation, this would not be a burden for students or faculty members. Indeed, having dissertation manuscripts ready to submit is advantageous to advisers, given the pressure to mentor doctoral students to publication (De Jong et al., 2005). Although it is not applicable to Sarai's current situation, she may use her lived experience to advocate in her new program for a manuscript-style dissertation, instituting a pathway for her future students' success.

• • •

Chapter 31

Do I Compromise to Get Published? Responding to Reviewers' Feedback

Jesse Fox

2014 *ACA Code of Ethics* Standards Addressed

- G.4.a. Accurate Results

• • •

Professor Banner worked with a research team composed of faculty and students at three universities. In their study, they had focused on investigating what theoretical principles and interventions were most influential in how counselors worked with their clients. They recognized that a qualitative study was appropriate to answer their research question, as it allowed them as researchers to delve deeply into the conscious and unconscious processes counselors used to make clinical decisions. This information was important to know because theory occupies a precarious role in the counseling field. On the one hand, theory may provide counselors with a needed structure, framework, or starting place for conceptualizing their clients and selecting interventions to address problems and pursue goals. On the other hand, by examining outcomes, researchers have uncovered that the type of theory a counselor uses does not seem to be as important as trailblazers once thought in determining the quality of care provided to clients (Norcross, 2011). In light of this tension, Professor Banner's team wanted to know to what extent counselors use theoretical frameworks when selecting interventions to use with clients.

The researchers had adhered to best practices in qualitative research by selecting a rigorous methodology that had required using multiple investigators throughout the process of developing research questions, collecting and analyzing interviews (researcher triangulation), triangulating data sources, using an external auditor to review the research for fidelity to practice and methodological rigor, and transparently presenting results. The data were complex, and the researchers acted meticulously to ensure the rigor of the study.

After the initial review for consideration for publication in a flagship counseling journal, the editor-in-chief recommended in a decision letter that the manuscript be revised and resubmitted. The recommended changes from the two blind reviewers were minor. However, the associate editor (AE) requested a significant revision, and the editor-in-chief agreed with the AE's feedback. The AE recommended simplifying the findings of the study by combining the qualitative themes, therefore diminishing the complexity of the study. Clarifying themes can aid in the dissemination of the findings. However, the team was concerned that the degree to which the AE wanted to simplify the themes compromised the integrity of the study. Rather than clarifying the meaning of the themes, the AE requested the team collapse and subsume some of the themes within other themes, which would have resulted in their being eliminated. This was concerning because it could affect the presentation and meaning of the findings. The rationale for the suggested changes focused on the clarity of presentation. The AE believed readers would have a difficult time understanding the results in their present form because of their complexity. If the themes were simplified, the AE reasoned, readers would more readily grasp their meaning and the implications for clinical practice.

Case Analysis and Discussion

Scientific review is inherently adversarial, which means all assertions are held up for scrutiny, counterevidence, or disconfirmation (Cozby & Bates, 2015). Clarifying the results of a study using different language, adjusting visual representations (i.e., tables or figures), or even correcting errors in results are all requests researchers can expect during the review process. Through this process, researchers uphold the ethical principles of fidelity and veracity. These ethical principles are included as foundational precepts of professional ethical behavior in the *ACA Code of Ethics* (American Counseling Association, 2014). When applied to counseling research, fidelity and veracity promote honoring promises and agreements, ensuring loyalty in relationships between researcher(s) and participant(s), as well as accounting for and upholding broader public interests. One of the primary aims of counseling research is to use accurate information to contribute to the knowledge base for the profession (Heppner et al., 2016). When counseling research ceases to be accurate, it becomes less reliable and less useful. The *ACA Code of Ethics* requires scholars to conduct research and report results accurately without distorting or misrepresenting data (Standard G.4.a.). The American Psychological Association (2020) provides step-by-step guidance for preparing scientific manuscripts for blind review to uphold these ethical principles.

Blind review is essential for ethical research. It encourages accurate reporting of counseling research because it removes the human tendency to personalize disconfirming feedback that is inevitable in the review process. Removing the identity of authors, as well as reviewers, helps prevent biases based on identity when interpreting findings (i.e., if a reviewer knows an author, they might be inclined to think that because the author is accomplished their field they must be reporting the information accurately). Thus, blind review prevents individuals from nonmajority identities from being excluded from contributing to the research base of the field. Any *ad hominin* arguments are squelched, with the focus remaining on the examination of the quality of the arguments, theories, methodologies, and evidence in any given study. One of the realities of the scientific process, exercised through blind review, is that diverse perspectives are assumed, encouraged, and welcomed because all status quos and majority opinions can be questioned, refined, reformed, or otherwise evolved and changed in light of new evidence.

The review process is also an imperfect system. Typically at the editor-in-chief and AE levels, names are disclosed, along with feedback. This introduces a level of bias previously accounted for during blind review. Along with the prestige and reputation of a journal, the editorial board generally reflects the quality of the journal. Thus, scholars who have earned a reputation in their field for quality research are charged with the responsibility of overseeing ongoing research in their profession. They can exert significant influence on the development of manuscripts to their final form by virtue of their reputation or status. Disagreeing with or pushing back on a review can create tension with highly influential individuals in the field. The degree to which disagreements become less focused on the evidence and more about the identities of authors and reviewers is not always clear. Plus, there is the possibility that not changing a manuscript to align with the editorial board's perspective can result in either significant delays in publication or rejection of the manuscript. What makes the critical incident in question significantly more complicated is that the feedback originated with the AE, not the reviewers, with the approval of the editor-in-chief. Therefore, the researchers' response to the feedback on the themes could be more decisive in determining whether the study will be published.

Behind the scenes of this critical incident, which may appear to be part and parcel of the process of scientific reporting, several influential factors are being held in balance, all simultaneously competing with one another. They are creating pressure points that can affect what to do next and inform the subjectivity of the researchers and reviewers alike. One source of pressure originates with the editorial board. They are charged with the responsibility of screening research using all available tools at their disposal to ferret out poor methodologies that contaminate results and the conclusions drawn from them. If poor research is published, they shoulder some of the responsibility for the effect it may have on the counseling profession and the public.

Another source of pressure originates with the researchers. They may feel unsurmountable pressure to publish, as their jobs may depend on their ability to do so, as it coincides with their tenure and promotion clocks. There is also the allure of being perceived as an intelligent and rigorous researcher with an influential track record of informing the field. Researchers can feel the draw of celebrity status in their field. There are well-publicized examples of such pressures corrupting the integrity of researchers by leading them to falsify findings. In one high-profile incident, falsified results in the *Lancet* misled large sections of the public to think vaccines cause autism (Wakefield et al., 1998).

Editors and AEs are not immune to the pressures of promotion or celebrity influence. They may manifest differently, such as in the need to appear credible to capable authors to assume their roles as guardians of research. As a result, reviewers and editors may dig into their initial opinions of research, which could be based more on ego and saving face than on methodological integrity. Thus, no matter how well crafted a response to editorial board comments may be, a manuscript may still be rejected for failing to meet the editorial board's standards of rigor, even if those standards could be misplaced. In the critical incident described here, each point of pressure from either the reviewers or the researchers could potentially influence the direction the research team takes in their response.

Professor Banner's research team clearly needed to think deeply about the integrity of the findings when revising the manuscript. They had to grapple with the implications and ramifications of removing entire themes from the findings as directed. In the process, the research team had to confront several potentially problematic questions. Would the reconfigured themes represent the findings accurately? Could these themes be reconfigured without losing their meaning? Does simplifying results help counselors be critical consumers of empirical research and enhance their practice, or is simplified information really misinformation? Should the researchers write to the perceived level of counseling practitioners, or is that underestimating practitioners' abilities to consume research critically?

Actions and Outcomes

At first, the research team thought removing themes would potentially misinform readers by oversimplifying the process of conducting effective counseling to a few easily applied theoretical principles and therefore misrepresent the findings. One possible course of action was to defer to the AE. This would have been the path of least resistance in getting the findings published, as AEs have influence over the resubmission process. This would have plausibly been the quickest route to publishing the manuscript in a high-profile journal. The researchers recognized that this pathway would support their need to publish for their jobs and to assume a higher level of visibility in the field. However, it could be a short-term gain for their curriculum vitae but potentially a long-term loss for their integrity as researchers. Another potential course of action was to reject the AE's request for revisions. In processing this option, the researchers recognized from their collective experience in publishing research that going against a reviewer at any level of the editorial board could be a death knell to the manuscript.

The researchers were able to pinpoint two major areas of consideration that could affect their decision. First, they decided the first option was nonnegotiable for them. They reasoned that if there was no way to reconfigure the results without losing their meaning and distorting the accuracy of reporting, they would keep the results in their present form and note this in their response letter to the reviewers. Second, and more problematic for them, was that they had to be honest with themselves that their egos could also be tied to how they presented the results. One reason scientific review is adversarial is because human beings tend to become attached to certain ways of seeing evidence through their own perspectives and preconceived assumptions. This is potentially a powerful source of influence in how research findings are interpreted by researchers and later presented in their manuscripts. Professor Banner and his research team had to reckon with the possibility that part of their objection to the AE's comments could simply be their own way of seeing things, and this could be altered without compromising the integrity of the findings.

After considering these options, the researchers identified a way of reconfiguring the findings while keeping the substance of the themes intact. They reasoned that they could do this by clarifying how the themes stemmed from important underlying meanings they saw as vital to convey to readers. Thus, the researchers saw adequate room to compromise without sacrificing the integrity of the study or their sense of personal responsibility and ethical standing. However, in planning, they agreed that if the editorial board, during the second review, required further simplification that distorted the results, they would notify the editor immediately about their concerns and be ready to remove the manuscript from consideration for the journal. They agreed to submit the manuscript to another journal if the editorial board remained unyielding in their opinion.

Conclusion

The integrity of the scientific process depends on several cardinal principles, including transparency of methodology, accurate reporting of results, and accounting for biases in researchers and peer reviewers, among others. Without these hinge points, the information disseminated in peer-reviewed journals and the sources that cite it (e.g., textbooks, trade books, magazines, online forums) might be misinformation presented as fact. Poor information might later be used for high-stakes decision-making (e.g., determining appropriate client interventions, resolving ethical dilemmas, making admissions and hiring decisions for educational and career paths). Thus, preserving the integrity of the publishing process is vital for the ongoing growth and development of the counseling profession.

Reflection Questions

1. What are some steps authors may take to ensure they critically review editorial board feedback without taking the feedback personally?
2. Do you agree with the decision of Professor Banner's team? Would you have chosen a different option? Why?

Critical Incident Response

A. Stephen Lenz, Diana Camilo, and Megan Speciale

This critical incident rings true for those who endeavor to publish their research findings. At some point, our vision for using the scientific method comes into conflict with how editorial staff believe our project may be better expressed and represented. The intersecting interests of authors, editorial board members, AEs, and editors converge on each manuscript and create many pathways for consideration, especially when substantial changes are requested.

To this point, it is important to consider that editorial boards are constructed with intention and thoughtfulness. In the most ideal of scenarios, editorial board members are topical, methodological, and process experts who act as an invaluable gate to ensure that the scientific inputs and outputs of a manuscript are both relevant and defensible to the target audience. Similarly, AEs offer additional expertise with an accompanying awareness of the similarities and differences between a given author's manuscript and those in the journal's backlog. This provides a depiction of a manuscript's value with, as well as its value added, to the corpus of previously accepted works. The editor acts as the final gate—a determining party whose dispositions are informed by intentions of being a harbinger of actionable science that is relevant to readership interests, representing the affiliated organization's mission, and increasing citation and sharing to promote the journal's vitality. Given the complex nature of these interests, nuanced considerations of responses to feedback are recommended in favor of dichotomous them-versus-me positions.

In response to the critical incident, Professor Banner and the research team chose the middle path, one represented by holding steadfast to initial positions while being flexible and open to considering those of the editorial staff. This was a wise choice. According to the Journal Article Reporting Standards for Qualitative Research (JARS-Qual; Levitt et al., 2018), there are some considerations to keep in mind to mitigate the intensity of such a critical incident. First, in alignment with the JARS-Qual, authors should include in the submission letter to the editor details related to the method used, the phenomenon explored, and the type of participant data studied. This can help guide the editor's selection of reviewers and an AE who represents the closest available fit. Second, authors should synthesize depictions of complex thematic representations. This guideline provides one example of defensibility for both Professor Banner's team and the editorial staff, because when data representation remains complex, clarity and synthesis can be facilitated by a well-designed visual depiction (Healy, 2018). Within the JARS-Qual there are considerations for anticipating the complexities of the review process and mitigating their influence on reviewer and author experiences.

Finally, this case illustrates the importance of asking oneself "How much is my personal stuff informing my reaction to this feedback?" This purposeful conversation highlights the importance of self-reflection and personal awareness-raising among authors during the publication process. Despite differences in the roles and functions of editorial team members, they all share a common interest: publishing the soundest scholarship that is relevant to readership and therefore has the potential to confirm existing practices or advance the field in some way. A disposition of revise and resubmit, even when it entails major revisions, indicates that the editorial staff views the work with promise. Professor Banner and his research team present a fine example of how taking the middle path may be both functional and adaptive for managing compromise throughout the publication process.

• • •

Resources

Check for Plagiarism: Plagiarism Consequences (https://www.checkforplagiarism.net/plagiarism-consequences)

Chronicle of Higher Education: "Why We Don't Report All of the Cheating We Detect" (https://www.chronicle.com/article/Why-We-Don-t-Report-All-of/247675)

Committee on Publication Ethics (https://publicationethics.org)

Copyright Advisory Network (https://librarycopyright.net)

Elsevier: "Co-Authors Gone Bad—How to Avoid Publishing Conflicts" (https://www.elsevier.com/connect/co-authors-gone-bad-how-to-avoid-publishing-conflicts)

Inside Higher Ed: "Plagiarize This!" (https://www.insidehighered.com/views/2019/12/06/essay-plagiarism)

Inside Higher Ed: "We Need to Talk About Authorship Abuse" (https://www.insidehighered.com/views/2019/09/12/academe-must-develop-greater-sense-ethical-responsibility-dealing-authorship-abuse)

Office of Research Integrity (https://ori.hhs.gov)

Online Ethics Center for Engineering and Science: The Co-Authorship Controversy (https://onlineethics.org/cases/graduate-research-ethics-cases-and-commentaries-volume-2-1998/co-authorship-controversy)

Springer: Publishing Ethics for Journals (https://www.springer.com/gp/authors-editors/editors/publishing-ethics-for-journals/4176)

Times Higher Education: "Authorship Wars: Academics Outline the Rules for Recognition" (https://www.timeshighereducation.com/features/authorship-wars-academics-outline-rules-recognition)

Part IV
Leadership and Advocacy

Section 1
Professional Organization Leadership 255

Section 2
Leadership and Advocacy in the Local Community 287

Section 3
Diversity and Inclusion Within Counselor Education Programs 305

Leadership and advocacy are long-standing hallmarks of doctoral-level counselor education and supervision. However, these functions are only newly addressed in the 2016 Council for Accreditation of Counseling and Related Educational Programs (CACREP) Standards, which denote the responsibility of doctoral programs to prepare students to "assume positions of leadership in the profession and/or their area(s) of specialization" (CACREP, 2016, Section 6, Standard A.2.d.). Standards around preparation highlight the importance of both theoretical foundations of leadership and preparation specific to leading within professional organizations, administering counselor preparation programs, and advocating or engaging within local communities. Although the *ACA Code of Ethics* (American Counseling Association, 2014) has sections dedicated to research, teaching, and supervision, there is a lack of clear guidance regarding leadership ethics and practices.

Still, counselor educators are often heavily involved in administering programs, and many serve their local communities in complex and meaningful ways. Likewise, local, state, and national professional counseling organizations are often powered by volunteer leaders who must navigate relationships among many stakeholders. The critical incidents in this section address leadership and advocacy within three primary settings: (a) professional counseling organizations, (b) the local community, and (c) counselor education programs.

Professional Organization Leadership

Professional counseling organizations are vital to the continued growth and development of the counseling profession. It was not until the adoption of the 2016 CACREP Standards (CACREP, 2016), however, that CACREP adopted leadership and advocacy as a core curricular area for doctoral programs, ushering in new attention to leadership within professional orientation coursework and, sometimes, dedicated leadership coursework. However, most counselor educators who lead learn by doing, sometimes stumbling onto key issues they may not even know are issues.

Volunteer leaders may be surprised by the depth of responsibility they hold as elected officers in professional organizations. Organizational leaders are charged with carefully balancing duties of care, loyalty, and obedience with potential conflicts of interest. The process of discerning conflicts of interest can be compounded when one is serving organizations closely aligned with specialty areas and expertise. "Is There a Conflict? Balancing Fiduciary Responsibility" features a member of the American Counseling Association's Governing Council who is working passionately to advocate for a population at risk; however, doing so raises questions regarding whether the advocacy may inadvertently jeopardize the organization. Conflicts of interest can also arise when one is serving multiple organizations simultaneously. "Who Are You Representing? Serving Two Professional Organizations" highlights one counselor educator who finds himself in a position to vote on an initiative he created with another organization.

Professional counseling organizations are often grassroots organizations in that they emerge from networks of professionals with similar interests and passions. These professionals are often practitioners or counselor educators first and engage with the organizations as part of their broader professional development. Leaders may find themselves surprised to be in increasingly complex and demanding positions of leadership. "True to Our Mission: Establishing an Identity as a Professional

Organization" highlights a professional leader who has followed an organization's development from its inception as an online discussion list to its establishment as an official professional association. The case highlights critical issues around differentiating networking and professional organizations.

Finally, professional counseling journals are critical to the continued development of counseling professionals. Yet the double-blind nature of the review process and safeguards for confidentiality can make journal processes largely invisible. Still, editors must work to provide direction to journals, mentoring editorial boards and ensuring a lasting vision for the journal. "It's All About Mentorship: Managing Professional Journals" provides a window into one organization's creative process for bringing editorial board members and aspiring scholars together as part of a journal community.

Leadership and Advocacy in the Local Community

Counselor educators are also active in their local communities, sometimes bringing specialty expertise to their advocacy or pro bono work. Local community organizations experience similar issues as professional counseling associations; however, dynamics may be complicated by the local, interdisciplinary context in which they work. "What Should We Fund? Addressing Budget Issues on a Community Board" follows a counselor educator who serves as a volunteer member of a nonprofit board and has to help the board navigate contentious issues regarding priorities while experiencing a declining budget.

Likewise, counselor educators will find themselves navigating tensions of conflicting organizational rules and expectations. Many counselor educators understand the special need for professional advocacy in moving the field forward, and learning about advocacy is an essential part of the master's-level curriculum. These expectations for advocacy may conflict with university policies that restrict faculty members' engagement in legislative professional advocacy. "My Hands Are Tied: Navigating University Prohibitions on Advocacy" highlights a new counselor educator who inadvertently finds herself in violation of a lobbying restriction she did not know existed and who in turn finds creative ways to ensure students learn advocacy skills.

Diversity and Inclusion Within Counselor Education Programs

The CACREP Standards (CACREP, 2016) require doctoral-level counselor educators and supervisors to learn advocacy models and skills, "strategies of leadership in relation to current multicultural and social justice issues" (Section 6, Standard B.5.k.), and "leadership in counselor education programs" (Section 6, Standard B.5.c.). The last set of critical incidents in this section highlight counselor educators' responsibilities for addressing issues of climate within counselor preparation programs, simultaneously illustrating how counselor educators' own identities and experiences of marginalization come into play. In "Do We Practice What We Preach? Diversity and Inclusion Plans," a counselor preparation program finds itself with a nicely developed, aspirational plan for recruiting and retaining diverse students and faculty members as required by the CACREP Standards. Yet as with many experiences related to the Multicultural and Social Justice Counseling Competencies (Ratts et al., 2015), members of marginalized communities may note discrepancies between the intent of policies and practices and their actual implementation or effects. Likewise, "Maybe I Can Change This: Addressing Marginalization in a Program" highlights experiences of marginalization for one doctoral student and illustrates how a faculty member works to raise awareness among faculty, create spaces for diverse students, and engage university initiatives. At the same time, the responses remind us of the potential costs of such initiatives.

Finally, issues related to diversity and inclusion are not just experienced by students. Diverse faculty members also navigate oppressive systems within academia on an ongoing basis. "You Can't Treat Me That Way! Microaggressions and Bullying" highlights the experience of a junior faculty member who encounters frequent microaggressions and bullying behavior from a senior peer that affect his scholarly productivity and raise questions regarding his connection to the program.

Section 1
Professional Organization Leadership

Chapter 32

Is There a Conflict? Balancing Fiduciary Responsibility

Leigh Falls Holman

2014 *ACA Code of Ethics* Standards Addressed

- I.1.b. Ethical Decision Making

• • •

Janet was an active member of the International Association of Addictions and Offender Counselors (IAAOC) and was serving on IAAOC's board of directors as the Governing Council (GC) representative to the American Counseling Association (ACA). Previously Janet had served as IAAOC's Sex Offender Committee chair, secretary, president-elect, president, and past-president. Through her leadership, she worked to raise awareness of racial disparities in the justice system and the negative impact of the Sex Offender Registration and Notification Act (SORNA) on the mental health and well-being of juvenile sex offenders (JSOs; Adam Walsh Child Protection and Safety Act, 2006; 18 U.S.C. 2241—Aggravated Sexual Abuse, 2011; Office of Sex Offender Sentencing, Monitoring, Apprehending, Registering, and Tracking, 2011). Specifically, Janet highlighted evidence that the registry does not decrease offending rates, in particular among juveniles who are unlikely to sexually reoffend in the future, but does negatively impact the mental health and well-being of kids publicly identified as sex offenders (Caldwell, 2010; Calley, 2008; Hanson et al., 2018; Human Rights Watch, 2013; Lobanov-Rostovsky, 2017; Shah, 2018; J. Shaw & Lee, 2019; Stern et al., 2017).

Janet's advocacy increased her professional profile and contributed to her ongoing leadership in IAAOC. Given her experience, Janet expressed excitement at the prospect of bringing national attention to her advocacy work with her new position as a GC representative. She realized many members of ACA worked with victims of sexual assault but knew little about sex offenders as a potentially vulnerable population. In addition, she felt strongly that the negative mental health effects and racial disparities associated with the JSO registry were injustices ACA's GC should advocate against.

As a new ACA GC member, Janet attended an orientation about her role. She learned the GC was the board of directors for ACA. In addition, she learned that her fiduciary duty was to ACA and that she was not supposed to represent IAAOC's concerns to the GC, poll IAAOC membership on issues before the GC, or otherwise put addictions or offender issues before the good of the ACA membership. This was true even though she was serving simultaneously on IAAOC's board of directors. In addition, Janet learned that the GC was largely responsible for overseeing resource allocation and developing a strategic plan that directed limited resources.

During her first year as a GC member, Janet tested the waters by developing a social justice advocacy position to address racial and socioeconomic disparities in the justice system. She partnered with representatives of the Association for Multicultural Counseling and Development and Counselors for Social Justice to draft a resolution that passed with little debate, as it was consistent with ACA's strategic plan focused on social justice. The following year, Janet developed a new resolution that specifically stated ACA would advocate against the JSO registry. This new resolution required the allocation of monetary and human resources from ACA for activities such as lobbying and educating ACA members and the public about disparities in implementation of the registry and about the negative effects on JSOs.

During the debate on the resolution, several GC members expressed concerns that Janet was advancing her personal research and advocacy agenda to raise her profile within the profession. They argued she was not considering the potential harm such advocacy could have on the organization as a whole. Specific concerns included public relations fallout and membership loss if ACA advocated for sex offenders. Board members also expressed concerns about whether expenditures for resources could be justified under ACA's current vision, mission, values, and strategic plan. Board members concerned about these issues reiterated the fact that each member of a nonprofit board had fiduciary duties to consider when voting on the resolution.

Case Analysis and Discussion

The word *fiduciary* comes from the Latin *fiducia*, meaning "trust." People who have fiduciary duties are trusted to make legal and financial decisions for another party. Nonprofit board members have three primary fiduciary duties: the duty of care, the duty of loyalty, and the duty of obedience (Price, 2018). Thus, they are required to demonstrate loyalty to the organization, honesty and integrity in their decision-making regarding limited organizational resources, and care for and consideration of the organization's beneficiaries (Paine, 1994). ACA GC members are fiduciaries of the organization, and the beneficiaries in this case are ACA's members and the counseling profession. Prior to deciding regarding whether to support this motion, GC members must consider their duties of care, loyalty, and obedience alongside potential conflicts of interest that might violate these duties.

The duty of care concerns whether the board manages the organization's resources in a reasonable manner, the degree to which a reasonable person would identify foreseeable injury to the members or profession, and the proximate relationship between the board's decision and potential harm that could result to the beneficiaries of the organization. Board members must seek out and critically evaluate "material information that is reasonably available to them" rather than simply relying on information that is presented to them (*Smith v. Van Gorkom*, 1985, p. 889). The GC must consider what financial resources would be needed to pay for educational and lobbying activities. They would also need to consider the amount of time ACA staff would need to spend on these activities and alternative activities staff might not be able to perform. Stakeholders must ask whether Janet's proposal would cost the organization too much or result in other activities (e.g., lobbying for licensure portability or Medicare reimbursement) not being pursued.

According to the duty of loyalty, board members must act in the best interest of the organization, its members, and the profession. It is problematic for board members to use their positions to seize opportunities for themselves at the expense of the organization, its members, or the profession. In this case, Janet made an interested transaction with the potential to benefit from organizational resources (e.g., money or staff time; Wagenmaker & Oberly, 2017). Although it is not relevant to Janet's case, the duty of loyalty also concerns disclosing private organizational information, board deliberations, or plans to those who are not fiduciaries of the organization (Wagenmaker & Oberly, 2017). When an organizational fiduciary (i.e., Janet) makes decisions that benefit the fiduciary personally or professionally at the expense of the beneficiary (i.e., ACA members), it is considered a conflict of interest. Consistent with their roles as fiduciaries of ACA, some GC members expressed concerns that Janet had a conflict of interest, given that her scholarly production was related to the topic of the resolution. To determine whether a conflict actually exists, one must ask whether Janet's career will benefit at the expense of the organization. Although it may be easy to determine that Janet's career may benefit from the resolution passing, it may be more complicated to determine whether this would harm members of ACA or the profession.

To determine the potential for harm, one must consider that ACA's membership had decreased in the previous 2 years, and the prevailing belief was that the decreased membership was correlated with several high-profile social advocacy positions the organization had taken that some counselors did not believe were reflective of their own values. In consideration of this, several board members expressed concern about the public relations impact if the organization and profession were seen as advocating for sex offenders rather than victims of sexual violence. Such a perception could result in even more reduced membership and related economic impact.

Although Janet could understand the public relations concerns, those supporting the resolution articulated that social justice movements often have social costs. They presented strong arguments that the racial and socioeconomic disparities in the adjudication and registration of JSOs were consistent with both the ACA Advocacy Competencies (Toporek & Daniels, 2018) and the Multicultural and Social Justice Counseling Competencies (Ratts et al., 2015). In discussing the ACA Advocacy Competencies, Janet emphasized the Systems Advocacy Counselor Competencies, which state that advocacy-oriented counselors in organizational leadership should collaborate to

- Provide and interpret data as well as share research and expertise to show the urgency for change.
- In collaboration with other stakeholders, develop a vision to guide change.
- Analyze the sources of political power and social influence within the system.
- Develop a step-by-step plan for implementing the change process, attending to possible ethical issues.
- Develop a plan for dealing with probable responses to change.
- Recognize and deal with resistance.
- Assess the effect of counselors' advocacy efforts on the system and constituents. (Toporek & Daniels, 2018, pp. 7–8)

In addition, Janet argued that ACA had a role in addressing this as a public policy initiative under the Collective Action section of the ACA Advocacy Competencies, which included duties "to address environmental and systemic issues, and inform the public as well as policy makers" about issues of oppression (Toporek & Daniels, 2018, p. 8) reflected within the JSO registry.

Both sides raised valid concerns about ACA's role in social advocacy as well as the potential costs to the organization's financial health. This led the GC to consider their duty of obedience next. The duty of obedience requires that the board not engage in unauthorized or illegal activities as they work to carry out the organization's mission (Price, 2018). According to the ACA website, the organization's mission is to "promote the professional development of counselors, advocate for the profession, and ensure ethical, culturally-inclusive practices that protect those using counseling services" (ACA, n.d.). In considering their duty of obedience, several GC members discussed concerns that ACA not expend resources on something not directly related to the ACA mission and noted that any resolution should have a clear connection to the current strategic plan developed to carry out that mission. At the time, the 3-year strategic plan articulated several related values, including the following:

- Diversity, equity, and inclusion, defined as "valu[ing] every person for the differences of identity, ideas, and interests they bring" and "actively work[ing] to engage with those people and their differences."
- Integrity, specifically being "honest, transparent and aligned with our values through communication, advocacy and action—always."
- Proactive leadership, defined as "be[ing] at the front of the profession, leading the way" and "creat[ing] a vision for the profession and tak[ing] action to turn it into reality."
- Professional community and relationships, including "creat[ing] opportunities for real and virtual networking, collaboration, and lifelong learning."
- Scientific practice and knowledge, meaning "ground[ing] our profession and our work in evidence-based methodologies and practices."
- Social justice and empowerment, meaning "stand[ing] with and for every person in pursuit of high-quality mental health care and wellness." (ACA, n.d.)

In considering the mission and values articulated in the strategic plan, Janet argued that the resolution was based on evidence from peer-reviewed research and concerns for social justice for people with mental health concerns, in particular because current law disproportionately impacted people of color and those from lower socioeconomic backgrounds. She stated that to demonstrate integrity in living ACA's values, it was important to be proactive leaders by supporting those who were marginalized by unjust laws. For these reasons, Janet believed the resolution upheld ACA's mission by ensuring the use of ethical and culturally inclusive practices to protect JSOs who used counseling services. If the GC passed the resolution, ACA could expend resources on professional development for counselors.

Janet and those in support of the resolution focused on how it aligned with the mission and values stated in ACA's strategic plan, emphasizing their fiduciary duty of obedience. Those who opposed the resolution emphasized concerns over a perceived conflict of interest between the advancement of Janet's career and the potential public relations fallout from the perception that ACA supported sex offenders, holding that the resolution might negatively impact membership and ultimately the financial resources ACA might have to carry out its mission.

Conclusion

The majority of board members voted in opposition to the motion because of concerns for the organization's overall financial health and potential negative fallout from committing financial and human organizational capital to advocate for a controversial population. Janet and those who voted in favor of the motion were angry because they believed the GC had avoided an opportunity for bold leadership in advocating for a marginalized population in spite of evidence that the registry does not decrease offending rates and results in harm to the well-being of JSOs.

Reflection Questions

1. Some ACA divisions ask their GC representative to also sit on the division board. How might being on two boards present a problem? How could the representative manage such a situation?
2. What do you think about the argument that Janet's activities could have potentially harmed the organization? Explain your reasoning.

Critical Incident Response

Philip B. Clarke and Michelle R. Ghoston

If we zoom out, we see this case is largely about organizational ethics. Organizational ethics involves three or more individuals in an interconnected system working together with a purpose and similar goal in mind (C. Johnson, 2018). Ethics includes many different considerations, such as for judging actions alongside an individual's character, moral compass (C. Johnson, 2018), and integrity. On a basic level, "organizational ethics applies moral standards and principles to the organizational context" (C. Johnson, 2018, p. 7).

Several aspects of this case work together to create a dilemma around organizational ethics. On beginning her role with the ACA GC, Janet seemed to understand the organizational purpose and goals of ACA. She also fully knew and embraced her passion for shedding light on the social injustice of SORNA and its mental health impacts on youth. For Janet, someone who ascribed to the *ACA Code of Ethics* (ACA, 2014), embracing and promoting social justice was paramount. Having to balance organizational ethics with her own sense of ethical responsibility may have created an unintended personal and professional conflict for Janet.

As we examined this case, we struggled with the following question: If Janet's situation entailed a conflict of interest, how was the initial proposition to "address racial and socioeconomic disparities in the justice system" passed? It seems this advocacy issue was one Janet was pursuing in conjunction with IAAOC. If this is the case, she was imposing a platform she and IAAOC had developed onto the ACA docket. This appears to violate one of the functions of GC members in the ACA Policy Manual: "To remain representative of their constituencies but not to be representative for their constituencies" (ACA, 2019, p. 15). It could be that the involvement of other ACA divisions served as a check and balance of sorts in ensuring that this proposition was not Janet's platform via IAAOC. In addition, there may have been less at stake because no financial support from ACA was required in the initial proposition.

However, there is still a perceived discrepancy in the GC accepting the justice system proposal but deeming advocacy against the JSO registry a conflict of interest. Another function of GC members mentioned in the ACA Policy Manual is to "forward issues from constituencies" (ACA, 2019, p. 15). Again, the accepted proposition is one Janet was not simply forwarding to ACA on behalf of IAAOC; it is one she had taken a lead in developing with IAAOC. How then would advocating against SORNA be any different for ACA?

Janet's experiences highlight the possibility that similar conflicts of interest arise frequently for organizational leaders in counseling and other professions. How do people extricate and distance themselves from advocacy issues they are passionate and knowledgeable about so as not to breach their leadership role? If they have researched a social justice issue, observed it in their life, observed it in their clinical work, and sought to make positive change related to it, how do they avoid imposing this topic onto the agendas of other organizations?

Thankfully, organizations have conflict of interest policies that stipulate how these dilemmas are to be handled. ACA Policy 301.6.B states that GC members should inform the ACA President of conflicts of interest and recuse themselves from voting on these proposals (ACA, 2019). Janet and the GC need to be vigilant for other ways in which the conflict of interest could manifest. For example, if Janet published a book on bias in the justice system or if funding opportunities were provided for counselor research in this area and Janet applied, these circumstances would need to be scrutinized. In the ACA Policy Manual (ACA, 2019), the conflict of interest discussion extends to prospective personal and/or financial gain that could be inappropriate for ACA volunteer leaders. ACA also includes a "Disclosure of Other Interests" form on which leaders declare any potential personal or financial conflicts of interest (p. 92).

We agree that Janet's cause fits within ACA's strategic plan and that her cause is an example of meaningful advocacy, thus fulfilling the duty of obedience. However, Janet may not be maintaining her duty of loyalty to not represent IAAOC's concerns to the GC, as noted by the author. In sum, we believe a conflict of interest has occurred. The checks and balances put in place by ACA provide a framework for addressing the situation. If IAAOC is the sole organization championing the proposal against SORNA, and Janet has been involved in these social justice efforts with IAAOC, Janet should recuse herself from voting on whether ACA funds this cause.

• • •

Chapter 33

Who Are You Representing? Serving Two Professional Organizations

Kristopher M. Goodrich and Renée C. Howells

2014 *ACA Code of Ethics* Standards Addressed

- I.1.b. Ethical Decision Making
- I.2.c. Consultation

• • •

Raul was a tenured faculty member at an institution classified as very high research activity. As part of workload requirements, he pursued service opportunities in various counseling organizations. As a faculty member of color, he had received a great deal of mentorship in his graduate program about the importance of representation to ensure that persons from historically marginalized groups had space at the table. Raul had taken that mentorship to heart and become an active member the Association for Multicultural Counseling and Development (AMCD), of the Association for Counselor Education and Supervision (ACES), and Chi Sigma Iota (CSI) early in his career. Noting his strong leadership skills, his placement at a prestigious university, and his identity as a scholar from a marginalized community, leaders in these organizations called on him to serve in roles of increasing significance.

Raul's service across organizations never presented a conflict, as each organization had different areas of focus and work, so overlap was typically very minimal. However, as the roles he took in multiple organizations increased in scope and significance, he came to serve on the executive boards of two organizations simultaneously. As an executive board member, Raul understood his fiduciary responsibility to act in accordance with each organization's bylaws, mission, vision, and budgetary confines. He also knew he had a responsibility to represent the organization's members' interests, not his own, in his votes as a board member.

At a recent board meeting, Raul noticed his first conflict as an executive board member. AMCD was holding a fundraiser at an upcoming American Counseling Association (ACA) conference that was meant to support a local nonprofit organization that served persons of color in the community where the ACA conference was going to be held. As an AMCD board member, Raul had the integral goal of ensuring the success of this activity and was part of a planning committee tasked with soliciting other ACA divisions to support these efforts. However, Raul also identified as a board member of ACES who would need to vote on whether ACES would donate funds to support AMCD's fundraiser. Although he saw this activity in line with ACES's mission, vision, and policies on donating to external organizations, he was unsure whether his role as an AMCD board member and planner of the fundraiser would pose a conflict of interest. Raul wanted ACES to support the fundraiser, but he did not want other ACES board members or the general membership of the organization to question his personal and professional ethics. Raul knew that he needed to register some kind of vote as an ACES board member, and he did not want other members of the board to think that an abstention or negative vote demonstrated concern he had for the event or negative feelings for the organization.

Case Analysis and Discussion

It is important to address the key issues presented in this case. Namely, what was Raul's ethical responsibility as an executive board member of multiple organizations? He identified a potential conflict of interest between AMCD's funding request and his voting position as an ACES officer. What was the best course of action for Raul to undertake to resolve ethical discrepancies in this scenario? This section begins with a review of the literature regarding counseling leadership as well as culturally linked experiences of underrepresented faculty members. Following this, we discuss relevant information from the *ACA Code of Ethics* (ACA, 2014) and the importance of using ethical decision-making models when conflicts arise. We then make a step-by-step analysis of the issue using a specific ethical decision-making model.

Participation in leadership is a cornerstone of counselor education (Luke & Goodrich, 2010). The 2016 Council for Accreditation of Counseling and Related Educational Programs (CACREP) Standards (CACREP, 2016) outline active participation in ACA divisions and other counseling organizations as pivotal to the longevity and welfare of the counseling profession. Leadership within these organizations fosters greater visibility of counselor professional identity across disciplines (Kaplan & Gladding, 2011). This perspective is further evidenced by CSI, which articulates leadership in counseling organizations as key to promoting professional excellence. Although the importance of leadership within the field is well documented, focused research on navigating multiple leadership roles ethically is warranted.

As leadership within counseling organizations becomes more diversified, it is imperative that faculty members have access to culturally responsive resources for negotiating roles and responsibilities. Raul was a seasoned faculty member with extensive mentorship and leadership experience. He was known for his significant abilities and contributions to leadership and scholarship. Counseling organizations routinely sought him out when leadership positions became available. His experience and reputation may imply a certain level of comfort navigating ethical dilemmas. However, making such an assumption is dangerous. Raul may indeed feel competent addressing this ethical quandary, but his personhood as a faculty member of color must be validated and contextualized.

Faculty members from historically and culturally marginalized groups face additional hardship in academia, which includes domains of service and leadership (Writer & Watson, 2019). Issues of tokenism and hypervisibility often result in faculty members of color feeling undersupported and overworked in service and leadership (Flores Niemann, 2016; Martinez et al., 2018; Writer & Watson, 2019). Faculty members of color are often pigeonholed in organizations and academia as the primary "caretakers of diversity" (Writer & Watson, 2019, p. 28). Thus, Raul may encounter implicit or explicit pressure to safeguard AMCD's fundraising efforts during the ACES meeting; at the same time, he may receive the same pressure from ACES that his primary role is within that organization and other organizational work is tertiary. Regardless of how Raul chooses to use his voting power, his personal and professional ethics may be questioned by others within AMCD and ACES, especially because faculty members from marginalized groups are regularly viewed as less competent and effective in their professional roles (Writer & Watson, 2019). Therefore, following an ethical decision-making process is vital to Raul's success and welfare.

To determine Raul's ethical responsibility and recommended course of action, we must consult relevant ethical standards outlined in the *ACA Code of Ethics* (ACA, 2014). The Introduction to Section I states that counselors aim to resolve ethical dilemmas with "direct and open communication among all parties involved and seek consultation with colleagues and supervisors when necessary" (p. 19). Given that Raul was unsure whether a conflict of interest had been breached, communication and consultation became essential components of timely resolution. Raul could have sought out trusted colleagues within AMCD and ACES to solicit their feedback on how to proceed with the upcoming ACES vote. Consultation is imperative to ethical decision-making because it can protect veracity, minimize bias and blind spots, and reveal alternative possibilities (Standard I.2.c.). Because Raul was concerned about his ethics being questioned by board members and the general membership, consultation with knowledgeable colleagues may have engendered clarity in responsibilities and course of action.

In addition, counselors should document dilemmas using an ethical decision-making model (ACA, 2014, Standard I.1.b.). An increasing number of ethical decision-making models exist within the counseling literature, evidencing the growing need for ethical guidance in a complex, pluralistic society (Heller-Levitt et al., 2015; Luke et al., 2013a, 2013b). Common steps in ethical decision-making models include (a) documentation, (b) a thorough review of relevant laws and ethical standards, (c) the generation of possible outcomes, (d) an analysis of the risks and benefits of potential actions, and (e) the determination of a decision (Heller-Levitt et al., 2015; Kaplan et al., 2017).

In Raul's case, leadership in multiple organizations had culminated in a potential fiduciary conflict of interest. Raul's positionality as an executive board member for both AMCD and ACES constitutes an ethically ambiguous circumstance. The efficacy of decision-making models has been a source of debate among scholars, as theoretical knowledge does not always clearly translate into multidimensional practice (Luke et al., 2013b). An issue of translation is present in this case, as a simple solution is not easily discernable, and two or more courses of action have collided. Raul was cognizant of his responsibility to uphold the creeds of both organizations, yet he recognized the need for objectivity when casting his vote. Although he believed AMCD's efforts to obtain funding aligned with ACES's mission and policies, his involvement on the fundraising planning committee may compromise his perceived objectivity by others. By engaging in consultation and an ethical decision-making process, Raul would be better able to demonstrate his awareness and communicate his rationale during the ACES board meeting.

Actions and Outcomes

Raul had not taken any action as he was aware that consultation and a review of ethical decision-making models were necessary before moving forward. It was imperative that Raul select an ethical decision-making model to guide his actions in this case. As the *ACA Code of Ethics* (ACA, 2014) does not explicitly address leadership, consulting the *Principles and Practices of Leadership Excellence* (CSI Academy of Leaders, 1999) would be important, as they note leadership practice across 10 different principles. In particular, Raul might attend to the first seven principles as well as the last, with the greatest attention to Principle 6, which addresses the financial responsibility board members have to their organization and its members.

The intercultural model of ethical decision-making (Luke et al., 2013a) felt most comfortable to Raul, as it takes into account cultural factors not explicitly addressed in other models but very relevant to this case and his life. In Step 1, Raul engaged in awareness raising and fact finding. He was aware that he had been presented with an ethical dilemma and he needed to take stock of all relevant facts before moving forward. This process included reviewing handbooks and other documentation related to mission, vision, and strategic planning. He also acknowledged and reviewed previous history and communication with both organizations.

In Step 2, Raul outlined relevant cultural, religious, and worldview (CRW) factors present within the case across each of the stakeholders, including Raul himself (Luke et al., 2013a). This involved exploring his own beliefs and values as well as any biases he might hold. During Step 3, he researched policies, procedures, and relevant law related to the case as well as ethics codes. This included exploring handbooks on organizational policy and procedure for both groups as well as consulting the *ACA Code of Ethics* (ACA, 2014) and the *Principles and Practices of Leadership Excellence* (CSI Academy of Leaders, 1999).

Step 4 required that Raul determine whether he needed external consultation (Luke et al., 2013a). It was important for Raul to receive consultation in both legal and ethical concerns related to this situation as well as the CRW factors present in the case. Raul consulted with previous leaders of AMCD and ACES and with a trusted mentor outside the organizations. He received their insight and processed the best ways to proceed.

Step 5 involved writing down each possible process action and then recording each potential decision or course of action that might resolve the situation. This included voting for ACES support of the AMCD fundraiser, voting against the proposal, and abstaining from the vote. Step 6 involved identifying and analyzing the CRW factors related to the process and decisions items in Step 5. Raul was aware that certain communities struggled with funding and support; if ACES did not support the fundraiser, at-risk groups might have experienced undue hardship. Raul was also aware that ACES had a culture as an organization of its own, and some members may not have shared the same values or appreciated membership dollars being spent on a cause they did not support. Raul was aware of the impressions people had of leaders from historically and culturally marginalized groups and that he might lose esteem from others if he voted in a certain way. He acknowledged he was setting precedent with any action he took as a board member.

Finally, Step 7 involved Raul making a choice, acting on that decision, and documenting and evaluating the outcome. Through research, external consultation, and the process of self-reflection, Raul decided it would be important to declare his potential conflict of interest during the ACES board meeting but state he felt it necessary to vote on this matter. He noted that he had arrived at this decision by considering the mission and vision of both organizations, reviewing policy and procedure manuals, and considering feedback from trusted mentors and colleagues who also helped him to consider CRW factors. Raul voted yes on the proposal, and it passed the board unanimously. Raul felt comfortable registering his vote because he clearly articulated the potential conflict and dilemma he faced, but he also noted how he arrived at his decision. Other board members later spoke to him about appreciating hearing his process and what Raul had shared with the board, as they could use this in future decision-making.

Conclusion

Learning to gracefully navigate potential ethical dilemmas within leadership is central to the development of counselor educators. The case of Raul illustrates how one might identify, document, and determine a course of action when presented with a conflict of interest in leadership roles. Not all issues related to role conflict were reviewed in this case; some professional organizations may have specific policies surrounding conflict of interest and/or ask members to sign contracts or agreements demonstrating awareness of these policies. In these circumstances, these policies and contracts should be considered in Steps 3 (policies) and 4 (legal concerns) of the intercultural model of ethical decision-making before any decisions are made (Luke et al., 2013a). However, we hope to highlight the fact that no leadership decision should be made lightly or without considering the full context of decisions for the organizations for which one serves.

Reflection Questions

1. To what degree do you believe Raul's dual affiliation created a conflict of interest?
2. How can the counseling profession attend to leadership and voice without continuing to overburden and tokenize leaders with minoritized identities?

Critical Incident Response

Marty Jencius

Raul was involved with multiple organizations and was in a problematic situation by having potentially divided allegiance. As organizations look to diversify leadership and draw from a limited available pool of diverse members, the few diverse members can be asked and overcommitted for multiple roles. Using an ethical decision-making model strengthened Raul's approach to handling conflicting roles. It provided independent guidance and allowed him to take a more objective approach to forming a solution to his situation. I also appreciate Raul's transparency throughout the process. He let those in both associations know about how his alliances could be considered a fiduciary conflict when voting on whether one association should fund the other association.

The problem is not with Raul's approach but with the lack of guidance associations have around addressing such conflicts. Professional counseling associations should have methods to inform them when candidates for leadership roles may have other professional commitments that could present undue influence or conflicts. Associations can ask for full transparency and set up rules to ensure leadership candidates do not have other unnecessary burdens or potential conflicts among multiple roles. By not having a formal process for handling conflicts of interest, associations falter in giving direction to their board members.

ACA provides members of its Governing Council with an orientation and a series of documents, including the Code of Leadership and the *ACA Policy Manual* (ACA, 2019). This helps board members understand their roles and duties, how to engage in the leadership process, and what is expected of them as board members. In addition, ACA has a Conflict of Interest Statement board members and leaders must sign. This document addresses financial and contractual arrangements that may pose a conflict of interest. The Code of Leadership covers service, organizational well-being, inclusion, personal conduct, reliability, accessibility, decision-making, and fiscal responsibility. The *ACA Policy Manual* includes Policy 301.6 (Conflict of Interest), which states that board members identify possible conflicts of interest that may prevent them from voting in the best interest of ACA. When a conflict of interest exists between two boards, it is to be resolved by giving "primary consideration to the welfare of the American Counseling Association" (ACA, 2019, p. 19). To follow this policy, Raul would need to vote in the best interest of ACES. According to Policy 301.6, board members who are unable to resolve conflicts of interest between a representing entity and ACA should give notice to the ACA President and, after giving such notification, refrain from voting. This policy frees board members from voting on actual or perceived conflicts of interest. A similar policy would encourage Raul to abstain from the ACES vote on funding for AMCD.

According to Robert's Rules of Order (Robert et al., 2020), voting members can abstain from a vote if there is potential for an actual or perceived conflict of interest. Raul went to significant lengths to explain his relationship with AMCD to ACES members. Although he made his conflict of interest public to members who were present, members who were not consulted may interpret his vote on funding as an inappropriate dual relationship. Despite feeling like he had practiced ethical decision-making, Raul did not consider how his vote could be perceived by the membership, which might assume the funding to AMCD passed because of his influence and not on its own merit.

The process of calling for a motion, discussing the motion, and voting allows for full consideration of a proposal's merits. A vote in the affirmative may look as if Raul is favoring his relationship with AMCD instead of his fiduciary responsibility to ACES. An alternative consideration for Raul would be to abstain from voting. Abstentions are not part of the total vote and can be made for various reasons. In this case, abstaining would allow Raul to separate his dual roles with both boards. Raul could use the discussion period to evaluate the board's support for the motion, express his support for the motion, and explain his principled reasoning for abstaining to avoid any appearance of taking advantage of ACES by promoting AMCD. From that discussion, Raul should be able to see the group's will in terms of support for the motion. Given what he might see as general support, he could get a sense of whether the board was likely to support or reject the motion. If the motion was headed for failure, it would not fall on Raul's shoulders but could be more an issue with the motion itself or the board's will.

• • •

Chapter 34

True to Our Mission: Establishing an Identity as a Professional Organization

Marty Jencius

2014 *ACA Code of Ethics* Standards Addressed

- Not applicable

• • •

Talisa, an African American counselor educator working at a state institution, had earned tenure with promotion in her seventh year of appointment. Her primary area of scholarship focused on clinical counselors in prison settings. She was an active member of the Association for Clinical Correctional Counseling (ACCC), an association formed in the past 8 years with a slowly growing membership of 600 practitioners, faculty, and students. The mission of ACCC was to promote professional education and training for counselors working with the incarcerated. Talisa had served on ACCC committees and as treasurer. She was now president of ACCC, which involved a 2-year term as president-elect, a 2-year term as president, and a 2-year term as past-president.

ACCC had started with a few faculty members who had felt the need for a professional association that represented counselors serving incarcerated individuals. The group had expanded to an online discussion list; then one member had begun the process of creating a professional association, which required the development of a board. The board met annually during the conference of another national association that all board members attended. It had occasional online meetings to address upcoming issues for members. The meetings had no collaboratively developed agenda and involved freeform discussions around concerns the president brought to the meeting, with others contributing new issues as they saw fit. Not much attention was given to infrastructure or running the association.

When Talisa had become involved with the association, she had brought her previous work experience as a financial auditor. During her tenure as treasurer, she had discovered and corrected some financial issues; this had led to her eventual election as president. Given her financial acumen, she was encouraged by those in the association to assist with setting up a member dues process. The financial bookkeeping consisted of a spreadsheet and a rolling checkbook of expenses and revenues. It had become apparent to Talisa that ACCC had to move from being an unincorporated entity to being an incorporated professional association with nonprofit status. She had begun that process during her time as president-elect.

Now as president, Talisa's board consisted of two counselor educators from the membership, two practitioners from the at-large membership, the past-president, the newly elected president-elect, and the newly elected treasurer (all practitioners) plus a student representative elected from the general membership. Talisa was one of three ethnically diverse people on the board, and she was the only president from an underrepresented group. All members served 2-year terms, with presidents serving a total of 6 years sequentially through the position.

ACCC had yet to develop bylaws and procedures. Beyond a mission statement and some rules of organization (e.g., officers, duties, elections, and meeting structures), there were no priorities, directions, or goals for the association. Thus, ACCC had not matured enough to assume direction as a professional association and still acted as a member-based club. It had not developed a strategic long-term plan and fell into the pattern of the president setting their own agenda, which often reflected the personal investment of the person in that office.

Talisa believed the association should not be driven by presidential initiatives. Her plans were to dissolve that practice and move to one that used strategic planning. She had 2 years during her presidential term to establish this new way of working. It engendered some consternation from the president-elect, who would take over the presidency in 2 years, as they saw the change as a move to prevent them from leaving their own footprint on the association.

Three of the board members (the newly elected president-elect, treasurer, and student representative) approached Talisa with the idea of emphasizing social justice issues, in particular injustices experienced by prisoners housed in criminal justice facilities. They wanted ACCC to address the rights of those adjudicated for crimes. The president-elect indicated that he had had conversations with the leader of a criminal justice welfare association on the topic of prisoner conditions and had assured them of ACCC's support of the effort. On hearing this, Talisa wanted to discourage the social justice direction, as she believed the board needed to focus on infrastructure and support for its members. However, she did not want to discourage those on the board from taking initiative and decided to ask the group to put this on the agenda for the next board meeting.

Case Analysis and Discussion

This scenario reflects an educational gap in counselor education professional development: the lack of training in organizational dynamics and the nuts and bolts of running professional associations. The 2016 Council for Accreditation of Counseling and Related Educational Programs (CACREP) Standards (CACREP, 2016) have begun to address leadership, but most of the andragogy focuses on theory and visioning (Barreto, 2012; Fassinger & Schullman, 2017) with little or no focus on structure, components, processes, or the management of people in organizations. ACCC has both structural (how the association is organized) and process (how the association performs its duties) concerns. The structural issues involve a lack of clarity in purpose (mission) and goals (vision) for the association as driven by the bylaws and direction that is driven by officer interest instead of a strategic plan. Process issues involve how communication happens and how decisions are made.

Structural Issues

A mission statement is an essential piece of an association's structural organization (Drucker, 1990). The ACCC mission statement ("to promote professional education and training for counselors working with the incarcerated") establishes the purpose of the association. At this point, the mission statement stands without a vision statement. Vision statements are developed from mission statements and embody the organization's vision for its members and/or its world. A vision statement is an outcome of the work of the association. In the case of ACCC, a vision statement might be "Every incarcerated inmate has access to an ACCC professionally trained counselor" or "Every counselor working with the incarcerated has professional training from ACCC." The vision statement establishes a long-term aim of the association and can be used to develop a strategic plan. Talisa is in a position to help the board see the importance of having a vision statement and developing a strategic plan to guide their work instead of relying on the whims of presidential initiatives.

Bylaws are another essential structural aspect of ACCC that needs to be addressed. When it files for nonprofit status, an organization should develop a complete set of bylaws. Basic sections of organizational bylaws include Article I, which states the name of the organization, and Article II, which includes a statement of the organization's purpose or mission and restrictions on that purpose (i.e., activities in which the organization will not engage). ACCC could very well decide to be an educational organization for its members and restrict itself from engaging in political campaigning or speaking out on political issues. Article II of the bylaws also articulates the objectives of the association, which are typically extensions of the mission statement. Article III on fairness addresses the fact that not all issues for the association can be included within the bylaws and contains guidelines on how to handle disagreements that may arise. Article IV on membership includes guidance on eligibility for voting and running for office. Article V covers the board of directors or governance board, including its role, its size, its composition, meetings, terms and elections, quorum, and notice. Article VI focuses on the duties of the various board positions, and Article VII addresses the role of the executive director and any staff (and is currently not applicable to ACCC). Article VIII speaks to finances, including working funds, permanent funds, gifts, banking practices, and interest. Article IX focuses on committees and their development and operations. Article X provides the process for the bylaws to be amended.

ACCC has developed some structure, with a name, a purpose, and officers, but the organization lacks other structural aspects of a nonprofit organization that are codified in bylaws. There are many free resources for groups that want to write bylaws (Vick, 2015) as well as online templates one can download and adapt. Because bylaws must conform to the laws of the jurisdiction in which the association is incorporated, they should be vetted by an attorney who specializes in nonprofit or association law. For example, some jurisdictions do not allow boards to vote through email and will only allow voting to occur at face-to-face meetings. It is only through an astute legal consultation that these jurisdictional discrepancies will be identified.

ACCC will also be required to maintain financial records of dues and expenditures and have regular audits of its books to stay within the legal confines of nonprofit associations. This will require moving from a rolling checkbook that gets passed from one treasurer to another to an annualized budgeting process. Budgeting involves anticipating regular annual expenses, anticipating special projects that may come up during the year, and making an annual forecast of finances. Talisa saw the need to manage finances but did not have a full scope of expertise; securing a certified financial consult would benefit ACCC.

The lack of a strategic plan is problematic for ACCC's structure. Drucker (2008) suggested that prior to developing a strategic plan organizations ask five essential questions to set their direction: What is our mission? Who is our customer? What does the customer value? What are our results? and What is our Plan? ACCC's answers to these questions might lead them to see the value of the member as a customer of the association.

The strategic planning process (Katsioloudes, 2006) involves using the mission statement, goals of the organization (vision statement), and objectives (from Article II of the bylaws) to begin discussing strategy formulation and strategy implementation. Formulation and implementation occur in a reciprocal loop that is evaluated throughout the cycle. ACCC has a mission statement but nothing else at this point. The ACCC board needs to establish goals and objectives. Goals are open-ended statements of planned accomplishments, similar to the vision statement. Objectives are the desired end results of these accomplishments. Objectives provide specificity to goals. Drucker (1990) recommended that to be successful with objectives organizations keep in mind three "musts": look at strength and performance (do better what you do well), look outside at the opportunities (look for competence outside your organization), and look at what you really believe in (missions are not impersonal).

If ACCC adopts the vision that "every counselor working with the incarcerated has professional training from ACCC," objectives might be statements of numbers of ACCC-trained counselors (e.g., "ACCC will enroll 200 counselors each year in a basic training for working with the incarcerated"). This may be a premature objective, as ACCC has not established the what, when, where, and how of any training for members. An objective that fits the development of training might be "ACCC will develop a day-long workshop for members on basic methods for working with the incarcerated by the end of the calendar year." Another objective around the development of training could be "ACCC will explore, choose, and invest in an online platform for training delivery." Creating and ordering objectives by priority and sequence is the function of the board in strategic planning.

As part of its strategic plan, ACCC needs to determine what can be done with the human resources available to them. Will some strategic objectives be delegated to member-chaired committees (already established in the bylaws by vote of the membership), or will the tasks be taken on by board members (the least effective method when trying to develop an involved organizational culture)? The final, continuous function of strategy evaluation involves monitoring the results of a strategy. Changes can be made in strategic implementation as needed, and information from evaluations can impact future strategic formulations. One of ACCC's process issues is that it does not appear to have any method of evaluating progress toward goals.

Process Issues

Process issues are related to how a board performs. ACCC needs guiding principles for how and when the board meets (Article V of the bylaws) and how official communication will be handled by board members. Outside their official capacity as board members for an association, board members should establish boundaries by only referencing the official public record of the board meetings. Likewise, board members cannot make promises or alliances on behalf of the association. All actions should come to the full board for debate and vote.

Another process issue involves preparation for and management of board meetings. Board members need to be educated in how to be a board member, which includes having an orientation for all new board members (Sand, 2005). Many board members do not know how meetings are run using Robert's Rules of Order, nor do they know how to formulate motions or follow the process of how motions are acted on. To that end, all board meetings should have previously established agendas, and prior notice should be given to all board members should they want to contribute items for the meeting. Items for discussion are best submitted in the form of motions because they then have the potential to become actionable items. Once presented in the form of a motion, an item can be discussed and voted on or tabled for discussion at another meeting. Any action needs to be brought before the board in the form of a motion that can be discussed.

Talisa faces her own developmental challenges as a leader of the association. She began her engagement with the association following a servant leadership model (Greenleaf, 1970), choosing to serve as she did in the role of treasurer and later making a decision to lead as president. Other board members may still see her as one who serves the association and may not have begun to appreciate her leadership role. Her underrepresented status could play into how others project bias on her ability to lead. Talisa may need to shift her leadership style to accommodate current board conditions. The conditions call for Talisa to lead from a position of situational leadership, in which she will influence others through both directive and supportive behaviors (Northouse, 2019). Alternatively, Talisa may wish to engage in adaptive leadership, focusing on helping others on the board do the work they need to do and adapt as they face challenges.

It may be helpful for Talisa and the board to look at a leadership assessment such as the Leadership Practices Inventory (Kouzes & Posner, 2012). This inventory helps identify leadership strengths and areas that might need attention. The Leadership Practices Inventory identifies the degree to which a leader models the way, inspires a shared vision, challenges the process, enables others to act, and encourages the heart, all positive qualities of leaders. Talisa may find that her primary leadership strength is modeling the way (i.e., setting an example for others by aligning actions with organizational values). To generate more investment in working on structural and process issues with ACCC, she may have to inspire a shared vision among fellow board members or challenge the current process to move the board in a professional direction.

Given the structural and process problems the board faces it would be best for Talisa to be more directive in her leadership style. Her first engagement should be to address the three board members who made promises on behalf of ACCC without board authorization. As suggested earlier, Talisa should generate an agenda with input from other board members and encourage the social justice initiative issue to be placed on the agenda in the form of a motion for discussion. As president, Talisa needs to inspire a shared vision structurally, with fully defined bylaws and a functional set of strategic initiatives. After considering strategic priorities and associated resources, the board will have to make judicious decisions about whether engaging in an external social justice initiative fits the mission and is realistic at this time.

Talisa should address process issues, including procedures for meetings, with board training regarding how meetings are run. She should familiarize the board with methods for proposing motions and be willing to help others adjust to the new working process. She may also encourage engagement from the membership, perhaps by populating committees on strategic initiatives with members who express interest. It will be important for members to have a sense of value from being part of ACCC so they feel they are getting the benefits of membership.

Conclusion

The problems Talisa and ACCC face are fairly common among grassroots and volunteer-led professional organizations. Although newly formed organizations can sustain themselves briefly by working without standard procedures and bylaws, they risk liability issues if they do not become incorporated. With status as an incorporated association come responsible procedures that, once adopted, lead to a better and more equitable organization.

Reflection Questions

1. What are the primary problems Talisa faces?
2. What management and leadership skills does Talisa need to develop?

Critical Incident Response

Natoya Hill Haskins

As noted, Talisa's priorities should be to ensure that fundamental organizational aspects are developed and implemented during her term (Katsioloudes, 2006). Her focus on refining the mission and vision as well as developing the bylaws is critical to the longevity and efficiency of the organization. Considerations such as leadership support, expansion, and style are also at play.

African American women and other individuals in leadership thrive when they receive mentorship (L. C. Jackson & Bouchard, 2019). Being mentored can help individuals attain authority and influence while increasing their credibility by enhancing their networks. Consequently, Talisa should seek out a colleague who has served as president of a national organization and from whom she can receive support. Mentoring will be almost necessary in this particular situation, as most of Talisa's role will be developing an organization from almost the ground up, and skillsets of the other board members are unknown.

Drafting a strategic plan requires time and an understanding of members' needs. Talisa may want to expand her leadership team to successfully create and implement a strategic plan using varied strategies. This may begin with a poll of the membership. Then Talisa may plan a strategic planning meeting or retreat in which she invites representatives and other organizational leaders to share in the development of the plan, allowing for expanded membership buy-in (Olivarius et al., 2010). Next Talisa may develop or appoint a strategic planning committee that would include various members of the executive board and other members of the organization. This committee would meet throughout the year with opportunities for board feedback at distinct points in the process. Finally, Talisa may consider forming a regional leadership advisory team; these would be members who have held positions in similar organizations at the state or regional level. Their role would be to provide insight to the president and help ensure that the mission, vision, bylaws, and strategic plan address the needs of members in their region and are consistent with best practices, are culturally responsive, and are ethical (Olivarius et al., 2010).

Although there are a number of leadership styles one can use as president of an organization (e.g., servant leadership, transformational leadership, adaptive leadership), it is important to note that African American women have unique life experiences that influence their leadership traits, behaviors, and styles (Parker & ogilvie, 1996). African American women engage in leadership that connects to their counterstories and lived oppression (Sims & Carter, 2019). As a result, Talisa's leadership style may encompass creativity, risk taking, boundary spanning, divergent thinking, and behavioral complexity (see Parker & ogilvie, 1996). In terms of creativity, Talisa's focus on addressing new ways of being would be clearly connected to her notions of change and improvement. Talisa would use boundary spanning to navigate her social identities with the knowledge that she exists within a bicultural system. Behavioral complexity would require that Talisa lean into the complex and sometimes competing tasks and relationships within the organization (Denison et al., 1995) as she becomes a visionary, advocate, creator, inspector, delegator, and mentor (Quinn, 1988).

Following these recommendations would allow Talisa to focus on the organizational and structural needs of the organization while working with members to address some of their appeals (e.g., injustices experienced by prisoners housed in criminal justice facilities). Consequently, Talisa may identify small groups or task forces to develop recommendations to address social justice issues or other timely issues. In a time when injustices prevail, it would be challenging to disregard critical justice and mental health issues that may affect the membership.

• • •

Chapter 35

It's All About Mentorship: Managing Professional Journals

Cirecie A. West-Olatunji and S. Anandavalli

2014 *ACA Code of Ethics* Standards Addressed

- Not applicable

• • •

When I (Cirecie A. West-Olatunji) assumed the position of editor-in-chief of the *Journal of Multicultural Counseling and Development* (*JMCD*), I noticed four critical issues my predecessor had begun to address and wanted to continue addressing. First, many members of the editorial review board consistently declined invitations to review manuscripts. Declining invitations creates significant delays in the review process. This is perplexing because editorial board members are aware of the significance of publications in scholars' lives, especially for those moving toward tenure and promotion. I reached out to editorial review board members who were not honoring their commitment to the journal. It became clear that many of them had competing obligations and were overwhelmed with work, home, and personal demands. Their circumstances personified the research on faculty of color and their disproportionate service load coupled with insufficient support within their institutions (Butz et al., 2019).

The second critical concern was the limited involvement of Emerging Reviewers (ERs) who were advanced doctoral students in counseling programs nationally. The ER position was a unique position within journal operations and had been the vision of the previous editor-in-chief. I called a meeting with the ERs to discuss their expectations and invite them to talk about the mentoring experience. The ERs indicated they wanted to be more actively involved with the associate editors but did not know how to reach out to them.

The third critical issue concerned the use of the Consulting Elders. This position was also unique to *JMCD* and reflected the mission and cultural values of the Association for Multicultural Counseling and Development (AMCD), a division of the American Counseling Association (ACA). Rather than sending senior scholars out to pasture as they advanced in their years as multicultural scholars, the *JMCD* editorial team preferred to defer to their wisdom and experience. The Consulting Elders desired to receive more communications about the journal's activities and serve as informal mentors to the editors. In essence, they did not have a clear understanding of their role but were hoping to feel more connected to the community.

The fourth critical issue was the associate editors' desire for more connection to the history of *JMCD* in advancing the core values and mission that had been established at inception. After several discussions, the associate editors articulated the need to be more intentional in their work, have a more strategic focus, and be more responsive to current issues in society.

Based on information gathered from interactions with Consulting Elders, ERs, associate editors, editorial assistants, and editorial review board members, I surmised that a more relational culture was needed within the journal operations. I then developed an action plan based on an understanding of the ethical issues relating to mentoring and organizational administration as well as prior research in multicultural counseling and mentoring.

Case Analysis and Discussion

A few key studies highlight dangers when ethics guidelines are violated in mentoring relationships (W. Johnson & Nelson, 1999). Despite addressing roles in supervision, teaching, and counseling, the current *ACA Code of Ethics* (ACA, 2014) does not explicitly address ethical concerns around mentorship. Mentorship is vital for the professional development of most, if not all, counselor educators during their professional careers (Borders et al., 2011). This presents a unique opportunity for counselor educators to reflect on how principles of ethics inform the complex mentoring process.

In addition to concerns around potential exploitation of mentees through sexual and emotional manipulation, other plausible ethical concerns must be addressed in mentoring relationships. The actual competence of mentors can often go unevaluated. This is especially the case for new faculty members who may undertake mentorship without fully understanding its pitfalls. The *ACA Code of Ethics* (ACA, 2014) addresses this concern by reminding educators and supervisors to work within the boundaries of their competence.

With rapid advances in higher education and the constant influx of new faculty and scholars, mentorship assumes a valuable role in academia. Although several papers focus on mentorship experiences (Baltrinic et al., 2018; Butz et al., 2019; Shannonhouse & West-Olatunji, 2013; West-Olatunji et al., 2018), there is little consensus on a universal definition of mentoring. The lack of a clear definition may pose several challenges, specifically raising doubts regarding the validity of studies pertaining to mentoring (Benishek et al., 2004). Given the lack of a singular definition of mentorship, there is only limited clarity on how to best support mentees.

Sorcinelli (2000) identified 10 principles of good practice in mentoring early career faculty that focus on using clear communications, high expectations, and concrete support to facilitate scholarly success. As research on mentoring relationships continues to expand, there are several areas of focus, including (a) defining mentoring in the context of counselor education, (b) exploring the direct effect of mentoring on the career success of early career faculty, and (c) establishing ethics guidelines to govern mentorship in counselor education.

The dearth of mentorship of minoritized faculty is of grave concern. For instance, in a survey of 115 female faculty, Hill et al. (2005) found that more than 45% reported they had no mentoring programs available to them. The limited opportunity for individuals from minoritized groups—such as women; people of color; lesbian, gay, bisexual, transgender, and queer (LGBTQ+) individuals; and people with disabilities—to receive meaningful mentorship is grounded in several factors. In one study, mentors were reluctant to address race and ethnicity in their mentoring relationships because they minimized the need for cultural conversations in academia or felt awkward broaching such conversations with their minoritized mentees (Butz et al., 2019).

Despite strong reasons to have courageous conversations about racism and cultural issues in mentoring relationships, few mentors are engaging in this practice (Butz et al., 2019). Effective mentoring is a key factor in the self-beliefs, persistence, and academic/professional success of faculty and student mentees from minoritized groups (Byars-Winston et al., 2018; Griffin et al., 2010). In addition, trust is an issue in cross-cultural mentorship relationships, specifically in counselor education (E. M. Brown & Grothaus, 2019).

Actions Taken and Not Taken

After considering ethical concerns and prior research in the area of mentoring, the associate editors and I (Cirecie A. West-Olatunji) collectively took action to address the four critical issues. It is imperative that mentors serve as role models of engaging in ethical practices, maintaining an effective work-life balance, and setting clear boundaries to avoid carrying an inordinate service load. To address the first critical issue, I reached out to the editorial board members who had felt challenged to complete several service commitments. Conversations with members of the editorial team members necessitated a relational approach, wherein I often adopted the role of a mentor, encouraging them to reflect on their current workload and self-efficacy. I also expanded the number of associate editors from three to four to decrease the average number of submissions each associate editor would review, thus providing reviewers with the opportunity to think more deeply and intentionally about the papers they were reviewing and spend more time with their assigned ERs.

Given that both mentors and mentees experience role ambiguity, the team of editors worked to expand and clarify the ER position description. The editors collectively drafted a position description and then approached current ERs to ask whether they were interested in continuing, given the new definition. Some stayed and others did not. Then an announcement was posted on social media platforms to solicit applications for new ERs with the expanded qualifications, and both advanced doctoral students and early career counselor educators had the opportunity to apply.

Mentoring theories in counseling are predominantly based on Western or Eurocentric worldviews (Benishek et al., 2004). With the increased number of students and faculty of color in the counseling profession, a multicultural lens is vital for effective mentorship. One core value of Western culture is individualism. At *JMCD*, the editorial team took pride in engaging in collectivist leadership and mentorship. In fact, collectivist wisdom was one of the underlying philosophies guiding the formation of the Consulting Elders Council and used to address the second and third critical issues. For instance, fostering stronger ties among ERs while clarifying their roles at *JMCD* allowed this group of nascent leaders to build meaningful connections among themselves. Nurturing relationships among ERs and between ERs and their assigned mentors (associate editors) resulted in the formation of a supportive community for these emerging professionals. ERs were paired with an editor to assist in reviewing submissions as well as developing the Editors' Commentary for an issue. As a group, the ERs also revised the *JMCD* website, drafted protocols for the new book review program, and assumed responsibility for coordinating the annual meeting held during the ACA conference. The ERs went on to collaborate on several scholarly initiatives, producing conference presentations and manuscripts. They have also invited other early career scholars to apply for ER positions at *JMCD*, which indicates the catalytic validity of a collectivist approach to mentorship.

Recognizing the wealth of information and wisdom that elders have, the editors enhanced the role of the Consulting Elders Council, involving them as ad hoc reviewers and asking them to serve as consultants in the review of manuscripts for the annual Outstanding Paper Award. In addition, the editors restructured the annual board meeting to provide face-to-face interaction and honor editorial board members who were rotating off the board with a reception.

The editors also expanded the number of editorial assistants from one to three to create more mentoring opportunities for graduate counseling students. The editorial assistants' responsibilities were divided into three roles: corresponding within and beyond the editorial staff, coordinating ER efforts, and preparing papers for publication. By dividing the work, I could spend more time with each student and provide higher quality mentoring experiences. The editors also created the Editors' Commentary, which provides a brief introduction to each issue, applying papers to current events and linking them to broader theoretical discussions within the discipline. Most important, the editors initiated strategic planning that began with surveying the readership, AMCD membership, and editorial team. A final analysis of the findings will inform future changes within the journal.

To address the fourth critical issue, the editors decided to schedule quarterly meetings. These meetings allowed editorial review board members the opportunity to see the faces of the editors and their peers while helping them to improve the quality of their reviews and better understand the review process. The editors typically schedule one face-to-face meeting at the ACA conference, another face-to-face meeting during an Association for Counselor Education and Supervision or Southern Association for Counselor Education and Supervision conference, and two virtual meetings. For instance, the quarterly editorial review board meeting at the 2018 Southern Association for Counselor Education and Supervision annual conference was held shortly after a hurricane had come through, causing major flooding and wind damage to property. This disaster allowed the *JMCD* editorial community to discuss how sociopolitical issues and natural disasters offer social justice advocates a unique opportunity to meet the needs of local communities.

The actions not taken highlight the challenges the editors faced. The editors frequently shared their experiences with heavy service loads as they faced work issues, health concerns, and family trials. As an African American female counselor educator, I also experienced many of the issues discussed in the literature, such as disproportionate service obligations and implicit bias from peers. As a leader in the profession, I often provided consultation, informal mentoring, assessment, emotional support, and recommendation letters for a host of students (undergraduate as well as graduate), early and midcareer faculty (within and outside of counseling), and colleagues. Future actions should focus on providing more structural relief measures for the editor-in-chief and associate editors.

Conclusion

These responsive actions have increased engagement among all members of our editorial community. In addition, there is now increased visibility of editorial assistants, review board members, ERs, Consulting Elders, and editors among AMCD members as well as the broader journal readership. The standing of the journal has also improved, and it has a substantially higher impact factor; *JMCD* is now the highest ranked journal within counselor education. Finally, the changes implemented have increased mentorship at multiple levels, both horizontally as well as vertically. Mentoring matters, and it's all about mentorship.

Reflection Questions

1. How did the community-based approach to mentorship reflect the values of AMCD?
2. How did the approach to mentorship match the developmental needs of editorial board members?

Critical Incident Response

Kathy Ybañez-Llorente

Not having served on an editorial board leadership team, I appreciate the authors' insight into structural difficulties experienced by journal leadership and the role mentorship played in resolving their four critical concerns. Reading about these critical concerns brought mentoring to the forefront, and I wondered, *Were these editorial board members mentored to decline invitations to review manuscripts to better manage their work-life balance?* Likely the answer is no, in particular if the mentors realized these denials could also contribute to a backlog or delay in publication for early career faculty members. The authors pointed out an important reality contributing to these denials: faculty members protecting their time, especially faculty members of color who are often stretched thin with service responsibilities and lack of support.

From an outsider's perspective, no mentoring appears to have taken place for ERs, as evidenced by the lack of contact with associate editors. Perhaps they did not know how to reach out, or they thought it was not appropriate to take the initiative to contact the associate editors for help. Similarly, the Consulting Elders appeared to play an honorary role with no clear expectation of assisting the division membership. How was the role defined that it allowed elders to remain disconnected from the larger division membership? Addressing each of these areas through a relational approach to mentorship clearly helped the editors establish expectations through shared power, mutuality, authenticity, and relational images and competencies. These exact variables were found by Cannon et al. (2019) to be critical in research mentorship of women doctoral counseling students and to represent "an important step toward the development of culturally inclusive research mentoring practices" (p. 10).

The lack of diverse faculty in academia continues, despite emphases on recruitment and retention in the *ACA Code of Ethics* (ACA, 2014) and 2016 Council for Accreditation of Counseling and Related Educational Programs (CACREP) Standards (CACREP, 2016). Lack of representation among senior faculty means fewer mentors are available to model paths to success in academia. Quality mentorship experiences and relationships are important at the beginning of academic training and throughout one's professional career. Cartwright et al. (2018) documented the interview experiences of faculty members from underrepresented groups and highlighted how minoritized faculty may be disadvantaged based on express assumptions of hiring committees and programs. The myriad diversity concerns expressed by participants should be a call to all faculty to examine their own environments for, treatment of, and perceptions of minoritized faculty well before inviting prospective faculty to interview with their program. Cross-cultural peer mentoring experiences are likely to be the norm for faculty from underrepresented populations, so issues of mentor competency should be addressed at the beginning of relationships. This could include broaching topics of race and ethnicity, discussing past mentor relationships, and examining ways to build safe and trusting relationships.

The decision to intentionally address critical needs through structured approaches to mentorship is similar to approaches to building social capital through peer mentor programs for women in academia (Esnard et al., 2015). Independent women's groups are created for the express reasons of helping one another thrive and persist in their home institutions while increasing opportunities for collaboration in research (Agosto et al., 2016). Informal peer mentorship groups may provide members with supportive spaces, new mentorship experiences, and opportunities for the development and maintenance of social capital in their respective fields (Agosto et al., 2016; Esnard et al., 2015). Similarly, counselor education programs and professional organizations can benefit from establishing faculty interest groups for underrepresented faculty (Follins et al., 2015) as a way to support faculty members as they are recruited, retained, and promoted within academia.

• • •

Section 2
Leadership and Advocacy in the Local Community

Chapter 36

What Should We Fund? Addressing Budget Issues on a Community Board

Nicole R. Hill

2014 *ACA Code of Ethics* Standards Addressed

- F.10.f. Extending Educator-Student Boundaries

• • •

When Professor Marija Foster graduated with her doctoral degree in counselor education and accepted her tenure-track position at Glennmore College, she was excited to embark on a new adventure and bring her deep commitment to client advocacy to the work of preparing counselors. She arrived on campus and immediately began meeting counselors in the community with the hopes of beginning a part-time private practice. But as Marija came to understand more thoroughly the demands of her teaching and supervision, she decided to postpone starting her practice.

In initial conversations with community members, Marija was introduced to a small group of counselors who were focused on advocating for adolescents and providing growth opportunities that fostered their resilience. Seeing this as a way to engage in client advocacy and connect with the community, Marija began volunteering at Counselors for Impact, a 501(c)(3) nonprofit coalition of licensed professional counselors who were passionate about their mission to promote the well-being, social-emotional learning, and resilience of all adolescents in the tristate area. Her volunteer work resonated with her work in the classroom in terms of professional values and also because two of her master's students were actively involved in the organization. After her first year as a counselor educator, Marija became a board member of Counselors for Impact. Two years later, she was serving as chairperson of the board. One of the board members, Scott, was a master's student in the clinical mental health counseling program at Glennmore

College, and the other five members were licensed professionals who provided counseling in schools and agencies.

Glennmore College was situated in a community in which 35% of residents met federal guidelines for poverty. The leading employer in Glennmore, Houghton Steel, had recently transitioned its factory to an off-shore location, which had displaced 2,300 workers. Mounting financial pressures in families paralleled financial challenges impacting nonprofit community organizations. In recent years, revenue for Counselors for Impact had decreased steadily by 5–10% every fiscal year. As funding became more limited, the board struggled to decide how to allocate funds to support the four signature programs they provided to the community: College Readiness Initiative, Food for Families, Project STEAM, and Youth Mentoring Collaborative.

Planning for the upcoming fiscal year's budget was complicated, as Marija knew budgetary realities would curtail their ability to fund their signature programs at the same level. In the past two board meetings, board members had become increasingly entrenched in their viewpoints about how to move forward. Faced with 15% fewer funds, Marija emphasized that there would need to be changes in how monies were allocated for the coming year. A tentative budget presented at the previous meeting had recommended all program areas be reduced by 17%.

Scott and another board member became increasingly aggressive about the need to prioritize the two programs that created pathways to future work for teens: Project STEAM and College Readiness Initiative. They argued that the only way for Glennmore to recover economically was for teens to be empowered and skilled in pursuing technical and professional careers. They argued for other programs to be reduced to increase Project STEAM and College Readiness Initiative funding by 5%. The three other board members reacted strongly and insisted that all funds be invested in Food for Families to prioritize the fundamental need for food security. Marija had adjourned the last meeting abruptly as one member had accused Scott of being "elitist" and focused on "the privilege of a few instead of the need of many."

Following the meeting, Marija spoke with each board member privately and tried to use her skills of persuasion to create solutions and find places of commonality. She emphasized the mission of Counselors for Impact and encouraged each board member to reflect on the broad spectrum of needs in Glennmore and surrounding communities. Each phone call started off promising, but they all seemed to dissolve into unproductive and frustrating spaces within about 15 minutes. Vivienne, a board member who was a high school counselor, accused another board member, Salvatore, of wanting to focus on Food for Families because his uncle owned a restaurant that benefitted from the allocation of funds. Even when Marija highlighted the fact that Vivienne had also wanted to invest available funds into Food for Families, Vivienne continued to focus on Salvatore's conflict of interest rather than a shared commitment to alleviating food insecurity. Marija assumed her connection as Scott's professor would assuage his displeasure and encourage him to be more responsive to the viewpoints of other board members. Their phone conversation ended with Scott asserting, "They haven't seen the depth of my resolve yet. They are living under a delusion that a short-term mentality will translate into a long-term solution. Professor Foster, you have to see that the only way to make meaningful change is through making certain every teenager in this area is prepared for their future. If the other board members can't see that, they are short sighted and delusional."

As time the next board meeting and the deadline for passing a budget approached, Marija had no idea how to resolve the highly contentious disagreement among board members. Over and over again, she reminded herself that her role as chair of the Counselors for Impact board was volunteer service in addition to her work as a counselor educator. Her role was supposed to help her build professional networks and advocate for change in the community. All arguments and the desire to allocate funds to multiple programs were valid, but the reality of the budget necessitated a novel approach. Marija's biggest worry about finalizing the upcoming budget was the interpersonal attacks happening among board members. She needed to figure out a path forward for Counselors for Impact.

As Marija prepared the agenda for the board meeting, she interpreted the blinking cursor on the empty page as a symbol of her paralysis. She was paralyzed by unanswered questions: How should we move forward? What is most important? Is the board dysfunctional? What is my role as leader in managing the dynamics of the board? What are the financial responsibilities of the board members? How does my student's behavior on the board impact my evaluation of him in the program? What will all this mean for the community? What should I have done to orient the board when I assumed the role of chair? How can we discuss and move to a decision when the board members are upset? How much more energy can this require of me right now as I am trying to grade midterm prepracticum tapes and biopsychosocial assessments? Am I taking care of myself? Which top priority will be the funded priority?

Case Analysis and Discussion

Professional service is critical within the professoriate, and many counselor educators assume responsibility for association leadership early in their professional careers (Gibson, Dollarhide, & McCallum, 2010). Leadership in professional organizations is an opportunity for counselor educators to enact professional values while also meeting expectations for promotion and tenure (Meany-Walen et al., 2013). Having the training and skills to navigate the demands of professional leadership while sustaining expectations of the academy is a critical area of development across counselor education and for individual faculty members.

Leadership competence is a domain that requires attention in scholarship, professional standards of practice, and training programs. Yet leadership development has been largely ignored in research, and attention to leadership within professional accreditation standards, ethical mandates, and standards of practice continues to be undeveloped. In a content analysis of counseling leadership research, McKibben et al. (2017) found that across 40 years of professional counseling discourse, only 33 manuscripts focused on leadership in counseling. With such a lack of professional discourse, counselor educators like Marija have inconsistent, sometimes absent, mentoring and training in how to navigate challenging leadership positions (Gibson, Dollarhide, & McCallum, 2010). Counselor educators who provide leadership within professional associations, community-based groups, and universities must develop an identity and skillset as a counselor educator-leader (Hill & Friedman, 2018).

In her service as board chairperson for Counselors for Impact, Marija must harness leadership awareness, knowledge, and skills that are informed by accreditation standards, ethical regulations, and professional standards. Leadership decision-making needs to be grounded in these guidelines while also attending to matters of equity, inclusion, fiduciary responsibility, dual relationships, and conflicts of interest.

In this case, the most prominent responsibility Marija holds is that of fiduciary. The Internal Revenue Service (2018) specifies in *Compliance Guide for 501(c)(3) Public Charities* that governing bodies should be "informed and active in overseeing a charity's operations and finances" (p. 20). Leaders of all nonprofit organizations are beholden to the duties of care and loyalty, which require leaders to exercise the utmost integrity and engage in informed, deliberate, and careful decisions that advance the mission of the organization (R. Harris, 2010). Harris described fiduciary responsibilities as emerging from the duties of care and loyalty and as representing a "relationship of confidence or trust … [through which] the board has responsibility to protect the organization and its resources" (p. 14).

In her role as board chair, Marija has an ethical and professional responsibility to uphold her fiduciary responsibilities and to ensure the Counselors for Impact board does as well. At this point in the board's process, it is critical that Marija ground all board members in their fiduciary duties and focus them on the core mission of Counselors for Impact. If all board members are appropriately oriented to the fiscal responsibilities of serving on a 501(c)(3) governing body, then Marija should emphasize how their responsibility transcends individual agendas.

If Marija and her fellow board members did not receive a robust orientation regarding their fiscal duties, Marija should begin the next meeting with an explication of the fiscal duties of board members and expectations of how they are executed with the budget discussion. Critical reflexive questions for the board members that need to guide the process include the following: How do the duties of care and loyalty (R. Harris, 2010) impact our deliberations about the next fiscal year's budget? How comprehensive is our understanding of the budget and its declining balance across the past 5 years? How informed are we about the signature programs of Counselors for Impact and the related financial needs associated with each one? What, if any, potential conflicts of interest exist for us as board members regarding our budget decisions? How have potential conflicts of interest been disclosed and addressed? What is the most appropriate course of action to ensure we are protecting the resources of Counselors for Impact during a time of economic challenge?

Although counselor educator-leaders who are trained in doctoral programs accredited by the Council for Accreditation of Counseling and Related Educational Programs (CACREP; 2016) receive dedicated development in leadership, there continue to be gaps in how well prepared counselor educator-leaders are to navigate the fiduciary components of association and board service (Gibson, Dollarhide, & McCallum, 2010; Hill & Friedman, 2019; Meany-Walen et al., 2013). Many professional counseling associations are 501(c)(3) organizations; therefore, board leaders need to be highly proficient in understanding the fiduciary responsibilities of their leadership roles. Relevant to this specific case, the 2016 CACREP Standards (CACREP, 2016) detail curricular requirements for knowledge of theories and skills of leadership, leadership in professional organizations, management and administration in organizations, and social justice and multicultural leadership competence.

Given that Marija graduated from a CACREP-accredited program, she is expected to have foundational awareness, knowledge, and skill across these leadership domains. Section 6, Standard B.5.e., of the CACREP Standards focuses on management and administrative responsibilities for organizations, yet many counselors are not versed in the fiduciary responsibilities of serving in association or community-based positions. Hence, it is incumbent on Marija to ensure all board members are prepared to handle their responsibilities in an ethical and deliberate manner.

If Marija did not receive explicit training on fiduciary matters in her doctoral program or if a formal orientation to her board leadership (including fiscal duties) was insufficient, resources within the counseling profession can provide a framework for her ongoing leadership. The *ACA Code of Ethics* (American Counseling Association [ACA], 2014) does not provide any specific standards regarding fiscal responsibilities of counselor educators, yet Marija can ground herself in the overall values that inform counseling ethics: autonomy, nonmaleficence, beneficence, justice, fidelity, and veracity (p. 3). Nonmaleficence, beneficence, justice, and fidelity seem the most relevant to this case. The board members of Counselors for Impact need to make budgetary decisions that are grounded in their mission but also do not cause any harm for the youth that they serve in Glennmore. Board members must wrestle with matters of how well they are honoring their commitments (fidelity) and how equitable are they being in how they allocate funds to community-based initiatives (justice).

Furthermore, the Introduction to Section C of the *ACA Code of Ethics* (ACA, 2014) asserts, "Counselors aspire to open, honest, and accurate communication in dealing with the public and other professionals. Counselors facilitate access to counseling services, and they practice in a nondiscriminatory manner within the boundaries of professional and personal competence" (p. 8). Marija and her fellow counselors who serve on the board for Counselors for Impact need to consider their budget deliberations from the ethical expectations of nondiscriminatory decisions and accurate communication. Is Salvatore appropriately disclosing the potential conflict of interest arising from his family's engagement in the food industry? How accurate are board members being in their communication as tension has increased? Are personal conflicts impacting the name calling of board members by other board members? These are critical questions that need to be tackled for the board to move forward on ratifying a budget.

During this challenging time, Marija can use Chi Sigma Iota's (CSI) *Principles and Practices of Leadership Excellence* (PPLEs; CSI Academy of Leaders, 1999) as a framework for leadership ethics and decision-making. Three principles are particularly relevant to this case. First, in line with Principle 1 (Philosophy of Leadership), counselor educators serve in leadership positions to advance the profession and serve others. While balancing demands to meet expectations of promotion and tenure, Marija needs to ground herself in the servant leadership paradigm (Greenleaf, 1977) and emphasize that her motivation to serve as board chair is to serve the youth in the community of Glennmore. Second, Principle 2 (Commitment to Mission) emphasizes the criticality of leaders working individually and collectively to enact the mission of the organization. The mission of Counselors for Impact is to promote the well-being, social-emotional learning, and resilience of all adolescents in the tristate area. All board decisions need to advance this mission. Third, Principle 6 (Preservation of Resources) directs counselor educator-leaders to actively protect the human and financial resources of organizations in which they serve. The PPLEs focus Marija's role on serving youth in her community, advancing the mission of Counselors for Impact, and relentlessly safeguarding the organization's assets.

Marija seems to be leading Counselors for Impact from a humanistic stance with her focus on consensus building and using relational skills to solve the fiscal problem. The PPLEs (CSI Academy of Leaders, 1999) and the *ACA Code of Ethics* (ACA, 2014) provide principles to guide the reflections and actions of Marija and the other board members. Clearly demarcating the fiscal and ethical responsibilities of all board members is necessary to shepherd the board through this challenging time. Another important leadership skill is attending to questions of equity and inclusivity. The details in the case do not highlight Marija's multicultural competence, yet this is a critical domain that needs attention. As the board members deliberate on how to proceed, they must wrestle with complex questions about the impact of their decisions. Marija can facilitate a processing exercise during which board members discuss the following questions: How do our decisions about where to invest our resources disproportionately impact groups of adolescents in our area? What data exist on the sociodemographic characteristics of tristate area youth and on who accesses the programs funded by Counselors for Impact? What are the implications for access and equity when funding levels are changed for the upcoming year? Which groups of adolescents benefit from and which are disadvantaged by the budgetary allocation? Tackling these questions and infusing the discussion with data may facilitate a more complex understanding of the issues at play.

Marija's next steps as a counselor educator-leader and board chairperson need to be informed by the values of nonmaleficence, beneficence, fidelity, and justice (ACA, 2014) and by the PPLEs (CSI Academy of Leaders, 1999). One unique aspect of this case that also needs to be addressed is the relationship between Marija and Scott, the clinical mental health student at Glennmore College. The *ACA Code of Ethics* (ACA, 2014) addresses boundaries between educators and students. Having collaborative leadership experiences in professional associations is one of the "potentially beneficial interactions or relationships" that may warrant extending educator-student boundaries (ACA, 2014, Standard F.10.f.). Specifically, Marija is expected to

> discuss with students the rationale for such interactions, the potential benefits and drawbacks, and the anticipated consequences for the student. Educators clarify the specific nature and limitations of the additional role(s) they will have with the student prior to engaging in a nonprofessional relationship. Nonprofessional relationships with students should be time limited and/or context specific and initiated with student consent. (Standard F.10.f.)

It is unclear whether Marija and Scott have engaged in explicit discussions about their relationship as board members for Counselors for Impact. As Marija encounters challenges with Scott, her ability to effectively address them across multiple roles—as board chairperson and faculty member—is strongly aligned with how explicitly she addressed these relationships at the outset of their collaborations. Proactive and explicit broaching of these multiple relationships and potential areas of disadvantage is the responsibility of the counselor educator-leader.

Conclusion

New counselor educators and doctoral students embrace service in professional associations and community-based organizations as part of their professional commitment. This case exposes potential challenges that may not be explicitly addressed in professional training and leadership orientation programs. Counselor educators and doctoral students need to understand their fiduciary responsibilities when they accept a leadership position, and they must work diligently to be well informed of the ethical standards and leadership principles that influence their decisions about financial matters. Matters such as potential conflicts of interest, extended counselor educator-student roles, and fiscal duties must be explicitly addressed early on in the process before challenges such as the one experienced by Marija emerge.

Reflection Questions

1. What are some strategies Professor Foster could have implemented to ensure she was adequately prepared to assume her leadership role with Counselors for Impact?
2. How can students be better prepared to understand their fiduciary responsibilities as officers of professional associations or members of nonprofit organizations?

Critical Incident Response

Renée C. Howells and
Kristopher M. Goodrich

This case highlights several key issues about how organizations make decisions and about fiduciary responsibilities of board members. The author described thoughtful use of the *ACA Code of Ethics* (ACA, 2014), the PPLEs (CSI Academy of Leaders, 1999), and other scholarship on leadership to ground Professor Foster's decision-making. However, additional unanswered questions must be considered before Marija makes a final determination about the best course of action. For example, it is important to know the amount of training board members received prior to beginning their time on the board, what information was shared about conflicts of interest, and whether any conflict of interest disclosures or contracts were signed by board members at the start of their service. This information would help ground the conversation surrounding potential conflicts presented in the case. The background information could serve as a resource to use in a meeting or as a point of action board members must take as they continue their service within their community.

Vivienne's concerns about Salvatore's connection to Food for Families highlight a possible fiduciary conflict of interest. If Salvatore's uncle benefits directly from Salvatore's voting position on the board, this should be brought to the attention of the board in the next meeting by Salvatore and Professor Foster. This would allow Salvatore an opportunity to address the concerns raised, and board members should also have a brief period in which to respond. If the majority of the board agrees that a true fiduciary conflict exists, Salvatore should abstain from voting on priorities that benefit his family. If conflicts persist during his time on the board, the board leadership may need to reassess his service.

Professor Foster's employment as a tenure-track faculty member at Glennmore College is another possible conflict of interest that must be addressed. Although it is not alluded to in the case, it is possible that Professor Foster could experience institutional pressure from university administrators, especially if the university could benefit from monies being funneled toward certain signature community programs, such as College Readiness Initiative and Project STEAM. It is unclear whether Professor Foster addressed this potential concern in past meetings, but it should be addressed before the final budgetary vote. Should the board identify a conflict of interest, Professor Foster should also abstain from voting and reconsider her own placement on the board if this conflict becomes a persistent issue.

To ensure best practices are being upheld, board members should engage in self-reflection about their own possible conflicts of interest, fiduciary or otherwise, throughout their time on the board. Relationships change over time, and leaders must continually assess them when in service leadership positions. Multiple relationships were presented in this case, including the professor-student relationship between Professor Foster and Scott. Joining a board with student members is not necessarily an inappropriate decision, as such an opportunity may provide mutually beneficial relationships for all parties. Such affiliations may support students' academic and professional learning, as is often seen in CSI. However, in her role as a board member, Professor Foster may also see students act in ways that call their professional dispositions and behavior into question. Because she is a gatekeeper of the field, this can complicate her roles as board chair and faculty member.

Prior to beginning her role on the board, Professor Foster should have had an intentional conversation with any student board members and negotiated the roles she would need to play in both contexts. Professor Foster should have reminded Scott of this during their phone conversation. Although students' First Amendment rights to free speech should be protected, Professor Foster may now face a dilemma if Scott continues to behave unprofessionally while serving on the Counselors for Impact board. Professor Foster may need to consult an ethical decision-making model and review relevant policy information from her program or university for guidance on possible courses of action within the university setting.

To address these concerns, Professor Foster may consider scheduling a roles and responsibilities training for Counselors for Impact board members. This training could outline behavioral expectations for how board members should interact with one another during meetings. Hot-button issues like First Amendment rights and expectations of professional decorum could be explored. Ethical models for identifying possible conflicts of interest and recognizing multiple relationships could also be explicitly communicated and explored. Finally, it may be beneficial for the board to develop a strategic plan to provide structure for board actions, allocation of resources, and guidance for the sustained growth of the organization. If board members have a voice in further developing guideposts for Counselors for Impact, some decision points might be viewed with less difficulty and contention.

Overall, the author provided a clear synthesis of relevant literature and an articulated vision. Attention to organizational leadership and fiduciary responsibilities is notable. Additional elements to consider include an exploration of board members' possible conflicts of interest, the potential for formal board training on topics relevant to their decisions, and the development of strategic planning protocols for the organization. These additions may aid Professor Foster as she navigates her current dilemma.

• • •

Chapter 37

My Hands Are Tied: Navigating University Prohibitions on Advocacy

Kathy Ybañez-Llorente

2014 *ACA Code of Ethics* Standards Addressed

- A.7.a. Advocacy
- D.1.g. Employer Policies

• • •

Jessica was a new assistant professor completing her first year in a tenure-track position at a large state university. She was enjoying teaching a professional orientation course, and she believed she was making a significant impact by starting counselors-in-training off on the right foot in establishing their professional identity. Jessica regularly participated in professional development workshops for new professors focusing on teaching, learning styles, student resources, and faculty support for research. Much of the information covered in these sessions was helpful in guiding the work of a new tenure-track professor, but there was little emphasis on formal university policies and procedures. Jessica did not remember seeing specific policies that just might curtail the work she was doing in her free time or affect assignments she was proposing for students in her orientation course. These university policies came to Jessica's attention when the dean of her college asked her to meet about the use of university resources for a legislative professional advocacy activity Jessica had recently planned.

Prior to pursuing doctoral studies, Jessica had worked for 7 years with diverse clinical populations in a community mental health agency. She had started as a case manager and worked her way to becoming a qualified mental health provider, working with clients exhibiting high acuity. Along the way, Jessica had worked as an intake specialist, gathering information to determine level of need and qualification for services. While in this position, Jessica had seen many clients fall through the cracks and have difficulty accessing mental health services. Some barriers had been created by agency policies, but others were the result of state laws originally passed to increase the types of resources local mental health authorities could provide to residents within their catchment areas. A shortage of providers in her area had further complicated the accessibility of mental health services. Jessica had vowed to do what she could to make changes on behalf of her community and profession.

Jessica had pursued a doctoral degree in counselor education and supervision to train counselors who would learn about the impact of state and federal policies on mental health treatment. Jessica used this passion to become an active member of her state and national professional counseling associations, and she served on public policy committees that researched proposed legislation and issued calls to action. Jessica decided this was her calling.

Now Jessica sat before the dean, wondering what went wrong. The dean proceeded to tell Jessica she had been contacted by the procurement office when a reservation for a state-owned van had been placed on behalf of the department. Upon investigation, the dean had found that Jessica's scheduled trip to take professional counseling students to the state capitol might have violated university policies and state laws prohibiting the use of public funds or equipment to advocate for or against pending or proposed legislation.

The dean discussed university policies expressly prohibiting faculty members from using their positions or titles to engage in legislative advocacy, and she mentioned federal rules related to lobbying. She asked Jessica to provide details regarding the trip. Jessica shared that the purpose of the trip was legislative professional advocacy in which she and the students would speak with legislators about opposing legislation that would have a negative impact on the state's professional counselors. During this trip, Jessica planned to explore research opportunities by connecting with other counselors from across the state. The dean thanked Jessica and told her they would be in touch soon. Jessica was worried that her hands were tied and that there would be a negative impact on her work as an advocate for the profession, her role as instructor, and her connections for future research projects related to legislative professional advocacy.

Jessica immediately reflected back on her master's- and doctoral-level experiences. She had learned about and participated in advocacy-related activities throughout her programs. Her programs, accredited by the Council for Accreditation of Counseling and Related Educational Programs (CACREP), stressed the importance of ethical advocacy work as well, so she wondered what information she might have missed.

Case Analysis and Discussion

The importance of advocacy and leadership is evident throughout the 2016 CACREP Standards (CACREP, 2016). Section 1, Standard X, requires faculty to identify with the counseling profession and demonstrate sustained professional service and advocacy. Section 2, Standard F, refers to advocacy as foundational knowledge in two core curricular areas for master's students: (a) Professional Counseling Orientation and Ethical Practice and (b) Social and Cultural Diversity. Section 6, Standard A.3., requires that doctoral admission criteria include "potential for scholarship, professional leadership, and advocacy" (p. 34). Leadership and advocacy is one of five required doctoral core areas in Section 6, Standard B, with ethically and culturally relevant leadership and advocacy practices covered in the doctoral curriculum. Section 6, Standard C, requires that doctoral students have internship experiences in at least three of the five core areas. This means that Jessica's doctoral internship could have excluded leadership and advocacy, leaving her unaware of important university policies and laws affecting state employees and the use of university resources.

The *ACA Code of Ethics* (American Counseling Association [ACA], 2014) defines *advocacy* as "promotion of the well-being of individuals, groups, and the counseling profession within systems and organizations. Advocacy seeks to remove barriers and obstacles that inhibit access, growth, and development" (p. 20). Standard A.7.a. allows counselors to advocate for clients at various levels, but the standard does not eliminate the concurrent responsibility to follow rules, laws, or guidelines affecting advocacy work. Jessica's lack of awareness of university policies, state laws, and federal rules related to lobbying resulted in her setting up an educational experience that students would not have been able to complete and that could have resulted in disciplinary action. Standard D.1.g. reminds counselors that "the acceptance of employment . . . implies that counselors are in agreement with its general policies and principles." As part of the onboarding process, human resource officers typically maintain specific requirements for all new employees, including letters of attestation verifying the new employee was notified of policies and procedures. That packet should have contained a document explaining the regulation of political activities by public employees, including restrictions on the use of university resources for political activities.

In general terms, these policies clarify who can act on behalf of the university when involved in legislative activities. These rules also limit the use of official titles; the university's physical address, email address, and telephone number; and other university resources or equipment by most state employees. Policies typically remind employees that they are free to express political opinions and engage in political activities to the extent they wish, but they may only do so in an individual capacity that in no way appears as though they are speaking for the university. State and local laws regulating lobbying can differ widely in scope depending on the jurisdiction. When in doubt, one should check with the office of general counsel for one's university.

Legislative Professional Advocacy

Legislative professional advocacy is "advocacy related to legislation to improve or change policies that impact the counseling profession, clients, and counselors' ability to practice" (Farrell & Barrio Minton, 2019, p. 144). Ways of helping clients address issues faced in their everyday lives can vary from engaging in direct client advocacy to addressing larger professional issues that impact how professional counselors do their jobs and seek reimbursement for services. Hof et al. (2009) proposed a model of advocacy that postulates that social advocacy and professional advocacy can be practiced concurrently within four competencies: promoting professional identity, increasing the public image of counseling, developing inter- and intraprofessional collaboration, and promoting legislative/policy initiatives. Each competency resonated with Jessica and described the approach she believed was most effective in advocating for underserved populations. In her work with counselors-in-training, she attempted to model actions in each of the competencies.

It is important for mental health practitioners to actively engage in legislative professional advocacy while acknowledging that "a general lack of training, discussion, and focus on political systems further mystifies policy work" (L. S. Jordan & Seponski, 2017, p. 6). Brat et al. (2016) made a case regarding the importance of teaching advocacy, noting that "it is critical that counseling programs train and emphasize professional advocacy and professional identity with students as well as stress the interconnectedness" between professional advocacy and professional identity (p. 65). The authors went on to discuss activities that solidify professional counselor identity through assignments, making it more likely that future counselors will be involved in advocacy across multiple levels.

Despite national accreditation standards, codes of ethics, and models of advocacy, little research exists regarding the best way to incorporate advocacy into the counseling curriculum. There are also few resources for addressing university policies, procedures, and state or federal laws when advocating. When counselors advocate for the counseling profession, "clients often indirectly benefit from counselors' professional advocacy efforts. Counselors might advocate for themselves because they know that doing so also benefits the general public" (Milsom, 2018, p. 440). These beliefs led Jessica to push forward and find a way to advocate not only for the profession but also for the clients soon to be served by her program's counselors-in-training.

Actions and Outcomes

Similar to experiences of those who engage in legislative professional advocacy, Jessica "learned to negotiate which barriers to overcome and which barriers to accept . . . having little control over time, money, and job requirements. However, negotiating barriers was a way to pick battles" (Farrell & Barrio Minton, 2019, p. 152). With her initial plans cancelled, Jessica reminded herself of the importance of students becoming active participants in legislative professional advocacy.

Having experienced the power of participating in student organizations herself, Jessica collaborated with the chapter faculty adviser (CFA) of the local Chi Sigma Iota chapter. The CFA may have been the perfect person to work with, as "CFAs believed that their role allowed them opportunities to mentor students on advocacy and leadership" (McKinney et al., 2018, p. 62), contribute to student leadership, and improve programmatic cohesiveness. Chi Sigma Iota chapters often participate in legislative advocacy days sponsored by state and national professional counseling associations. Burns (2015) examined perspectives on membership in a state counseling association and found that participants valued the association "providing them with timely information on legislative updates offered through the state counseling association listserv, web site, and newsletter" (p. 39). Farrell and Barrio Minton (2019) also found that leaders in the counseling profession valued their advocacy experiences with professional organizations. Thus, Jessica and the CFA decided to collaborate with the closest professional counseling association to ensure advocacy training and experiences would be offered to students.

Together Jessica and the CFA developed a presentation for students on legislative professional advocacy. Topics were for students and state employees and included differentiating between grassroots advocacy that potentially used university resources and advocacy completed on the state employee's personal time. Jessica also began using her personal contact information, not her university contact information, to communicate with legislative staffers, officials, and students regarding legislative professional advocacy.

After the advocacy training, a group of students took it upon themselves to raise enough money to get them to their state capitol. Their state professional counseling association had already established advocacy days at which detailed training was provided to participants, and they were able to self-pace their experience. With the CFA's help and experience mentoring students in leadership roles and advocacy initiatives, Jessica streamlined the training and offered it across the program. To make it clear she was acting on her own and not as an employee of the university, Jessica had business cards made that listed her credentials and personal email, address, and phone number. This was an important demonstration that she was proud to have her professional identity clearly noted when communicating with legislators and other professionals but that she was following university policies by speaking for herself and not the university.

To ensure the participation of students from across the program, Jessica personally contacted classes to promote the training and direct them to the Chi Sigma Iota chapter for service opportunities, including leadership positions. As a way to look for systematic inequities, Jessica and other faculty members asked "difficult questions regarding which faculty member, staff, and student voices [were] heard and valued within program operations" (Cashwell & Barrio Minton, 2012, p. 173). This exercise helped to make student organizers aware of barriers to participation some students faced. By considering these barriers, student leaders were able to make accommodations for those who were limited by time, experience, or finances. This experience helped to bring things full circle for Jessica, as she saw the same passion and care she had for her mental health clients translated into care for her counselors-in-training.

Conclusion

Although being called in by the dean was daunting, Jessica could not help but feel proud of how she had handled and remedied the problem. She now had a clearer understanding of conflicts of interest state employees must avoid and of the importance of representing herself as a constituent, not as an agent of the university. These experiences also allowed Jessica to identify sources of support in the program, which ultimately facilitated students' professional development.

Reflection Questions

1. What is the long-term impact of counselor educators not focusing on leadership and advocacy within their counselor education programs?
2. How can counselor education programs ensure they are educating future counselor educators about university policies and state regulations?

Critical Incident Response

Nicole R. Hill

Jessica evidenced many dispositions and competencies that we expect from well-trained and highly engaged professionals: a deep commitment to professional advocacy, focused attention to CACREP learning outcomes, the creation of experiential and high-impact teaching strategies, and the modeling of professional roles (Brat et al., 2016; L. S. Jordan & Seponski, 2017). Jessica's experiences as a case manager, licensed professional counselor, and intake specialist galvanized her professional goal of shaping the next generation of counselors to advocate for access to mental health services for all community members.

Jessica's professionalism and commitment to learning a new culture at her new university are evident in her engagement in the formal orientation and mentoring programs offered. Her response to the dean's concerns and illumination of essential policies impacting state employees was prompt, professional, and resourceful. Policies around legislative advocacy are quite variable at state institutions of higher education, with some programs consistently hosting Day at the Capitol events, engaging in advocacy projects, and sponsoring student groups such as the Young Democrats or Young Republicans. Therefore, Jessica has a systems-level responsibility to ensure she is clearly informed about more stringent university policies around fiscal responsibilities and representation as a university employee.

The professional counseling context and identity drive more curricular and programmatic enactments of advocacy than other academic areas. Given 2016 CACREP Standards stipulating advocacy as a foundational knowledge competency for training professional counselors (e.g., Section 2, Standard F) and *ACA Code of Ethics* (ACA, 2014) standards around advocating across multiple systems, administrators should expect that incoming faculty members will need to be explicitly briefed on how to enact these professional competencies in state-funded institutions. Relying on human resources or a faculty orientation to address the nuances of how to engage in professional and legislative advocacy while a state employee is inadequate. As counselor educators advance in their careers and assume more programmatic and administrative leadership roles, they have a responsibility to ensure university policies, procedures, and standards of conduct are clearly and systematically articulated to new faculty members. Counseling leaders may also educate deans and other administrators about the role of advocacy in the professional identity development of counselor trainees.

As a first-year tenure-track counselor educator, being asked to meet with the dean and questioned about one's use of university resources and decision-making around a course assignment can be overwhelming and anxiety provoking. Jessica should initiate another meeting with the dean to summarize her choices and discuss how she was able to ensure the graduate students received the professional training necessary required by accreditation and ethical standards (ACA, 2014; CACREP, 2016). Jessica can also emphasize her appreciation of a more thorough understanding of state laws and university policies. Having a positive, working relationship with the dean is an important factor in Jessica's success. Following up with the dean and sharing how she addressed concerns and created meaningful cocurricular experiences for her students will showcase her professionalism and competence as a faculty member.

In addition, Jessica should request meetings with the department chair and program coordinator to highlight her decisions in response to concerns about following policies and to explore any additional steps she needs to take politically to ensure she is held in high regard by administrators, colleagues, and students. Such a meeting would also provide Jessica with an opportunity to ask whether there are other nuanced policies, procedures, or cultural expectations of which she needs to be aware to thrive in her tenure-track position.

Engaging in legislative professional advocacy can be a complicated process that requires a high level of awareness of political, systemic, and contextual factors as well as persistence, resourcefulness, and collaboration (Brat et al., 2016; Farrell & Barrio Minton, 2019). This experience is a critical learning moment Jessica can share with her students about the complexities and realities of needing to change course and implement new strategies to achieve desired outcomes. Professional counselors must be ethical and competent in navigating dual relationships and dialectics between different roles. Jessica may share with students how she had to balance state laws, university policies, CACREP Standards, and her own identity as a counselor while identifying other pathways to provide them with training in legislative advocacy. This may model how counselors can develop consultative, reflective, and critical thinking skills to manage tensions and conflicts among their roles. Jessica's experience exemplifies how to professionally and effectively navigate challenging situations from a growth orientation and ethical mind-set.

• • •

Section 3
Diversity and Inclusion Within Counselor Education Programs

Chapter 38
Do We Practice What We Preach? Diversity and Inclusion Plans

Christian D. Chan

2014 *ACA Code of Ethics* Standards Addressed

- F.2.b. Multicultural Issues/Diversity in Supervision
- F.6.b. Gatekeeping and Remediation
- F.7.c. Infusing Multicultural Issues/Diversity
- F.11.a. Faculty Diversity
- F.11.b. Student Diversity
- F.11.c. Multicultural/Diversity Competence

• • •

Professor X was a white, cisgender, able-bodied, heterosexual male who was serving as department chair of a teaching institution in the Midwest. Professor X had served in his role for 10 years and had received positive feedback from faculty colleagues and upper administrators. The department had master's programs and a newly minted doctoral program. The master's programs, with four specialty areas, were accredited by the Council for Accreditation of Counseling and Related Educational Programs (CACREP), and the doctoral program in counselor education and supervision, which had been established 3 years ago, had recently received CACREP accreditation.

Professor X was satisfied with the construction and development of the doctoral program, and the program had thus far not been found deficient in meeting any of the CACREP Standards (CACREP, 2016). The department consisted of 14 faculty members and nearly 140 students across its counseling programs. Although the faculty represented diverse social identities and cultural backgrounds (e.g., in terms of gender identity, sexual orientation, and ability status), the department suffered from a lack of racial diversity among its faculty; there had been no tenured faculty of color within the history of the department. Moreover, only three faculty members of color had been granted professor status in the history of the entire institution.

During the CACREP site visit, the site team raved about the department's field experience, curriculum, and course sequencing but expressed concerns about the lack of diversity among faculty and students. The site team, however, appreciated documents shared related to a plan to recruit diverse faculty and students. Following the visit, the department received a tenure-track faculty line and successfully hired Professor G, a pretenure, cisgender, pansexual, able-bodied female faculty member of color who had expertise in trauma and assessment. In addition, the newest cohort of master's students was the most racially and ethnically diverse in the history of the program. Professor X hoped these changes would move the department toward a spirit of diversity, equity, and inclusion with the goal of bolstering its reputation as a department focused on multicultural and social justice issues.

At the start of the spring semester, Professor X received a report from Lee, a student of color, that Sasha, a white student, had committed a series of microaggressions in their master's-level counseling research methods course. Professor X met with Lee in person to gain additional background regarding the incidents. Lee noted that Sasha had used racial slurs to refer to other students in the class, and the faculty instructor, Professor F, had not intervened or addressed the issue publicly. Instead, Professor F consistently praised Sasha for their thoughtful and intelligent contributions to critical thinking during class discussions. Professor F indicated to students that a discussion of similar issues concerning diversity would be more relevant in one of Professor G's classes. Lee disclosed that many students in the course and the cohort, especially students of color, felt unsafe transitioning into their second semester. To address the issue, Professor X created a task force of three faculty members and four doctoral students to address policies, gatekeeping procedures, remediation, and andragogical practices related to diversity, equity, and inclusion.

Case Analysis and Discussion

This incident is a two-pronged issue that reflects a situation of institutional racism and institutional culture along with gatekeeping and remediation concerns for Sasha. To successfully implement culturally responsive and equitable strategies, counselor educators must incorporate interpersonal domains and the broader institutional culture into their decision-making (Ahmed, 2012; C. D. Chan et al., 2018; Guth et al., 2019; Ratts et al., 2016).

Institutional Racism and Institutional Culture

One concern highlights the profound impact of microaggressions and explicit racism occurring within a classroom setting (see Pérez Huber & Solorzano, 2018; Sue et al., 2019). It is clear that a white student perpetuated a multitude of microaggressions and harmful racialized interactions within the classroom (Darvin, 2018; Doharty, 2019). Microaggressions can surface as interpersonal and systemic indignities that reinforce stereotypes and prejudices while perpetuating histories and structures of power (Nadal et al., 2014). The conglomeration of microaggressions, explicit racism, and faculty failure to intervene reflects the norms of an institution (Ahmed, 2012; Bonilla-Silva, 2018; Hughey et al., 2017). Even more concerning, instances of racialized interactions maintain a status quo that can be upheld by white communities and communities of color within an institution (Ahmed, 2012). Institutional and departmental cultures can affect the climate and the pipeline for faculty and students of color. Thus, it is imperative for counselor educators to consider the long-term ramifications and cultural implications of their actions and inaction.

Professor F's interactions illustrate another issue related to systemic microaggressions. Professor F's discomfort and lack of awareness resulted in him redirecting the discussion and placing the burden on Professor G simply because of her cultural capital and intersections (Koshino, 2016). His arguments mirror historical and structural insights into color-blind ideologies, images, and stereotypes impacting faculty of color (Doharty, 2019). Professor F instilled a tokenizing dynamic by involving Professor G and absolving himself of culpability in a critically important situation with racial tension (Ahmed, 2012; Hughey et al., 2017). Rather than recognizing his own privileges and power in the classroom, he used a faculty member of color to forward his interests and obscure the racial issue at hand (Bell, 2016; Delgado Bernal & Villalpando, 2016). The department could suffer from two additional core issues: (a) using faculty of color to indicate a more multicultural and social justice–focused department and (b) positioning faculty of color as unwilling teachers and representatives of multiculturalism and social justice (Morales, 2020; Sanchez, 2019). In addition, the department could suffer from failing to retain students and faculty of color as an outcome of inadequate support and protection (Brezinski et al., 2018; Koshino, 2016).

Another portion of the vignette indicates the need for faculty to receive training surrounding diversity, equity, and inclusion within their curriculum and andragogy (Doharty, 2019; Singh, 2019a). Counselor educators can benefit from reflecting on the messages they send with their practices (Malott et al., 2015). Interactions with students reflect action or inaction on issues related to diversity, equity, and inclusion (Darvin, 2018), and counselor educators cannot assume that one multicultural course can serve as the exclusive holding place for a number of these issues (Remley & Herlihy, 2020). Rather, multiculturalism and social justice should be integrated into the entire curriculum (Ratts et al., 2015; Remley & Herlihy, 2020). Counselor educators have an ethical responsibility to publicly address instances of racism and maintain psychological safety in the classroom (C. D. Chan et al., 2018; Malott et al., 2015). When these interactions go unaddressed, students of color can feel unsafe as outsiders as a result of the racial climate at predominantly white institutions (Brezinski et al., 2018; Koshino, 2016; Sanchez, 2019). Counselor educators need to be attentive to racial climate within their academic units, campuses, and surrounding communities and actively broach these critical discussions in their classrooms and advising (Day-Vines et al., 2018).

Professor F's position reinforces the same power structure established in the classroom (C. D. Chan et al., 2018). It is highly concerning that Professor F failed to address the student directing racial slurs at other students and also continued to compliment the student for their intellectual contributions. Counselor educators are charged with intervening in teacher-student and student-student interactions (Darvin, 2018; Pérez Huber & Solorzano, 2018). Failures to address disparities can discourage students from engaging in the learning environment and maintaining trust in the faculty and department (Doharty, 2019; Sanchez, 2019). Note that students of color can feel a sense of institutional betrayal when facing multiple experiences of harm and distrust from faculty, which can lead to additional distress and emotionality (C. P. Smith & Freyd, 2014). Students can seemingly trust an institution to protect them but instead experience a set of incidents, policies, and lack of reparations that fail to legitimize their perspectives (C. P. Smith & Freyd, 2014). In this scenario, students would have likely expected Professor F to intervene. Professor F's failure to intervene created distrust of faculty and reinforced a culture that supports whiteness. Counselor educators must recognize the power relations among themselves and students along with their responsibility to protect students in the classroom (C. D. Chan et al., 2018) by detecting and responding to racialized experiences and incidents of bias (Haskins & Singh, 2015; Pérez Huber & Solorzano, 2018).

Another area in the case vignette relates to the disconnect between departmental policy and explicit practices associated with diversity, equity, and inclusion (Ahmed, 2012; C. V. Harris, 2016). Departmental policies and diversity statements often reflect public intentions to radically alter the culture of a department through documenting core dispositions (Spurgeon, Gibbons, & Cochran, 2012). Detailed and public documents position stakeholders with a mission to augment multicultural and social justice competencies critical to the professional identity of counselors (see Cashwell & Barrio Minton, 2012; Ratts et al., 2015, 2016). However, there may be a disconnect between public documents and commitment to individual practice (Ahmed, 2012). A more alarming concern surfaces when departments assume they are successfully integrating values of multiculturalism and social justice without addressing long-standing gaps, vulnerabilities, and biases (see DiAngelo, 2018; C. V. Harris, 2016). Consistent with the case vignette, the CACREP site team praised the faculty for developing documents to increase diversity. Despite calls for the recruitment and retention of diverse faculty and students (American Counseling Association [ACA], 2014), a persistent lack of environmental and cultural supports often leads to attrition among students of color and early departures among faculty of color (Koshino, 2016).

Cultural Issues in Gatekeeping and Remediation

This case presents an additional issue regarding gatekeeping and remediation. Although the observable data do not include interactions with clients, it is clear that Sasha's racialized behavior and interpersonal dispositions could predict future attitudes and behaviors toward clients (Ziomek-Daigle, 2019). Note that the 2016 CACREP Standards communicate how crucial it is to evaluate students on an ongoing basis to ensure adequate attention to professional dispositions (CACREP, 2016). *ACA Code of Ethics* Standards F.2.b., F.6.b., F.7.c., and F.11.c. also address counselor educators' and supervisors' duties for engaging in gatekeeping and infusing multiculturalism into supervision and counselor education (ACA, 2014). Other counseling scholars have reinforced the claim that programs and departments are tasked with the necessary duty of assessing students and the overall program culture (e.g., Cashwell & Barrio Minton, 2012; Spurgeon, Gibbons, & Cochran, 2012), in particular in light of the Multicultural and Social Justice Counseling Competencies (Ratts et al., 2015) and the ACA Advocacy Competencies (Toporek & Daniels, 2018). The counselor education faculty in this scenario were actively modeling standards and cultural norms for gatekeeping through their action or inaction.

Actions and Outcomes

The department's response should involve multiple strategies on multiple systems levels. The task force must map out the contextual, interpersonal, and individual factors that make up the cultural problems within the department (Ahmed, 2012). Although the task force may consider this an isolated incident, it is highly likely that it occurred on more than one occasion within the department. Thus, the task force would need to elicit long-term change by engaging in a series of actions to systematically address issues of diversity, equity, and inclusion in the department beyond merely attending to this one andragogical issue (Hughey et al., 2017). The task force can actively tackle the root of the problem attached to the history of the department and institution (Ahmed, 2012; Cashwell & Barrio Minton, 2012) while also initiating short-term initiatives for remediation (Ziomek-Daigle, 2019).

The task force can take a primary step toward publicly addressing the issue and condemning acts of racism without naming specific individuals involved. Taking such action could mitigate the effects of institutional betrayal students of color might face (C. P. Smith & Freyd, 2014) and enhance the racial climate for students and faculty of color (C. V. Harris, 2016). This type of public action illustrates the importance of microaffirmations to ensure that people of color are seen, heard, and validated (C. V. Harris, 2016; Sue et al., 2019). The task force would also illustrate the main goals of the 2016 CACREP Standards (CACREP, 2016) and the *ACA Code of Ethics* (ACA, 2014) by signifying attunement to power, privilege, and oppression within and outside the classroom (Malott et al., 2015). Consistent with *ACA Code of Ethics* Standards F.11.a. and F.11.b., creating additional supports within the environment would augment the department's commitment to recruiting and retaining diverse faculty and students.

The task force must address how Professor F handled the classroom situation while also providing ongoing training for all faculty and students surrounding racial and cultural issues. It is important for the task force to emphasize broaching cultural factors as a daily practice with clients, students, and one another (Day-Vines et al., 2018; Singh, 2019b). The task force must continue to examine gaps within faculty training and cultivate long-term initiatives that uphold counselor educators as advocates of multiculturalism and social justice (C. D. Chan et al., 2018; Haskins & Singh, 2015). For example, the task force can map a series of trainings required for all faculty. Given constraints on time and responsibility, the task force can also assign texts faculty members can read together at various points of time and perhaps discuss during a retreat. These recommendations would especially connect to *ACA Code of Ethics* Standard F.11.c., which requires continued training on and infusion of multicultural and social justice practices (ACA, 2014).

The members of the task force can also use an intersectionality-based policy analysis (see Hankivsky et al., 2014) to assist the department in developing a systematic plan of action while interrogating their own personal biases and intersections of social identities. An intersectionality-based policy analysis uses multiple dimensions grounded in intersectionality to (a) inquire about personal biases, privilege, and oppression; (b) map previous responses to issues; (c) illustrate current policies and measures designed to address the current issue; (d) determine the distinct actions for stakeholders (e.g., specific faculty, the department chair) to address; and (e) outline a systematic plan for evaluating, measuring, and implementing the change to enhance diversity, equity, and inclusion (Hankivsky et al., 2014). Given the context of the vignette, the task force should apply this information to all faculty training, where they can address their biases and racial identity development (Singh, 2019b). As an outcome, the task force would reinforce a proactive stance, in which strategies do not apply only to one problematic faculty member. Instead, the task force would magnify the priority for diversity, equity, and inclusion practices as a cultural norm rather than a passive set of statements integrated into a policy (Ahmed, 2012). Similarly, the task force would encourage faculty and students to engage in antiracist approaches individually and collectively (Kendi, 2019; Singh, 2019b). Rather than integrating an exemplary analysis at one point in time (e.g., strategic planning), the task force could generate multiple intervals, such as the beginning of each semester, for faculty in the department to participate in an intersectionality-based policy analysis.

Conclusion

Consistent with the 2016 CACREP Standards (CACREP, 2016), initiating ongoing efforts can exemplify a myriad of sustainable changes for the learning environment, infusion of multiculturalism and social justice across the core curriculum, and recruitment and retention of diverse faculty and students. Counselor educators are called to be proactive and consistent in addressing these issues rather than intervening only in the midst of a critical incident. Consistently planning for and explicitly discussing these types of racialized issues will strengthen the racial climate of an academic unit and procedures for responses to bias.

Reflection Questions

1. How can counselor education faculty members in your department, program, or academic unit create sustainable initiatives that promote long-term changes for equity?
2. How can counselor education faculty members intervene in racialized incidents and racial microaggressions within your department, program, or academic unit?

Critical Incident Response

S. Anandavalli and
Cirecie A. West-Olatunji

As the author noted, there is often a significant gap between principles and philosophies guiding counselor education work and everyday experiences within counselor training programs. This critical incident highlights several vulnerable and, regrettably, common incidents in the counselor education community (C. D. Chan et al., 2018). Experiences of chronic microaggressions are common among faculty and students of color (C. D. Chan et al., 2018; Day-Vines et al., 2018; Haskins & Singh, 2015). In this context, taking a systematic approach to handling a sensitive issue is commendable and offers a framework for programs facing similar threats to enhancing their diversity and representativeness. The critical incident has several layers of complexity that require careful attention by affected students and faculty members in addition to a deeper examination of culture at the department and university level. Multiple strengths in the chair's approach communicate a strong commitment to moving toward inclusivity and antiracism within the department (Kendi, 2019).

First, Lee felt safe approaching the department chair and discussing his concerns regarding Sasha and Professor F. From an observer's standpoint, the fact that a student feels comfortable approaching the department chair to discuss a vulnerable situation indicates that the chair has demonstrated potential rapport and approachability. It also potentially communicates a culture of open communication embedded in the department.

Second, the department chair used his race, gender, and ascribed position-based privilege to enforce the core values of multiculturalism and social justice (Ratts et al., 2015). Using his intersecting sources of power (Crenshaw, 1989), Professor X set out to address a historic and oppressive narrative within the campus. With deep awareness of his own privileges and sources of cultural capital, he used this situation to move the department toward a more progressive, inclusive, and socially just trajectory.

Third, the approach to addressing and dismantling the toxic incidents was systematic and democratic. The chair gave the issue the attention and seriousness it deserved and developed a task force to carefully examine the happenings. The carefully structured task force, which comprised both students and faculty members, offered an opportunity for meaningful discussion and problem-solving.

Finally, the chair considered multiple sources for dismantling racism. He discussed trainings and readings in addition to theoretical models to learn from this critical incident. His actions communicate a long-term willingness to adopt a tutorial stance and engage in meaningful and deeper antiracist work.

A couple additional measures may help the chair further goals for an inclusive and diverse department. Mentorship is especially important for faculty of color. Marginalized faculty members experience historical barriers in addition to the challenges of entering academia, and new and emerging faculty of color can benefit from meaningful mentorship from established faculty (Borders et al., 2011). In the current vignette, Professor G (and other faculty of color in the department in the past) is likely to have experienced similar microaggressions on a chronic basis. If current, structured mentorship infrastructure is not already in place for new faculty members of color, it might be a helpful strategy to enhance retention.

Furthermore, the chair drew significantly from the works of Crenshaw (1989), Kendi (2019), and Sue and colleagues (2019). The author rightly acknowledged that antiracist work cannot be relegated to a single course. Instead, core values of the department, such as microinterventions, antiracism, and intersectionality, can be infused into new student orientations and regular brown bag series for students to be reminded of the department's stance on racism.

This critical incident has much to offer to counselor education programs that seek to enhance and retain diversity among students and faculty. The author's careful description of the incident and the measures taken by the chair indicates that increasing representation within a department is an intentional and deliberate effort that requires an ongoing tutorial stance and openness to learning.

• • •

Chapter 39

Maybe I Can Change This: Addressing Marginalization in a Program

Natoya Hill Haskins, Unity Walker, Aiesha Lee, and Huijuan Li

2014 *ACA Code of Ethics* Standards Addressed

- F.11.a. Faculty Diversity
- F.11.b. Student Diversity
- F.11.c. Multicultural/Diversity Competence

• • •

A first-year doctoral cohort had recently begun their second semester at Elsewhere University. After class one day, the cohort members gathered to discuss their experience in the program thus far. Sitting at the table were Rebecca, a straight white woman; Sam, a straight white woman; Chris, a straight white man; James, a straight white man; and Jessica, a queer Black woman. During the discussion, members shared their assignments and responsibilities.

Rebecca began discussing a research project in which her adviser, Professor Carlson, had invited her to participate. Although the project did not completely align with her research interests, she was excited to begin engaging in research. Then Sam began discussing a project in which she was currently engaged with her adviser, Professor Smith. Sam explained that Professor Smith had suggested Sam participate to get exposure to the research process. Sam expressed gratitude for Professor Smith's insistence, as she was learning a lot about conducting research. James told the cohort about the conference proposal he had just submitted with his adviser, Professor O'Neill. James explained that the proposal topic was not something in which he was very interested, but he had been able to learn how to write and submit a strong conference proposal, an important skill. Chris also began discussing the research study on which a faculty member, Professor Roberts, had invited him to assist. Chris explained how excited he was to be working on this particular study, as it aligned perfectly with his interests. Jessica asked Chris more about the research study. While he explained, Chris asked Jessica why she was not on the study with him because Professor Roberts was also Jessica's adviser.

Jessica told the group that she had not been invited to participate in the study. In an attempt to alleviate their discomfort, Chris explained that it was possible Professor Roberts had not invited her to participate because the study did not align with her research interests. Noticing her distress, Chris invited Jessica to work on references and formatting for the project, saying he would ask Professor Roberts to make sure it was OK. Jessica nodded and remained quiet throughout the remainder of the discussion, feeling isolated, confused, disempowered, invisible, and ignored.

Over the next several weeks, Jessica tried to connect with some of her cohort members and students in other doctoral programs to design a research study she could present at a conference in the near future. Jessica reached out to a few others who shared her underrepresented identities in the program, only to realize that they were having the same experience. Feeling discouraged yet somewhat validated, she reached out to Professor Roberts, who signed off on the research, in hopes of receiving some support.

About a week later, Professor Fisk, a tenured associate professor and the sole faculty member of color, casually checked in with Jessica and several other students of color. The students quickly asked her to talk privately. In Professor Fisk's office, the students shared that they had not been experiencing the same support as their white counterparts. Specifically, they had not been asked to be on research teams by their advisers or other faculty members despite repeatedly asking for support; instead, they had been rebuffed and brushed off. Professor Fisk was appalled that these doctoral students were not developing the same skillsets as other students, and she recognized that their lack of support might impact their job prospects and career success in the academy. Although Professor Fisk had only been at Elsewhere University for 2 years, she had been in the field for almost 10 years; she realized she had to find a way to support and advocate for these students.

Case Analysis and Discussion

Jessica's experience of discrimination in her program has several implications for the field of counselor education as a whole. The 2016 Council for Accreditation of Counseling and Related Educational Programs (CACREP) Standards (CACREP, 2016) require accredited programs to promote the success of marginalized students through purposive recruitment and retention of diverse students and faculty. Although doctoral students are the most diverse of all groups in counselor education, their transition into faculty falls short, as counselor education faculty are the least diverse of all counselor education groups.

Professor Fisk focused on advocating around three issues: underrepresentation of faculty and students from diverse backgrounds, inequitable support for underrepresented students, and lack of relevant curriculum and research experiences for underrepresented students. The Preamble to the *ACA Code of Ethics* (American Counseling Association [ACA], 2014) states that the profession of counseling should be "honoring diversity and embracing a multicultural approach in support of the worth, dignity, potential, and uniqueness of people within their social and cultural context" (p. 3). The *Code* provides a clear rationale for creating and cultivating equity and inclusion in training programs and with students and faculty (Standard F.11.a.). Furthermore, the *Code* highlights the importance of recruiting and retaining a diverse student body and notes that "counselor educators demonstrate commitment to multicultural/diversity competence by recognizing and valuing the diverse cultures and types of abilities that students bring to the training experience" (Standard F.11.b.). Finally, the *Code* requires members of the profession to ensure that the curriculum represents diverse perspectives (Standard F.11.c.).

Actions Taken

Professor Fisk's response reflected all aspects of the *Code* described above. First, she invited several students to participate on her research teams. African American students' interactions with faculty are important for their academic achievement and significantly impact their overall educational satisfaction (Fountaine, 2012; Horsford, 2014; McGaskey, 2015). Furthermore, queer graduate students report pressure to avoid identity-related topics in academia, invalidation of their experiences, and objectification by faculty (Bryan, 2018), and queer students of color benefit positively from their relationships with faculty (Mobley & Hall, 2020). African American students who have multiple marginalized identities experience unique microaggressions their cisgender, heterosexual, or white counterparts do not (Bryan, 2018). Underrepresented students who receive mentoring and support from faculty who share their identities have greater persistence and retention (Cockrell & Shelley, 2011; McGee et al., 2016; Mobley & Hall, 2020).

Second, Professor Fisk advocated at the program level on behalf of the underrepresented students. She presented her concerns to the faculty regarding a lack of support for students from marginalized backgrounds, citing their lack of research opportunities and recognition for departmental awards. Several faculty members commented that they had reached out to several underrepresented students and that the students had declined opportunities for engagement, whereas others commented that they did not realize that there was a disparity and that the students' lack of inclusion was not intentional. In some instances, broaching multicultural issues can bring awareness and potential behavior change (Allan, 2011; Aryan & Guzman, 2010; Costner et al., 2010). In this case, several faculty members became hypervigilant in their efforts to reach out to underrepresented students to participate on research and writing projects, whereas the behavior of others remained unchanged.

Professor Fisk also advocated for students at the individual level. She focused on helping Jessica and other students begin to develop their own advocacy skills while also creating a supportive community. Professor Fisk created two affinity groups for graduate students: one for African American women and the other for lesbian, gay, bisexual, transgender, and queer (LGBTQ+) students. The groups ran for 3 years and focused on helping students develop strategies for navigating the academy and advocating for themselves.

Marginalized students also benefit from nonacademic supportive relationships and experiences, as they provide benefits such as self-confidence, self-esteem, and motivation (Welton et al., 2010). Affinity groups or sanctuary spaces offer safety and a sense of belonging, healing, and restoration for underrepresented graduate students attending predominantly white institutions (Carter et al., 2013). Participants in sanctuary spaces promote the development of professional networks, mentorship, engagement in critical conversation, and information regarding how to navigate graduate school (Cockrell & Shelley, 2011; Felder, 2010; McGee et al., 2016; Neal-Barnett et al., 2011). Sanctuary spaces serve as a respite from the challenges of graduate school and address the unique needs of underrepresented graduate students. Affinity groups provide a space for participants to engage in critical, in-depth conversation around their identities and prepare for conversations with other identity groups (Tauriac et al., 2013), thus promoting conversations and building relationships and cohesion among students with different identities.

In an effort to create more support for Jessica and other Black women and LGBTQ+ students, Professor Fisk advocated at the institutional level, working with the diversity and inclusion office to convene the first African American Intersections of Identity Research Conference at the university. The provost's office and several university partners funded the conference. More than 60 graduate students and 20 underrepresented faculty members came together to explore the hidden curriculum with topics such as navigating microaggressions, job searching, and scholarly writing and publishing.

Hidden information, requirements, and expectations can have significant impacts on students' achievement and personal confidence (Alsubaie, 2015). By definition, a *hidden curriculum* refers to "the unspoken or implicit values, behaviors, procedures, and norms that exist in an educational setting" (Alsubaie, 2015, p. 125). Professor Fisk addressed the hidden curriculum that Jessica and other students noted as a significant issue within their program. Simultaneously, Professor Fisk worked with the School of Education's Diversity Committee to advocate for an associate dean for diversity, whose role would be to hold the school accountable for its diversity efforts. Over several years, Professor Fisk worked with the team to build a rationale for the position, collecting data from the university, students, faculty, and staff.

Outcomes

Jessica went on to publish four manuscripts with Professor Fisk while a doctoral student. She participated in both of Professor Fisk's affinity groups for 2 years. In addition, Jessica helped plan the university's African American Intersections of Identity Research Conference. She then went on to serve on the faculty of a top university. Professor Fisk saw many of the master's students who participated in the affinity groups go on to doctoral programs at rates that were significantly higher than before their implementation. Many of the faculty members Professor Fisk broached during their departmental meeting noted that the meeting was a pivotal moment in illuminating their blind spots and changing how they saw themselves as allies and advocates.

Although Professor Fisk eventually left the university where she first met Jessica, their shared experience continued to be the impetus for her advocacy work at programmatic and institutional levels. Recognizing the barriers to including queer experiences even within spaces for underrepresented students (Mobley & Hall, 2020), Professor Fisk advocated for a yearly training related to queer issues for her department. In addition, Professor Fisk worked to update language in departmental policies to include the identities of underrepresented graduate students (Bryan, 2018).

In response to the devaluing of research topics and qualitative methodologies designed to illuminate, examine, or critique the experiences of marginalized populations (Dotson, 2012), Professor Fisk used her experiences to develop a fellows program. The program provided faculty with access and opportunities to develop, design, and execute research in the areas of equity, diversity, and inclusion while also mentoring burgeoning social justice scholars. The program included monthly professional development activities with leaders in critical race theory, social justice, cultural responsiveness, and equity education (J. Rodriguez & Haskins, 2020).

In addition, Professor Fisk developed an Advanced Social Justice and Diversity course to ensure that doctoral counselor education students knew how to teach, supervise, and conduct research from critical and cultural lenses. Professor Fisk tasked students with writing a manuscript using constructs from the course. Students presented outlines of these manuscripts during the course to mimic conference presentations. Students also read *White Fragility* (DiAngelo, 2018) as the impetus for engagement around topics of privilege, heteronormativity, cultural humility, and oppression. In many ways, Professor Fisk presented a curriculum that embodied the experiences of underrepresented students (Haskins & Singh, 2015), thereby shaping how future counselor educators would interact with diverse students.

Conclusion

As an advocate for social justice and diversity in counselor education, Professor Fisk invested in Jessica and her peers to provide a supportive environment. However, not all programs have a faculty member who is willing and able to address situations of cultural discrimination in such an expedited and passionate manner. Programs must resist relying on one or two faculty members to support underrepresented students. Rather, faculty members must become active in creating a programmatic culture that emphasizes support for all students. Shared understanding of personal and professional support is key to implementing this culture. Coming to this consensus and shifting the culture of a program is a process. To support students like Jessica, institutions must consider hiring qualified marginalized faculty members like Professor Fisk to begin or propel institutional change. In addition, counselor educators must encourage cross-institutional support for marginalized students who may not have faculty members to whom they can turn for diversity-related support and research (Alvarez et al., 2016). Cross-institutional support could provide the modeling and leadership necessary to empower counselor educators in situations similar to Jessica's. Finally, counselor educators should conduct research related to supporting marginalized doctoral students to better inform interventions.

Reflection Questions

1. What would you consider barriers to implementation in this case?
2. How might you change the climate in the department to address the needs of underrepresented students?

Critical Incident Response

Christian D. Chan

This case demonstrates a range of implicit behaviors that reflect structural issues in counselor education, and these inequalities dovetail with current societal problems. The case illustrates a far too common experience within higher education and forms an important platform for examining the cultural climate of institutions. Similar situations reflect a myriad of social conditions that pervade faculty affairs, student affairs, and doctoral education. Despite the profession's historical attachment to multiculturalism and social justice, counselor education is not distant from perpetuating chronic and severe forms of inequity.

Counselors and counselor educators alike are called to embody virtue ethics that actively challenge internalized biases (Singh, 2019a). The 2016 CACREP Standards (CACREP, 2016) and *ACA Code of Ethics* (ACA, 2014) emphasize that the actions required of white counselor educators and white students are rooted in foundational rather than specialized training. Counselor educators must hold one another accountable and engage in self-critique around multiple dimensions of privilege consistent with the Multicultural and Social Justice Counseling Competencies (Ratts et al., 2015) and cultural humility (see Guth et al., 2019; Hook et al., 2017).

This case indicates multiple instances of implicit and harmful privilege. There were numerous opportunities for white students and faculty to intervene in the exclusion of a queer Black woman. Instead, they disallowed a marginalized student from mentorship and professional opportunities in the academic system. More poignantly, the privileged faculty and peers attempted to capitalize on the labor and capital Jessica provided. This situation resembles secondary oppression, in which privileged communities benefit from their complicity in the oppression of marginalized communities (see Gnilka et al., 2018).

A structural issue that could have been further explicated in the case is the burden often placed on women of color, in particular Black women, to fix a broken system (Shavers & Moore, 2019). Encouraging Professor Fisk to advocate, endure, and implement tasks associated with equity can empower historically marginalized faculty and students to productively connect to meaningful changes (Casado Pérez, 2019). However, the insidious costs of tokenism and undue burden set up an inequitable structure that fails to hold white faculty, colleagues, and students accountable for making reparations to historically marginalized communities.

At worst, allowing these structural issues to occur sends a litany of messages. First, this dilemma represents a larger microcosm of the profession in which training in multiculturalism and social justice is siloed in a single multiculturalism class and often the responsibility of historically marginalized faculty members. Second, although the actions in the case are important for increasing the belongingness and cultural capital of historically marginalized students, they did not address the racial and cultural climate perpetuated by the white faculty and students. Overlooking opportunities to name and denounce actions perpetuated by white faculty members and students can lead to tacit endorsement of social conditions of whiteness in the learning environment (Matias et al., 2014). This can exacerbate the unwelcoming space already present for historically marginalized communities in academia (Shavers & Moore, 2019).

Third, the story details a sense of empowerment for both Professor Fisk and Jessica. Witnessing Professor Fisk take on these responsibilities can potentially incite feelings of exhaustion and sadness and ultimately culminate in racial battle fatigue (see W. A. Smith et al., 2016). Patterns of chronic daily experiences with racism result in race-based trauma and spirit murdering across the preschool to workforce educational system (Love, 2017). Although Professor Fisk created important avenues for Jessica's survival and promoted her growth, the environment of the academic unit should be addressed to prevent further instances of marginalization for students like Jessica and faculty members like Professor Fisk.

This scenario details layers of Jessica's experience as she faced marginalization through racism, genderism, sexism, and heterosexism. Given the attention to intersectionality in counselor education (see C. D. Chan et al., 2018; Haskins & Singh, 2015; Singh et al., 2020), counselor educators can use this case to understand the social context that elicited different forms of power for Jessica and Professor Fisk. These experiences of marginalization and cultural capital play a crucial role in systematically mapping out how to alter structural inequities within counselor education and this specific academic unit.

• • •

Chapter 40

You Can't Treat Me That Way! Microaggressions and Bullying

Philip B. Clarke and Michelle R. Ghoston

2014 *ACA Code of Ethics* Standards Addressed

- F.11.a. Faculty Diversity
- G.5.e. Agreement of Contributors

• • •

Chris was well prepared, excited, and enthusiastic to be joining the faculty of an esteemed counselor education program directly after graduating from his doctoral program. Although excited and prepared to start his first full-time tenure-track job, Chris recalled several messages received from his mother, such as "Always bring your 'A' game . . . we can't afford to make any mistakes" and "Once a Black person gets their foot in the door, their job is not complete. In fact, the real work begins!" Chris planned to arrive early, stay late, and volunteer for as many opportunities as possible all while ensuring he was treated with dignity and respect.

As Chris prepared for his first day in the office, he was informed there would be a meeting with Maggie, a senior faculty member, for onboarding. Chris was eager to meet Maggie for the first time face to face. After they exchanged pleasantries, Maggie noted that she had expected Chris to be in the office at 8 a.m., even though their meeting was not scheduled until 10 a.m. This was said as a joke, and they both laughed. As they talked, Maggie shared a wealth of information about the layout of the department, connections with information technology personnel, and the location of classroom materials. As the meeting concluded, Maggie said, "Don't disappoint me—I really fought to hire someone like you!" This statement stayed with Chris throughout his first year on the job.

Chris initially elected not to speak much in faculty meetings out of respect for longer standing faculty members and to get a clear sense of department meeting procedures.

However, 3 months after he began in the position, tensions arose among faculty over how to increase the number of applicants to the counseling program. Chris felt compelled to share his thoughts. Before he could finish speaking, Chris was shocked to hear Maggie interrupting in a raised voice and irritated tone, stating, "Chris, we were hoping to hear from the more seasoned faculty regarding this matter. Furthermore, the chair indicated she would like to move on from this topic." Chris was shocked and embarrassed. After the meeting, Chris felt increasingly angry over what had occurred. He was determined to speak more during faculty meetings and not be deterred by this experience. As the year progressed, Chris got more involved in discussions during meetings.

On another occasion that first year, Maggie asked Chris to serve on a committee she was chairing. Chris had mixed feelings about working closely with Maggie but was excited to be part of the innovative work being done by this committee. Maggie assigned Chris to several menial and time-consuming tasks. Chris soon realized that the other committee members had been assigned significantly fewer tasks. Yet when the committee decided to develop a presentation and journal article based on their work, he was not invited to participate in any discussion on author order and was listed second to last. Chris thought about stating his concerns directly to Maggie, but he did not take action at this time.

A few weeks after his discovery about the presenter order and authorship, Chris walked to Maggie's office to problem solve an issue. As he approached Maggie's door, Chris noticed Maggie ending a meeting with another faculty member. Chris sat down in the waiting area and overheard Maggie say, "I don't care whether it's committee meetings or faculty meetings, Chris means well but comes across as angry whenever he's giving a take on things. I think he is going to be great, but he has to learn to make points so people can receive them. And he has to earn everyone's respect first." Chris quickly left the building instead of meeting with Maggie. He felt incensed, devastated, and more confused than ever. He now worried about being able to remain composed when addressing these issues with Maggie.

Case Analysis and Discussion

Workplace bullying involves a person with more authority purposefully inflicting a pattern of unfavorable behaviors on a coworker who may have few options for addressing the bullying (Bartlett & Bartlett, 2011). Workplace bullying can be work related (e.g., assigning too much or too little work, assigning work that the person is overqualified to do, engaging in ethically questionable assessment of an employee's work or ability to progress in rank in the organization) or personal (e.g., being unresponsive with work correspondence, gossiping, being intimidating or threatening; Bartlett & Bartlett, 2011). Scholars have most often written about bullying that involves preventing the target from achieving success or progressing in their career (Keashly & Neuman, 2010). These factors were at work with Chris, who, as a new faculty member, was weary of asserting himself to end the work-related and personal workplace bullying he was experiencing.

In the U.S. Workplace Bullying Survey (Namie, 2017), nearly 1 in 5 people reported being bullied at work; 40% of these people said bullying had a negative influence on their health. Female, Black, and Latinx participants were more likely to report being bullied than male and white participants. Workplace bullying may be connected to posttraumatic stress and issues with mental and physical health, according to a meta-analysis of 54 studies (Nielsen & Einarsen, 2012).

Several variables in academia increase the risk for workplace bullying. The professoriate places a strong emphasis on faculty producing a high quantity and quality of scholarship and/or maintaining a high course load (Goodboy et al., 2019). Department chairs balance aiding faculty while safeguarding their independence (Goodboy et al., 2019). Independence is treasured in higher education but paradoxically can enable faculty to bully each other in an unchecked manner (Keashly & Neuman, 2010). Jealousy is a catalyst for bullying as educators vie for prestige within their department (Sedivy-Benton et al., 2015). One by-product of this is faculty omitting others from important decisions (Sedivy-Benton et al., 2015). In this case, Maggie was not reasonably collaborative in determining authorship and presenter order. Her behavior may have been spurred by her desire to attain the rank of full professor and her need to demonstrate leadership in conducting impactful scholarship (Goodboy et al., 2019). Maggie also tried to omit Chris from admissions discussions during the faculty meeting while speaking to him in an aggressive and demeaning manner.

The *ACA Code of Ethics* (American Counseling Association [ACA], 2014) offers additional insight into the workplace bullying Chris experienced. Maggie appears to have violated research ethics in not determining an appropriate order of authorship based on the amount of work Chris had committed to the research (Standard G.5.e.). Even if the order of authorship were correct, Chris was not given the opportunity to partake in a discussion of authorship with Maggie and the research team. This case also raises concerns regarding ethical responsibility to demonstrate cultural sensitivity in all roles as counselor educator (Standard F.11.c.). Faculty serve as powerful models for students in developing multicultural competence (A. W. Chan et al., 2015). Maggie's microaggression and implication that Chris was hired because he identified as Black, Indigenous, and people of color (BIPOC) raises questions regarding the cultural climate of the program for students and faculty.

Academia, Bullying, and Marginalization

Bullying within higher education can often be observed within the relationships of junior and senior faculty members and of tenured and untenured faculty members. By their very nature, these relationships establish a hierarchy of power within departments. Furthermore, these relationships can become problematic when senior, tenured faculty members are white and represent the dominant culture. According to the Council for Accreditation of Counseling and Related Educational Programs (CACREP; 2018), 71.38% of faculty members in CACREP-accredited programs identify as white.

Although these hierarchical relationships are powerful, there is evidence that the climate of the department is even more significant for BIPOC faculty members and relates to faculty satisfaction. Chris, who identified as Black, was having direct and indirect contentious interactions with Maggie, who was white and tenured with years of experience. This likely impacted the climate of the department and Chris's ability to thrive personally and professionally as he decided how to respond to Maggie's behaviors. The climate of a department greatly impacts feelings of satisfaction with the job (Holcomb-McCoy & Addison-Bradley, 2005).

During Chris's initial years in the department, there was some indication that going along to get along would be less stressful and time consuming than challenging senior faculty, yet doing so was simply intolerable for Chris. Chris recalled being told by mentors and his mother that the work of marginalized faculty members was not done when they got the job. Diggs et al. (2009) indicated numerous unintended barriers that impact the tenure process for tenure-track BIPOC faculty: sexism, racism, and marginalization. Faculty representing the BIPOC population tend to have numerous points of intersectionality that are not recognized or honored by their senior colleagues or the university at large. These areas of intersectionality include sexism (e.g., being a woman, a woman of color, a woman of color with a family, a woman of color who does not identify as a cisgender female). When sexism is coupled with systemic racism embedded within a department, social marginalization can exist (Diggs et al., 2009). The negative things Maggie said about Chris to other faculty members are examples of social marginalization at work.

The climate and barriers experienced by BIPOC faculty lead to feelings of dissatisfaction and are further connected to how junior untenured BIPOC faculty members respond to microaggressions experienced on a daily basis. This is evident in this case: Chris presented as eager to engage and be a productive member of the department but was met with microinsults and microassaults from a senior faculty member.

Oppression against BIPOC faculty members in higher education continues to show up in the forms of tokenism (Joseph & Hirshfield, 2013), challenges to one's positional role and research (Misawa, 2015), and microaggressions and discrimination (Eagan & Garvey, 2015; Louis et al., 2016). *Racial microaggressions* are "brief, commonplace, and subtle indignities (whether verbal, behavioral, or environmental) that communicate negative or denigrating messages to people of color" (Constantine et al., 2008, p. 349). Constantine et al. (2008) found a number of themes regarding how microaggressions gravely impact BIPOC faculty members: (a) having their qualifications challenged or questioned, (b) receiving little to no mentorship in the workplace, and (c) needing to develop coping strategies to address and deal with the microaggressions. These themes also apply to Chris's experiences with Maggie.

Prevention and Intervention

Faculty targets of bullying choose a variety of ways to manage the issue. Linvill and Connaughton (2019) identified emotion-focused (managing feelings) and problem-focused approaches. Social support was the mode of emotion-focused coping most frequently endorsed by targets in their qualitative study. Withdrawal was used by the majority of study participants. This entailed stepping down from the job or increasing the extent to which one bypassed the job site or the bully. Problem-focused coping involved broaching the issue with the perpetrator of the bullying, human resources, or leaders in the workplace. Problem-focused strategies also included invoking cognitive behavioral methods. Another study indicated that reporting the issue to department or university leadership, ignoring the bullying, imploring the bully to discontinue the behavior, reporting to human resources, and filing a "formal complaint" had negative implications for targets (Keashly & Neuman, 2013, p. 14). Conversely, disclosing to social supports, steering clear of the bully, seeking assistance from contemporaries, and "ask[ing] for transfer" had positive effects (Keashly & Neuman, 2013, p. 14). Chris seemed to use problem-focused coping in this case: He was undaunted by the incident during the faculty meeting and elected to engage in committee work with Maggie rather than steering clear of her.

Scholars of workplace bullying have proposed prevention and intervention strategies. C. King and Piotrowski (2015) purported that universities should develop and publicize policies underscoring the problem and consequences of bullying. They also advised providing objective resources external to one's department to which one can disclose bullying confidentially and using a panel to administer policy decisions. Department chairs and leaders are also charged with nurturing a workplace that is not conducive to bullying, "in which leadership and staff have collaboration and civility woven into performance standards" (Hollis, 2017, p. 66). In addition, universities and departments can train faculty and staff in conflict management and mediation skills they could use if bullying issues arise (Keashly & Neuman, 2010). Self-care and assertiveness skills are critical for targets of bullying (Dereshiwsky, 2020). Chris pondered taking an assertive response to Maggie by considering dialoguing with her about the bullying.

Recommendations

We recommend several steps for responding to workplace bullying and microaggressions. Seeking assistance from contemporaries can be helpful in cases of workplace bullying (Keashly & Neuman, 2013). Louis et al. (2016) further noted the importance of consulting with another colleague who also identifies as BIPOC; doing so may help Chris feel less isolated. Another option would be for Chris to speak with Maggie about his concerns. In doing so, Chris should use assertiveness skills to maximize the likelihood of a positive outcome from the dialogue with Maggie (Dereshiwsky, 2020).

If the bullying continues or the conversation in which Chris confronts Maggie is unsuccessful, Chris could inform the department leader regarding the bullying that has occurred and seek out university resources for filing complaints (Keashly & Neuman, 2010). The university ombudsperson is a confidential safeguard charged with helping faculty and staff understand options and navigate difficult situations. Chris may then assess whether the university and departmental response was satisfactory. To remain at the institution, Chris would likely need to enact coping skills (e.g., infusing wellness into his nonwork life; Linvill & Connaughton, 2019) and cull meaning from other aspects of work (Sedivy-Benton et al., 2015). Chris can also elect not to remain at the institution (Wieland & Beitz, 2015).

Mentoring is a resource for preventing or minimizing the effects of workplace bullying. Meaningful mentoring opportunities should help doctoral students prepare for academia and navigate any bullying that might occur. Counseling departments can provide continuity of mentorship through faculty-to-faculty mentoring programs (see Borders et al., 2011). Furthermore, the Workplace Bullying Institute (https://workplacebullying.org/) has numerous resources on bullying prevention and intervention that may be useful to counselor educators.

Conclusion

Faculty-on-faculty bullying in counselor education has not been frequently researched. However, workplace bullying can occur in counselor education as a result of the marginalization of faculty members (Diggs et al., 2009), a need to excel (Goodboy et al., 2019), jealousy (Sedivy-Benton et al., 2015), or independence in the undertakings of faculty members in academia (Keashly & Neuman, 2010). Counselor educators should work to pinpoint bullying, increase awareness of its hazards, and prevent and attend to these concerns.

Reflection Questions

1. How do you differentiate bullying and racism? Does this differentiation change your approach to the case?
2. What steps could you take to address or prevent bullying in your academic unit?

Critical Incident Response

Leigh Falls Holman

This case response encourages established faculty to provide welcoming environments, establish policies that support junior faculty, create mentoring structures, and intentionally seek out the voices of BIPOC faculty members in decision-making. These best practices are consistent with our stated mission as counselors and counselor educators. However, given that the misuse of structural power is both difficult to anticipate and common for BIPOC faculty members (Constantine et al., 2008), it is important for new faculty members to be proactive in establishing networks of supports to help them navigate such situations. As with any crisis situation, it is helpful to prepare prior to it happening so one can respond quickly and move toward a productive trajectory almost without thinking (James & Gilliland, 2020).

Navigating academic infrastructure is often challenging for newer faculty members. Establishing communication and support networks prior to feeling vulnerable as a result of a bullying incident will make reaching out to these networks easier if bullying occurs. Doing so can help faculty members feel they have some control in vulnerable situations involving microaggressions or the misuse of power. These networks can also help with accessing emotion-focused coping and problem-focused coping, as discussed in the case (Linvill & Connaughton, 2019).

Counselor education doctoral programs should integrate attention to methods for establishing mentoring relationships with more experienced faculty members, consistent with the 2016 CACREP Standards (CACREP, 2016). If they do, graduates will have supports before they enter the job market. This can be particularly helpful because there are ways to explore the possibility of bullying behavior prior to accepting a job, and experienced mentors can help new members of the professoriate evaluate them strategically. Doctoral advisers are often natural mentors for new graduates; however, there are other ways to build relationships in the counselor education community in larger universities. Once established, these networks can provide alternative methods of support.

One of the best ways to establish mentoring networks is through professional organizations. Specific divisions of ACA tend to draw large numbers of faculty members with similar lived experiences as minoritized people and professionals (e.g., the Association for Multicultural Counseling and Development; Counselors for Social Justice; the Society for Sexual, Affectional, Intersex, and Gender Expansive Identities; and the Association for Spiritual, Ethical, and Religious Values in Counseling). Although mentoring programs change over time, new professionals should inquire about mentorship programs within these organizations. Similarly, state and regional counseling organizations and Chi Sigma Iota have leadership and mentorship programs with strong multicultural emphases. Although mentors may work at different universities, situations such as bullying occur across universities, so they are likely to provide valid advice even if they are not familiar with a particular university. In some cases, an outsider's perspective may be helpful for understanding the concern.

One organization in which all doctoral candidates and new faculty members should participate is the Association for Counselor Education and Supervision. Specifically, the New Faculty Interest Network allows pretenure members to post anonymous questions about how to navigate a variety of situations in academia. Responding to bullying is one of the most powerful issues for which this group can provide support. Similarly, there are closed Facebook groups for faculty members (e.g., Academic Mamas*) in which individuals may find support. Finally, understanding the structure and culture of the university is important. Most universities have an ombudsperson. This may be one of the best people to connect with on campus. These individuals are among the most knowledgeable about junior faculty concerns, trends within departments and colleges, and potential bullying situations on a campus because they are often the final resort for faculty members. Although what they hear is confidential, ombudspersons are likely to provide wise advice to new faculty members, especially as those who engage in bullying often have a history of such behavior on campus. This makes ombudspersons well positioned to suggest specific actions or pathways to address the concern in context.

• • •

Resources

Websites

American Counseling Association: Government Affairs and Public Policy
www.counseling.org/PublicPolicy/

Center for Lobbying in the Public Interest
https://www.betterevaluation.org/en/resources/guides/Center_for_Lobbying_in_Public_Interest

CHANGE (Center for Health and Gender Equity)
www.genderhealth.org/

Chi Sigma Iota: Professional Advocacy
www.csi-net.org/advocacy

Congress.gov
https://www.congress.gov/

Mental Health Liaison Group
www.mhlg.org

National Alliance on Mental Illness
www.nami.org

National Research Mentoring Network: Research Mentor Training
https://nrmnet.net/

Printed Works

Daniel, H. J., Aponte, J., Chao, G., Cuevas, H., Locke, B., Matthews, J., & Koocher, G. (2006). *Introduction to mentoring: A guide for mentors and mentees*. American Psychological Association. https://www.apa.org/education/grad/mentoring

Helms, J. E. (2020). *A race is a nice thing to have: A guide to being a white person or understanding the white persons in your life* (3rd ed.). Cognella.

Matias, C. E. (2016). *Feeling white: Whiteness, emotionality, and education*. Sense.

Office of the Attorney General of Texas. (n.d.). *Public Information Act handbook 2018*. https://www.texasattorneygeneral.gov/sites/default/files/files/divisions/open-government/2018_Public-Information-Handbook.pdf

Saad, L. F. (2020). *Me and white supremacy: Combat racism, change the world, and become a good ancestor*. Sourcebooks.

Singleton, G. E. (2015). *Courageous conversations about race: A field guide for achieving equity in schools*. Corwin.

Storlie, C. A., Parker-Wright, M., & Woo, H. (2015). Multicultural leadership development: A qualitative analysis of emerging leaders in counselor education. *Journal of Counselor Leadership and Advocacy, 2*(2), 154–169. http://doi.org/gf4bzk

References

Aasheim, L. (2012). *Practical clinical supervision for counselors: An experiential guide.* Springer.

Abraham, P. (2000). Duplicate and salami publications. *Journal of Postgraduate Medicine, 46*(2), 67–69. www.jpgmonline.com/text.asp?2000/46/2/67/313

Abrica, E., & Martinez, E., Jr. (2016). Strategies for navigating financial challenges among Latino male community college students: Centralizing race, gender, and immigrant generation. *Journal of Applied Research in the Community College, 23*(2), 59–72.

Acuff, J. (2018). Confronting racial battle fatigue and comforting my blackness as an educator. *Multicultural Perspectives, 20*(3), 174–181. http://doi.org/dpcg

Adam, D. (2019, April 19). Universities grapple with student-faculty relationships. *The Scientist.* https://www.the-scientist.com/news-opinion/universities-grapple-with-student-faculty-relationships-65766

Adam Walsh Child Protection and Safety Act, H.R. 4472. (2006). https://www.justice.gov/archive/olp/pdf/adam_walsh_act.pdf

Agosto, V., Karanxha, Z., Unterreiner, A., Cobb-Roberts, D., Esnard, T., Wu, K., & Beck, M. (2016). Running bamboo: A mentoring network of women intending to thrive in academia. *NASPA Journal About Women in Higher Education, 9*(1), 74–89. https://doi.org/10.1080/19407882.2015.1124785

Ahmed, S. (2012). *On being included: Racism and diversity in institutional life.* Duke.

Albert, T., & Wager, E. (2003). *How to handle authorship disputes: A guide for new researchers.* Committee on Publication Ethics. http://doi.org/dp8m

Ali, S., & Lee, C. C. (2019). Using creativity to explore intersectionality in counseling. *Journal of Creativity in Mental Health, 14*(4), 510–518. https://doi.org/fdwc

Allan, E. (Ed.). (2011). Women's status in higher education: Equity matters [Special issue]. *ASHE Higher Education Report, 37*(1). http://doi.org/dhzzx8

Allen, L., O'Connell, A., & Kiermer, V. (2019). How can we ensure visibility and diversity in research contributions? How the contributor role taxonomy (CRediT) is helping the shift from authorship to contributorship. *Learned Publishing, 32*(1), 71–74. http://doi.org/gf4jjv

Alsamadani, H. A. (2011). The effects of the 3-2-1 reading strategy on EFL reading comprehension. *English Language Teaching, 4*(3), 184–191. http://doi.org/dtktbf

Alsubaie, M. A. (2015). Hidden curriculum as one of current issue of curriculum. *Journal of Education and Practice, 6*(33), 125–128. https://www.iiste.org/Journals/index.php/JEP/article/view/27376/28066

Alvarez, A. N., Liang, C. T. H., & Neville, H. A. (Eds.). (2016). *The cost of racism for people of color: Contextualizing experiences of discrimination*. American Psychological Association.

American Counseling Association. (n.d.). *Our vision and mission: ACA's strategic plan*. https://www.counseling.org/about-us/about-aca/our-mission

American Counseling Association. (2012). ACA graduate student committee launches mentorship initiative. *Counseling Today, 54*(9), 68–69.

American Counseling Association. (2014). *ACA code of ethics*. https://www.counseling.org/resources/aca-code-of-ethics.pdf

American Counseling Association. (2019, May). *ACA policy manual*. https://www.counseling.org/docs/default-source/governance/policy-manual---may-2019.pdf

American Psychological Association. (2015). *Publication practices and responsible authorship*. www.apa.org/research/responsible/publication/

American Psychological Association. (2020). *Publication manual of the American Psychological Association* (7th ed.).

American School Counselor Association. (2016a). *ASCA ethical standards for school counselors*. https://www.schoolcounselor.org/getmedia/f041cbd0-7004-47a5-ba01-3a5d657c6743/Ethical-Standards.pdf

American School Counselor Association. (2016b). *The school counselor and students with disabilities*. https://www.schoolcounselor.org/Standards-Positions/Position-Statements/ASCA-Position-Statements/The-School-Counselor-and-Students-with-Disabilitie

American School Counselor Association. (2019). *ASCA school counselor professional standards and competencies*. https://www.schoolcounselor.org/getmedia/a8d59c2c-51de-4ec3-a565-a3235f3b93c3/SC-Competencies.pdf

American School Counselor Association. (2020). *Eliminating racism and bias in schools: The school counselor's role*. https://www.schoolcounselor.org/getmedia/542b085a-7eda-48ba-906e-24cd3f08a03f/SIP-Racism-Bias.pdf

Ametrano, I. (2014). Teaching ethical decision making: Helping students reconcile personal and professional values. *Journal of Counseling & Development, 92*(2), 154–161. http://doi.org/dqqs

Ancis, J. R., & Marshall, D. S. (2010). Using a multicultural framework to assess supervisees' perceptions of culturally competent supervision. *Journal of Counseling & Development, 88*(3), 277–284. http://doi.org/fzfx7g

Anderson, S. (2020). *Audio visual aids in education*. Ed-Tech.

Arao, B., & Clemens, K. (2013). From safe spaces to brave spaces: A new way to frame dialogue around diversity and social justice. In L. M. Landreman (Ed.), *The art of effective facilitation: Reflections from social justice educators* (pp. 135–150). Stylus.

Aryan, B., & Guzman, F. (2010). Women of color and the PhD: Experiences in formal graduate support programs. *Journal of Business Studies Quarterly, 1*(4), 69–77. http://citeseerx.ist.psu.edu/viewdoc/download?doi=10.1.1.653.4311&rep=rep1&type=pdf

Association for Counselor Education and Supervision Taskforce. (2011). *Best practices in clinical supervision.* https://acesonline.net/wp-content/uploads/2018/11/ACES-Best-Practices-in-Clinical-Supervision-2011.pdf

Association for Counselor Education and Supervision Teaching Initiative Taskforce. (2016). *Best practices in teaching in counselor education.* https://acesonline.net/wp-content/uploads/2019/05/ACES-Teaching-Initiative-Taskforce-Final-Report-Oct-1-2016.pdf

Association for Spiritual, Ethical, and Religious Values in Counseling. (2009). *Competencies for addressing spiritual and religious issues in counseling.* https://www.counseling.org/docs/default-source/competencies/competencies-for-addressing-spiritual-and-religious-issues-in-counseling.pdf?sfvrsn=aad7c2c_8

Atieno Okech, J. E., & Geroski, A. M. (2015). Interdisciplinary training: Preparing counselors for collaborative practice. *The Professional Counselor, 5*(4), 458–472. https://doi.org/10.15241/jeo.5.4.458

Atkins, S. L., Fitzpatrick, M. R., Poolokasingham, G., Lebeau, M., & Spanierman, L. B. (2017). Make it personal: A qualitative investigation of white counselors' multicultural awareness development. *The Counseling Psychologist, 45*(5), 669–696. https://doi.org/10.1177/0011000017719458

Bahrick, A. S. (1990). *Role induction for counselor trainees: Effects on the supervisory working alliance* [Doctoral dissertation, The Ohio State University]. OhioLINK. https://etd.ohiolink.edu/apexprod/rws_olink/r/1501/10?clear=10&p10_accession_num=osu1217871239

Bain, K. (2004). *What the best college teachers do.* Harvard University Press.

Baker, C. A., Gaulke, K., & Smith, K. (2015). Counselor education cultural climate: Underrepresented master's students' experiences. *Journal for Multicultural Education, 9*(2), 68–84. http://doi.org/dnfc

Baker, D. F. (2017). Teaching empathy and ethical decision making in business schools. *Journal of Management Education, 41*(4), 575–598. http://doi.org/dwvn

Baltrinic, E. R., Moate, R. M., Hinkle, M. G., Jencius, M., & Taylor, J. Z. (2018). Counselor educators' teaching mentorship styles: A Q methodology study. *The Professional Counselor, 8*(1), 46–59. http://doi.org/dqt5

Barbeau, P., & Mahfood, S. (2012). Considering human and spiritual formation in distance learning: A question of relationality. *Colloquy, 20*(2), 33–35.

Barden, S. M., Sherrell, R. S., & Matthews, J. J. (2017). A national survey on multicultural competence for professional counselors: A replication study. *Journal of Counseling & Development, 95*(2), 203–212. http://doi.org/dtjb

Barreto, A. (2012). Counseling for the training of leaders and leadership development: A commentary. *The Professional Counselor, 2*(3), 226–234. http://doi.org/dxhh

Bartlett, J. E., & Bartlett, M. E. (2011). Workplace bullying: An integrative literature review. *Advances in Developing Human Resources, 13*(1), 69–84. http://doi.org/dsfk7f

Baum, N. (2016). Therapist self-care to mitigate secondary traumatization. In S. Maltzman (Ed.), *Oxford handbook of treatment processes* (pp. 136–145). Oxford University Press.

Bell, D. A. (2016). Who's afraid of critical race theory? In E. Taylor, D. Gillborn, & G. Ladson-Billings (Eds.), *Foundations of critical race theory in education* (2nd ed., pp. 31–42). Routledge.

Bellas, M. L., & Gossett, J. L. (2001). Love or the "lecherous professor": Consensual sexual relationships between professors and students. *Sociological Quarterly, 42*(4), 529–558. https://doi.org/fr5x98

Benishek, L. A., Bieschke, K. J., Park, J., & Slattery, S. M. (2004). A multicultural feminist model of mentoring. *Journal of Multicultural Counseling and Development, 32*(extra), 428–442.

Berdrow, I. (2010). King among kings: Understanding the role and responsibilities of the department chair in higher education. *Educational Management Administration & Leadership, 38*(4), 499–514. https://doi.org/10.1177/174114321036814

Berger, R., & Quiros, L. (2014). Supervision for trauma-informed practice. *Traumatology, 20*(4), 296–304. https://doi.org/fgtt

Bernard, J. M. (1979). Supervisor training: A discrimination model. *Counselor Education and Supervision, 19*(1), 60–68. http://doi.org/fx2vdc

Bernard, J. M., & Goodyear, R. K. (2019). *Fundamentals of clinical supervision* (6th ed.). Pearson.

Berry, J. W. (2003). Conceptual approaches to acculturation. In K. M. Chun, P. Balls Organista, & G. Marín (Eds.), *Acculturation: Advances in theory, measurement, and applied research* (pp. 17–37). American Psychological Association. https://doi.org/10.1037/10472-004

Bloch, S., Reibstein, J., Crouch, E., Holroyd, P., & Themen, J. (1979). A method for the study of therapeutic factors in group psychotherapy. *British Journal of Psychiatry, 134*(3), 257–263. http://doi.org/fvjj56

Blume-Marcovici, A. C., Stolberg, R. A., & Khademi, M. (2013). Do therapists cry in therapy? The role of experience and other factors in therapists' tears. *Psychotherapy: Theory, Research, Practice, Training, 50*(2), 224–234. http://doi.org/f425vm

Blume-Marcovici, A. C., Stolberg, R. A., & Khademi, M. (2015). Examining tears: Therapists' accounts of crying in therapy. *American Journal of Psychotherapy, 69*(4), 399–421. http://doi.org/drhw

Bonilla-Silva, E. (2018). *Racism without racists: Color-blind racism and the persistence of racial inequality in America* (5th ed.). Rowman & Littlefield.

Borders, L. D., & Brown, L. L. (2005). *The new handbook of counseling supervision*. Routledge.

Borders, L. D., Glosoff, H. L., Welfare, L. E., Hays, D. G., DeKruyf, L., Fernando, D. M., & Page, B. (2014). Best practices in clinical supervision: Evolution of a counseling specialty. *The Clinical Supervisor, 33*(1), 26–44. http://doi.org/dn6r

Borders, L., Gonzalez, L., Umstead, L., & Wester, K. (2019). New counselor educators' scholarly productivity: Supportive and discouraging environments. *Counselor Education and Supervision, 58*(4), 293–308. http://doi.org/dn9s

Borders, L. D., Wester, K. L., Granello, D. H., Chang, C. Y., Hays, D. G., Pepperell, J., & Spurgeon, S. L. (2012). Association for Counselor Education and Supervision guidelines for research mentorship: Development and implementation. *Counselor Education and Supervision, 51*(3), 162–175. http://doi.org/ggfqhn

Borders, L. D., Young, J. S., Wester, K. L., Murray, C. E., Villalba, J. A., Lewis, T. F., & Mobley, K. (2011). Mentoring promotion/tenure-seeking faculty: Principles of good practice within a counselor education program. *Counselor Education and Supervision, 50*(3), 171–188. http://doi.org/fxqkk3

Boswell, J. N., Wilson, A. D., Stark, M. D., & Onwuegbuzie, A. J. (2015). The role of mentoring relationships in counseling programs. *International Journal of Mentoring and Coaching in Education, 4*(3), 168–183. https://doi.org/10.1108/IJMCE-03-2015-0007

Bradley, C., & Holcomb-McCoy, C. (2011). African American counselor educators: Their experiences, challenges, and recommendations. *Counselor Education and Supervision, 43*(4), 258–273. http://doi.org/fxq99d

Brat, M., O'Hara, C., McGhee, C. M., & Chang, C. Y. (2016). Promoting professional counselor advocacy through professional identity development efforts in counselor education. *Journal of Counselor Leadership and Advocacy, 3*(1), 62–70. http://doi.org/gf4b2k

Brezinski, K. J., Laux, J., Roseman, C., O'Hara, C., & Gore, S. (2018). Undergraduate African-American student's experience of racial microaggressions on a primarily white campus. *Journal for Multicultural Education, 12*(3), 267–277. https://doi.org/10.1108/JME-06-2017-0035

Broderick, N. A., & Casadevall, A. (2019, January 30). Meta-research: Gender inequalities among authors who contributed equally. *eLife, 8*, e36399. https://doi.org/fdtr

Broome, M. E. (2018). The manuscript option dissertation: Dissemination and challenges. *Nurse Author & Editor, 28*(1), 1–10. https://doi.org/10.1111/j.1750-4910.2018.tb00007.x

Brown, B. (2010). *The gifts of imperfection: Let go of who you think you're supposed to be and embrace who you are*. Hazelden.

Brown, E. M., & Grothaus, T. (2019). Experiences of cross-racial trust in mentoring relationships between Black doctoral counseling students and white counselor educators and supervisors. *The Professional Counselor, 9*(3), 211–225. http://doi.org/dqt6

Bryan, S. E. (2018). Types of LGBT microaggressions in counselor education programs. *Journal of LGBT Issues in Counseling, 12*(2), 119–135. http://doi.org/dmn8

Burns, S. T. (2015). Perspectives on membership in a state counseling association. *Journal of Counselor Leadership and Advocacy, 2*(1), 29–50. http://doi.org/gf4bzr

Burns, S. T. (2019). Students' ethical decision-making when considering boundary crossings with counselor educators. *Counseling and Values, 64*(1), 53–71. https://doi.org/10.1002/cvj.12115

Burt, I., Gonzalez, T., Swank, J., & Ascher, D. L. (2011). Addressing the technology gap in counselor education: Identification of characteristics in students that affect learning in college classrooms. *The Journal of Counselor Preparation and Supervision, 3*(1), 18–33. http://doi.org/dth7

Butler, S. K., Evans, M. P., Brooks, M., Williams, C. R., & Bailey, D. F. (2013). Mentoring African American men during their postsecondary and graduate school experiences: Implications for the counseling profession. *Journal of Counseling & Development, 91*(4), 419–427. https://doi.org/10.1002/j.1556-6676.2013.00113.x

Butz, A. R., Spencer, K., Thayer-Hart, N., Cabrera, I. E., & Byars-Winston, A. (2019). Mentors' motivation to address race/ethnicity in research mentoring relationships. *Journal of Diversity in Higher Education, 12*(3), 242–254. http://doi.org/dqt7

Byars-Winston, A., Womack, V. Y., Butz, A. R., McGee, R., Quinn, S. C., Utzerath, E., Saetermoe, C. L., & Thomas, S. (2018). Pilot study of an intervention to increase cultural awareness in research mentoring: Implications for diversifying the scientific workforce. *Journal of Clinical and Translational Science, 2*(2), 86–94. http://doi.org/dqt8

Caldwell, M. (2010). Study characteristics and recidivism base rates in juvenile sex offender recidivism. *International Journal of Offender Therapy & Comparative Criminology*, *54*(2), 194–212. http://doi.org/b48hkb

Calley, N. G. (2008). Juvenile sex offenders and sex offender legislation: Unintended consequences. *Federal Probation*, *72*(3), 37–41. https://www.uscourts.gov/sites/default/files/72_3_5_0.pdf

Cannon, Y., Haiyasoso, M., & Tello, A. (2019). Relational aspects in research mentoring of women doctoral counseling students. *Journal of Creativity in Mental Health*, *15*(3), 1–14. https://doi.org/10.1080/15401383.2019.1689213

Carter, S., Blumenstein, M., & Cook, C. (2013). Different for women? The challenges of doctoral studies. *Teaching in Higher Education*, *18*(4), 339–351. http://doi.org/dxhp

Cartwright, A. D., Avent-Harris, J. R., Munsey, R. B., & Lloyd-Hazlett, J. (2018). Interview experiences and diversity concerns of counselor education faculty from underrepresented groups. *Counselor Education and Supervision*, *57*(2), 132–146. https://doi.org/10.1002/ceas.12098

Caruso, R., Bowen, G., & Adams-Dunford, J. (2006). Student affairs and service learning: Promoting student engagement. *College Student Affairs Journal*, *25*(2), 186–198.

Casado Pérez, J. F. (2019). Everyday resistance strategies by minoritized faculty. *Journal of Diversity in Higher Education*, *12*(2), 170–179. https://doi.org/10.1037/dhe0000090

Cashwell, C. S., & Barrio Minton, C. A. (2012). Leadership and advocacy in counselor education programs: Administration and culture. In C. Y. Chang, C. A. Barrio Minton, A. L. Dixon, J. E. Myers, & T. J. Sweeney (Eds.), *Professional counseling excellence through leadership and advocacy* (pp. 165–184). Taylor & Francis.

Cavazos Vela, J. (2020). *Teaching and learning in counselor education*. American Counseling Association.

Center for Substance Abuse Treatment. (2009). *TIP 52: Clinical supervision and professional development of the substance abuse counselor* (HHS Publication No. [SMA] 14-4435). Substance Abuse and Mental Health Services Administration.

Center for the Treatment and Study of Anxiety. (n.d.). *PE certification requirements*. https://www.med.upenn.edu/ctsa/certification_requirements.html

Centers for Disease Control and Prevention. (2020, March 2). *The Tuskegee timeline*. https://www.cdc.gov/tuskegee/timeline.htm

Cerny, M. S. (1995). Treating the "heroic treater." In C. R. Figley (Ed.), *Compassion fatigue: Coping with secondary traumatic stress disorder in those who treat the traumatized* (pp. 131–149). Brunner/Mazel.

Chan, A. W., Yeh, C. J., & Krumboltz, J. D. (2015). Mentoring ethnic minority counseling and clinical psychology students: A multicultural, ecological, and relational model. *Journal of Counseling Psychology*, *62*(4), 592–607. http://doi.org/f7vmcr

Chan, C. D., Cor, D. N., & Band, M. P. (2018). Privilege and oppression in counselor education: An intersectionality framework. *Journal of Multicultural Counseling and Development*, *46*(1), 58–73. https://doi.org/10.1002/jmcd.12092

Chan, Y. (2019). *Best practices in addressing diversity in clinical supervision: A survey of experienced supervisors* [Unpublished doctoral dissertation]. Pepperdine University.

Chao, R. C.-L., Wei, M., Good, G. E., & Flores, L. Y. (2011). Race/ethnicity, color-blind racial attitudes, and multicultural counseling competence: The moderating effects of multicultural counseling training. *Journal of Counseling Psychology, 58*(1), 72–82. http://doi.org/fc5ssd

Chapman, C., Laird, J., Ifill, N., & KewalRamani, A. (2010). *Trends in high school dropout and completion rates in the United States: 1972–2009* (NCES 2012-006). National Center for Education Statistics.

Chi Sigma Iota Academy of Leaders. (1999). *Principles and practices of leadership excellence.* www.csi-net.org/?Leadership_Practices

Cholewa, B., Burkhardt, C. K., & Hull, M. F. (2018). Are school counselors impacting underrepresented students' thinking about postsecondary education? A nationally representative study. *Professional School Counseling, 19*(1), 144–154. https://doi.org/fgt2

Chun, E., & Evans, A. (2016). Rethinking cultural competence in higher education: An ecological framework for student development. *ASHE Higher Education Report, 42*(4), 7–162. http://doi.org/dpch

Chung, R. C. Y., Bemak, F., & Talleyrand, R. M. (2007, March). Mentoring within the field of counseling: A preliminary study of multicultural perspectives. *International Journal for the Advancement of Counselling, 29,* 21–32. http://doi.org/cdptcf

CNA & Healthcare Providers Service Organization. (2019). *Counselor liability claim report: 2nd edition: Minimizing risk, achieving excellence.* www.hpso.com/Documents/Risk%20Education/individuals/Claim-Reports/Counselor/HPSO-CNA-Counselor-Claim-Report-2019.pdf

Cockrell, C., & Shelley, K. (2011). The relationship between academic support systems and intended persistence in doctoral education. *Journal of College Student Retention, 12*(4), 469–484. http://doi.org/fsdrzg

Collier, L. (2016). Is it ok to cry? *gradPSYCH, 14*(1), 38. https://www.apa.org/gradpsych/2016/01/therapy-tears

Committee on Publication Ethics. (2020). *Redundant publication.* https://publicationethics.org/category/keywords/redundant-publication

Constantine, M. G., Smith, L., Redington, R. M., & Owens, D. (2008). Racial microaggressions against Black counseling and counseling psychology faculty: A central challenge in the multicultural counseling movement. *Journal of Counseling & Development, 86*(3), 348–355. http://doi.org/fxsqbk

Cook, R. M., Welfare, L. E., & Romero, D. E. (2018). Counselor-in-training intentional non-disclosure in onsite supervision: A content analysis. *The Professional Counselor, 8*(2), 115–130. http://doi.org/dsv3

Corey, G., Corey, M. S., & Corey, C. (2019). *Issues and ethics in the helping professions* (10th ed.). Cengage Learning.

Corse, B. (2011). Internationalization of the higher education classroom: Strategies to facilitate intercultural learning and academic success. *International Journal of Teaching and Learning in Higher Education, 23*(3), 388–395. www.isetl.org/ijtlhe/pdf/IJTLHE1056.pdf

Costner, K. L., Daniels, K., & Clark, M. T. (2010). The struggle will not continue: An examination of faculty attitudes toward teaching African American students. *Journal of Black Studies, 41*(1), 40–55. http://doi.org/dvtxb9

Council for Accreditation of Counseling and Related Educational Programs. (2016). *2016 CACREP standards.* http://www.cacrep.org/for-programs/2016-cacrep-standards/

Council for Accreditation of Counseling and Related Educational Programs. (2018). *CACREP vital statistics 2017: Results from a national survey of accredited programs.* www.cacrep.org/wp-content/uploads/2019/05/2017-CACREP-Vital-Statistics-Report.pdf

Cozby, P. C., & Bates, S. C. (2015). *Methods in behavioral research* (12th ed.). McGraw-Hill.

Cranton, P. (2016). *Understanding and promoting transformative learning: A guide to theory and practice* (3rd ed.). Stylus.

Crenshaw, K. W. (1989). Demarginalizing the intersection of race and sex: A Black feminist critique of antidiscrimination doctrine, feminist theory and antiracist politics. *University of Chicago Legal Forum, 1989*(1), 139–167. https://chicagounbound.uchicago.edu/uclf/vol1989/iss1/8

Creswell, J. W., & Poth, C. N. (2018). *Qualitative inquiry and research design: Choosing among five approaches* (4th ed.). Sage.

Cross, W. E., Jr. (1991). *Shades of Black: Diversity in African American identity*. Temple University Press.

Dancy, T. E., II, & Gaetane, J. M. (2014). Faculty of color in higher education: Exploring the intersections of identity, impostorship, and internalized racism. *Mentoring & Tutoring: Partnership in Learning, 22*(4), 354–372. http://doi.org/dsqj

Darby, F. (2019, April 17). How to be a better online teacher: Advice guide. *The Chronicle of Higher Education.* https://www.chronicle.com/interactives/advice-online-teaching

Darvin, J. (2018). Becoming a more culturally responsive teacher by identifying and reducing microaggressions in classrooms and school communities. *Journal for Multicultural Education, 12*(1), 2–9. https://doi.org/10.1108/JME-03-2017-0020

Davis, L., & Fry, R. (2019, July 31). *College faculty have become more racially and ethnically diverse, but remain far less so than students*. Pew Research Center. https://www.pewresearch.org/fact-tank/2019/07/31/us-college-faculty-student-diversity/

Day-Vines, N. L., Booker Ammah, B., Steen, S., & Arnold, K. M. (2018). Getting comfortable with discomfort: Preparing counselor trainees to broach racial, ethnic, and cultural factors with clients during counseling. *International Journal for the Advancement of Counselling, 40*(2), 89–104. http://doi.org/dpdq

Day-Vines, N. L., Cluxton-Keller, F., Agorsor, C., Gubara, S., & Otabil, N. A. A. (2020). The multidimensional model of broaching behavior. *Journal of Counseling & Development, 98*(1), 107–118. https://doi.org/10.1002/jcad.12304

de Beurs, E., Warmerdam, L., & Twisk, J. (2018). Bias through selective inclusion and attrition: Representativeness when comparing provider performance with routine outcome monitoring data. *Clinical Psychology and Psychotherapy, 26*(4), 430–439. https://doi.org/fdsm

De Jong, M., Moser, D., & Hall, L. (2005). The manuscript option dissertation: Multiple perspectives. *Nurse Author & Editor, 15*(3), 3–4. https://doi.org/fd74

De Stefano, J., Hutman, H., & Gazzola, N. (2017). Putting on the face: A qualitative study of power dynamics in clinical supervision. *The Clinical Supervisor, 36*(2), 223–240. https://doi.org/gf2jxz

Decker, K. M., Manis, A. A., & Paylo, M. J. (2016). Infusing social justice advocacy into counselor education: Strategies and recommendations. *The Journal of Counselor Preparation and Supervision, 8*(3), Article 1. http://dx.doi.org/10.7729/83.1092

Degges, W. S. E., Colon, B. R., & Borzumato, G. C. (2013). Counseling supervision within a feminist framework: Guidelines for intervention. *The Journal of Humanistic Counseling, 52*(1), 92–105. http://doi.org/dn7h

Delgado Bernal, D., & Villalpando, O. (2016). An apartheid of knowledge in academia: The struggle over the "legitimate" knowledge of faculty of color. In E. Taylor, D. Gillborn, & G. Ladson-Billings (Eds.), *Foundations of critical race theory in education* (2nd ed., pp. 77–92). Routledge.

Denison, D. R., Hooijberg, R., & Quinn, R. E. (1995). Paradox and performance: Toward a theory of behavioral complexity in managerial leadership. *Organization Science, 6*(5), 509–601. https://doi.org/10.1287/orsc.6.5.524

Dereshiwsky, M. I. (2020). Bullying and harassment of faculty in higher education. In R. Papa (Ed.), *Handbook on promoting social justice in education* (pp. 1209–1227). Springer.

DeRicco, J. N., & Sciarra, D. T. (2005). The immersion experience in multicultural counselor training: Confronting covert racism. *Journal of Multicultural Counseling and Development, 33*(1), 2–16. http://doi.org/fzms6r

DiAngelo, R. (2018). *White fragility: Why it's so hard for white people to talk about racism.* Beacon Press.

Dietlin, O., Loomis, J., & Preffer, J. (2019). Pedagogy of authenticity in the online learning environment: An interdisciplinary overview. In L. Kyei-Blankson, J. Blankson, & E. Ntuli (Eds.), *Care and culturally responsive pedagogy in online settings* (pp. 214–229). IGI Global.

Diggs, G. A., Garrison-Wade, D., Estrada, D., & Galindo, R. (2009). Smiling faces and colored spaces: The experiences of faculty of color pursuing tenure in the academy. *The Urban Review, 41*(4), 312–333. http://doi.org/dm6jtg

Doharty, N. (2019). "I felt dead": Applying a racial microaggressions framework to Black students' experiences of Black History Month and Black history. *Race, Ethnicity & Education, 22*(1), 110–129. https://doi.org/10.1080/13613324.2017.1417253

Dollarhide, C. T., Berendts, A. M., Gibbs, T. A., Gorby, S. R., & Oehrtman, J. P. (2018). Counselor education from a postmodern perspective: Empowering students. In M. B. Scholl & J. T. Hanson (Eds.), *Postmodern perspectives on contemporary counseling issues: Approaches across diverse settings* (pp. 287–309). Oxford University Press.

Dotson, K. (2012). A cautionary tale: On limiting epistemic oppression. *Frontier, 33*(1), 24–47. http://doi.org/gf9f8k

Douglas, B. D., McGorray, E. L., & Ewell, P. J. (2020). Some researchers wear yellow pants, but even fewer participants read consent forms: Exploring and improving consent form reading in human subjects research. *Psychological Methods*. Advance online publication. https://doi.org/fdsn

Dow, G. (2015). Do cheaters never prosper? The impact of examples, expertise, and cognitive load on cryptomnesia and inadvertent self-plagiarism of creative tasks. *Creativity Research Journal, 27*(1), 47–57. https://doi.org/10.1080/10400419.2015.992679

Drucker, P. (1990). *Managing the non-profit organization: Practices and principles.* Routledge.

Drucker, P. (2008). *The five most important questions you will ever ask about your organization*. Wiley.

Duan, C., & Brown, C. (2016). *Becoming a multiculturally competent counselor*. Sage.

Duffey, T., Haberstroh, S., & Vecchio-Scully, D. D. (2020). Responding to community violence and community trauma. In T. Duffey & S. Haberstroh (Eds.), *Introduction to crisis and trauma counseling* (pp. 227–246). American Counseling Association.

Dworkin, S. H., & Pope, M. (Eds.). (2012). *Casebook for counseling lesbian, gay, bisexual, and transgender persons and their families*. American Counseling Association.

Eagan, M. K., Jr., & Garvey, J. C. (2015). Stressing out: Connecting race, gender, and stress with faculty productivity. *The Journal of Higher Education, 86*(6), 926–954. http://doi.org/dpcb

The Education Trust. (2019). *School counselors matter*. https://edtrustmain.s3.us-east-2.amazonaws.com/wp-content/uploads/2019/01/30161630/School-Counselors-Matter.pdf

Eggert, L. D. (2011). Best practices for allocating appropriate credit and responsibility to authors of multi-authored articles. *Frontiers in Psychology, 2*, 196. http://doi.org/bshjxs

18 U.S.C. 2241 - aggravated sexual abuse. (2011). https://www.govinfo.gov/app/details/USCODE-2011-title18/USCODE-2011-title18-partI-chap109A-sec2241

Ellis, M. V. (2006). Critical incidents in clinical supervision and in supervisor supervision: Assessing supervisory issues. *Training and Education in Professional Psychology, S*(2), 122–132. http://doi.org/fc8t53

Else-Quest, N. M., & Hyde, J. S. (2016). Intersectionality in quantitative psychological research: I. Theoretical and epistemological issues. *Psychology of Women Quarterly, 40*(2), 155–170. http://doi.org/f8qmmf

Equal Employment Opportunity Commission. (2008). *ADA Amendments Act of 2008*. https://www.eeoc.gov/statutes/ada-amendments-act-2008

Esnard, T., Cobb-Roberts, D., Agosto, V., Karanxha, Z., Beck, M., Wu, K., & Unterreiner, A. (2015). Productive tensions in a cross-cultural peer mentoring women's network: A social capital perspective. *Mentoring & Tutoring: Partnership in Learning, 23*(1), 19–36. https://doi.org/10.1080/13611267.2015.1011035

Estrada, F., & Rigali-Oiler, M. (2016). Interest in the teaching alliance and its associations with multicultural counseling education among a sample of students in the United States. *International Journal for the Advancement of Counselling, 38*(3), 204–217. http://doi.org/dthm

Eva, K. W. (2017). How would you like your salami? A guide to slicing. *Medical Education, 51*(5), 456–457. https://doi.org/fg8f

Evans, A. M., Levitt, D. H., & Henning, S. (2013). The application of ethical decision-making and self-awareness in the counselor education classroom. *The Journal of Counselor Preparation and Supervision, 4*(2), 39–48.

Fallon, K. M., Dobmeier, R. A., Reiner, S. M., Casquarelli, E. J., Giglia, L. A., & Goodwin, E. (2013). Reconciling spiritual values conflicts for counselors and lesbian and gay clients. *Adultspan Journal, 12*(1), 38–53. http://doi.org/dqqv

Farrell, I. C., & Barrio Minton, C. A. (2019). Advocacy among counseling leaders: The three-tiered legislative professional advocacy model. *Journal of Counselor Leadership and Advocacy, 6*(2), 144–159. http://doi.org/dqvf

Fassinger, R. E., & Schullman, S. L. (2017). Leadership and counseling psychology: What should we know? Where could we go? *The Counseling Psychologist, 45*(7), 927–964. http://doi.org/gcp8q7

Felder, P. (2010). On doctoral student development: Exploring faculty mentoring in the shaping of African American doctoral student success. *Qualitative Report, 15*(2), 455–474. www.nova.edu/ssss/QR/QR15-2/felder.pdf

Fickling, M. J., Tangen, J. L., Graden, M. W., & Grays, D. (2019). Multicultural and social justice competence in clinical supervision. *Counselor Education and Supervision, 58*(4), 309–316. https://doi.org/fdv2

Fisher, C. B. (1997). A relational perspective on ethics-in-science decision-making for research with vulnerable populations. *IRB: Ethics & Human Research, 19*(5), 1–4. https://doi.org/ftzzv3

Flamez, B., Lenz, A. S., Balkin, R. S., & Smith, R. L. (2017). *A counselor's guide to the dissertation process: Where to start and how to finish*. American Counseling Association.

Flores Niemann, Y. (2016). The social ecology of tokenism in higher education. *Peace Review, 28*(4), 451–458. http://doi.org/dqb9

Follins, L. D., Paler, L. K., & Nanin, J. E. (2015). Creating and implementing a faculty interest group for historically underrepresented faculty. *Community College Journal of Research and Practice, 39*(9), 839–851. https://doi.org/10.1080.10668926.2014.917595

Forester-Miller, H., & Davis, T. E. (2016). *Practitioner's guide to ethical decision making*. American Counseling Association.

Foster, J. M., Leppma, M., & Hutchinson, T. S. (2014). Students' perspectives on gatekeeping in counselor education: A case study. *Counselor Education and Supervision, 53*(3), 190–203. http://doi.org/dq5r

Foster, R., & Ray, D. (2012). An ethical decision-making model to determine authorship credit in published faculty–student collaborations. *Counseling and Values, 57*(2), 214–228. http://doi.org/ggm3rv

Fountaine, T. P. (2012). The impact of faculty-student interaction on Black doctoral students attending historically Black institutions. *The Journal of Negro Education, 81*(2), 136–147.

Fox, M., & Beall, J. (2014). Advice for plagiarism whistleblowers. *Ethics & Behavior, 24*(5), 341–349. http://doi.org/dn96

Freeman, S., Jr. (2018). The manuscript dissertation: A means of increasing competitive edge for tenure-track faculty positions. *International Journal of Doctoral Studies, 13*, 273–292. https://doi.org/fd75

Freire, P. (1970). *Pedagogy of the oppressed*. Continuum.

Fuller, R. G. (2012). Building empathy in online courses: Effective practical approaches. *International Journal of Information and Communication Technology Education, 8*(4), 38–49. http://doi.org/dthf

Gannon, K. (2019, September 2). Teaching online will make you a better teacher in any setting. *The Chronicle of Higher Education*. https://www.chronicle.com/article/Teaching-Online-Will-Make-You/247031

Gardner, S. K., & Barnes, B. J. (2007). Graduate student involvement: Socialization for the professional role. *Journal of College Student Development, 48*(4), 369–387. https://doi.org/frb7vh

Garrett, M. T., Borders, D. L., Crutchfield, L. B., Torres-Rivera, E., Brotherton, D., & Curtis, R. (2001). Multicultural superVISION: A paradigm of cultural responsiveness for supervisors. *Journal of Multicultural Counseling and Development, 29*(2), 147–158. http://doi.org/fzzqsc

Gatmon, D., Jackson, D., Koshkarian, L., Martos-Perry, N., Molina, A., Patel, N., & Rodolfa, E. (2011). Exploring ethnic, gender, and sexual orientation variables in supervision: Do they really matter? *Journal of Multicultural Counseling and Development, 29*(2), 102–113. http://doi.org/fx34bh

Gaughan, M., & Bozeman, B. (2016). Using the prisms of gender and rank to interpret research collaboration power dynamics. *Social Studies of Science, 46*(4), 536–558. http://doi.org/gbzp76

Gentry, E. (2016). *Forward facing trauma therapy: Healing the moral wound*. Compassion Unlimited.

George, M., Lim, H., Lucas, S., & Meadows, R. (2015). Learning by doing: Experiential learning in criminal justice. *Journal of Criminal Justice Education, 26*(4), 471–492. http://doi.org/d47v

Gerdes, C. (2004). The case for university consensual relationship policies. *Wayne Law Review, 49*(4), 1031–1050.

Gibson, D. M., Dollarhide, C. T., & McCallum, L. J. (2010). Nontenured assistant professors as American Counseling Association division presidents: The new look of leadership in counseling. *Journal of Counseling & Development, 88*(3), 285–292. http://doi.org/tztjcd

Gibson, D. M., Dollarhide, C. T., & Moss, J. M. (2010). Professional identity development: A grounded theory of transformational tasks of new counselors. *Counselor Education and Supervision, 50*(1), 21–36. http://doi.org/fx5zx7

Giordano, A. L., Schmit, M. K., & Schmit, E. L. (2021). Best practice guidelines for publishing rigorous research in counseling. *Journal of Counseling & Development, 99*(2), 123–133. https://doi.org/10.1002/jcad.12360

Gnilka, P. B., O'Hara, C., & Chang, C. Y. (2018). Social justice counseling. In D. G. Hays & B. T. Erford (Eds.), *Developing multicultural counseling competence: A systems approach* (3rd ed., pp. 66–91). Pearson.

Gomez-Arostegui, H. T. (2008). What history teaches us about copyright injunctions and the inadequate-remedy-at-law requirement. *Southern California Law Review, 81*, 1197–1281. https://ssrn.com/abstract=1101974

Goodboy, A. K., Martin, M. M., Mills, C. B., & Clark-Gordon, C. V. (2019). Bullying in academia among college professors. In R. West & C. S. Beck (Eds.), *The Routledge handbook of communication and bullying* (pp. 155–163). Routledge.

Goodstein, D. (2011). How science works. In National Research Council (Ed.), *Reference manual on scientific evidence* (3rd ed., pp. 37–54). National Academies Press. http://doi.org/dtzh

Grant, J., Schofield, M. J., & Crawford, S. (2012). Managing difficulties in supervision: Supervisors' perspectives. *Journal of Counseling Psychology, 59*(4), 528–541. http://doi.org/f4cp3g

Grassie, W. (2010). *The new sciences of religion: Exploring spirituality from the outside in and bottom up*. Palgrave Macmillan.

Greene, J. H., Braden, S. M., Richardson, E. D., & Hall, K. G. (2014). The influence of film and experiential pedagogy on multicultural self-efficacy and multicultural counseling competencies. *Journal of the Scholarship of Teaching and Learning, 14*(5), 63–78. https://doi.org/fcq4

Greenleaf, R. K. (1970). *The servant as leader*. Greenleaf Center for Servant Leadership.

Greenleaf, R. K. (1977). *Servant leadership: A journey into the nature of legitimate power and greatness*. Paulist Press.

Griffin, K. A., Pérez, D., Holmes, A. P. E., & Mayo, C. E. P. (2010). Investing in the future: The importance of faculty mentoring in the development of students of color in STEM. *New Directions for Institutional Research, 148*, 95–103. https://doi.org/10.1002/ir.365

Guth, L. J., Nitza, A., Pollard, B., Puig, A., Chan, C. D., Singh, A., & Bailey, H. (2019). Ten strategies to intentionally use group work to transform hate, facilitate courageous conversations, and enhance community building. *The Journal for Specialists in Group Work, 44*(1), 3–24. https://doi.org/10.1080/01933922.2018.1561778

Hagler, M. A. (2020). LGBQ-affirming and -nonaffirming supervision: Perspectives from a queer trainee. *Journal of Psychotherapy Integration, 30*(1), 76–83. https://doi.org/10.1037/int0000165

Halpert, S. C., Reinhardt, B., & Toohey, M. J. (2007). Affirmative clinical supervision. In K. J. Bieschke, R. M. Perez, & K. A. DeBord (Eds.), *Handbook of counseling and psychotherapy with lesbian, gay, bisexual, and transgender*. American Psychological Association.

Handelsman, M. M., Gottlieb, M. C., & Knapp, S. (2005). Training ethical psychologists: An acculturation model. *Professional Psychology: Research and Practice, 36*(1), 59–65. http://doi.org/dcg7r4

Hankivsky, O., Grace, D., Hunting, G., Giesbrecht, M., Fridkin, A., Rudrum, S., Ferlatte, O., & Clark, N. (2014). An intersectionality-based policy analysis framework: Critical reflections on a methodology for advancing equity. *International Journal for Equity in Health, 13*(1), 50–78. https://doi.org/10.1186/s12939-014-0119-x

Hansell, L. (2017). *Perceptions of supervisor ethical behavior by psychology interns* [Unpublished doctoral dissertation]. Pepperdine University.

Hanson, R. K., Harris, A. J. R., Letourneau, E., Helmus, L. M., & Thornton, D. (2018). Reductions in risk based on time offense-free in community: Once a sexual offender, not always a sexual offender. *Psychology, Public Policy, and Law, 24*(1), 48–63. http://doi.org/gc2n57

Harper, A., Finerty, P., Martinez, M., Brace, A., Crethar, H. C., Loos, B., Harper, B., Graham, S., Singh, A., Kocet, M., Travis, L., Lambert, S., Burnes, T., Dickey, L. M., & Hammer, T. R. (2013). Association for Lesbian, Gay, Bisexual, and Transgender Issues in Counseling Competencies for counseling with lesbian, gay, bisexual, queer, questioning, intersex, and ally individuals. *Journal of LGBT Issues in Counseling, 7*(1), 2–43. https://doi.org/10.1080/15538605.2013.755444

Harris, C. V. (2016). Still eating in the kitchen: The marginalization of African American faculty in majority white academic governance. In P. A. Matthew (Ed.), *Written/unwritten: Diversity and the hidden truths of tenure* (pp. 165–177). The University of North Carolina Press.

Harris, R. (2010). *Board roles and goals for associations – chambers – nonprofits*. https://www.nspe.org/sites/default/files/resources/pdfs/LeadershipToolbox/BoardExcellenceLONG7-10.pdf

Harvey, V. S., & Struzziero, J. A. (2008). *Professional development and supervision of school psychologists: From intern to expert*. National Association of School Psychologists.

Haskins, N., & Singh, A. (2015). Critical race theory and counselor education pedagogy: Creating equitable training. *Counselor Education and Supervision, 54*(4), 288–301. http://doi.org/dqc5

Haskins, N., Whitfield-Williams, M., Shillingford, M. A., Singh, A., Moxley, R., & Ofauni, C. (2013). The experiences of Black master's counseling students: A phenomenological inquiry. *Counselor Education and Supervision, 52*(1), 162–177. http://doi.org/dms4

Hays, D. G., & Singh, A. A. (2012). *Qualitative inquiry in clinical and educational settings*. Guilford Press.

Hays, P. A. (2016). *Addressing cultural complexities in practice: Assessment, diagnosis, and therapy* (3rd ed.). American Psychological Association.

Healthcare Providers Service Organization. (2019). *Counselor liability claim report: 2nd edition: Minimizing risk, achieving excellence*. www.hpso.com/risk-education/individuals/Counselor-Claim-Reports

Healy, K. (2018). *Data visualization: A practical introduction*. Princeton University Press.

Heller-Levitt, D., Farry, T. J., & Mazzarella, J. R. (2015). Counselor ethical reasoning: Decision-making practice versus theory. *Counseling and Values*, *60*(1), 84–99. http://doi.org/dqcb

Helms, J. (1992). *Race is a nice thing to have*. Content Communications.

Henfield, M. S., Woo, H., & Washington, A. (2013). A phenomenological investigation of African American counselor education students' challenging experiences. *Counselor Education and Supervision*, *52*(2), 122–136. http://doi.org/ggjwcd

Heppner, P., Wampold, B., Owen, J., Wang, K., & Thompson, M. (2016). *Research design in counseling* (4th ed.). Cengage Learning.

Hersey, P., Blanchard, K., & Johnson, D. (2012). *Management of organizational behavior: Leading human resources* (10th ed.). Pearson.

Hiemstra, A. M. F., Derous, E., & Born, M. (2017). Psychological predictors of cultural diversity support at work. *Cultural Diversity and Ethnic Minority Psychology*, *23*(3), 312–322. https://doi.org/gbfh7h

Hill, N. R., & Friedman, E. N. (2019). Professional leadership at the state, regional, national, and international levels. In J. E Atieno Okech & D. J. Rubel (Eds.), *Counselor education in the 21st century*. American Counseling Association.

Hill, N. R., Leinbaugh, T., Bradley, C., & Hazler, R. (2005). Female counselor educators: Encouraging and discouraging factors in academia. *Journal of Counseling & Development*, *83*(3), 374–380. http://doi.org/fzmb94

Hines, E. M., Borders, L. D., & Gonzalez, L. M. (2015). "It takes fire to make steel": Stories of two African American males finding purpose through their college experiences. *Journal for Multicultural Education*, *9*(4), 225–247. http://doi.org/dq9r

Hines, E. M., Vega, D., Mayes, R. D., Harris, P. C., & Mack, M. (2019). College and career readiness: School psychologists and school counselors as collaborators. *Journal for Multicultural Education*, *13*(3), 190–202. http://doi.org/dszg

Hipolito-Delgado, C. P. (2009). Cultural identity: Understanding the development and integration of its multiple dimensions. In C. C. Lee, D. Burnhill, A. Butler, C. P. Hipolito-Delgado, M. Humphrey, O. Munoz, & H. J. Shin (Eds.), *Elements of culture in counseling*. Allyn & Bacon.

Hipolito-Delgado, C. P. (2016). Using punk rock to invite dialogues on diversity and inclusion. *Faculty Focus Special Report: Diversity and Inclusion in the College Classroom*, pp. 19–20. https://provost.tufts.edu/celt/files/Diversity-and-Inclusion-Report.pdf

Hipolito-Delgado, C. P., Cook, J., Avrus, E., & Bonham, E. (2011). Developing counseling students' multicultural competence through the multicultural action project. *Counselor Education and Supervision*, *50*(6), 402–421. http://doi.org/fx3n9r

Hipolito-Delgado, C. P., Cook, J., Avrus, E., & Bonham, E. (2013). The lived experience of cultural immersion. *The Journal of Humanistic Counseling*, *52*(2), 191–207. http://doi.org/dnfd

Hipolito-Delgado, C. P., Estrada, D., & Garcia, M. (2017). Diversifying counsellor education: A case study of U.S. students of colour. *British Journal of Guidance and Counselling*, *45*(5), 473–488. http://doi.org/dnff

Hipolito-Delgado, C. P., Pharaoh, T., & Hermosillo, J. (2016). Empathy and advocacy: Successfully serving communities of color. *The Journal of Humanistic Counseling, 55*(1), 37–54. https://doi.org/10.1002/johc.12023

History.com Editors. (2017, November 15). *Eugenics*. https://www.history.com/topics/germany/eugenics

Hoeft, M. E. (2012). Why university students don't read: What professors can do to increase compliance. *International Journal for the Scholarship for Teaching and Learning, 6*(2), 1–12. https://doi.org/fd6h

Hof, D. D., Dinsmore, J. D., Barber, S., Suhr, R., & Scofield, T. R. (2009). Advocacy: The T.R.A.I.N.E.R. model. *Journal of Social Action in Counseling and Psychology, 2*(1), 15–28. https://openjournals.bsu.edu/jsacp/article/view/219

Holcombe, A. O. (2019). Contributorship, not authorship: Use CRediT to indicate who did what. Publications, 7(3), Article 48. http://doi.org/gghnrr

Holcomb-McCoy, C., & Addison-Bradley, C. (2005). African American counselor educators' job satisfaction and perceptions of departmental racial climate. *Counselor Education and Supervision, 45*(1), 2–15. http://doi.org/fzcnzh

Hollis, L. (2017). Evasive actions: The gendered cycle of stress and coping for those enduring workplace bullying in American higher education. *Advances in Social Sciences Research Journal, 4*(7), 59–68. http://dx.doi.org/10.2139/ssrn.3030904

Homrich, A. M., & Henderson, K. L. (Eds.). (2018). *Gatekeeping in the mental health professions*. American Counseling Association.

Hook, J. N., Davis, D., Owen, J., & DeBlaere, C. (2017). *Cultural humility: Engaging diverse identities in therapy*. American Psychological Association.

Hook, J. N., Farrell, J. E., Davis, D. E., DeBlaere, C., Van Tongeren, D. R., & Utsey, S. O. (2016). Cultural humility and racial microaggressions in counseling. *Journal of Counseling Psychology, 63*(3), 269–277. https://doi.org/f8k5s9

hooks, b. (2003). *Teaching community: A pedagogy of hope*. Routledge.

Hooley, E. M. (2019). Power, diversity, and relational process within supervision. *Training and Education in Professional Psychology, 13*(3), 212–215. https://doi.org/fd22

Horsford, S. (2014). *The interface of risks and protective factors among African American women in clinically focused graduate programs* (Order No. 3618103) [Doctoral dissertation, Michigan State University]. ProQuest Dissertations and Theses Global.

Houser, R. A. (2020). *Counseling and educational research: Evaluation and application* (4th ed.). Sage.

Howard, T. C. (2003). Culturally relevant pedagogy: Ingredients for critical teacher reflection. *Theory Into Practice, 42*(3), 195–202.

Hughey, M. W., Rees, J., Goss, D. R., Rosino, M. L., & Lesser, E. (2017). Making everyday microaggressions: An exploratory experimental vignette study on the presence and power of racial microaggressions. *Sociological Inquiry, 87*(2), 303–336. https://doi.org/10.1111/soin.12167

Human Rights Watch. (2013). *Raised on the registry: The irreparable harm of placing children on sex offender registries in the US*. https://www.hrw.org/sites/default/files/reports/us0513_ForUpload_1.pdf

Hunt, B. (2011). Publishing qualitative research in counseling journals. *Journal of Counseling & Development, 89*(3), 296–300. http://doi.org/fx28s5

Hunt, K. A., Trent, M. N., Jackson, J. R., Marquis, J. M., Barrett-Williams, S., Gurvitch, R., & Metzler, M. W. (2016). The effect of content delivery media on student engagement and learning outcomes. *Journal of Effective Teaching, 16*(1), 5–18.

Hutton, C. (2019). Using role models to increase diversity in STEM: The American workforce needs every capable STEM worker to keep American in a global leadership position. *Technology and Engineering Teacher, 79*(3), 16–19.

Interiano, C. G., & Lim, J. H. (2018). A "chameleonic" identity: Foreign-born doctoral students in US counselor education. *International Journal for the Advancement of Counselling, 40*(3), 310–325. https://doi.org/ggbxn2

Internal Revenue Service. (2018). *Compliance guide for 501(c)(3) public charities* (Publication 4221). https://www.irs.gov/pub/irs-pdf/p4221pc.pdf

International Coaching Federation. (2015). *ICF code of ethics*. https://coachingfederation.org/app/uploads/2021/01/ICF-Code-of-Ethics.pdf

Ivers, N., Johnson, D., Clarke, P., Newsome, D., & Berry, R. (2016). The relationship between mindfulness and multicultural counseling competence. *Journal of Counseling & Development, 94*(1), 72–82. http://doi.org/dthn

Ivers, N. N., Rogers, J., Borders, L. D., & Turner, A. (2017). Using interpersonal process recall in clinical supervision to enhance supervisees' multicultural awareness. *The Clinical Supervisor, 36*(2), 282–303. http://doi.org/dthp

Jackson, D. (2013). Multiple outputs from single studies: Acceptable division of findings vs. "salami" slicing. *Journal of Clinical Nursing, 23*(1–2), 1–2. http://doi.org/dpcc

Jackson, L. C., & Bouchard, M. M. (2019). Mentoring: A key success factor for African American women in the U.S. Federal Senior Executive Service. *SAM Advanced Management Journal, 84*(4), 35–56.

Jafar, A. (2003). Consent or coercion? Sexual relationships between college faculty and students. *Gender Issues, 21*(1), 42–58. https://doi.org/fvtt5b

James, R. K., & Gilliland, B. E. (2020). *Crisis intervention strategies* (6th ed.). Cengage.

Janghorban, R., & Azarkish, F. (2019). Salami publication in qualitative research: An ethical challenge. *Iranian Journal of Public Health, 48*(8), 1551–1552.

Jerry, P., & Collins, S. (2005). Web-based education in the human services: Use of web-based video clips in counseling skills training. *Journal of Technology in Human Services, 23*(3–4), 183–199. http://doi.org/fjg5rz

Johns Hopkins Medicine. (2020). *Honoring Henrietta: The legacy of Henrietta Lacks*. https://www.hopkinsmedicine.org/henriettalacks/

Johnson, C. (2018). *Organizational ethics: A practical approach*. Sage.

Johnson, W., & Nelson, N. (1999). Mentor-protégé relationships in graduate training: Some ethical concerns. *Ethics & Behavior, 9*(3), 189–210. http://doi.org/bqfj4k

Johnson, Z. D., & Labelle, S. (2017). An examination of teacher authenticity in the college classroom. *Communication Education, 66*(4), 423–439. http://doi.org/gfb559

Jones, C. T., & Branco, S. F. (2020). Trauma-informed supervision: Clinical supervision of substance use disorder counselors. *Journal of Addictions & Offender Counseling, 41*(1), 2–17. https://doi.org/fd23

Jones, C., Welfare, L. E., Melchior, S., & Cash, R. (2019). Broaching as a strategy for intercultural understanding in clinical supervision. *The Clinical Supervisor, 38*(1), 1–13. http://doi.org/dn6s

Jordan, L. S., & Seponski, D. M. (2017). Public participation: Moving beyond the four walls of therapy. *Journal of Marital and Family Therapy, 44*(1), 5–18. http://doi.org/gc5bcj

Jordan, P. J. (2018). *Counselor educators' perceptions of nontraditional master's-level counseling students and how those perceptions shape teaching practices* [Unpublished doctoral dissertation]. Western Michigan University.

Joseph, T., & Hirshfield, L. (2013). "Why don't you get somebody new to do it?" Race, gender, and identity taxation in the academy. In M. A. Chesler, A. A. Young, & R. L. Beale (Eds.), *Faculty identities and the challenge of diversity: Reflections on teaching in higher education* (pp. 153–170). Paradigm.

Jun, H. (2018). *Social justice, multicultural counseling, and practice: Beyond a conventional approach* (2nd ed.). Springer. http://doi.org/dthq

Kagan, N. I. (1976). *Influencing human interaction*. Mason Media.

Kaplan, D. M. (2014). Ethical implications of a critical legal case for the counseling profession: *Ward v. Wilbanks*. *Journal of Counseling & Development, 92*(2), 142–146. https://doi.org/fd2z

Kaplan, D. M., Francis, P. C., Hermann, M. A., Baca, J. V., Goodnough, G. E., Hodges, S., Spurgeon, S. L., & Wade, M. E. (2017). New concepts in the 2014 *ACA Code of Ethics*. *Journal of Counseling & Development, 95*(1), 110–120. http://doi.org/dqcc

Kaplan, D. M., & Gladding, S. T. (2011). A vision for the future of counseling: The 20/20 principles for unifying and strengthening the profession. *Journal of Counseling & Development, 89*(3), 367–372. http://doi.org/fxjm65

Karaman, M. A., Schmit, M. K., Ulus, I. C., & Oliver, M. (2018). International counseling students' perception of ethics. *Journal of International Students, 8*(2), 677–695. https://doi.org/10.32674/jis.v8i2.98

Katsioloudes, M. I. (2006). *Strategic management: Global cultural perspectives for profit and non-profit organizations*. Elsevier.

Kaye, J. B. (2004). *The complete guide to service learning: Proven practical ways to engage students in civic responsibility, academic curriculum, and social action*. Free Spirit.

Keashly, L., & Neuman, J. H. (2010). Faculty experiences with bullying in higher education: Causes, consequences, and management. *Administrative Theory & Praxis, 32*(1), 48–70. http://doi.org/fvqpdz

Keashly, L., & Neuman, J. H. (2013). Bullying in higher education: What current research, theorizing, and practice tell us. In J. Lester (Ed.), *Workplace bullying in higher education* (pp. 1–22). Routledge.

Keith-Spiegel, P. (2014). *Red flags in psychotherapy: Stories of ethics complaints and resolutions*. Routledge.

Kemer, G. (2020). A comparison of beginning and expert supervisors' supervision cognitions. *Counselor Education and Supervision, 59*(1), 74–92. https://doi.org/10.1002/ceas.12167

Kemer, G., & Borders, L. D. (2017). Expert clinical supervisors' descriptions of easy and challenging supervisees. *The Journal of Counselor Preparation and Supervision, 9*(1), Article 3. http://doi.org/dn6v

Kemer, G., Borders, L. D., & Yel, N. (2017). Expert clinical supervisors' priorities when working with easy and challenging supervisees. *Counselor Education and Supervision, 56*(1), 50–64. http://doi.org/dn6w

Kendi, I. X. (2019). *How to be an antiracist*. One World.

Kerr, M. M., & Frese, K. M. (2017). Reading to learn or learning to read? Engaging college students in course readings. *College Teaching, 65*(1), 28–31. https://doi.org/fcq8

Khatib, M., Sarem, S. N., & Hamidi, H. (2013). Humanistic education: Concerns, implications, and applications. *Journal of Language Teaching and Research, 4*(1), 45–51. https://doi.org/ggc8qb

Killermann, S. (2012). *30+ examples of heterosexual (straight) privileges.* https://www.itspronouncedmetrosexual.com/2012/01/29-examples-of-heterosexual-privilege/

Kim, D., & Otts, C. (2010). The effect of loans on time to doctorate degree: Differences by race/ethnicity, field of study, and institutional characteristics. *The Journal of Higher Education, 81*(1), 1–32. https://doi.org/ft58pf

King, C., & Piotrowski, C. (2015). Bullying of educators by educators: Incivility in higher education. *Contemporary Issues in Education Research, 8*(4), 257–262.

King, K. M., & Jones, K. (2018). An autoethnography of broaching in supervision: Joining supervisee and supervisor perspectives on addressing identity, power, and difference. *The Clinical Supervisor, 38*(1), 17–37. https://doi.org/fdvz

Kinser, P. A., & Robins, J. (2013). Control group design: Enhancing rigor in research of mind-body therapies for depression. *Evidence-Based Complementary and Alternative Medicine, 2013*, Article 140467. http://doi.org/gbcv3d

Kitchener, K. S. (1984). Intuition, critical evaluation, and ethical principles: The foundation for ethical decisions in counseling psychology. *The Counseling Psychologist, 12*(3), 43–55. http://doi.org/fnzs2n

Knight, C. (2018). Trauma-informed supervision: Historical antecedents, current practice, and future directions. *The Clinical Supervisor, 37*(1), 7–37. https://doi.org/gf2jx3

Kocet, M. M., & Herlihy, B. (2014). Addressing value-based conflicts within the counseling relationship: A decision making model. *Journal of Counseling & Development, 92*(2), 180–186. https://doi.org/10.1002/j.1556-6676.2014.00146.x

Koch, J. M., Procopio, S. J., Knutson, D., Loche, R. W., III, Jayne, A., Jayne, C., & Loche, L. (2018). Counseling psychology students' perceptions of faculty multicultural competence. *Scholarship of Teaching and Learning in Psychology, 4*(3), 140–150. https://doi.org/10.1037/stl0000116

Kolb, D. A. (1984). *Experiential learning: Experience as the source of learning and development* (1st ed.). Prentice Hall.

Kolb, D. A. (2015). *Experiential learning: Experience as the source of learning and development* (2nd ed.). Pearson.

Koocher, G. P., & Keith-Spiegel, P. (2016). *Ethics in psychology and the mental health professions: Standards and cases.* Oxford University Press.

Koshino, K. (2016). Campus racial climate and experiences of students of color in a Midwestern college. In F. Tuitt, C. Haynes, & S. Stewart (Eds.), *Race, equity, and the learning environment: The global relevance of critical and inclusive pedagogies in higher education* (pp. 98–111). Stylus.

Kouzes, J. M., & Posner, B. Z. (2012). *The Leadership Practices Inventory* (4th ed.). Wiley.

Kozlowska, K., Nunn, K., & Cousens, P. (1997). Training in psychiatry: An examination of trainee perceptions: Part 1. *Australian and New Zealand Journal of Psychiatry, 31*(5), 628–640. http://doi.org/bzpqfd

Kruse, S. D., Rakha, S., & Calderone, S. (2018). Developing cultural competency in higher education: An agenda for practice. *Teaching in Higher Education, 23*(6), 733–750. http://doi.org/dpcj

Kumi-Yeboah, A., & Smith, P. (2016). Relationships between minority students online: Learning experiences and academic performance. *Online Learning, 20*(4). http://doi.org/dxht

Kwon, Y. (2009). Factors affecting international students' transition to higher education institutions in the United States: From the perspective the Office of International Students. *College Student Journal, 43*(4), 1020–1036.

Ladany, N. (2004). Psychotherapy supervision: What lies beneath. *Psychotherapy Research, 14*(1), 1–19. http://doi.org/d45v3c

Ladany, N., Ellis, M. V., & Friedlander, M. L. (1999). The supervisory working alliance, trainee self-efficacy, and satisfaction. *Journal of Counseling & Development, 77*(4), 447–455. http://doi.org/fx87ht

Ladany, N., Mori, Y., & Mehr, K. E. (2012). Effective and ineffective supervision. *The Counseling Psychologist, 41*(1), 28–47. http://doi.org/dwzt

Ladany, N., O'Brien, K. M., Hill, C. E., Melincoff, D. S., Knox, S., & Petersen, D. A. (1997). Sexual attraction toward clients, use of supervision, and prior training: A qualitative study of predoctoral psychology interns. *Journal of Counseling Psychology, 44*(4), 413–424. http://doi.org/dqjpqg

Ladson-Billings, G. (1994). *The dreamkeepers*. Jossey-Bass.

Ladson-Billings, G. (1995a). But that's just good teaching! The case for culturally relevant pedagogy. *Theory Into Practice, 34*(3), 159–165. http://doi.org/c7gt92

Ladson-Billings, G. (1995b). Towards a theory of culturally relevant pedagogy. *American Educational Research Journal, 32*(3), 465–491. http://doi.org/dx3gcj

Lai, C. K., Marini, M., Lehr, S. A., Cerruti, C., Shin, J. L., Joy-Gaba, J. A., & Nosek, B. A. (2014). Reducing implicit racial preferences: A comparative investigation of 17 interventions. *Journal of Experimental Psychology: General, 143*(4), 1765–1785. https://doi.org/10.1037/a0036260

Lam, C. B., McHale, S. M., & Updegraff, K. A. (2012). Gender dynamics in Mexican American families: Connecting mothers', fathers', and youths' experiences. *Sex Roles, 67*(1–2), 17–28. https://doi.org/f32bj2

Lambda Legal (n.d.). *Your rights*. https://www.lambdalegal.org/your-rights

Lane, J. A. (2012). The ethical implication of bartering for mental health services: Examining interdisciplinary ethical standards. *Michigan Journal of Counseling, 39*(2), 4–7.

Langellier, K. A., Astramovich, R. L., & Doughty Horn, E. A. (2020). Infusing service learning into the counselor education curriculum. *The Professional Counselor, 10*(2), 194–203. https://doi.org/10.15241/kal.10.2.194

Lanning, W. (1986). Development of the supervisor emphasis rating form. *Counselor Education and Supervision, 25*(3), 191–196. http://doi.org/fx2qv4

Lechuga, V. M. (2011). Faculty-graduate student mentoring relationships: Mentors' perceived roles and responsibilities. *Higher Education, 62*(6), 757–771. https://doi.org/10.1007/s10734-011-9416-0

Levitt, H. M., Bamberg, M., Creswell, J. W., Frost, D. M., Josselson, R., & Suárez-Orozco, C. (2018). Journal article reporting standards for qualitative primary, qualitative meta-analytic, and mixed methods research in psychology: The APA Publications and Communications Board task force report. *American Psychologist, 73*(1), 26–46. https://doi.org/gctpzh

Linvill, J. S., & Connaughton, S. L. (2019). Coping with workplace incivility. In R. West & C. S. Beck (Eds.), *The Routledge handbook of communication and bullying* (pp. 116–126). Routledge.

Lloyd-Hazlett, J. (2018). Enhancing student counselor program evaluation training through creative community service learning partnerships. *Journal of Creativity in Mental Health, 13*(4), 467–478. http://doi.org/d47s

Lobanov-Rostovsky, C. (2017). Recidivism of juveniles who commit sexual offenses. In K. Baldwin & S. Faupel (Eds.), *Sex offender management assessment and planning initiative* (pp. 251–267). Office of Sex Offender Sentencing, Monitoring, Apprehending, Registering, and Tracking. https://www.smart.gov/SOMAPI/pdfs/SOMAPI_Full%20Report.pdf

Lock, J., Clancy, T., Lisella, R., Rosenau, P., Ferreira, C., & Rainsbury, J. (2016). The lived experiences of instructors co-teaching in higher education. *Brock Education, 26*(1), 22–35. https://files.eric.ed.gov/fulltext/EJ1148312.pdf

Louis, D. A., Rawls, G. J., Jackson-Smith, D., Chambers, G. A., Phillips, L. L., & Louis, S. L. (2016). Listening to our voices: Experiences of Black faculty at predominantly white research universities with microaggression. *Journal of Black Studies, 47*(5), 454–474. http://doi.org/dmvb

Love, B. L. (2017). *We want to do more than survive: Abolitionist teaching and the pursuit of educational freedom*. Beacon.

Luft, J. (1961). The Johari window. *Human Relations Training News, 5*(9), 6–7.

Luke, M., & Bruner, S. L. (2022). That's my idea: Taking someone else's work as their own. In J. M. Swank & C. A. Barrio Minton (Eds.), *Critical incidents in counselor education: Teaching, supervision, scholarship, leadership, and advocacy* (pp. 187–194). American Counseling Association.

Luke, M., & Goodrich, K. M. (2010). Chi Sigma Iota chapter leadership and professional identity development in early career counselors. *Counselor Education and Supervision, 50*(1), 56–78. http://doi.org/fx5zx7

Luke, M., Goodrich, K. M., & Gilbride, D. D. (2013a). Intercultural model of ethical decision making: Addressing worldview dilemmas in school counseling. *Counseling and Values, 58*(2), 177–194. http://doi.org/dn98

Luke, M., Goodrich, K. M., & Gilbride, D. D. (2013b). Testing the intercultural model of ethical decision making with counselors-in-training. *Counselor Education and Supervision, 52*(3), 222–234. http://doi.org/dn99

Mack, M. H. (1999). Regulating sexual relationships between faculty and students. *Michigan Journal of Gender & Law, 6*(1), 79–112. https://repository.law.umich.edu/mjgl/vol6/iss1/3

Macpherson, C. C. (2001). Research ethics: Beyond the guidelines. *Developing World Bioethics, 1*(1), 57–68. http://doi.org/ddn4x5

Malott, K. M., Paone, T. R., Schaefle, S., & Gao, J. (2015). Is it racist? Addressing racial microaggressions in counselor training. *Journal of Creativity in Mental Health, 10*(3), 386–398. https://doi.org/10.1080/15401383.2014.988312

Manis, A. A. (2012). A review of the literature on promoting cultural competence and social justice agency among students and counselor trainees: Piecing the evidence together to advocate pedagogy and research. *The Professional Counselor, 2*(1), 48–57. http://doi.org/d2d3

Marshall, C., & Rossman, G. B. (2015). *Designing qualitative research* (6th ed.). Sage.

Martinez, M. (2019). Toxic masculinity: An outcome of colonialism and its effects on the Latinx/Chicanx LGBTQ+ community. *McNair Research Journal SJSU, 15*(1), Article 6. https://scholarworks.sjsu.edu/mcnair/vol15/iss1/6

Martinez, M. A., Nino, J. M., & Torres, I. (2018). Examining intersectionalities among male faculty of color on the tenure-track. *Intersections: Critical Issues in Education* 2(2), 57–75. https://digitalrepository.unm.edu/intersections/vol2/iss2/3

Matias, C. E., Viesca, K. M., Garrison-Wade, D. F., Tandon, M., & Galindo, R. (2014). "What is critical whiteness doing in our nice field like critical race theory?" Applying CRT and CWS to understand the white imaginations of white teacher candidates. *Equity & Excellence in Education, 47*(3), 289–304. https://doi.org/10.1080/10665684.2014.933692

Matthew, P. A. (Ed.). (2016). *Written/unwritten: Diversity and the hidden truths of tenure*. The University of North Carolina Press.

Mawdsley, R. (2009). The tangled web of plagiarism litigation: Sorting out the legal issues. *Brigham Young University Education and Law Journal, 2009*(2), Article 3. https://digitalcommons.law.byu.edu/elj/vol2009/iss2/3

McArthur, N. (2017). Relationships between university professors and students: Should they be banned? *Ethics & Education, 12*(2), 129–140. https://doi.org/gfn86t

McGaskey, F. G. (2015). Facilitating the creation of knowledge: An investigation of the factors that influence the research productivity of Black doctoral students at predominantly white institutions. *The Journal of Negro Education, 84*(2), 187–201.

McGee, E. O., White, D. T., Jenkins, A. T., Houston, S., Bentley, L. C., Smith, W. J., & Robinson, W. H. (2016). Black engineering students' motivation for PhD attainment: Passion plus purpose. *Journal for Multicultural Education, 10*(2), 167–193. http://doi.org/dxhr

McKay, R. B., Kidwell, L. A., & Kling, J. A. (2007). Faculty ethics from the perspective of college of business administrators. *Proceedings of the Academy of Legal, Ethical and Regulatory Issues, 10*(1), 105–124.

McKeachie, W. J., & Svinicki, M. (2006). *McKeachie's teaching tips: Strategies, research, and theory for college and university teachers*. Houghton Mifflin.

McKibben, W. B., Borders, L. D., & Wahesh, E. (2019). Factors influencing supervisee perceptions of critical feedback validity. *Counselor Education and Supervision, 58*(4), 242–256. http://doi.org/dn69

McKibben, W. B., Cook, R. M., & Fickling, M. J. (2019). Feminist supervision and supervisee nondisclosure: The mediating role of the supervisory relationship. *The Clinical Supervisor, 38*(1), 38–57. http://doi.org/dtmd

McKibben, W. B., Umstead, L. K., & Borders, L. D. (2017). Identifying dynamics of counseling leadership: A content analysis study. *Journal of Counseling & Development, 95*(2), 192–202. http://doi.org/gfb554

McKinney, R., West, E., Fye, M., Bradley, R., & Storlie, C. A. (2018). Chi Sigma Iota chapter faculty advisors' experiences of professional counselor identity. *Journal of Counselor Leadership and Advocacy, 5*(1), 56–70. http://doi.org/gf4b3k

McLean, C. P., & Foa, E. B. (2011). Prolonged exposure therapy for post-traumatic stress disorder: A review of evidence and dissemination. *Expert Review of Neurotherapeutics, 11*(8), 1151–1163. http://doi.org/d7mbdd

McNeil, B. W., & Stoltenberg, C. D. (2015). *Supervision essentials for the integrative developmental model*. American Psychological Association.

McNutt, L. A., Waltermaurer, E., Bednarczyk, R. A., Carlson, B. E., Kotval, J., McCauley, J., Campbell, J. C., & Ford, D. E. (2008). Are we misjudging how well informed consent forms are read? *Journal of Empirical Research on Human Research Ethics, 3*(1), 89–97. https://doi.org/dqhvpt

Meany-Walen, K. K., Carnes-Holt, K., Barrio Minton, C. A., Purswell, K., & Pronchenko-Jain, Y. (2013). An exploration of counselors' professional leadership development. *Journal of Counseling & Development, 91*(2), 206–215. http://doi.org/dtkh

Meier, S. T., & Davis, S. R. (2011). *The elements of counseling*. Brooks/Cole.

Melamed, L., Casado Pérez, J. F., & Hunt, B. (2020). Teaching strategies for incorporating the Multicultural and Social Justice Counseling Competencies. *The Journal of Counselor Preparation and Supervision, 13*(2), Article 2. http://dx.doi.org/10.7729/42.1350

Merritt, A. C., Effron, D. A., & Monin, B. (2010). Moral self-licensing: When being good frees us to be bad. *Social and Personality Psychology Compass, 4*(5), 344–357. http://doi.org/cwj8g6

Miller, S. M., Larwin, K. H., Kautzman-East, M., Williams, J. L., Evans, W. J., Williams, D. D., Abramski, A. L., & Miller, K. L. (2020). A proposed definition and structure of counselor dispositions. *Measurement and Evaluation in Counseling and Development, 53*(2), 117–130. https://doi.org/10.1080/07481756.2019.1640618

Milne, D. (2016). How can video recordings best contribute to clinical supervisor training? *The Cognitive Behaviour Therapist, 9*, e25. http://doi.org/dwzv

Milsom, A. (2018). Advocating for the counseling profession. In B. Erford (Ed.), *Orientation to the counseling profession: Advocacy, ethics, and essential professional foundations* (3rd ed., pp. 435–457). Pearson.

Minnix, G. M. (2018). Reconciling counselors' Christian beliefs and lesbian, gay, bisexual, and transgender affirmation: A grounded theory. *Counseling and Values, 63*(1), 110–128. http://doi.org/dqqz

Misawa, M. (2015). Cuts and bruises caused by arrows, sticks, and stones in academia: Theorizing three types of racist and homophobic bullying in adult and higher education. *Adult Learning, 26*(1), 6–13. https://doi.org/10.1177/1045159514558413

Mitcham, M., Greenidge, W., & Smith, S. D. (2013). Teaching the multicultural counseling course: Facilitating courageous conversations and transformational multicultural pedagogy. In *VISTAS 2013*. https://www.counseling.org/docs/default-source/vistas/teaching-the-multicultural-counseling-course-facilitating-courageous-conversations-and-transformational-multicultural-pedagogy.pdf?sfvrsn=bc6aac5c_13

Mobley, S. D., Jr., & Hall, L. (2020). (Re)defining queer and trans* student retention and "success" at historically Black colleges and universities. *Journal of College Student Retention: Research, Theory & Practice, 21*(4), 497–519.

Mock, R. P., Savage, A., & Simkin, M. G. (2010). The ethics of indemnity clauses in academic publication contracts. *Issues in Accounting Education, 25*(2), 267–278. http://doi.org/d65hv4

Morales, E. (2020). "Beasting" at the battleground: Black students responding to racial microaggressions in higher education. *Journal of Diversity in Higher Education*. Advance online publication. https://doi.org./10.1037/dhe0000168

Morrison, M. A., & Lent, R. W. (2018). The working alliance, beliefs about the supervisor, and counseling self-efficacy: Applying the relational efficacy model to counselor supervision. *Journal of Counseling Psychology, 65*(4), 512–522. http://doi.org/gdwqxn

Morrissey, J., & Tribe, R. (2001). Parallel process in supervision. *Counselling Psychology Quarterly, 14*(2), 103–110. http://doi.org/d6txkk

Mullen, C. (2005). *Mentorship primer*. Peter Lang.

Murdock, J., Williams, A., Becker, K., Bruce, M. A., & Young, S. (2012). Online versus on-campus: A comparison study of counseling skills courses. *The Journal of Human Resource and Adult Learning, 8*(1), 105–118.

Myers, J. E., & Sweeney, T. J. (2004). The indivisible self: An evidence-based model of wellness. *Journal of Individual Psychology, 60*(3), 234–245.

Myrick, R. D. (2003). Accountability: Counselors count. *Professional School Counseling, 6*(3), 174–179. https://www.jstor.org/stable/42732426

Nadal, K. L., Griffin, K. E., Wong, Y., Hamit, S., & Rasmus, M. (2014). The impact of racial microaggressions on mental health: Counseling implications for clients of color. *Journal of Counseling & Development, 92*(1), 57–66. https://doi.org/10.1002/j.1556-6676.2014.00130.x

Namie, G. (2017). *From 2017 Workplace Bullying Institute (WBI) U.S. workplace bullying survey.* https://www.uwsp.edu/conted/Documents/FOCUS/C5%20and%20E2%20See%20handout_workplace%20bullying%20stats.pdf

National Association of Social Workers. (2017). *Code of ethics.*

National Center for Education Statistics. (2019). *The condition of education 2019.* https://nces.ed.gov/pubsearch/pubsinfo.asp?pubid=2019144

National Center on Safe Supportive Learning Environments. (n.d.). *School climate improvement.* https://safesupportivelearning.ed.gov/school-climate-improvement

National Commission for the Protection of Human Subjects of Biomedical and Behavioral Research. (1979, April 18). *The Belmont report: Ethical principles and guidelines for the protection of human subjects of research.* https://www.hhs.gov/ohrp/regulations-and-policy/belmont-report/read-the-belmont-report/index.html

Neal-Barnett, A., Stadulis, R., Murray, M., Payne, M. R., Thomas, A., & Salley, B. B. (2011). Sister circles as a culturally relevant intervention for anxious Black women. *Clinical Psychology Science and Practice, 18*(3), 266–273. http://doi.org/d5v97c

Nettles, M. T., & Millett, C. M. (2006). *Three magic letters: Getting to Ph.D.* Johns Hopkins University Press.

Neufeldt, S. A. (2007). *Supervision strategies for the first practicum* (3rd ed.). American Counseling Association.

Ng, K. M. (2006). International students in CACREP-accredited counseling programs. *Journal of Professional Counseling: Practice, Theory & Research, 34*(1–2), 20–32. http://doi.org/dq56

Nielsen, M. B., & Einarsen, S. (2012). Outcomes of exposure to workplace bullying: A meta-analytic review. *Work & Stress, 26*(4), 309–332. http://doi.org/gd3zdj

Noddings, N. (2005). *The challenge to care in schools: An alternative approach to education* (2nd ed.). Teachers College Press.

Norcross, J. (Ed.). (2011). *Psychotherapy relationships that work: Therapist contributions and responsiveness to patients* (2nd ed.). Oxford University Press.

Norem, K., Magnuson, S., Wilcoxon, S. A., & Arbel, O. (2006). Supervisees' contributions to stellar supervision outcomes. *Journal of Professional Counseling: Practice, Theory & Research, 34*(1&2), 33–48. http://doi.org/dn6x

Norman, G. (2014). Data dredging, salami-slicing, and other successful strategies to ensure rejection: Twelve tips on how to not get your paper published. *Advances in Health Science Education, 19*(1), 1–5. http://doi.org/dpcd

Northouse, P. G. (2019). *Leadership* (8th ed.). Sage.

Odegard, M. A., & Vereen, L. G. (2010). A grounded theory of counselor educators integrating social justice into their pedagogy. *Counselor Education and Supervision, 50*(2), 130–149.

Office for Civil Rights. (2020, November 19). *Title IX of the Education Amendments of 1972.* https://www.hhs.gov/civil-rights/for-individuals/sex-discrimination/title-ix-education-amendments/index.html

Office for Civil Rights. (2021, May). *Title IX and sex discrimination.* https://www2.ed.gov/about/offices/list/ocr/docs/tix_dis.html

Office of Sex Offender Sentencing, Monitoring, Apprehending, Registering, and Tracking. (2011). *The national guidelines for sex offender registration and notification.* www.ojp.usdoj.gov/smart/pdfs/final_sornaguidelines.pdf

O'Hara, C., Clark, M., Hays, D. G., McDonald, C. P., Chang, C. Y., Crockett, S. A., Filmore, J., Portman, T., Spurgeon, S., & Wester, K. L. (2016). AARC standards for multicultural research. *Counseling Outcome and Research and Evaluation, 7*(2), 67–72. http://doi.org/dpbc

Okahana, H., Klein, C., Allum, J., & Sowell, R. (2018). STEM doctoral completion of underrepresented minority students: Challenges and opportunities for improving participation in the doctoral workforce. *Innovative Higher Education, 43*(4), 237–255. http://doi.org/dpcm

Olivarius, N., Kousgaard, M. B., Reventlow, S., Quelle, D. G., & Tulinius, C. (2010). Dynamic strategic planning in a professional knowledge-based organization. *Journal of Research Administration, 41*(1), 35–48. https://files.eric.ed.gov/fulltext/EJ886791.pdf

Overholser, J. C. (1991). The Socratic method as a technique in psychotherapy supervision. *Professional Psychology, 22*(1), 68–74. http://doi.org/cqqvxm

Owen, J. (2013). Early career perspectives on psychotherapy research and practice: Psychotherapist effects, multicultural orientation, and couple interventions. *Psychotherapy, 50*(4), 496–502. http://doi.org/dn7n

Owen, J., Imel, Z., Tao, K., Wampold, B., Smith, A., & Rodolfa, E. (2011). Cultural ruptures in short-term therapy: Working alliance as a mediator between clients' perceptions of microaggressions and therapy outcomes. *Counseling and Psychotherapy Research, 11*(3), 204–212. http://doi.org/c732s8

Owens, E. W., & Neale-McFall, C. W. (2014). Counselor identity development: Toward a model for the formation of professional identity. *Journal of Counselor Leadership and Advocacy, 1*(1), 16–27. https://doi.org/gf4bxx

Paine, L. S. (1994, March–April). Managing for organizational integrity. *Harvard Business Review.* http://hbr.org/1994/03/managing-for-organizational-integrity

Paone, T. R., Malott, K. M., Pulliam, N., & Shannon, J. (2019). Experiences of counselor students of color in the classroom: A qualitative study. *Race Ethnicity and Education.* Advance online publication. https://doi.org/10.1080/13613324.2019.1579186

Paquette, P. (2016). Instructing the instructors: Training instructors to use social presence cues in online courses. *Journal of Educators Online, 13*(1), 80–108. https://eric.ed.gov/?id=Ej1087698

Parker, P. S., & ogilvie, d. t. (1996). Gender, culture, and leadership: Toward a culturally distinct model of African-American women executives' leadership strategies. *The Leadership Quarterly, 7*(2), 189–214. https://doi.org/10.1016/S1048-9843(96)90040-5

Pease-Carter, C., & Barrio Minton, C. A. (2012). Counseling programs' informed consent practices: A survey of student preferences. *Counselor Education and Supervision, 51*(4), 308–319. http://doi.org/dq5t

Pérez Huber, L., & Solorzano, D. G. (2018). Teaching racial microaggressions: Implications of critical race hypos for social work praxis. *Journal of Ethnic & Cultural Diversity in Social Work, 27*(1), 54–71. https://doi.org/10.1080/15313204.2017.1417944

Perlstein, M. (2009). Virgins and veterans: Culturally sensitive supervision in the LGBT community. *Women & Therapy, 33*(1), 85–100. https://doi.org/fgfv7g

Perry, A. R., Wallace, S. L., Moore, S. E., & Perry-Burney, G. D. (2015). Understanding student evaluations: A Black faculty perspective. *Reflections: Narratives of Professional Helping, 20*(1), 29–35.

Pink, D. H. (2009). *Drive: The surprising truth about what motivates us*. Riverhead.

Pope, K. S., Sonne, J. L., & Greene, B. (2006). *What therapists don't talk about and why: Understanding taboos that hurt us and our clients* (2nd ed.). American Psychological Association.

Powers, M. B., Halpern, J. M., Ferenschak, M. P., Gillihan, S. J., & Foa, E. B. (2010). A meta-analytic review of prolonged exposure for posttraumatic stress disorder. *Clinical Psychology Review, 30*(6), 635–641. http://doi.org/bt6n4b

Price, N. (2018, March 12). *The fiduciary responsibilities of a nonprofit board of directors*. https://www.boardeffect.com/blog/fiduciary-responsibilities-nonprofit-board-directors/

Project Implicit. (2011). *Sexuality Implicit Association Test*. https://implicit.harvard.edu/implicit/takeatest.html

Prosek, E. A., & Gibson, D. M. (2021). Promoting rigorous research by examining lived experiences: A review of four qualitative traditions. *Journal of Counseling & Development, 99*(2), 167–177. https://doi.org/10.1002/jcad.12364

Pulliam, N., Paone, T. R., Malott, K. M., & Shannon, J. (2019). The experiences of students of color at a predominantly white institution: Implications for counselor training. *Journal of Multicultural Counseling and Development, 47*(4), 239–255. https://doi.org/10.1002/jmcd.12156

Purarjomandlangrudi, A., & Chen, D. (2019). A causal loop approach to uncover interrelationship of student online interaction and engagement and their contributing factors. *Research in Learning Technology, 27*, 1–15. https://doi.org/10.25304/rlt.v27.2058

Queer Café. (2017). *Questions*. https://queercafe.net/questions.htm

Quinn, R. E. (1988). *Beyond rational management: Mastering the paradoxes and competing demands of high performance*. Jossey-Bass.

Ramos-Sánchez, L., Esnil, E., Goodwin, A., Riggs, S., Touster, L. O., Wright, L. K., Ratanasiripong, P., & Rodolfa, E. (2002). Negative supervisory events: Effects on supervision and supervisory alliance. *Professional Psychology: Research and Practice, 33*(2), 197–202. http://doi.org/cmsr2t

Rash, A. S., Skinner, A. J., Cline, D. M., & Blanch, K. D. (2008). Non-traditional students: "Needs and challenges." *The College Student Experience, CNS 572*, Paper 6. http://digitalcommons.wku.edu/cns/6

Rathvon, N. (2008). *Effective school interventions: Evidence-based strategies for improving student outcomes* (2nd ed.). Guilford Press.

Ratliff, D. A., Wampler, K. S., & Morris, G. H. (2000). Lack of consensus in supervision. *Journal of Marital and Family Therapy, 26*(3), 373–384. http://doi.org/ffh5kr

Ratts, M. J., Singh, A. A., Nassar-McMillan, S., Butler, S. K., & McCullough, J. R. (2015). *Multicultural and social justice counseling competencies*. Association for Multicultural Counseling and Development. http://www.counseling.org/docs/default-source/competencies/multicultural-and-social-justice-counseling-competencies.pdf?sfvrsn=20

Ratts, M. J., Singh, A. A., Nassar-McMillan, S., Butler, S. K., & McCullough, J. R. (2016). Multicultural and social justice counseling competencies: Guidelines for the counseling profession. *Journal of Multicultural Counseling and Development, 44*(1), 28–48. http://doi.org/dn4b

Ravitch, S. M., & Mittenfelner Carl, N. (2016). *Qualitative research: Bridging the conceptual, theoretical, and methodological*. Sage.

Remley, T. P., & Herlihy, B. (2020). *Ethical, legal, and professional issues in counseling* (6th ed.). Pearson.

Richards, T. N., Crittendon, C., Garland, T. S., & McGuffee, K. (2014). An exploration of policies governing faculty-to-student consensual sexual relationships on university campuses: Current strategies and future directions. *Journal of College Student Development, 55*(4), 337–352. https://doi.org/f5522c

Rigazio-DiGilio, S. A., Daniels, T. G., & Ivey, A. E. (1997). Systemic cognitive-developmental supervision: A developmental-integrative approach to psychotherapy supervision. In C. E. Watkins (Ed.), *Handbook of psychotherapy supervision* (pp. 223–245). Wiley.

Robert, H. M., III, Honemann, D. H., Balch, T. J., Seabold, D. E., & Gerber, S. (2020). *Robert's rules of order* (12th ed.). Public Affairs.

Robinson, E. H., III, & Curry, J. R. (2009). Institutional review boards and profession counseling research. *Counseling and Values, 53*(1), 39–52. http://doi.org/fzk2d8

Rodriguez, A. (2019). Feminists betraying feminism to restrict faculty-student romances. *Sexuality & Culture, 23*(4), 1345–1349. https://doi.org/d8th

Rodriguez, J., & Haskins, N. (2020). Fellows program: Training the next generation of EDI researchers. In S. Burrell Storms, S. Donovan, & T. Williams (Eds.), *Breaking down silos for equity, diversity, and inclusion (EDI): Teaching and collaboration across disciplines* (pp. 71–78). Rowman & Littlefield.

Rogers, C. R. (1969). *Freedom to learn*. Merrill.

Rogers, C., & Freiberg, H. J. (1993). *Freedom to learn* (3rd ed.). Merrill.

Rogers, J. L. (2006). Role-modeling authenticity in higher education. *Spirituality in Higher Education Newsletter, 3*(1), 1–5. https://www.spirituality.ucla.edu/docs/newsletters/3/Rogers.pdf

Rose, C. A., & Gage, N. A. (2017). Exploring the involvement of bullying among students with disabilities over time. *Exceptional Children, 83*(3), 298–314. https://doi.org/gbmhjf

Rose, J. S., Kocet, M. M., Thompson, I. A., Flores, M., McKinney, R., & Suprina, J. S. (2019). Association for Lesbian, Gay, Bisexual, and Transgender Issues in Counseling's best practices in addressing conscience clause legislation in counselor education and supervision. *Journal of LGBT Issues in Counseling, 13*(1), 2–27. http://doi.org/dqq2

Rosenthal, L., & Lobel, M. (2016). Stereotypes of Black American women related to sexuality and motherhood. *Psychology of Women Quarterly, 40*(3), 414–427. http://doi.org/f8z5ht

Rothschild, B. (2000). *The body remembers: The psychophysiology of trauma and trauma treatment*. Norton.

Rothschild, B. (2017). *The body remembers: Vol. 2. Revolutionizing trauma treatment*. Norton.

Rucks-Ahidiana, Z. (2019, June 7). The inequities of the tenure-track system. *Inside Higher Ed*. https://www.insidehighered.com/advice/2019/06/07/nonwhite-faculty-face-significant-disadvantages-tenure-track-opinion

Rutherford, P. (2002). *Why didn't I learn this in college? Teaching and learning in the 21st century*. Just ASK.

Sadler, G. R., Lee, H. C., Lim, R. S., & Fullerton, J. (2010). Recruitment of hard-to-reach population subgroups via adaptations of the snowball sampling strategy. *Nursing & Health Sciences, 12*(3), 369–374. https://doi.org/b652bj

Saef, R. M., Porter, C. M., Woo, S. E., & Wiese, C. (2019, April). Getting off on the right foot: The role of openness to experience in fostering initial trust between culturally dissimilar partners. *Journal of Research in Personality, 79*, 176–187. https://doi.org/fgmt

Salazar, C. F. (2009). Strategies to survive and thrive in academia: The collective voices of counseling faculty of color. *International Journal for the Advancement of Counselling, 31*(3), 181–198. http://doi.org/cdrknr

Sanchez, M. E. (2019). Perceptions of campus climate and experiences of racial microaggressions for Latinos at Hispanic-serving institutions. *Journal of Hispanic Higher Education, 18*(3), 240–253. https://doi.org/10.1177/2F1538192717739351

Sand, M. A. (2005). *How to manage an effective nonprofit organization*. Career Press.

Sandelowski, M. (1986). The problem of rigor in qualitative research. *Advances in Nursing Science, 8*(3), 27–37. http://doi.org/dq9s

Sandler, J. C., & Russell, B. L. (2005). Faculty-student collaborations: Ethics and satisfaction in authorship credit. *Ethics & Behavior, 15*(1), 65–80. http://doi.org/c7w5fn

Schaefers, K. (2012). Working for good: The encore career movement. *Career Planning and Adult Development Journal, 28*(2), 84–95.

Scharff, D. P., Mathews, K. J., Jackson, P., Hoffsuemmer, J., Martin, E., & Edwards, D. (2010). More than Tuskegee: Understanding mistrust about research participation. *Journal of Health Care for the Poor and Underserved, 21*(3), 879–897. https://doi.org/dpzt2v

Schwartz, C. E., Chesney, M. A., Irvine, J., & Keefe, F. J. (1997). The control group dilemma in clinical research: Applications for psychosocial and behavioral medicine trials. *Psychosomatic Medicine, 59*(4), 362–371. http://doi.org/dsqk

Seaman, J. E., Allen, I. E., & Seaman, J. (2018). *Grade increase: Tracking distance education in the United States*. http://onlinelearningsurvey.com/reports/gradeincrease.pdf

Sedivy-Benton, A., Strohschen, G., Cavazos, N., & Boden-McGill, C. (2015). Good ol' boys, mean girls, and tyrants: A phenomenological study of the lived experiences and survival strategies of bullied women adult educators. *Adult Learning, 26*(1), 35–41. http://doi.org/gd8dj3

Seward, D. X. (2014). Multicultural course pedagogy: Experiences of master's-level students of color. *Counselor Education and Supervision, 53*(1), 62–79. http://doi.org/dnfg

Shah, R. S. (2018, December 5). *Five facts about juvenile sex offender registration*. American Bar Association. https://www.americanbar.org/groups/litigation/committees/childrens-rights/practice/2018/five-facts-about-juvenile-sex-offender-registration/

Shannonhouse, L., & West-Olatunji, C. (2013). *One counselor-trainee's journey toward multicultural counseling competence: The role of mentoring in executing intentional cultural immersion*. https://www.shsu.edu/dotAsset/10ca6ff0-c865-4526-ba95-d2f181356a30.pdf

Shapiro, R. (2010). *The trauma treatment handbook: Protocols across the spectrum.* Norton.

Shavers, M. C., & Moore, J. L. (2019). The perpetual outsider: Voices of Black women pursuing doctoral degrees at predominantly white institutions. *Journal of Multicultural Counseling and Development, 47*(4), 210–226. https://doi.org/10.1002/jmcd.12154

Shaw, J., & Lee, H. N. (2019). Race and the criminal justice system response to sexual assault: A systematic review. *American Journal of Community Psychology, 64*(1–2), 256–278. http://doi.org/dw3m

Shaw, S. (2016, December 27). Practicing cultural humility. *Counseling Today*. https://ct.counseling.org/2016/12/practicing-cultural-humility

Sheperis, D. S., Coker, J. K., Haag, E., & Salem-Pease, F. (2020). Online counselor education: A student–faculty collaboration. *The Professional Counselor, 10*(1), 133–143. https://doi.org/10.15241/dss.10.1.133

Sheperis, D. S., Ordway, A., & Lamar, M. (2020). Legal and ethical challenges in online counselor education. *The Professional Counselor, 10*(1), 106–119. https://doi.org/10.15241/dss.10.1.106

Simon, D. J., & Swerdlik, M. E. (2017). *Supervision in school psychology: The developmental, ecological, problem-solving model*. Routledge.

Sims, C. M., & Carter, A. D. (2019). Revisiting Parker & ogilvie's African American women executive leadership model. *Journal of Business Diversity, 19*(2), 99–112. https://doi.org/10.33423/jbd.v19i2.2058

Singh, A. A. (2019a). Multicultural and social justice leadership and learning in the classroom. In L. R. Haddock & J. S. Whitman (Eds.), *Preparing the educator in counselor education: A comprehensive guide to building knowledge and developing skills* (pp. 59–77). Routledge.

Singh, A. A. (2019b). *The racial healing handbook: Practical activities to help you challenge privilege, confront systemic racism, and engage in collective healing*. New Harbinger.

Singh, A. A., Appling, B., & Trepal, H. (2020). Using the Multicultural and Social Justice Counseling Competencies to decolonize counseling practice: The important roles of theory, power, and action. *Journal of Counseling & Development, 98*(3), 261–271. https://doi.org/10.1002/jcad.12321

Skovholt, T. M., & Trotter-Mathison, M. (2016). *The resilient practitioner: Burnout prevention and self-care strategies for counselors, therapists, teachers, and health professionals* (3rd ed.). Routledge.

Smart, P. (2017). Redundant publication and salami slicing: The significance of splitting data. *Developmental Medicine & Child Neurology, 59*(8), 775. http://doi.org/dpcf

Smith v. Van Gorkom, 488 A. 2d 858. (1985). https://scholar.google.com/scholar_case?case=15445043763196054007&q=Smith+v.+Van+Gorkom,+488+A.2d+858,+1985&hl=en&as_sdt=6,43&as_vis=1

Smith, C. P., & Freyd, J. J. (2014). Institutional betrayal. *American Psychologist, 69*(6), 575–587. https://doi.org/10.1037/a0037564

Smith, W. A., Mustaffa, J. B., Jones, C. M., Curry, T. J., & Allen, W. R. (2016). "You make me wanna holler and throw up both my hands!" Campus culture, Black misandric microaggressions, and racial battle fatigue. *International Journal of Qualitative Studies in Education, 29*(9), 1189–1209. https://doi.org/10.1080/09518398.2016.1214296

Snow, W. H., Lamar, M. R., Hinkle, J. S., & Speciale, M. (2018). Current practices in online counselor education. *The Professional Counselor, 8*(2), 131–146. http://doi.org/dthg

Sorcinelli, M. (2000). *Principles of good practice: Supporting early-career faculty. Guidance for deans, department chairs, and other academic leaders* (ED450634). ERIC. https://files.eric.ed.gov/fulltext/ED450634.pdf

Spielmans, G. I., Biehn, T. L., & Sawrey, D. (2009). A case study of salami slicing: Pooled analyses of duloxetine for depression. *Psychotherapy and Psychosomatics, 79*(2), 97–106. http://doi.org/crr7v2

Spieth, P. M., Kubasch, A. S., Penzlin, A. I., Illigens, B. M. W., Barlinn, K., & Siepmann, T. (2016). Randomized controlled trials—a matter of design. *Neuropsychiatric Disease and Treatment, 12*, 1341–1349. http://doi.org/dsqm

Spruill, D. A., & Benshoff, J. M. (2011). Helping beginning counselors develop a personal theory of counseling. *Counselor Education and Supervision, 40*(1), 70–80. https://doi.org/fzpqz4

Spurgeon, S. L., Gibbons, M. M., & Cochran, J. L. (2012). Creating personal dispositions for a professional counseling program. *Counseling and Values, 57*(1), 96–108. https://doi.org/10.1002/j.2161-007X.2012.00011.x

Spurgeon, S. L., Woodside, M., McClam, T., Heidel, E., & Catalana, M. (2012). Prepracticum students and cognitive complexity. *Journal of Counseling, Research, and Practice, 2*(1), 3–11.

Stadler, H. A. (1986). Making hard choices: Clarifying controversial ethical issues. *Counseling and Human Development, 19*, 1–10.

Steen, S., Henfield, M. S., & Booker, B. (2014). The achieving success everyday group counseling model: Implications for professional school counselors. *The Journal for Specialists in Group Work, 39*(1), 29–46. http://doi.org/d44p

Stern, A., Guckenburg, S., & Petrosino, A. (2017, June). *Juvenile sexual offender registration: A research review*. WestED Justice & Prevention Research Center. https://jprc.wested.org/wp-content/uploads/2017/06/WestEd-JPRC-Juvenile-Sexual-Offender-Registration-Review-Report-June-2017.pdf

Stoltenberg, C. D., & McNeill, B. W. (2010). *IDM supervision: An integrative developmental model for supervising counselors and therapists* (3rd ed.). Routledge.

Stoltenberg, C. D., McNeill, B., & Delworth, U. (1998). *IDM supervision: An integrated developmental model for supervising counselors and therapists*. Jossey-Bass.

Stone, C., & Springer, M. (2019). Interactivity, connectedness and "teacher-presence": Engaging and retaining students online. *Australian Journal of Adult Learning, 59*(2), 146–169.

Strandberg, S. E. (2015). *The ability of supervisors and supervisees to recognize ethical violations within the supervisory relationship* [Unpublished doctoral dissertation]. William James College.

Substance Abuse and Mental Health Services Administration. (2014). *TIP 57: Trauma-informed care in behavioral health services* (HHS Publication No. [SMA] 14-4816).

Sue, D. W., Sue, D., Neville, H. A., & Smith, L. (2019). *Counseling the culturally diverse: Theory and practice* (8th ed.). Wiley.

Swank, J. M., & Houseknecht, A. (2019). Teaching competencies in counselor education: A Delphi study. *Counselor Education and Supervision, 58*(3), 162–176. doi.org/10.1002/ceas.12148

Swank, J. M., Houseknecht, A., & Puig, A. (2019). Authorship decision-making: A national survey of counselor educators. *The Journal of Counselor Preparation and Supervision*, *12*(2). https://repository.wcsu.edu/jcps/vol12/iss2/6

Swank, J. M., Houseknecht, A., & Puig, A. (2020). Authorship decision-making: A qualitative exploration of counselor educator practices. *Counseling and Values*, *65*(2), 222–234. https://doi.org/fk6t

Swank, J. M., & Lambie, G. W. (2016). Development of the Research Competencies Scale. *Measurement and Evaluation in Counseling and Development*, *49*(2), 91–108. http://doi.org/dn92

Swift, J. K., Callahan, J. L., Rousmaniere, T. G., Whipple, J. L., Dexter, K., & Wrape, E. R. (2015). Using client outcome monitoring as a tool for supervision. *Psychotherapy*, *52*(2), 180–184. http://doi.org/dwzx

Szucs, L. E., Shipley, M., McNeill, E. B., Housman, J., & Vinal, C. (2019). Developing preservice teachers' cultural competency through urban immersion. *American Journal of Health Studies*, *34*(2), 69–79.

Tangen, J. L., & Borders, L. D. (2016). The supervisory relationship: A conceptual and psychometric review of measures. *Counselor Education and Supervision*, *55*(3), 159–181. http://doi.org/dtmf

Tauriac, J. J., Kim, G. S., Sarinana, S. L., Tawa, J., & Kahn, V. D. (2013). Utilizing affinity groups to enhance intergroup dialogue workshops for racially and ethnically diverse students. *The Journal for Specialists in Group Work*, *38*(3), 241–260. http://doi.org/dqc7

Tenenbaum, G., Naidu, S., Jegede, O., & Austin, J. (2001). Constructivist pedagogy in conventional on-campus and distance learning practice: An exploratory investigation. *Learning and Instruction*, *11*(2), 87–111.

Tillman, D. R., Hof, D. D., Chasek, C. L., & Dinsmore, J. A. (2014). Title IX and the Clery Act: What counselor educators must know. In *VISTAS 2014*. https://www.counseling.org/docs/default-source/vistas/article_26.pdf?sfvrsn=a4a17c2c_10

Tobin, D. J., Willow, R. A., Bastow, E. K., & Ratkowski, E. M. (2009). Reflective learning within a counselor education curriculum. *The Journal of Counselor Preparation and Supervision*, *1*(1), Article 2. http://doi.org/dw37

Topor, D. R., AhnAllen, C. G., Mulligan, E. A., & Dickey, C. C. (2018). Using video recordings of psychotherapy sessions in supervision: Strategies to reduce learner anxiety. *Academic Psychiatry*, *41*(1), 40–43. http://doi.org/dwz2

Toporek, R. L., & Daniels, J. (2018). *American Counseling Association advocacy competencies*. American Counseling Association. https://www.counseling.org/docs/default-source/competencies/aca-advocacy-competencies-updated-may-2020.pdf?sfvrsn=f410212c_4

Toporek, R. L., Ortega-Villalobos, L., & Pope-Davis, D. B. (2011). Critical incidents in multicultural supervision: Exploring supervisees' and supervisor experiences. *Journal of Multicultural Counseling and Development*, *32*(2), 66–83. http://doi.org/fz4b3j

Trauma-Informed Community Network. (2018). *The trauma-informed supervisor* (3rd ed.). https://www.acesconnection.com/g/becoming-a-trauma-informed-and-beyond/fileSendAction/fcType/0/fcOid/475599658546455450/filePointer/475599658546455545/fodoid/475599658546455539/3rd%20Edition%20TI%20Supervisor%20Workbook.pdf

Vandiver, B. J., Fhagen-Smith, P. E., Cokley, K. O., Cross, W. E., & Worrell, F. C. (2001). Cross's nigrescence model: From theory to scale to theory. *Journal of Multicultural Counseling and Development*, *29*(3), 174–200. http://doi.org/fxq5gx

Vehviläinen, S., Löfström, E., & Nevgi, A. (2018). Dealing with plagiarism in the academic community: Emotional engagement and moral distress. *Higher Education, 75*(1), 1–18. http://doi.org/gcp8bk

Vick, S. (2015). *Nonprofit bylaws made easy: The complete guide to writing your nonprofit bylaws.* NonprofitAlly.com

Vontress, C. E. (2009). A conceptual approach to counseling across cultures. In C. C. Lee, D. A. Burnhill, A. L. Butler, C. P. Hipolito-Delgado, M. Humphrey, O. Muñoz, & H. J. Shin (Eds.), *Elements of culture in counseling* (pp. 19–30). Pearson.

Wachter Morris, C. A., Wester, K. L., Vaishnav, S., & Austin, J. L. (2018). Introduction. In C. A. Wachter Morris & K. L. Wester (Eds.), *Making research relevant: Applied research designs for the mental health practitioner* (pp. 1–13). Routledge.

Wagenmaker & Oberly. (2017, September 27). *Wearing the right "hat": The duty of loyalty.* https://wagenmakerlaw.com/blog/wearing-right-%E2%80%9Chat%E2%80%9D-duty-loyalty

Wager, E. (2013). *What to do if you suspect ghost, guest or gift authorship.* Committee on Publication Ethics. https://publicationethics.org/files/Ghost.pdf

Wakefield, A. J., Murch, S. H., Anthony, A., Linnell, J., Casson, D. M., Malik, M., Berelowitz, M., Dhillon, A. P., Thomson, M. A., Harvey, P., Valentine, A., Davies, S. E., & Walker-Smith, J. A. (1998). Retracted: Ileal-lymphoid-nodular hyperplasia, non-specific colitis, and pervasive developmental disorder in children. *The Lancet, 351*(9103), 637–641. http://doi.org/cntj8h

Walker, V. L. (2009). 3D virtual learning in counselor education: Using Second Life in counselor skill development. *Journal of Virtual World Research, 2*(10), 4–14. http://doi.org/dthh

Walter, G. (1999). Salami: Kosher and unkosher. *Australian and New Zealand Journal of Psychiatry, 33*(5), 766–767. http://doi.org/c77x64

Ward v. Polite, 667 F.3d. 727 (U.S. Ct. App., 6th Cir. 2012).

Ward v. Wilbanks, 700 F. Supp. 2d. 803 (Dist. Ct., S.D. Mich. 2010).

Warner, L. R., & Shields, S. A. (2013). The intersections of sexuality, gender, and race: Identity research at the crossroads. *Sex Roles, 68*(11–12), 803–810. http://doi.org/f42wft

Watson, B., Robinson, D. H. Z., Harker, L., & Jacob-Arriola, K. R. (2016). The inclusion of African-American study participants in web-based research studies: Viewpoint. *Journal of Medical Internet Research, 18*(6), e168. http://doi.org/f83k3j

Watt, S. K. (2007). Difficult dialogues, privilege and social justice: Uses of the privileged identity exploration (PIE) model in student affairs practice. *College Student Affairs Journal, 26*(2), 114–126. https://files.eric.ed.gov/fulltext/EJ899385.pdf

Watts, R. E. (2015). Research and publication. In B. Herlihy & G. Corey, *ACA ethical standards casebook* (7th ed., pp. 273–279). American Counseling Association.

Welton, A., Pei-Ling, L., & Young, M. (2010). The lived experiences of female educational leadership doctoral students. *Journal of Educational Administration, 48*(6), 727–740. http://doi.org/bm7js6

West, J. D., Bubenzer, D. L., Cox, J. A., & McGlothlin, J. M. (2013). *Teaching in counselor education: Engaging students.* Association for Counselor Education and Supervision.

West-Olatunji, C., Williams, K., & Chan, C. (2018). The role of mentoring in counselor education. In J. S. Whitman & L. R. Haddock (Eds.), *Preparing the educator in counselor education: A comprehensive guide to building knowledge and developing skills* (pp. 213–230). Routledge.

Wester, K. L. (2011). Publishing ethical research: A step-by-step overview. *Journal of Counseling & Development, 89*(3), 301–307. https://doi.org/fzs2n7

Wheeler, A. M., & Bertram, B. (2019). *The counselor and the law* (8th ed.). American Counseling Association.

White, M., & Epston, D. (1990). *Narrative means to therapeutic ends*. Norton.

Whitman, J. S., & Bidell, M. P. (2014). Affirmative lesbian, gay, and bisexual counselor education and religious beliefs: How do we bridge the gap? *Journal of Counseling & Development, 92*(2), 162–169. http://doi.org/gfxcxd

Wieland, D., & Beitz, J. M. (2015). Resilience to social bullying in academia: Phenomenological study. *Nurse Educator, 40*(6), 289–293. https://doi.org/10.1097/NNE.0000000000000169

Wilkinson, B. D., & Dewell, J. A. (2019). Cognitive complexity: Differentiation and integration in counseling training and practice. *Journal of Counseling & Development, 97*(3), 317–324. http://doi.org/dxhv

Williams, M. T. (2019). Cultural competence 101: Teaching about race and racism. In M. T. Williams, D. C. Rosen, & J. W. Kanter (Eds.), *Eliminating race-based mental health disparities: Promoting equity and culturally responsive care across settings* (pp. 129–146). Context.

Wind, S. A., Cook, R. M., & McKibben, W. B. (2021). Supervisees' of differing genders and races perceptions of power in supervision. *Counselling Psychology Quarterly, 34*(2), 275–297. https://doi.org/10.1080/09515070.2020.1731791

Wisdom, J., & Creswell, J. W. (2013). *Mixed methods: Integrating quantitative and qualitative data collection and analysis while studying patient-centered medical home models*. (AHRQ Publication No. 13-0028-EF). Agency for Healthcare Research and Quality. https://pcmh.ahrq.gov/sites/default/files/attachments/MixedMethods_032513comp.pdf

Wolpe, J. (1969). *The practice of behavior therapy*. Pergamon Press.

Wong, L. C. J., Wong, P. T. P., & Ishiyama, F. I. (2013). What helps and what hinders in cross-cultural clinical supervision: A critical incident study. *The Counseling Psychologist, 41*(1), 66–85. http://doi.org/f4jgwz

Wrenn, C. G. (1962). The culturally encapsulated counselor. *Harvard Educational Review, 32*(4), 444–449.

Writer, J. H., & Watson, D. C. (2019). Recruitment and retention: An institutional imperative told through the storied lenses of faculty of color. *Journal of the Professoriate, 10*(2), 23–46.

Xu, D., & Xu, Y. (2019, March). *The promises and limits of online higher education: Understanding how distance education affects access, cost, and quality*. The American Enterprise Institute. https://www.aei.org/wp-content/uploads/2019/03/The-Promises-and-Limits-of-Online-Higher-Education.pdf

Yin, S. (2016, August 27). The accidental plagiarist in all of us. *The New York Times*. https://www.nytimes.com/2016/08/27/science/cryptomnesia-demi-lovato-plagiarism.html

Youmans, R. (2011). Does the adoption of plagiarism-detection software in higher education reduce plagiarism? *Studies in Higher Education, 36*(7), 749–761. http://doi.org/b7b5qv

Young, M. E. (2017). *Learning the art of helping: Building blocks and techniques* (6th ed.). Merrill Prentice Hall.

Zeligman, M., Prescod, D. J., & Greene, J. H. (2015). Journey toward becoming a counselor education doctoral student: Perspectives of women of color. *The Journal of Negro Education, 84*(1), 66–79. http://doi.org/dmtc

Ziomek-Daigle, J. (2019). Admissions and gatekeeping processes. In J. E. Atieno Okech & D. J. Rubel (Eds.), *Counselor education in the 21st century: Issues and experiences* (pp. 73–90). American Counseling Association.

Zur, O. (2008, November/December). Bartering in psychotherapy and counselling: Complexities, case studies and guidelines. *New Therapist, 58,* 18–26. Drzur.com/media/barter_therapy.pdf

Index

Tables are indicated by "t" following the page number.

A

AARC (Association for Assessment and Research in Counseling), 218
Abstentions of executive board members, 264, 268–269, 294
ACA Code of Ethics (American Counseling Association)
on advocacy, 299, 302
on bullying in workplace, 323
on collaboration and authorship, 190, 197
on communication with other professionals, 15, 139
on competency development of students, 46
on counseling plan development, 149
on counselor educator issues, 2
on counselor impairment, 34, 129, 156, 161, 164
on cultural competence, 205
on dignity and welfare of clients, 39
on diversity, 170, 284, 309
on dual relationships, 81, 82
on duplicate submissions, 231
on equity and inclusion in training programs, 314–315
on ethical dilemma resolution, 265
on ethics vs. law, 102
on faculty competence, 94–95
on fees for clients and bartering, 101, 104
on fidelity and professional responsibility, 15, 19, 39
on gatekeeping role of educators, 82, 308
on informed consent, 211, 225
on institutional regulations for research, 210
on interdisciplinary teams, 205
on internship monitoring, 137–138
on mentorship, 280
on monitoring supervisees' performance, 31
on multiculturalism, 46, 50, 63
on nonprofit boards, 291–292
on online and hybrid class formats, 87
on plagiarism, 2–3, 22, 239
on power, privilege, and oppression, 309
on practice within boundaries of competency, 112
on professional boundaries, 31
on remediation of students, 42
on research and publication, 184, 188, 191, 197, 225, 231, 244
on research participants, 214, 217–218
on self-growth, 2–3, 16, 50, 71
on self-knowledge and cognitive distortion, 71
on sexual harassment, 81, 177
on site supervisor issues, 145–146, 149, 153, 161
on students' rights, 31–32
on supervision, 108
on supervision of former colleagues, 177
on teaching, 7
on values and beliefs of counselors, 120–121, 124, 169, 171
Academic integrity, 188. *See also* Plagiarism
ACCC (Association for Clinical Correctional Counseling), 271–278
Acculturation, 53–54, 122
Acculturation model (Berry), 122
ACES. *See* Association for Counselor Education and Supervision
Achieving Success Everyday group counseling model (Steen), 209
Active learning, 6
Advocacy, 298, 299, 302. *See also* Leadership and advocacy
Affinity groups, 315–316
Affirmation, 122, 309
Affirmative supervision, 180–181
Agaskar, Vaibhavee R., 19, 93
Age-related issues. *See* Nontraditional students
Alcohol use and impairment, 159–165
Ali, S., 173
Ambrose, Heather J., 149, 159

AMCD (Association for Multicultural Counseling and Development), 121, 263–269, 280. *See also* Multicultural and Social Justice Counseling Competencies
American Counseling Association. *See also ACA Code of Ethics;* Association for Multicultural Counseling and Development
fiduciary responsibilities of Governing Council representatives, 255–261
mentorship and, 19, 326
orientation and documents for members, 268
American Psychological Association, 184, 198, 239, 244
American School Counselor Association (ASCA), 95, 211, 213–214
Americans with Disabilities Act of 1990, 32
Ametrano, I., 121
Anandavalli, S., 279, 311
Ancis, J. R., 152
ASERVIC (Association for Spiritual, Ethical, and Religious Values in Counseling), 120
Assignments
group projects
inequitable contributions to, 13–20, 17*t*
student resistance to, 45–51
plagiarism and, 21–27
readings, lack of student preparation and, 5–11
reflections on service-learning projects, 40–41
Assimilation, 8, 53–55
Association for Assessment and Research in Counseling (AARC), 218
Association for Clinical Correctional Counseling (ACCC), 271–278
Association for Counselor Education and Supervision (ACES)
Best Practices in Clinical Supervision, 96, 108, 112, 121, 125, 178
Best Practices in Teaching in Counselor Education, 2
Guidelines for Research Mentorship, 184, 188, 197
New Faculty Interest Network, 95, 327
representation of, 263–269
Teaching Initiative Taskforce, 2, 96
Association for Multicultural Counseling and Development (AMCD), 121, 263–269, 280. *See also* Multicultural and Social Justice Counseling Competencies
Association for Spiritual, Ethical, and Religious Values in Counseling (ASERVIC), 120
Atkins, S. L., 73
Attrition in research studies, 223–228
Authenticity
cultural encapsulation and, 75–76
group experiences and, 48
multicultural counseling and, 56–59
pedagogy of care and, 86
role-modeling, 88–90
Authorship. *See* Collaboration and authorship
Autonomy
community advocacy boards and, 291
counselor impairment and, 129
ethical dilemmas and, 95
job satisfaction and, 89, 91
of research participants, 210, 218–220
site supervisor issues and, 146, 157

B

Bahrick, A. S., 138
Baker, D. F., 139
Barrio Minton, Casey A., 26, 300
Bartering, 101
Basic principles of ethics (Kitchener), 94–95, 146
Baum, N., 129, 131
Belmont Report (National Commission for the Protection of Human Subjects of Biomedical and Behavioral Research), 218, 227
Beneficence
community advocacy boards and, 291
counselor impairment and, 129
faculty competence and, 95
research subjects and, 210, 218, 227–228
service-learning projects and, 39
site supervisor issues and, 146
value conflicts of counselors and, 121
Benshoff, J. M., 174
Bernard, J. M., 138, 177
Berry, J. W., 122
Bertram, B., 125
Best Practices in Clinical Supervision (ACES Supervision Taskforce), 96, 108, 112, 121, 125, 178
Best Practices in Teaching in Counselor Education (ACES Teaching Initiative Taskforce), 2
Bias
attrition bias, 225
blind review of research to avoid, 244–245
consulting other professionals to minimize, 265
ethnocentrism and, 71
modeling disclosure, 67
multicultural courses and, 55–57
performance bias, 225
positivism and, 207
race and ethnicity, 283, 309–310
school counselors and, 213
selection bias, 224–225
in supervisor relationships, 167–174
underrepresented populations in studies and, 204–205, 208
virtue ethics to challenge, 318
Bias, implicit, 26, 204–205, 207–208, 283
Bidell, M. P., 120
Billing and sliding scale fees, 100–105
Black racial identity development model (Cross), 170, 176
Blind review of research, 244–245
Blind spots, 67, 204, 265, 316
Boundaries
acquaintances as research participants, 215–222
babysitting supervisor's children, 129, 133
community advocacy boards, students and educators serving together, 292, 295
extensions in service learning, 37–43
maintenance during skills practice, 29–35
overinvolvement and deep attachments to clients, 129
savior complexes and, 129–130
site supervisor issues and, 161
supervision of former colleagues and, 177–178
supervisor attraction to supervisee, 175–181
Title IX and faculty–student relationships, 77–84

Boundary spanning, 278
Bracketing skills, 50–51, 122
Brat, M., 300
Bratton, Imelda N., 77
Brave spaces concept, 58
Broaching feedback conversations
  bullying in workplace, 324
  cultural factors, 51, 156, 170, 309, 315
  mentors and, 281, 285
  modeling, 51–52
  multiple relationships, 292
  power dynamics and, 190
  racial issues, 177
Broderick, N. A., 201
Broome, M. E., 241
Brown, Brené, 88
Bruner, Sherrie L., 187, 201
Budget issues of community boards, 287–295
Bullying, 213–214, 321–328
Burnout, 151–157
Burns, S. T., 129, 300
Bylaw statements of organizations, 273–274

C

Camilo, Diana, 195, 248
Cannon, Y., 284
Care duty in fiduciary responsibility, 256–257, 290
Care ethical approach, 22–23, 26
Cartwright, A. D., 284
Casadevall, A., 201
Cavazos Vela, J., 41
CF (compassion fatigue), 128, 130, 131–132
Challenger, Clewiston D., 13, 34
Chan, Christian D., 305, 318
Chan, Y., 162
Chang, Catherine Y., 61, 90
Chien, Jenny L., 50, 85
Chi Sigma Iota (CSI)
  legislative advocacy and, 300–301
  mentorship through, 326
  Principles and Practices of Leadership Excellence, 263, 291–292
  representation of, 263, 264, 266
  support network through, 19
Choudhuri, Devika Dibya, 135, 180
Chung, R. C. Y., 197
Citing of quotations, 23
City University of New York at Hunter, plagiarism information, 23
Civil Rights Act of 1964, 73
Clarke, Philip B., 260, 321
Classroom preparation and discussions, 5–11
Client interest and well-being in counseling. *See also* Beneficence; Nonmaleficence
  billing and fees, 100–105
  boundary extensions in service learning, 37–43
  impairment of counselors and, 127–134, 159–165
  intern exhaustion and burnout, 151–157
  practice within boundaries of competency, 111–118
Client interest and well-being in research and scholarship, 184–185, 209–228
  acquaintances as research participants, 215–222
  IRB approval and, 209–214
  withdrawing from studies, 223–228
Coaching, 137, 140. *See also* Mentorship
Cochran, J. L., 16, 64
Code of ethics. *See ACA Code of Ethics*
Cognitive counseling skills in discrimination model, 112, 114–115
Cognitive distortions, 71–73
Coker, J. K., 90
Colburn, Anita A. Neuer, 119, 133
Collaboration and authorship, 184, 187–208. *See also* Group projects
  authorship agreements, 200, 202
  bullying in workplace and, 322–323
  collaboration gone wrong, 203–208
  contested authorship, 195–202
  support groups for women in academia, 285
  taking someone else's work as own, 187–194
Collectivism, 218, 221, 282
Colonization, 67
Committee on Publication Ethics, 198, 232
Communal learning environments, 47–48
Community leadership. *See* Local community leadership and advocacy
Compassion fatigue (CF), 128, 130, 131–132
Competencies for Addressing Spiritual and Religious Issues in Counseling (ASERVIC), 120
Competencies for Counseling with Lesbian, Gay, Bisexual, Queer, Questioning, Intersex, and Ally Individuals (Society for Sexual, Affectional, Intersex, and Gender Expansive Identities), 121
Competency issues. *See also* Cultural competence
  overemotional counselors, 128, 130
  personal issues impacting, 32
  practice within boundaries of competency, 111–118
  remediation for, 42, 71, 73
  skills practice and, 31
Compliance Guide for 501(c)(3) Public Charities (IRS), 290
Confidentiality
  bullying in workplace and, 324–325, 327
  counselor education and, 64
  in research, 210–213, 217, 219–220, 225, 228
  skill practice and, 31, 34
Conflicts of interest
  on community boards, 288, 290–291, 294–295
  fiduciary responsibilities and, 255–261
  internships and, 141
  representation of multiple organizations and, 263–269
Connaughton, S. L., 324
Consensual relationships, 77–84
Consent. *See* Informed consent
Consortia Advancing Standards in Research Administration Information, 198
Constantine, M. G., 324
Constructivism, 207
Consulting other professionals
  on ethical dilemmas, 104, 265–266

(Continued)

Consulting other professionals *(continued)*
on internship site issues, 138
skill practice in, 30
Contact hypothesis, 76
Contested authorship, 195–202
Contributor Roles Taxonomy (CRediT), 198
Control groups for research studies, 223–228
Cook, R. M., 161
Copyright law, 199
Core conditions for facilitative learning (Rogers & Freiberg), 86
Corey, G., 94
Council for Accreditation of Counseling and Related Educational Programs (CACREP) Standards
ACA Code of Ethics on, 2
on advocacy and leadership, 298–299, 302
on advocacy models and skills of supervisors, 253
on assessing student learning, 16, 19
on diversity and recruitment of faculty, 284
faculty competence and, 94–95
on leadership in professional organizations, 264
on leadership preparation of doctoral students, 252, 290–291
on marginalized students' success, 314
on mentorship, 19
Multicultural and Social Justice Counseling Competencies and admissions processes, 3
on multicultural counseling, 73
on online and hybrid formats, 87
on professional organization identity and development, 272–273
on race of faculty, 323
on remediation of students, 308
on research and publication, 184
on reviewing supervisees' recordings, 109
on self-growth, 3, 16
on self-knowledge and cognitive distortion, 72
on site internship and supervisor qualifications, 138–139
on site supervisor issues, 157
on student review, remediation, or dismissal, 34
on supervision, 108, 148, 178
on teaching as core area, 2
Counseling performance skills in discrimination model, 112
Counselor impairment. *See* Impairment of counselors
Counselors for Impact, 287–295
Countertransference, 117, 129, 170–171, 178, 180
Course evaluations, 57
Credibility of research findings, 231
CRediT (Contributor Roles Taxonomy), 198
Credit for work. *See* Collaboration and authorship
Crenshaw, K. W., 312
Critical epistemologies, 207
Critical thinking and questioning skills, 56–57, 122
Cross, William, 170, 176
Crying of counselors, 127–134, 167–168
Cryptomnesia, 24–25
CSI. *See* Chi Sigma Iota
Cultural awareness, 62, 74, 173–174, 178
Cultural competence
cultural encapsulation and, 97
culturally relevant teaching and, 47
instructor competency to teach specialty courses and, 97
multicultural courses and, 53–59
research participants and bias toward, 203–205, 208
of supervisors, 149
values of counselors and, 172
Cultural considerations
in authorship determinations, 197, 201–202
broaching feedback conversations on, 51, 156, 170, 309, 315
cultural encapsulation and racism, 69–76
cultural humility and, 173, 318
culturally affirmative remediation and, 122
culturally relevant teaching and, 47
ethical decision-making, model for, 189–191, 266
in gatekeeping and remediation, 308–309
institutional culture and, 306–307
international students and, 8, 11
research subjects and, 203–205, 208, 221
site supervisor issues and, 143–150, 152–153, 156
student preparation and, 8, 10–11
in trauma counseling, 115
Cut-and-paste plagiarism, 23–24

D

Davis, T. E., 144
Decolonizing teaching materials, 67
Deep learning, 88
DeLorenzi, Leigh D., 151
Diambra, Joel F., 143, 173
Dietlin, Olga R., 50, 85, 88
Differently abled children, 209–214
Diggs, G. A., 323
Digital classes, faculty preparedness for, 85–91
Discrimination. *See* Diversity and inclusion; Race, ethnicity, and racism
Dismissals from graduate programs, 139–140, 142
Dissertations, 187–194, 237–242
Diversity and inclusion, 3–4, 53–84. *See also* Race, ethnicity, and racism
blind review of research and, 245
within counselor education programs, 253–254, 305–328
diversity and inclusion plans, 305–312
marginalization and, 313–319
microaggressions and bullying, 321–328
cultural encapsulation and racism, 69–76
discrimination model and, 112–115, 117, 131, 172
multicultural courses and, 53–59
race and ethnicity, 61–68, 225
Title IX and faculty–student relationships, 77–84
Dixon, Natasha K., 223–228
Doci, Erich, 187
Doctoral student supervisors, 110, 167–181
attraction to supervisees, 175–181
supervisee's bias, 167–174
Douglas, B. D., 228
Drucker, P., 274
Dual relationships, 77–84, 215–222, 295
Due process policies, 26, 113, 125, 139
Duplicate submissions for publication, 231

E

EBP (evidence-based practice), 114–115, 231
Editors and associate editors of journals, 243–249
EDMDAC (ethical decision-making model to determine authorship credit, R. Foster & Ray), 189–192
Education Trust, 213
Educause, 88
Eggert, L. D., 190
Emerging Reviewers (EMs), 279, 282, 284
Emotional distress of counselors, 127–134. *See also* Impairment of counselors
Empathy, 76, 88, 168, 170
English language learners, 8, 11
Equity audits, 202
Ethical acculturation model (Handelsman), 122
Ethical bracketing, 122
Ethical decision-making models (EDMMs)
  acquaintances as research participants, 217–219
  authorship credit, 188–192
  counselor competency to teach specialty courses, 94–96
  faculty–student consensual relationships, 84
  representation of multiple organizations, 265–266
  site supervisor issues, 144–148
  value conflicts of counselors, 121
Ethical Standards for School Counselors (ASCA), 214
Ethics and ethical dilemmas. *See also ACA Code of Ethics;* Fidelity
  alcohol use and impairment of site supervisors, 160–165
  assessing skills of aspiring counselors and, 22
  authorship issues, 196, 323
  boundary crossing, 129
  client attraction to counselor and, 177
  client harm and, 31
  collectivism and, 218
  community advocacy boards and, 290–292
  dual relationships and, 81, 82–83
  of executive board members, 263–269
  faculty preparedness in, 99–105
  fees and, 100–105
  informed consent forms, research participants' understanding of, 228
  mentorship and, 280–281
  online classes and, 91
  organizational, 260
  plagiarism and, 22–23
  publication issues, 230, 239, 244
  self-serving motivations and, 139
  supervisor attraction to supervisee and, 179, 181
  values and beliefs of counselors and, 121–122
  veracity and, 39, 42
  virtue ethics, 318
Ethnicity. *See* Race, ethnicity, and racism
Ethnocentrism, 71
Eugenics, 208
Evaluations
  of faculty and courses, 57
  of students, 64, 83
Evidence-based practice (EBP), 114–115, 231
Executive board members, 263–269
Experiential activities. *See also* Group projects; Internships
  advocacy opportunities, 302
  boundary maintenance during skills practice, 29–35
  in online courses, 87
  unprepared or unengaged students and, 5–11
Experiential teaching philosophy, 5, 7, 10

F

Faculty. *See also* Leadership and advocacy
  bullying in workplace and, 321–328
  consulting on issues, 30, 104, 138, 265–266
  course evaluations and, 57
  as gatekeepers. *See* Gatekeeping policies
  interest groups for, 285
  from marginalized groups, 57, 318–319
  as mentors. *See* Mentorship
  as models of behavior. *See* Modeling behaviors
  power and privilege of, 55, 64–65
  professional development for, 68
  promotion and tenure of, 230, 234, 323–324
  race and ethnicity of, 8, 57, 225–226, 284–285, 307, 311–312, 314–315, 323
  relationships with students, 77–84
  in service-learning project preparation, 40–41, 43
  supervision and. *See* Supervision
  Title IX reports of student behavior, 179, 181
Faculty preparedness, 4, 85–105
  competency for specialty courses, 93–98
  for online delivery, 85–91
  unethical or illegal practice, 99–105
Fallon, K. M., 122
Farrell, I. C., 300
Fees, 100–105
Fellows programs, 317
Feminist-based supervisory approach, 115, 118
Fidelity
  community advocacy boards and, 291
  faculty competence and, 95
  group projects, inequitable contributions to, 15, 19
  review of research and, 244
  service-learning projects and, 39, 42
  site supervisor issues and, 146
Fiduciary responsibilities
  community board leadership and, 290, 294
  conflicts of interest and association board memberships, 255–261
  faculty–student relationships and, 82
  representation of multiple organizations and, 263, 265
First Amendment rights, 295
501(c)(3) organizations, 287–295
Flirting, 77–84
Ford, David Julius, Jr., 156, 175
Forester-Miller, H., 144
Foster, Marija, 287–295
Foster, R., 189
Fox, Jesse, 207, 243
Fraud, 101–102
Freeman, S., Jr., 242
Free-write assignments, 24

Freire, Paulo, 56, 58–59
Frese, K. M., 10
Fuller, R. G., 88

G

Gabe, Rowan, 151–157
Gage, N. A., 213
Gannon, K., 89
Garrett, M. T., 144
Gatekeeping policies. *See also* Remediation for students
 boundary extensions in service learning and, 42
 boundary maintenance during skills practice and, 32, 34–35
 cultural considerations, 308–309
 dual relationships and, 82–83, 295
 faculty competence and, 94
 internship monitoring and, 137–141
 online classes and, 91
 supervisors' role in, 121
 training in, 74
Gatmon, D., 144
Gender. *See* Women
George, Shanice, 86
Georgiou, Jean, 19, 93
Ghost authors, 198
Ghoston, Michelle R., 260, 321
Gibbons, M. M., 16, 64
Gibson, D. M., 241
Giordano, A. L., 241
Gonzalez, Tiphanie, 21
Goodrich, Kristopher M., 263, 294
Goodyear, R. K., 138, 177
Grading processes, 25
Grant proposals, 184
Group counseling
 boundaries maintenance during skills practice, 29–35
 IRB approval for study on, 209–214
 student resistance to group experience, 45–51
Group projects
 faculty–student relationships and, 83
 inequitable contributions, 13–20, 17*t*
 learning preferences and, 7, 9
Guest speakers in class, 99–105
Guidelines for Research Mentorship (ACES), 184, 188, 197

H

Hagler, M. A., 180
Handelsman, M. M., 122
Harris, Paul C., 203, 234
Harris, R., 290
Haskins, Natoya Hill, 277, 313
Healthcare Providers Service Organization, 84
Helms, J., 169
Henderson, Kathryn L., 29, 42
Herlihy, B., 122
Heterosexual privilege, 123
Hidden curriculum, 316
Hiemstra, A. M. F., 149
Hierarchical thinking, 72
Hill, Nicole R., 13, 34, 281, 287, 302
Hines, Erik M., 203, 234
Hipolito-Delgado, Carlos P., 53, 55, 57, 75, 76
HIV-positive status, 175–181
Hoeft, M. E., 10
Hof, D. D., 299
Holman, Leigh Falls, 255, 326
Hook, J. N., 173
hooks, b., 47
Houseknecht, A., 90
Howells, Renée C., 263, 294
Hudson, Denita N., 69, 97
Humanistic teaching philosophy, 5, 9, 10
Hunt, B., 239, 241
Hypervisibility, 265
Hypothetical-deductive method, 208

I

IAAOC (International Association of Addictions and Offender Counselors), 255–256, 260–261
Identity development
 intersectionality and, 46–47, 71, 173–174
 professional, 68, 201
 racial, 169–173, 176–177, 180, 310
 sexual, 180
IMED (Intercultural model of ethical decision-making, Luke), 189–192, 266
Impairment of counselors
 burnout and self-care, 156
 determining, 127–134
 people with disabilities and, 34
 role confusion and, 97
 session recordings and awareness of, 137–139
 of site supervisors, 159–165
 supervisor attraction to supervisee and, 177
Implicit bias, 26, 204–205, 207–208, 283
Individualism, 55, 282
Informed consent
 fee structures and, 104
 overinvolvement with clients and violations of, 129
 of research participants, 210–211, 217, 219, 225, 228
 supervisory, 125, 133, 146
Institutional culture, 306–307
Institutional racism, 306–307
Institutional review boards (IRBs), 185, 209–214, 218, 222
Instructors. *See* Faculty; Faculty preparedness
Insurance companies, 99–105
Integrated developmental model (Stoltenberg & McNeill), 131–132, 169
Intercultural model of ethical decision-making (IMED, Luke), 189–192, 266
Interdisciplinary teams, 184, 203–208
International Association of Addictions and Offender Counselors (IAAOC), 255–256, 260–261
International students, 8, 11

Internships. *See also* Site supervisor issues
faculty competency for teaching specialty courses, 93–98
reassignments of, 154
termination of, 146–147
Interpersonal process recall, 171
Intersectionality
of faculty, 97, 323–324
identity development and understanding of, 46–47, 71, 173–174
impairment of counselors and, 128, 131
marginalization in counselor education programs and, 319
microaggressions and, 307
Intersectionality-based policy analysis, 309–310
Intrapersonal communication, 71
IRBs (institutional review boards), 185, 209–214, 218, 222
Isolation of students, 226

J

Jamison, Ani, 187–194
JARS-Qual (Journal Article Reporting Standards for Qualitative Research), 248
Jealousy, 323
Jencius, Marty, 268, 271
Job satisfaction, 89, 91, 323–324
Johari's window, 48–49
Journal Article Reporting Standards for Qualitative Research (JARS-Qual), 248
Journal articles, 24. *See also* Research and scholarship
Journal management, 279–285
Journal of Multicultural Counseling and Development (JMCD), 279–285
Jun, H., 72
Justice. *See also* Social justice
community advocacy boards and, 291
as litmus test for courses of action, 147
research subjects and, 210, 218, 221, 227–228
site supervisor issues and, 146
value conflicts of counselors and, 121
Juvenile sex offenders, advocacy for, 255–261

K

Kaye, J. B., 40
Kemer, Gülşh, 141, 167, 168–169, 171
Kendi, I. X., 312
Kerr, M. M., 10
Killermann, S., 123
King, C., 324
Kitchener, K. S., 94–95, 146
Kocet, M. M., 122

L

Lacks, Henrietta, 214
Ladson-Billings, G., 47
Lai, C. K., 58
Lamar, M., 91
Leadership and advocacy
diversity and inclusion within counselor education programs, 305–328. *See also* Diversity and inclusion
in local community, 287–304. *See also* Local community leadership and advocacy
professional organization leadership, 255–286. *See also* Professional organization leadership
Leadership Practices Inventory (Kouzes & Posner), 275
Learning. *See also* Experiential activities
active, 6
assessing, 16, 19
communal learning environments, 47–48
deep, 88
self-directed, 10
service learning, 37–43
student formats for, 7, 9
transformative, 88
Least publishable unit, 229–235, 230*t*
Lee, Aiesha, 313
Lee, C. C., 173
Legal concerns
alcohol use and impairment, 160–165
copyright law and authorship issues, 199
dismissals of students from programs and, 140
legislative advocacy and, 297–303
online classes and, 91
for professional organizations, 274
sexual harassment and, 177
unethical or illegal practice and, 99–105
values and beliefs conflicts of counselors, 124–125
Lenz, A. Stephen, 195, 248
LGBT population
marginalization of students and, 313–319
mentorship and, 281
sexual harassment and, 177, 179
site supervisor issues and, 150
supervision of supervision and, 175–181
values and beliefs of counselors and, 119–125
Li, Huijuan, 313
Licensure boards, 179, 181
Linear thinking, 72
Linich, Kathryn P., 5, 67
Linvill, J. S., 324
Lobbying, 297–303
Local community leadership and advocacy, 253, 287–304
budget issues of community boards, 287–295
university prohibitions on, 297–303
Louis, D. A., 325
Loyalty duty as fiduciary responsibility, 257, 290
Luke, Melissa, 144, 187, 201

M

Managed care, 100–102
Manis, A. A., 46–47
Manuscript-style dissertations, 241–242
MAP (Multicultural Action Project), 57, 59
Marginalization. *See* Diversity and inclusion
Marshall, D. S., 152

Mason, Erin C. M., 61, 90
Matthew, P. A., 234
McKibben, W. Bradley, 111, 124, 289
Mediation, 192
Melchior, Shekila, 209, 221
Mentorship
- authorship issues and, 191–193
- bullying in workplace, prevention of, 325, 326–327
- Emerging Reviewers and, 279, 282, 284
- ethical considerations for, 280–281
- Guidelines for Research Mentorship of ACES, 184, 188, 197
- for journal management, 279–285
- for junior faculty, 95
- by peers, 19
- professional organizations and, 326
- professional socialization and, 188
- race and ethnicity of faculty and, 8, 226, 284–285, 311–312, 315
- race and ethnicity of leaders and, 277, 281
- research assistant positions and, 195–202
- by retired scholars, 280, 282, 284
- student development and, 19
- through team teaching, 98
- women and, 277, 281, 284–285

Meritocracy, 55
Microaffirmations, 309
Microaggressions
- addressing in class, 56
- bullying in workplace, 321–328
- by counselors, 173
- defined, 324
- diversity and inclusion policies and, 305–312
- financial incentives for international research participants and, 221
- lack of openness to diversity as, 205
- multiple marginalized identities and, 315

Minnix, G. M., 122
Misrepresentation of data in research, 231
Mission statements of organizations, 273–274
Modeling behaviors. *See also* Role modeling
- biases, faculty disclosure of, 67
- broaching feedback conversations, 50–51
- collaboration and authorship, 184
- ethical decision-making, 150, 160–161
- interventions recommended by supervisors, 178
- professional roles, 302
- student expectations and, 7

Morrissey, J., 178
Multicultural Action Project (MAP), 57, 59
Multicultural and Social Justice Counseling Competencies (MSJCC)
- advocacy positions with social costs, 257
- CACREP on, 3
- on clients' worldviews, 177
- developmental domains of, 63
- intersectionality and, 46–47, 50, 71
- marginalized students and, 318
- privilege and, 121
- self-awareness and, 97
- self-knowledge and cognitive distortion, 72

Multiculturalism. *See also* Cultural considerations; Intersectionality
- across curriculums, 307–308
- community advocacy and, 292
- courses on, 3, 53–59, 307
- cultural encapsulation and racism, 69–76
- faculty as advocates for, 309
- lens for teaching materials, 8
- marginalized students and, 313–319
- mentorship and, 281–282
- multicultural orientation model (Owen), 152, 157
- research participants and, 211
- site supervisor issues and, 162
- Standards for Multicultural Research of AARC, 218
- student tensions related to, 61–68
- supervision of supervision and, 167–174
- values and beliefs of counselors and, 120–122

Multiple professional organization representation, 263–269
Murdock, J., 87

N

Narrative supervision (White & Epston), 131–132
National Association of Social Workers, 137
National Center for Education Statistics, 225
National Commission for the Protection of Human Subjects of Biomedical and Behavioral Research, 218, 227
Neufeldt, S. A., 114
New Faculty Interest Network of ACES, 95
Ng, K. M., 8
Nigrescence model (Cross), 176
Noncompliance of students, 5–11
Nonmaleficence
- community advocacy boards and, 291
- counselor impairment and, 129
- faculty competence and, 95
- service-learning projects and, 39
- site supervisor issues and, 146, 150, 161
- skill practice and, 34
- supervisee bias and, 171
- value conflicts of counselors and, 121

Nonprofit organizations, 287–295. *See also* Professional organization leadership
Nontraditional students
- group counseling participation and, 45–51
- group projects, inequitable contributions to, 13–20
- multicultural courses and, 53–59
- technology gaps and, 22–23

Nowak, Sandy, 135–142

O

Obedience duty in fiduciary responsibility, 258–259
Ohrt, Jonathan H., 5, 67
Ombudspersons, 192, 325, 327
Online classes, faculty preparedness for, 85–91
Oppression, 54–55, 58–59, 208, 318, 324
Ordway, A., 91

Organizational ethics, 260
Orientation
for community advocacy boards, 290
for faculty on university policies, 302
gatekeeping policies reviewed during, 32
plagiarism prevention during, 27
racism education and, 312
for site supervisors, 144, 157
Overlapping research questions, 229–235

P

Paladino, Derrick A., 151, 164
Parallel processes in counseling, 172, 178
Paraphrasing as plagiarism, 23
Patel, Samir H., 5, 45
Pearson, Barb, 85–91
Pedagogy of care (Noddings), 86, 87–88, 90
Peer mentorships, 19
Peer support, 95. *See also* Consulting other professionals
People with disabilities, 32, 34, 209–214
Performance bias, 225
PE (prolonged exposure) therapy, 111–118
Phenomenological research design, 217–218
Philosophy of science, 207–208
Physical contact and touching, 177–178
Pink, D. H., 89
Piotrowski, C., 324
Placeres, Vanessa, 61
Plagiarism
ACA Code of Ethics on, 2–3, 22, 239
authorship and collaboration issues, 187–194
detection services for, 23, 25
prevention of, 23, 27
self-plagiarism, 23–24
similar topics of research studies and publications, 238, 239
in student assignments, 21–27
Positive school environments, 63–64
Positivism, 207
Postpositivism, 207
Posttraumatic stress, 322
Power differentials
authorship determinations and, 189–192, 197, 201
bullying in workplace and, 321–328
faculty–student relationships and, 80–83
faculty supervisors and, 133, 138, 178
racism and, 307–308
site supervisors and, 145, 153, 157, 161, 164–165
value conflicts of counselors and, 121
Practice-based model (Corey), 94
Pratt, Ezekiel, 187–194
Predominanty white institutions, 307, 315–316
Premium diversion, 101–102
Prescod, Diandra J., 213, 223
Principles and Practices of Leadership Excellence (CSI Academy of Leaders), 263, 291–292
Privacy. *See* Confidentiality
Privilege. *See also* Power differentials
blind spots, recognizing, 204
cultural encapsulation and, 75
diverse voices, lack of openness to, 205
heterosexual, 123
marginalized students and, 318
multicultural education and, 55, 64–65
student expectations based on, 26
tokenization of faculty of color and, 307
value conflicts of counselors and, 121
Professional behaviors. *See also* Ethics and ethical dilemmas; Modeling behaviors
basic principles of ethics, 94–95, 146
in discrimination model, 112–113
site supervisor issues and, 151–157
of students on community boards, 295
Professional development, 68, 156–157, 272. *See also* Mentorship; Orientation
Professional identity development, 68, 201
Professional organization leadership, 252–253, 255–286
fiduciary responsibility, 255–261
identity and development of organizations and, 271–278
journals, managing, 279–285
representing multiple organizations, 263–269
Professional Progression Plans, 35
Professional socialization, 188, 201
Project Implicit, 123
Prolonged exposure (PE) therapy, 111–118
Prosek, Elizabeth A., 215, 241
Publication Manual of the American Psychological Association (American Psychological Association), 184, 198
Publication process, 185–186, 229–249
already published research and, 237–242
compromising with reviewers' feedback, 243–249
least publishable unit, 229–235, 230*t*
Public speaking skills, 6, 9, 11

Q

Queer Café website, 123

R

Race, ethnicity, and racism. *See also* Cultural considerations; Diversity and inclusion; Intersectionality; Microaggressions; Multiculturalism
allies of communities of color, 76
assimilation and, 8, 53–55
bullying in workplace and, 321–327
collectivism and, 218, 221
cultural encapsulation and, 69–76
disproportionate service responsibilities and, 279, 283, 284
eugenics and, 208
of faculty and students, 8, 19, 57, 225–226, 284–285, 307, 311–312, 314–315, 323
institutional, 306–312
justice system disparities and, 255–257
mentorship and, 277, 281
mistrust of research studies, 214, 225
online courses and access to higher education, 87
(Continued)

Race, ethnicity, and racism *(continued)*
professional organizations, representation of, 263, 265
promotion and tenure stress, 234
race-based trauma and fatigue, 319
remediation for students and, 306, 308–309
research studies and, 213–214
school counselors' recognition of, 213
student tensions related to, 61–68
supervisory relationships and, 167–174, 177–178
targeted research and, 215–222
tokenism and, 265, 307, 318, 324
white savior complex and, 101, 168–172
Racial climate, 307–309, 323
Racial identity development, 169–173, 176–177, 180, 310
Ray, D., 189
Recruitment of research participants, 216, 221–222
Redundant publication, 229–235
Referrals, 109–110, 120–121, 124
Reflection
for cognitive distortion recognition, 72, 73
on conflicts of interest, 294–295
ethical decision-making models and, 267
researchers' responses to feedback and, 249
self-reflection, promotion of, 47
for service-learning projects, 40–41
in supervision, 170–171, 173
Relational equilibrium model (Minnix), 122
Religious beliefs, 119–125
Remediation for students
boundaries during skills practice and, 31–34
boundary extensions in service learning and, 42
cultural encapsulation and, 71–74
group projects, inequitable contributions to, 19
plagiarism and, 22, 27
practice within boundaries of competency, 113
racism and, 306, 308–309
session recordings, refusal to share, 139
supervisor impairment and, 164
value conflicts of counselors and, 121–125
Representation of multiple professional organizations, 263–269
Rescue Legion (RL), 135–142
Research and scholarship
client interest and well-being, 184–185, 209–228. *See also* Client interest and well-being in research and scholarship
collaboration and authorship, 184, 187–208. *See also* Collaboration and authorship
publication process, 185–186, 229–249. *See also* Publication process
Research assistant (RA) positions, 195–202
Research ethics, 323
Respect for research participants, 210, 218–219, 227–228
Retaliation, 133, 152–153, 162–164
Review of journal articles, 243–249, 279–285
Robert's Rules of Order, 269, 275
Rogers, J. L., 88
Role modeling
authenticity and, 88
counselor educator responsibility in, 7, 146
discussion or racism and multiculturalism, 74
mentors and, 281
race and ethnicity of faculty and, 226
Role plays, 29–35
Romantic relationships, 77–84, 175–181
Rose, C. A., 213
Rubrics for group performance, 16, 17*t*, 19
Rules ethical approach, 22–23, 26

S

Safe and supportive schools model of school climate (National Center on Safe Supportive Learning Environments), 63–64
SafeAssign (plagiarism detection service), 25
Safety. *See also* Trust
bullying in workplace and, 321–328
LGBT supervision and, 180
multicultural courses and, 54, 56, 58
nontraditional students and, 47–48, 50
positive school environments and, 63–64
racism and, 307–309
sanctuary spaces and, 315–316
supervisory relationships and, 178, 180–181
Salami slicing (redundant publication), 229–235
Sanctuary spaces, 315–316
Savior complex, 101, 129–130, 168–172
Scholl, Mark B., 37, 58
School counselors, 209–214
Scientific method, 207–208
Secondary oppression, 318
Secondary traumatic stress (STS), 128, 130, 131–132
Segregation in educational settings, 62, 73
Selection bias, 224–225
Self-assessment, 73, 170, 178. *See also* Self-reflection
Self-awareness
cultural, 71, 74, 97, 178
in discrimination model, 112, 114
emotional distress during sessions, 131
faculty competence and, 94
faculty–student relationships and, 82–83
group project participation and, 16, 47
LGBT population, attitudes toward, 123
of race and ethnicity, 63
in relation to clients, 169
researchers' responses to feedback and, 249
Self-care, 132, 151–157
Self-directed learning activities, 10
Self-disclosure, 30–31, 138, 171
Self-growth
ACA Code of Ethics on, 2–3, 16, 50, 71
counseling for, 33
cultural encapsulation and, 71
resistance to, 46
Self-plagiarism, 23–24
Self-reflection
bias and, 173
on conflicts of interest, 267, 294
cultural encapsulation and, 72
practice within boundaries of competency, 117
promotion in classrooms, 47
responding to reviewers' feedback and, 249

Self-reporting, 140
Service-learning (SL) projects, 37–43
Session recordings, not bringing to supervision, 135–142
Seward, D. X., 72
Sexism, 324
Sex Offender Registration and Notification Act (SORNA), 255, 260–261
Sex offenders, advocacy for, 255–261
Sexual harassment, 79–80, 82, 177, 179
Sexual identity development, 180
Sexuality Implicit Association Test (Project Implicit), 123
Sexual orientation, 119–125. *See also* LGBT population
Sheperis, D. S., 90, 91
Shields, S. A., 232
Site agreement forms, 136–137, 153
Site supervisor issues, 109–110, 143–165
- conflicts of interests and ethical dilemmas, 135–142
- impairment of supervisors, 159–165
- incongruence between supervisors, 143–150
- supervisor presenting differently to students, 151–157

Skills practice, boundary maintenance during, 29–35
Sliding scale fees, 100–105
Snowball sampling, 221
Socialization, professional, 188, 201
Social justice. *See also* Multicultural and Social Justice Counseling Competencies
- across curriculums and courses, 53–59, 307–311
- competency in, 71–74
- egalitarian teacher–student dialogue and, 58
- faculty as advocates for, 309
- juvenile sex offenders, advocacy for, 255–261
- marginalized students and, 313–319
- multicultural counseling and, 73–74
- race and ethnicity tensions in classrooms, 61–68

Society for Sexual, Affectional, Intersex, and Gender Expansive Identities, 121
Soleman, J., 93–98
Sorcinelli, M., 281
SORNA (Sex Offender Registration and Notification Act), 255, 260–261
Speciale, Megan, 195, 248
Specialty courses, faculty competency for, 93–98
Spirituality, 119–125
Spruill, D. A., 174
Spurgeon, Shawn L., 16, 64, 82, 99
Stadler, H. A., 147
Standards for Multicultural Research (AARC), 218
State counseling associations, 300
Statistical power and significance in research findings, 231
Steen, Sam, 209, 221
Stereotypes, 53–54, 169, 173, 306–307
Strategic plans for organizations, 274, 277
Stretch, LoriAnn Sykes, 69, 97
STS (secondary traumatic stress), 128, 130, 131–132
Student engagement and dispositions, 2–3, 5–51
- boundaries during skills practice, 29–35
- boundary extensions in service learning, 37–43
- group projects, 13–20, 17*t*, 45–51
- online classes, 90–91
- plagiarism, 21–27
- unprepared or unengaged students, 5–11

Student handbooks, 125
Sue, D. W., 312
Supervisee dispositions and behaviors, 108–109, 111–142. *See also* Supervision of supervision
- counselor impairment and, 127–134
- practice within boundaries of competency, 111–118
- session recordings, not bringing to supervision, 135–142
- value conflicts of counselors, 119–125

Supervision. *See also* Gatekeeping policies
- doctoral student supervisors, 110, 167–174. *See also* Doctoral student supervisors
- internships and faculty competence, 93–98
- multicultural and social justice counseling competencies, 73–74
- power differentials and, 133, 138, 145
- of service-learning projects, 37–43
- site supervisor issues, 143–165. *See also* Site supervisor issues
- supervisee dispositions and behaviors, 108–109, 111–142. *See also* Supervisee dispositions and behaviors

Supervision of supervision (SOS), 110, 167–181
- attraction to supervisees, 175–181
- supervisee's bias, 167–174

Swank, Jacqueline M., 90, 104, 193, 237
Syphilis study, 214
Systemic inequity, 202

T

Taxonomies of authorship, 190, 198, 201
Teaching Initiative Taskforce of ACES, 2, 96
Teams, interdisciplinary, 184, 203–208
Team teaching, 98
Technology
- faculty preparedness for, 85–91
- gaps in knowledge, 22–23

Text-to-speech software, 25
Theory of nigresence (Cross), 176
Thinking-aloud approach, 171
3-2-1 assignment, 48
Tillman, D. R., 179
Tirrell, Matthew, 175
Title IX, 77–84, 177, 179, 181
Tokenism, 265, 307, 318, 324
Topor, D. R., 140
Toporek, R. L., 144
Training. *See* Orientation
Transference, 117, 178, 180
Transformative learning, 88
Transparency, 34–35, 244, 268
Trauma
- cultural considerations and, 115
- posttraumatic stress, 322

(Continued)

Trauma *(continued)*
race-based trauma and fatigue, 319
secondary traumatic stress, 128, 130, 131–132
Trauma-informed principles, 130–133
Trauma-informed supervision (Knight), 131–132
Traumatic history, 128–130
Tribe, R., 178
Trust. *See also* Fidelity; Fiduciary responsibilities; Safety
authenticity and, 48
community advocacy boards and, 290
counseling relationships and, 31
faculty relationships and, 307–308
mentorship and, 8, 281
research participants and, 214
supervisor relationships and, 42, 145, 149, 153, 178
Turnitin (plagiarism detection service), 23, 25

U

Unethical or illegal practice, 99–105. *See also* Ethics and ethical dilemmas; Legal concerns
Universality, 147
University policies
on advocacy, 297–303
on bullying in workplace, 324–325
diversity and inclusion plans, 305–312
due process and, 26, 113, 125, 139
on institutional change, 313–319
institutional review boards and, 185, 209–214, 218, 222
on plagiarism
in faculty research, 192
in student assignments, 26
student handbooks, 125
on Title IX violation reporting, 179, 181
Unprepared or unengaged students, 5–11
U.S. Workplace Bullying Survey, 322

V

Value conflicts of counselors, 119–125, 139, 169, 171, 172
Vehviläinen, S., 22
Veracity, 244, 265
Vereen, Linwood G., 13, 34
Vicarious liability, 162
Virtue ethics, 318
Vision statements of organizations, 273–274
Volunteer work. *See* Local community leadership and advocacy; Mentorship; Professional organization leadership
Vontress, C. E., 56

W

Wachter Morris, C. A., 114
Walker, Unity, 313
Walter, G., 232
Ward v. Wilbanks (2010), 124
Warner, L. R., 232
Watts, Richard E., 193, 237
Watts, S. K., 193
Waxturn County Drug and Alcohol Recovery Program (WCDARP), 143–150
Weaver, Jo Lauren, 237
Webber, Jane M., 117, 127
West, J. D., 7–8
Wester, Kelly L., 188, 227, 229
West-Olatunji, Cirecie A., 279–285, 311
Wheeler, A. M., 125
White Fragility (DiAngelo), 317
White identity development model (Helms), 169
White privilege, 205
White savior complex, 101, 168–172
Whitman, J. S., 120
Wind, S. A., 115
Window of tolerance, 118, 128, 131
Withdrawing from studies, 223–228
Women
affinity groups for, 315–316
bullying in workplace and, 322
mentorship and, 277, 281, 284–285
online courses and access to higher education, 87
sexism and, 323–324
sexual harassment and, 79–80, 82
STEM education and, 204
stereotypes of, 169
support groups in academia, 285
Workplace bullying, 321–328
Workplace Bullying Institute, 325
Workplace Bullying Survey, U.S., 322
Works for hire, 191, 199
Writing styles, 24–25

Y

Ybañez-Llorente, Kathy, 284, 297
Youmans, R., 22